Feminism and Autobiography

Autobiography has become a staple of feminist scholarship. This new collection features essays by leading feminist academics from a variety of disciplines on the latest developments in autobiographical studies. The central questions addressed include whether autobiography is a genre, if so what it consists of, and whether it is the product of an internal urge or of external forms and pressures. Structured around the concepts of genre, intersubjectivity and memory, the book is situated within the tradition of feminist engagements with the autobiographical by a detailed historical introduction. Whilst exemplifying the very different levels of autobiographical activity going on in feminist studies, the contributions chart a movement from autobiography as genre to autobiography as cultural practice, and from the analysis of autobiographical texts to a preoccupation with autobiography as method. *Feminism and Autobiography* will be essential reading for students and academics working in feminist studies across the social sciences and humanities.

The contributors are: Trev Broughton, Mary Chamberlain, Marie-Françoise Chanfrault-Duchet, Tess Cosslett, Alison Easton, Gwendolyn Etter-Lewis, Mary Evans, Maggie Humm, Celia Lury, Ruth McElroy, Magda Michielsens, Nancy K. Miller, Susannah Radstone, Consuelo Rivera-Fuentes, Sara Scott, Sue Scott, Liz Stanley, Carolyn Steedman and Penny Summerfield.

Tess Cosslett is a Reader in Victorian Studies and Women's Writing at Lancaster University; **Celia Lury** is a Reader in Sociology at Goldsmiths College, University of London; and **Penny Summerfield** is Professor of Modern History at Manchester University.

Transformations: Thinking Through Feminism

Edited by:

Maureen McNeil, *Institute of Women's Studies, Lancaster University*
Lynne Pearce, *Department of English, Lancaster University*
Beverley Skeggs, *Department of Sociology, Manchester University.*

Other books in the series include:

Transformations: Thinking Through Feminism
Edited by S. Ahmed, J. Kilby, C. Lury, M. McNeil and B. Skeggs

Strange Encounters: Embodied Others in Post-Coloniality
S. Ahmed

Advertising and Consumer Citizenship: Gender, Images and Rights
A.M. Cronin

Mothering the Self: Mothers, Daughters, Subjects
S. Lawler

Feminism and Autobiography

Texts, theories, methods

**Edited by
Tess Cosslett, Celia Lury
and Penny Summerfield**

London and New York

First published 2000 by Routledge
11 New Fetter Lane, London EC4P 4EE

Simultaneously published in the USA and Canada
by Routledge
29 West 35th Street, New York, NY 10001

Routledge is an imprint of the Taylor & Francis Group

© 2000 Tess Cosslett, Celia Lury and Penny Summerfield, selection and
editorial matter; individual chapters, the contributors

Typeset in Baskerville by Taylor & Francis Books Ltd
Printed and bound in Great Britain by TJ International Ltd, Padstow,
Cornwall

British Library Cataloguing in Publication Data
A catalogue record for this book is available from the British Library

Library of Congress Cataloging in Publication Data
Feminism and autobiography: texts, theories, methods/ [edited by] Tess
Cosslett, Celia Lury, and Penny Summerfield.
p. cm. – (Transformations)
Includes bibliographical references and index.
1. Women's studies – Biographical methods. 2. Autobiography –
Women authors. 3. Feminist criticism. I. Cosslett, Tess. II. Lury, Celia.
III. Summerfield, Penny. IV. Series.
HQ1185 .F45 2000
305.42–dc21

00–032842

ISBN 0–415–23201–5 (hbk)
ISBN 0–415–23202–3 (pbk)

To all the participants in the seminar series 'Autobiography and the Social Self'

Autobiography

I have forgotten more than I remember:
Reinvent myself with strange stories
of a fragmented past.
A life blurred with dislocation, power misused, unbelonging.
Forty-five years later I emerge
Out of the shadow into the sun.
        (A poem sent by Catherine Williams to the editors)

Contents

Figures

Contributors

Trev Broughton teaches English and Women's Studies at the University of York. She has – to her great surprise – recently become a mother, and has, as a result, found 'auto/biography' to be even more complicated than she suspected. Among her publications are *Women's Lives/Women's Times: New Essays on Auto/biography*, edited with Linda Anderson (1997) and *Men of Letters, Writing Lives* (1999).

Mary Chamberlain is Professor of Modern Social History at Oxford Brookes University. Her recent publications include *Narratives of Exile and Return* (1997), *Caribbean Migration: Globalised Identities* (ed., 1998) and *Narrative and Genre* (ed. with Paul Thompson, 1998). She is currently completing a book (with Harry Goulbourne) on Caribbean families.

Marie-Françoise Chanfrault-Duchet teaches language sciences at the IUFM and the University F. Rabelais at Tours, France. Her research fields concern biography from the viewpoint of linguistics, literature, education and feminist theory. She recently published a book in German, *Adolf Wolfli: Autobiographie und Autofiktion* (1998), and is currently working on the linguistic construction of the self.

Tess Cosslett is Reader in Victorian Studies and Women's Writing at Lancaster University, and a member of the Institute for Women's Studies there. Her books include *Woman to Woman: Female Friendship in Victorian Fiction* (1986), *Women Writing Childbirth: Modern Discourses of Motherhood* (1994), *Victorian Women Poets, A Critical Reader* (1996) and *Women, Power and Resistance: An Introduction to Women's Studies* (ed. with Alison Easton and Penny Summerfield, 1996). She is currently working on children's fiction.

Alison Easton is Senior Lecturer in English at Lancaster University and a former Co-Director of its Institute for Women's Studies. She is author of *The Making of the Hawthorne Subject* (1994) and essays on nineteenth-century American and contemporary British women writers (including the African-Caribbean poet, Grace Nichols). She has edited the Penguin Sarah Orne Jewett, *The Country of the Pointed Firs* (1995) and is co-editor of *Women, Power and Resistance: An Introduction to Women's Studies* (1996).

Gwendolyn Etter-Lewis is Professor of English at Western Michigan University. Her specialisations include sociolinguistics, gender differences in language use, oral narratives and both African and African-American literature. She is the author of numerous scholarly publications including *My Soul is My Own: Oral Narratives of African American Women in the Professions* (1993) and *Unrelated Kin: Race and Gender in Women's Personal Narratives* (ed. with Michele Foster, 1996). She is currently completing a book on African women in higher education, using oral narrative methodology, and an edited volume (with Richard Thomas) entitled *Lights of the Spirit: A History of Black Baha'is in the Diaspora.*

Mary Evans teaches Sociology and Women's Studies at the University of Kent at Canterbury. Her most recent publication is *Missing Persons: The Impossibility of Auto/Biography* (1999) and her current projects are studies of love, and gender and sociological theory.

Maggie Humm is Professor in Cultural Studies, University of East London, where she teaches. She is the author of ten books, notably *Border Traffic* (1991), *Feminisms* (1992), *The Dictionary of Feminist Theory*, *Choice* Outstanding Academic Book (2nd edn, 1995). Her most recent book was *Feminism and Film* (1997). Currently she is Subject Editor for *The International Encyclopedia of Women's Studies*, and researching the photography and visual aesthetics of Virginia Woolf and other modernist women for her book *Borderline.*

Celia Lury is a Reader in Sociology at Goldsmiths College, University of London. Previously she was Co-Director of the Institute of Women's Studies at Lancaster University, where she helped organise the seminar series which was the inspiration for this volume. She has been interested in autobiography since her graduate studies, and has written on gender and identity, feminist theory and consumer culture. Recent publications include, *Prosthetic Culture* (1999) and *Global Nature, Global Culture* (with Sarah Franklin and Jackie Stacey, in press).

Ruth McElroy works as a Lecturer in English, Media and Welsh Studies at Trinity College, Carmarthen, Wales. Her areas of special interest include North and South American fiction, Welsh women's writing, and theories of cultural and national identity. She is currently working on a book entitled *Un/homely Britons: Belonging and its Discontents.*

Magda Michielsens teaches Women's Studies at the University of Antwerp (Belgium) and the University of Nijmegen (The Netherlands). As a philosopher working within the social sciences, her work is focused on the role of ideology in different aspects of women's lives. She has published on feminist theory, women and (new) media and gender scripts in biographical research. She is Director of the Centre of Women's Studies at the University of Antwerp and editor of *The European Journal of Women's Studies.*

Nancy K. Miller is Distinguished Professor of English and Comparative Literature at the Graduate Center, City University of New York. Her most recent book is *Bequest and Betrayal: Memoirs of a Parent's Death* (1998).

Susannah Radstone teaches in the Cultural Studies Department at the University of East London. She writes on cultural theory and film and has edited *Sweet Dreams: Sexuality, Gender and Popular Fiction* (1988) and *Memory and Method* (forthcoming). She is an editor of the volume series *Routledge Studies in Memory and Narrative* and recently co-organised 'Frontiers of Memory', an international conference. Her monograph *On Memory and Confession* is near completion.

Consuelo Rivera-Fuentes is a Chilean feminist writer now living in Britain. She is an EFL teacher and holds an MA in Sociology and Women's Studies from the University of Lancaster, where she is currently doing her PhD thesis on Lesbian Autobiographies, which combines literature, photography and oral narrations. She has published 'They Do Not Dance Alone: The Women's Movements in Latin America' in *Women, Power and Resistance* (ed. Tess Cosslett, Alison Easton and Penny Summerfield, 1996). She lives in North Wales with her lover, one of her sons and lots of animals.

Sara Scott is currently undertaking research on gender in the secure psychiatric sector as part of a Gender Training Initiative funded by the Department of Health. She is based in the Department of Sociology, Social Policy and Social Work at the University of Liverpool. In 1997/8 she held the first Sociological Review Fellowship at Keele University, writing up research undertaken with adult survivors of ritual abuse.

Sue Scott is Professor of Sociology at the University of Durham, having previously held posts at Stirling and Manchester. Her main research interests are in the sociology of gender, sexuality, the body and risk. She was a member of the Women Risk and AIDS Project (WRAP), and current research projects include: a study of sex education in Scottish schools funded by the MRC and a study of Children, Risk and Parental Risk Anxiety, funded by the ESRC. She hopes in the future to research siblings and their networks.

Liz Stanley is Professor of Sociology and Director of Women's Studies at the University of Manchester, and still thinks that 'Doctor' is the only academic title worth having. Her research and writing interests are concerned with 'autobiography', radical sociology and feminist epistemology; in the rest of her life, she enjoys the 'earthly pleasures' that Colette evokes so wonderfully. From 1999 to 2002 she will be involved in archive research concerning the complex relationship between imperialism and colonialism in southern Africa from 1890 to 1920.

Carolyn Steedman is Professor of History at the University of Warwick. She has written widely on the topic of self-writing. Her books include a biography of Margaret McMillan (*Childhood, Culture and Class in Britain*, 1990), *The Radical Soldier's Tale* (1988) and *Landscape for a Good Woman* (1986). She is currently working on the topic of eighteenth-century servants, service and servitude in the making of modern identity.

Penny Summerfield is Professor of Modern History at Manchester University. She has published several books on British women and the Second World War, most recently *Reconstructing Women's Wartime Lives: Discourse and Subjectivity in Oral Histories of the Second World War* (1998). Other publications include *Women Workers in the Second World War, Production and Patriarchy in Conflict* (1989) and (with Gail Braybon) *Out of the Cage, Women's Experiences in Two World Wars* (1987). She is currently working on a Leverhulme-funded project, 'The Gendering of Home Defence 1939–45: The Case of the Home Guard'.

Preface

Autobiography, the social self and ghosts

Maggie Humm

Shortly before undertaking my first weeks of research on Virginia Woolf's photo albums, my stepmother arrived with old family photographs including a photograph of me, perhaps aged two, in my bath. The photograph is somewhat out of focus, as were almost all of my father's early attempts, and taken with a Kodak 2A camera, one of the same camera models used by Virginia Woolf. The coincidence I took as a sign of wonder, clear proof that my research would be fruitful.

In my bath photograph I am supported by a ghostly hand, my mother's hand, which gave me a third image of my mother to add to the existing two photographs of her I owned. At some point during my research I came to understand that Virginia Woolf's mother was a ghostly revenant not only in Woolf's writing as critics uniformly argue, but also in Woolf's photography.

In the same way, the ESRC Autobiography Seminars, out of which this book grew, are already becoming traces, ghostly revenants in my palimpsest writing. Autobiographical identifications were as much part of the *process* of the seminar series as they were part of the *context* of the seminar lectures. Our academic 'autobiographies', our academic life journeys are never 'ours', can never be, should never be, purely personal.

I realise as I reflect on the seminar moments that I wanted these to reveal to me aspects of my own relationship to my work that I did not, or could not, know. I wanted the seminar moments to plot the story of my research. Walter Benjamin's term 'optical unconscious' for that which we cannot represent but which is always at the core of our representations best describes my desires.

The seminars were a prism through which I looked inside myself to see how bits of theory, odd empirical data, ideas from differing disciplines could tell my research story. Lectures only move us in relation to our own academic memories and academic desires and can then help us structure a sense of our academic identity. What I heard will not be what anyone else heard because everyone listens to lectures for clues about their individual academic existence. This is why questions to speakers are never simply commentary or requests for more information but come from a passionate desire for the speaker to recognise the questioner as a legitimate self. Hearing the lecture is to recognise myself in it. The lectures showed us, in part, what we want our own writing to be and also, sometimes, what our writing cannot be. But the seminar series did reveal unexpected ideas, bright flickers of recognition of what could, hopefully, become my writing identity.

(From a letter sent by Maggie Humm to the editors)

Acknowledgements

We would like to thank all the participants, speakers, organisers, helpers and caterers involved in the ESRC-funded seminar series 'Autobiography and the Social Self', held at the Universities of Lancaster and York in 1996–8, and in particular the secretaries in the Institute for Women's Studies at Lancaster University.

Special thanks to Mari Shullaw, our editor at Routledge, for her patience and support, to the anonymous reader who provided helpful comments on our original proposal, to Lynne Pearce for her careful reading and editing of the manuscript, and to Val Walsh for her comments on the 'Genre' section.

Excerpt from 'You Hated Spain' from *Birthday Letters* by Ted Hughes. Copyright © 1998 by Ted Hughes. Reprinted by kind permission of Farrar, Straus and Giroux, LLC and Faber and Faber Ltd. Excerpt from 'Annus Mirabilis' from *High Windows* by Philip Larkin. Copyright © 1974 by Philip Larkin. Reprinted by kind permission of Farrar, Strauss and Giroux, LLC and Faber and Faber Ltd. Thanks to Bloodaxe Books for permission to quote the lines from Gwyneth Lewis's *Parables and Faxes* (1995) on p. 252.

Introduction

The excitement of autobiography as a category of study is that it links together many different disciplines – literature, history, sociology, cultural studies. At the same time, within each of these fields, the study of autobiography explodes disciplinary boundaries and requires an understanding of other approaches, methods and practices. Autobiography makes trouble: it is difficult to define as a distinct genre,[1] on the borderline between fact and fiction, the personal and the social, the popular and the academic, the everyday and the literary (Marcus 1994). This kind of disruptive interdisciplinarity, the challenging of traditional boundaries and definitions, has also been central to the feminist project, especially as articulated in Women's Studies, and autobiography provides a meeting-place for many different kinds of feminist approach. Feminist approaches in turn have helped to revolutionise the study of autobiography, expanding its definition to include not just a literary genre or a body of texts but a practice that pervades many areas of our lives (Gilmore 1994; Gagnier 1991; Stanley and Broughton in this collection). A different way to put this would be that autobiographical practices are now seen to operate in many different written, spoken and visual genres, such as application forms, interviews and family photographs.

Indeed, the seminar series from which this collection grew,[2] took as its starting point the way in which, across a range of social and cultural practices – public and private – individuals are compelled to display self-knowledge through the creation and presentation of stories about the self. This focus was in recognition of the importance of autobiography in public and semi-public as well as private discourse. In psychotherapy and medicine, in law courts and workplaces autobiography is an increasingly visible means of confession, of accusation, of legitimation; it is a source of authority and of shame. The aim was not to ignore the importance of writing in autobiography, but to draw attention to the variety of media in which lives are represented, and to locate such mediations – whether they be text- or image-based, written or spoken – in specific practices. It also enabled us to ask whether the compulsion to tell stories about ourselves is best understood as an inner urge or an external requirement, a question which feminism's engagement with Foucault's notion of the disciplined subject had highlighted (Probyn 1993a). What was at issue was the value of the experience represented in autobiography (and to whom), and the implications of such presentations of self for the attribution of both agency and responsibility for actions.

Feminism offers a distinctive vantage point from which to view these concerns, highlighting the gendered constructions of self they typically assume, and the ethical and political consequences of such assumptions. Laura Marcus, for example, has provided a history of autobiography criticism within literary study that shows how the literary genre was constructed, pointing out that it is a way of writing that historically came to mark, and be marked by, the (usually masculine) privilege of self-possession (Marcus 1994). However, while feminism has posed a challenge to the genre of autobiography, feminism's engagement with the genre has, in turn, contributed to a critical re-evaluation of its own long-standing concerns including subjectivity, knowledge and power, differences, and collective identity. There has always been a strong feminist interest in the autobiographical, beginning with the attempt to connect the 'personal' with the 'political', and the concomitant emphasis on women's experience as a vital resource in the creation of women's knowledge (Skeggs 1995). As awareness has shifted from women's experience as a given, to the complex construction of gendered subjectivities, the field of autobiography has become a central preoccupation and testing-ground for feminism.

Feminist critiques of literary autobiography initially focused their attention on the absence of women's writing and women's voices from the canon (Anderson and Broughton 1997; S. Smith 1987; Brodzki and Schenck 1988). The traditional construction of the ideal autobiographer as a unified, transcendent subject, representative of the age, has favoured privileged white male writers who can fit into this role more easily than the marginalised and the dispossessed. The introduction of women's texts into the canon inevitably unsettled and problematised the genre: if women have more relational, or more fragmented selves, if they have difficulties with subjecthood, as Patricia Waugh has argued, their stories will take a different shape (Waugh 1989). Their selfhood and what it can report will not be so simple: fiction, and the biographies of others, will enter into their 'autobiographies' (S. Smith 1987; Stanley 1992). Feminist questioning of universalist assumptions has thus unsettled the definition of the literary genre 'autobiography'.

At the same time, the feminist insistence that 'the personal is political' has had profound effects on other genres. Feminist academics in several disciplines now insist that the subjective element must not be left out of the practice of research methods, such as the interview, or of theories of knowledge production (Skeggs 1995; Maynard and Purvis 1994; Reinharz 1992). Researchers must be self-reflexively aware of intersubjective relationships with their 'subjects'; knowledge is not objectively 'there', but is produced by subjects situated in particular social relations and historical discourses (Harding 1986; Skeggs 1995; D. Smith 1987). Again, this emphasis derives from a feminist questioning of universalist assumptions, and a realisation that knowledge is not 'objective', but has often been produced from a privileged white male-centred perspective that has pretended to universality and objectivity.

The realisation by feminists of the importance of further categories of difference such as race, class, sexual orientation, nationality and age – sometimes as a consequence of challenges to their own presumption of universality – has complicated and enriched understandings of autobiographical writing and practices. These concerns are central to this collection, and are most overtly present in the contributions by Rivera-Fuentes, McElroy, Steedman, Cosslett, Scott and Scott, Chamberlain, Miller, Easton, Michielsens and Etter-Lewis. These chapters focus on differences of sexual identity, nationality, age, class, culture and 'race'. Considerations of difference now pervade all areas of feminist autobiographical investigation.

In an attempt to rationalise and connect the wide range of texts, events and practices deemed autobiographical in this volume, we have divided our contributions into three main areas: genre,[3] intersubjectivity and memory. As we have already suggested, autobiography as a literary genre is immediately problematised by a feminist intervention. Carolyn Steedman develops this problematisation by questioning the assumption that autobiography's origins lie in the enlightened subjectivities of the male middle and upper classes. Instead, she finds a working-class origin for the genre in the life-stories extorted from the poor by officialdom. Her emphasis is on the *external requirement* to narrate one's life, not on the spontaneous production of autobiography by an inner 'self'. Liz Stanley explores the external impetus to produce autobiographies still further, by showing how, in the contemporary world, genres such as the CV require us to produce certain limited accounts of our selves. Marie-Françoise Chanfrault-Duchet demonstrates how narrative and mythic forms structure the accounts of her oral-history interviewees. While Steedman's prime example is a literary one – Jemima the wardress's story from Wollstonecraft's *Maria* – Chanfrault-Duchet takes the insights of literary criticism and applies them to the spoken stories of living respondents. Mary Evans, on the other hand, takes Sylvia Plath's semi-fictional novel *The Bell Jar* and argues for its importance as a different, and better, kind of feminist autobiography. The problematisation of the genre is implicated in the increasingly interdisciplinary perspectives of Women's Studies: oral narratives, CVs, fictional accounts, may today all be thought of as autobiographical practices.

The centrality of the idea that women's voices have been silenced to feminist concern with autobiography raises issues concerning the relationships in which the narrator is embedded. Hence the second section of this volume focuses on intersubjectivity, a term with at least a two-fold meaning. It may be used to refer, on the one hand, to the relationship between personal narratives and the public stories available within popular culture, and, on the other, to the relationship between the narrator and the audience. It thus enables us to ask about the ways in which experience is narratively and dialogically organised. Both of these relationships are crucial to the process of 'composure' by which a narrator produces a story of themselves with which they can live in relative psychic comfort. But the notion of silencing suggests that women's stories typically do not reach the public domain as readily as men's, and also places on feminist researchers an obligation to elicit the unspoken (and perhaps unspeakable) private story. Summerfield discusses whether both public silencing and the feminist focus on interiority unsettle the production and composition of women's narratives, leading not to 'composure' but to 'discomposure', as subjects confront the conflicting discourses of femininity.

Intersubjectivity, then, implies that the narration of a life or a self can never be confined to a single, isolated subjecthood. Others are an integral part of consciousness, events and the production of a narrative. Or, put more abstractly, the narration of a self cannot be understood in isolation from an other it acknowledges, implicitly or explicitly, and with which it is in a constitutive relationship. Moreover, this other may be either a concrete individual or a generalised subject. Gwendolyn Etter-Lewis, for example, charts the shifting subject position of Evva K. Heath in the letters she writes to her mother, positioning this 'moving subject' in relation to both the remembering and retelling of the circumstances of a particular life and to the collective narrative of African-American women.

The notion that women in particular have a more fluid sense of self, developed in their relationship to their mothers, has become one of the favourite sites of both psychoanalytic and literary engagements with the autobiographical in recent years (see p. 6 below), and is revisited in the chapters by Sue and Sara Scott, and by Tess Cosslett. Scott and Scott explore the effect of their mother's narratives on their own lives, complicating any essentialist notion of mother–daughter identification by introducing class position, and the differences as well as the similarities of sisters' lives. Cosslett questions and problematises the assumption that feminist autobiographers can restore subjectivity to the mother, by including her biography within their autobiographies. While daughters' accounts of their mothers' lives are clearly an important part of *their* subjectivities, the mothers are often denied full subjectivity. To posit the mother–daughter relationship so centrally to women's life-stories as 'dialogic' is not to deny that it is also power-inscribed, with the two parties struggling for control and self-actualisation. Yet whether, and how, the mother's subjectivity emerges varies in autobiographical practice and is more or less enabled by particular cultural practices. In Mary Chamberlain's account, Caribbean migrant women's accounts of their lives are shown to depend on a *collective*, familial sense of self, foreign to many white traditions. Her 'subjects', both mothers *and* daughters, conceive of themselves intersubjectively. They are women who are not separable from their mothers and grandmothers.

Our final category is memory. Autobiography is to do with recovering a past (as well as with the projection of a future), and depends on the deployment of an often shifting, partial and contested set of personal or collective memories. However, the uses of memory are various and sometimes confusing; so, for example, the notion of memory can mean both the stories we tell about our past and the ways in which we are changed by our experience (Kirmayer 1996). Feminists have begun to explore the many forms of memory, drawing attention to the role of media as 'memory texts' and pointing out that memories usually have neither an obvious source nor a single owner (Spence 1986; Kuhn 1995). Memory, too, then is intersubjective and dialogical, a function of personal identifications and social commitments. While it may be uniquely ours it is also objectified, a matter of public convention and shared rituals. The recovery of the past through personal testimony can have a political dimension depending on what is remembered and what is forgotten. The right to establish validity, authenticity or truth is never the story-teller's alone.

Criticism that attends to gender and other differences emphasises this dimension, exploring the conditions in which the stories we tell ourselves can be heard. Alison Easton investigates the power and the limitations of the slave narrative genre, as it persists in the autobiographies of later African-American women writers. 'Slavery' remains as a memory, in form as well as content. Magda Michielsens is also concerned with the forms of memory, the frames we use to narrate the past, and what happens when these lose their force. Susannah Radstone inserts the consideration of gender into postmodern preoccupations with temporality. She locates gender differences in the forms of different kinds of remembering. Finally, Nancy Miller reflects on the intersection of her own memories of the fifties, with the wider history of feminism, and the creation of a feminist past.

Genre, intersubjectivity and memory may thus be seen as overlapping frameworks central to a range of issues currently under debate in feminist autobiographical studies. In what follows, we consider these debates, discussing how they have impacted on the arguments presented in this collection, and how our approaches are relevant to them. The key issues we consider here are: subjectivities, testimony, personalist criticism, situated knowledges, and oral history.

Subjectivities

The promise of an exploration or revelation of a 'self' has made autobiography of immense interest to feminists, but has also highlighted problems and confusions within feminism. The derivation of the word 'autobiography' is often given as 'self-life-writing'. Both the notions of 'self' and 'life' have been put under close examination in recent years, as literary theory has focused on textuality, 'writing', as a linguistic game of endlessly deferred meaning without stable reference to 'real life' or 'real selves'. At the same time, there has been increasing recognition of the importance of the medium in which the 'writing' or representation of the self occurs, and growing interest in the use of images, especially photographs in autobiography (Spence 1986, 1991; Stanley 1992; Kuhn 1995; Stacey 1997). This move has contributed both to the view that textuality should be at the heart of the study of autobiography and, in other interpretations, to the dissolution of the distinctions between self-life-writing. This is especially clear when the medium in which the self is written is the body, an approach which is explored here in Ruth McElroy's discussion of the difficulties of situating a self between cultures.

If women have been categorised as 'objects' by patriarchal cultures, women's autobiography gives an opportunity for them to express themselves as 'subjects', with their own selfhood. But poststructuralist theory has deconstructed notions of a self and of a narrative necessary to the idea of a life-story. Patricia Waugh explains this process, recognising that it is occurring just as

> women writers are beginning … to construct an identity out of the recognition that women need to discover, and must fight for, a sense of unified selfhood, a rational, coherent, effective identity. As male writers lament its demise, women writers have not yet experienced that subjectivity which will give them a sense of personal autonomy, continuous identity, a history and agency in the world.
>
> (Waugh 1989: 6)

The 'self' has been put under pressure from within, by psychoanalysis, as a delusory product of unconscious processes, and from without, as a delusory product of ideologies or discourses. Waugh, however, argues that oppressed or marginalised groups have never had a sense of unified selfhood:

> For those marginalized by the dominant culture, a sense of identity as constructed through impersonal and social relations of power (rather than a sense of identity as the reflection of an inner 'essence') has been a major aspect of their self-concept long before post-structuralists and postmodernists began to assemble their cultural manifestos.
>
> (Waugh 1989: 3)

In the case of women, Waugh relates this fragmentary self to the idea of relationality, as pioneered by the feminist psychoanalyst Nancy Chodorow (1978). Chodorow argued that because the primary child-carers in our culture are usually women, boys and girls form their sense of identity in different ways. Boys define themselves against women, and emerge with closed-off, autonomous selves; girls define themselves in relation to women, and emerge with fluid, relational selves. Waugh sees this relational self as a product and cause of women's oppression, but also as a possible positive strength for women. Some feminist critics of autobiography have taken up this idea of relationality as the prime characteristic of women's autobiography, identifying a different kind of hitherto unvalued self (Jelinek 1980). Other critics, however, see this relationality as an effect of ideology or discourse – a way 'women' were constructed or had to present themselves, rather than as an expression of their 'real' nature (Brodzki and Schenck 1988; S. Smith 1987; Stanton 1987). Chodorow's work has been attacked as ahistorical and essentialist.[4] In our collection a 'relational' identity between mothers and daughters is a focus of Tess Cosslett's, Sue and Sara Scott's, Mary Chamberlain's and Gwendolyn Etter-Lewis's chapters, but it is differently conceptualised. For Chamberlain, it is a result of the ways culture shapes the 'self'; for the Scotts, it is to do with the handing on of formative narratives from one generation to the next; and for Cosslett, it is a matter of literary forms and strategies, and the effects of different kinds of feminist approach. For Etter-Lewis it is to do with all these and their interconnections.

Domna Stanton responds to the challenge of poststructuralism and postmodernism differently from Waugh, by excising the 'bio', that is the 'real life', from 'autobiography', to come up with two new formulations, 'autography' and 'autogynography', which imply that women are free to write themselves without any presupposition of referentiality or truth (Stanton 1989). But as Stanley points out in this collection, 'life' cannot be got rid of so easily. Instead 'relationality' has returned in a different guise. Smith and Watson list this rethinking of relationality among their future projects for autobiographical research (1998: 37). What is now on the agenda is what we have called 'intersubjectivity' – the ways in which all selves are structured by interactions with others, and a more general attention to the ways in which the self is framed and created by the social. The complexity of this relationship – in which neither the self nor the social are reduced to the other – is explored by Consuelo Rivera-Fuentes in her discussion of 'sym/bio/graphy'. This is a term Rivera-Fuentes introduces to acknowledge the symbiotic relationship she argues exists between herself, as a reader of lesbian autobiographies, and the writer, and the selves they jointly create. This is a relationship which is, for Riviera, 'beyond interpretation', a 'living together'.

Elsewhere in the volume, the new emphasis on 'life' in the triplet self-life-writing is most clearly evident in the pieces by Liz Stanley and Trev Broughton. Liz Stanley explores the ways in which autobiography is caught up within an audit culture, a culture of bureaucracy in which the self is represented and made accountable in relation to the techniques of management planning and prediction. The self is no longer an expression from within, but is extracted, moulded, created by outside forces. But not entirely – as Stanley's wish to 'have it all' attests, the self is both inner and outer. This emphasis on 'life' has gone along with the widening of the interest in autobiography beyond the literary and the textual: as Trev Broughton suggests, many critics are less interested in autobiography as a body of texts than in autobiographical practices, including everyone's everyday presentations of their selves in ordinary social encounters.

In a further dimension of thinking about autobiography as practice, the 'inner' part of the equation is being seen less as expression than as *performance* (Marcus 1994; Butler 1990), which not only removes any notion of an essential self, but also implies an audience, and brings us back to another of the meanings of intersubjectivity. It draws attention to the processual, dynamic nature of subjectivity; there is an emphasis on verbs, not nouns – writing, not texts. This also links with some of the 'dialogic' theorising around subjectivity, the gendered dimension of which has been developed by theorists such as Lynne Pearce (1994) out of Bakhtin's (1981) work on literary dialogics.

Another interesting development in the erosion of the idea of an autonomous and isolated self has been the investigation of *histories* of subjectivity: the subject is not a stable essence, but changes according to social and discursive changes and pressures (Gagnier 1991; Steedman 1995a and 1995b). Regenia Gagnier charts the ways in which the nineteenth-century middle-class literary autobiographical self was produced, and contrasts it with the self-writings of working-class people. These she finds marked and limited by bodily suffering.

Ironically, it is only in intersubjectivity, in communicating and cooperating with others, that these writers find a writing 'self': 'subjectivity cannot exist without intersubjectivity, whereas bodies in pain exist only as bodies in pain' (Gagnier 1991: 83). However, there is nothing necessarily liberating about narrative in itself, as Carolyn Steedman's contribution to the debate about class and subjectivity in this collection indicates. Some narrative subject positions are more or less enabling than others.

One of the most important contemporary autobiographical explorations of class and subjectivity is that provided by Jo Spence in her phototherapy work with Rosy Martin. In this practice, Spence and Martin re-enact fragments of their mothers' lives for the camera, with the intention of exploring the dynamic of the mother–daughter relationship, and the aim of reconstructing their residual subjectivity as working-class children. Out of this, they believe, comes an understanding and valuing of marginalised family histories (Spence 1991; Martin 1991). Valerie Walkerdine, too, works with photographs of herself as a child: colouring in portraits, highlighting shadows, she illustrates the ways in which emotions of greed, envy and anger can be deciphered as traces on the imaged body (Walkerdine 1991).

The practices of Spence and Walkerdine demonstrate that any notion of a unified and stable subjectivity is put under pressure from memory. As Annette Kuhn points out, 'Memory … has its own modes of expression: these are characterized by the fragmentary, non-linear quality of moments recalled out of time' (Kuhn 1995: 5). Critics of autobiography have long realised that at least two 'selves' are involved in the writing of a life: the self then, and the self now, doing the writing. Sidonie Smith sees memory as one of the necessary 'fictions' of autobiography (S. Smith 1987: 45). Kuhn, too, argues for the importance of what she calls 'memory work', suggesting that it is a powerful instrument of 'conscientization': 'the awakening of critical consciousness, through their own activities of reflection and learning, among those who lack power; and the development of a critical and questioning attitude towards their own lives and the lives of those around them' (Kuhn 1995: 8).

This gap between present and past selves exercises Nancy Miller in this collection, as she tries to use memory to connect with her own past, and to the past of feminism. The traumatic memories that interest several writers on testimony (see below) by definition comprise a wound or rift in the psyche, while the present self is haunted by dreams from a past experience. Alison Easton investigates this type of haunting in a longer historical context, as Black women writers seek to come to terms with and rewrite slave narratives from the past. Linda Anderson has suggested that memory is a space in which the self can be remade by women autobiographers (Anderson 1997: 8–12). How to write a self-in-process, changing in intersubjective relation to the social environment, is the problem that engages Mary Evans, in her chapter on Sylvia Plath. Interestingly, she finds the part-fiction of *The Bell Jar* a better medium for the exploration of women's multiple selves than traditional autobiography.

Testimony

In recent years, 'testimony' has become an increasingly important category of autobiographical practice. Like all such categories (memoirs, oral history, confessional writing, personalist criticism), it is not clearly separable from a distinctly defined 'autobiography' – it is another way of conceiving some of the same material. The concept of testimony comes partly from a legal framework – the testimony of witnesses in court. In this sense, it connects first-person narration to truth-telling. The aim of the court is to arrive as near as possible to the facts of the case, relying on the testimony of eye-witnesses. But of course from the legal point of view the unreliability and partiality of memory is a problem – the court cannot assume that witnesses' accounts are accurate, or unbiased. A second important derivation of the term 'testimony' is a religious one: testifiers bear witness to their conversions or beliefs. In both these senses, the term has important resonances for feminism, which begins with women speaking out about their hitherto unheard experiences, and also testifying to their feminist beliefs. The idea of difference between women of different ages, classes, races, nations also points towards the importance of many voices, all testifying to their own truths. Gayatri Spivak has however questioned whether the 'subaltern', the woman in a subordinate position, can ever 'speak', since she is required to use the dominant discourse of the oppressors that effectively silences her own voice (Spivak 1986).

The idea of testimony, then, seems to be re-emphasising the referentiality of autobiography (it refers to real things in the world, it isn't just a word-game). But it also dissolves into uncertainty when looked at more closely. The term has most often been used in connection with horrific events. Felman and Laub's pioneering book *Testimony: Crises of Witnessing* (1992), focuses on the testimony of Holocaust survivors, emphasising the difficulties of testifying to an event which was concealed and silenced with chilling efficiency by its perpetrators, who attempted to erase all witnesses. Felman writes both of stories which enable their tellers and others to survive, and of the determination to survive in order to tell the story. Laub argues for the emotional accuracy of even demonstrably inaccurate memories. In other words, there is a move away from a one-dimensional intepretation of truth. Both writers emphasise that testimony is an occurrence in the present, to do with the meaning of the past now, and facilitated by specific situations and interchanges. In particular, they stress the importance and the difficulty of listening to such testimony. Intersubjectivity is clearly central to this kind of personal story.

A further complication to this sort of testimony, is the effect of trauma, making rents in the tissues of memory as a result of an overwhelming event. Cathy Caruth (1995, 1996) has investigated this topic, which fascinated Freud. Freud noticed that traumatic events are not registered by the conscious mind at the time they occur; they are repressed but come back in the form of recurring dreams and repetitive behaviour. The dreams are not metaphorical as is typical in Freud's interpretation, but obsessively literal, a replaying of the event. This means that the traumatic event is not experienced until it is over. Freud used the

(German) word 'Nachträglichkeit', or 'afterwardsness', to signify this effect. Once again, testimony does not bring us unquestionably into contact with a past event. The plasticity of memory intervenes, as does the (intersubjective) relationship with the analyst who brings suppressed memories to the surface. The reliability of many such memories – especially those associated with the recall of sexual abuse – have been questioned by the proponents of 'false memory syndrome' (Kenny 1999).

It is interesting that Freud also made a similar move, in the process of arriving at his theory of repression, as he decided to attribute patients' memories of incestuous childhood abuse not to real occurrences, but to sexual fantasy. As many of these victims were and are women, there are implications here for feminism, but exactly what they are is hard to know. What is clear is that feminists need to consider the context in which trauma is remembered and to question the conventions by which it is brought into existence. In her article 'Not outside the Range: One Feminist Perspective on Psychic Trauma', Laura S. Brown questions existing legal definitions of trauma from a feminist perspective. Trauma is defined in legal discourse as an experience 'outside the normal range' of human experience. Brown points out that feminism has alerted us to the constructed and limited male-centred definition of 'normality'. Victims of incest and domestic violence lose out both because their experiences are not those of the dominant group, and because their experiences are so frequent as not to count as traumatic. Brown argues for a new, more political, definition of trauma that includes the everyday violence, mental and physical, done to the victims of the existing order (Caruth 1995: 100–12). This feminist redefinition of trauma explodes the whole concept of an out-of-the-ordinary event on which repression is based.

Work on testimony has taken yet another direction. While it seems at first the most authentic type of personal account, because of its connections with truth-telling, justice, belief and deeply experienced events, it has come to mean almost the opposite, in the context of certain contemporary cultural events. Here we are thinking, in particular, of televised talk-shows in which people testify on demand and before an audience to ever-more bizarre experiences. Internal lives are given theatrical expression. This tendency has been explored and criticised by Lauren Berlant (1997) and by Elaine Showalter (1997) from different points of view. Showalter sees it as an 'hysterical epidemic', whereas Berlant sees it more as a politically motivated performance to distract people from social problems by a focus on the narrowly personal. Testimony here intersects with performance – it is literally a 'show' for an audience. Such testimonies are produced not so much by the needs of the speakers, as by the demands of the media for specific types of sensational story. This argument echoes the contention of many of the contributors to this collection that autobiography is neither simply externally required or internally generated. It thus fits in with the arguments of other critics that subjectivity is an effect produced by autobiography – or rather in autobiographical practice – and does not precede it (Gilmore; Gagnier). The specific feminist relevance of this argument is that gender, too, is produced in discourse and/or performance.

Testimony as a dominant contemporary form of autobiography has been attacked in another way by Susannah Radstone (1999). She valorises an older form, confession, which implies guilt and implication on the part of the narrator, making possible, she believes, an ethical relation to our past. Testimony, on the other hand, as she defines it, is the story of the victim, totally innocent and passive, who narrates what has been done to her and is denied the possibility of revising her relation to the past. Listeners are encouraged to identify with this victim position, rather than to discover the perpetrator in themselves as well. Here Radstone's argument intersects with Berlant's in finding something infantilising about testimony: in this form, we identify with the helpless child.

Radstone's advocacy of confession is interesting, as this form is often taken as an early, superseded phase of feminism, but while she argues it may be more enabling than the current media fascination with testimony, she is also, in this collection, concerned to distinguish it from 'remembrance', a further mode of autobiography. Her concern in making this further distinction is to highlight the sexual politics of autobiographical time. She first identifies the view that while the confession's quest for truth aligns it with the modern concern with linear progress, transformation and truth, the non-linear revisions of memory staged in remembrance are in keeping with postmodern times. But then she goes on to show how both confession and remembrance challenge the notion of an epochal shift in temporality from modernity to postmodernity and its reliance on a construction of history as a homogeneous continuum.

Personalist criticism

While feminist interventions have helped to problematise and destabilise the definition of 'autobiography', autobiographical interventions have also produced radical changes in feminist theorising and critical practice. This process has especially affected the form, tone and style of the academic or critical article or essay. Jane Tompkins is often credited with initiating a movement away from abstract 'theory' to a more personal and accessible mode in her article 'Me and My Shadow' (1991). Here, Tompkins refuses the 'straitjacket' of the theoretical language she is supposed to be adopting, and introduces herself as an embodied presence. Famously, she reveals that she is about to go to the 'bathroom'. She also rejects the dismissive and combative stance of many academic articles, in favour of a more generous and inclusive listening to other women's words. Tompkins genders her approach by claiming that theory and objectivity are stereotypically 'male', while the personal and emotional have been mocked and undervalued because they are seen as 'female'. She wants to return to the feminist anger that first fuelled her research. There have been several attacks on or reworkings of Tompkins' argument (Veeser 1996; Miller 1991). Her gendered opposition of theory and feeling is especially vulnerable to criticism. But her piece is not as simplistic as critics, beguiled by her accessible style, have assumed.

The article was sparked off by an invitation to reply to another article by Ellen Messer-Davidow, whose 'theoretical' argument is about standpoint epistemology. As Tompkins puts it, 'what counts as knowledge is a function of situation and perspective' (1991: 1081). But Tompkins' whole piece is about her personal investment in her critical ideas: she enacts and embodies Messer-Davidow's theoretical argument. In the second version of the article (the one commonly reprinted) she readmits 'theory', if it connects to her feelings. In a recent interview, Tompkins and members of her writing group reject a theory/personal binary, and even the label 'personal', for what they are trying to do (Veeser 1996). Tompkins' intervention is often seen as ushering in a new movement towards a more 'personal' academic style, but earlier feminist critics already often combined the autobiographical and the theoretical in an accessible and exciting way (Rich 1977, 1979, 1987; Lorde 1984; Heilbrun 1988). The subsequent turn in feminist scholarship towards a highly abstract theoretical language is what made Tompkins' reiteration necessary.

If autobiography as a genre is problematised and complexified by feminist attention, the feminist use of the autobiographical in other contexts will take on this complexity. An autobiographical slant is therefore no guarantee of the kind of simplicity, directness and accessibility that Tompkins was aiming at (see, for instance, the writings of Peggy Phelan, Lauren Berlant and Gayatri Spivak in Veeser 1996). A more recent emphasis on performance, coming from Judith Butler's work, has led to ironical, reflexive and multi-layered writings. On the other hand, both Jane Tompkins and Nancy Miller have in their most recent autobiographical books moved outside the purely academic to address a wider audience in a simpler style (Tompkins 1991; Miller 1996).

Diane Freedman, Olivia Frey and Frances Murphy Zauhar have put together a number of autobiographical critiques, widely different in form and content, in their collection *The Intimate Critique* (1993). H. Aram Veeser's more recent collection (1996) includes arguments for and against the autobiographical turn, as well as examples of critics 'just doing it'. In both these collections, the majority of the contributors are women. The most successful of these essays (e.g. Marianne Hirsch in Veeser 1996) combine an autobiographical, anecdotal style, with an investigation of feelings, and a theoretical understanding. Several of the contributors to this book write autobiographically too, in major or minor ways (McElroy; Rivera-Fuentes; Cosslett; Scott and Scott; Summerfield; Miller).

Situated knowledges

Personalist criticism is one example of the ways in which an autobiographical approach has produced changes in the literary-critical article. Another, wider example of this kind of effect is the way in which autobiographical approaches have been adopted and adapted in feminist research in the social sciences. Here epistemological questions have become important: questions about how knowledge is produced. As Ellen Messer-Davidow argued, knowledge is an effect of who it is that does the knowing (Tompkins 1991).

Jane Tompkins questions the usefulness of this idea, arguing that knowing this does not in any way change the content of what she knows. But she misses the point: this kind of epistemological argument has a rhetorical force, preventing the dismissal of feminist knowledge as merely subjective, or merely biased. But it has also produced the criticism that feminism has fallen into a problematic relativism (Ramazanoglu 1993): if all knowledge, even that which claims to be objective, is seen as produced from a particular (political, gendered) standpoint, none can be excluded. A further step in this argument would be to see feminist knowledge as somehow privileged, because of its very standpoint, more valuable than other standpoints (D. Smith 1987). However, such privileging can lead to a simplistic competitiveness in knowledge claims.

Sandra Harding (1986) defines three types of feminist epistemology: feminist empiricism (based on women's authentic experience), feminist standpoint (based on a feminist angle of interpretation) and feminist postmodernism (a stance that rejects the possibility of any universal theory). There are many problems with all three positions, which are not always clearly distinguished. Mary Maynard points out that it is not always clear whether it is the experience and/or standpoint of women or of feminists that is being appealed to (Maynard and Purvis 1994: 20). Bev Skeggs questions the idea that 'only those who have the appropriate experience of oppression are able to speak about it', fearing that this leads to a competition between different identity politics (Skeggs 1995: 16). The concern with questions of difference within feminism means that there can no longer be any notion of one correct feminist standpoint. Women of different classes, 'races', nationalities, ages will all have their own standpoints.

What is happening now is less a search for the correct epistemology than a methodological concern to reveal the complex autobiographical underpinnings of feminist research. If, as feminists have argued, all research is situated, and pure objectivity is a pretence, it is ethically and politically right that feminist researchers should lead the way in coming clean on the way research is produced and lived by those producing it. As Maynard argues, 'a focus on autobiographical analysis of what it is actually like to do research can provide a useful insight into issues often hidden in conventional methodology textbooks' (Maynard and Purvis 1994: 1). More than this, Skeggs argues for the location of the researcher in her social position. She produces a list of autobiographical questions for researchers to ask themselves, about research as a process:

- why was the area of study chosen, what institutional, economic and socio-political factors underpinned the choice?
- which frameworks of established knowledge were used, referred to, challenged, ignored, and why?
- which methods were chosen for study and why? Why were other approaches not used?
- how did the initial questions and research relate to the final product?
- how did the process of writing influence the final product?

(Skeggs 1995: 4)

It is not a simple, anecdotal account of experience that she is asking for, but an informed and self-reflexive understanding:

> we can, however, explore the processes by which we are positioned, and hence come to see how our experiences and understandings of who we (and others) are, are always known and interpreted through the discourses and representations available to us.
>
> (Skeggs 1995: 17)

The ways in which the autobiography of the researcher is involved in the research are not just limited to the initial standpoint or subject position taken up. Research can have an impact on the researchers, changing their sense of self; and research may become a part of their 'private' lives, because of their intense feminist investment in it, and/or because they make use of the material to hand (Ahmed 1997; Fonow and Cook 1991). This making use of 'personal' material is evident in the chapters in this collection by Rivera-Fuentes, McElroy, Cosslett, Miller, and the Scotts. Rivera-Fuentes and a number of other contributors also place their research in their academic lives, revealing their projects, their changes of mind, their failed investigations. Liz Stanley has argued for the inclusion of an 'intellectual autobiography' in feminist work, specifically in the practice of biography, where the biographer's personal investment in the interpretation and construction of the biographee's life is usually hidden (1992). Contributors here reveal their intellectual affiliations, and how they have been led to the research they are doing, what frameworks they are using.

The focus on the autobiographical in feminist research processes necessarily also returns us to the issue of intersubjectivity. In the case of biography, at least two lives and their intersections are involved, and Stanley has further argued for a feminist emphasis on 'group biography' and friendship networks in the narration of women's lives (Stanley 1992). In our collection, Nancy Miller situates her own autobiographical memories within a 'group biography' of early feminism and its autobiographical connections (Stanley 1992; see also Marcus 1994: 281 on group biography). Valerie Walkerdine, together with her collaborators, has drawn on Jo Spence's work to develop a psychoanalytically informed practice in which the interpretation of the subjects of her research is situated in relation to an analysis of her own response. She writes that self-reflection requires the researcher 'to be able to attempt to bring to consciousness some of their own reactions, defences, the transferences through which the material brought up by others stirs emotional material of their own' (Spence 1997: 72). This process of self-reflection can, she suggests, be assisted by discussion amongst a group of researchers, since this practice can help identify the complex processes of transference at work.

Intersubjectivity is important in other ways too: Skeggs and Maynard write about the ways in which research impacts not only on the life of the researcher, but on the lives of the researched. Awareness of interpersonal dynamics has led to the feminist redesigning of interview techniques and interpretations of material from interview situations (Skeggs 1995; Maynard 1994). Maynard remarks on feminist awareness of 'the social nature of interpretation' (1994: 7). Elspeth Probyn has worried about the autobiographical focus in cultural studies, that it may exclude attention to others (1993b). Walkerdine emphasises, however, that while the researcher's struggle to explore her own investments in certain interpretations can be crucial to research if properly used, it is 'not equivalent' to recording the subject's own words (Walkerdine 1997: 74), nor is it a means of speaking 'for' them. Autobiographical references in themselves do not guarantee intellectual correctness, political authenticity or effectiveness. But this turn in feminist work nearly always goes along with a strong awareness of intersubjectivity, and nowhere more so than in feminist oral history, our next area of debate.

Oral history

Laura Marcus, from the point of view of a literary critic, remarks that 'another important development is the growing affinity between auto/biography and oral history' (Marcus 1994: 274). She notes that much influential work in oral history has been dedicated to recording working-class testimonies, as part of a revision of historical focus to include those previously left out of the history books (Thompson 1988). This aim has obvious similarities with the feminist project, and feminist oral historians have seen themselves as recovering women's lost voices and hidden history (Carroll 1976; Chamberlain 1975; Lewis 1981; Roberts 1984; Passerini 1989). The issues that we have discussed in the previous section have raised problems for this simple model of recording experience, and some feminist oral historians have developed complex and sophisticated methodologies to deal with these problems. In particular, ideas of intersubjectivity and relationship have been central to their endeavour. As Penny Summerfield has pointed out, 'the telling of life stories in response to a researcher's enquiries, is not a simple one-way process, but involves a set of relationships all of which are pervaded by gender' (Summerfield 1998: 2).

The problems involved in using accounts of 'lived experience' as history were first pointed out by Denise Riley. As she wrote:

> The trouble with the attempt to lay bare the red heart of truth beneath the discolourations and encrustations of thirty-odd years on, is that it assumes a clear space out of which voices can speak – as if, that is, ascertaining 'consciousness' stopped at scraping off history. That is not, of course, to discredit what people say as such, or to imply that considering the expression of wants is pointless. The difficulty is that needs and wants are never pure and undetermined in such a way that they could be fully revealed, to shine out with an absolute clarity, by stripping away a patina of historical postscripts and rewritings.

(Riley 1983: 191)

Riley went on to argue against the use of 'women' as a category in history, whose experiences could be recovered. Instead, the object of study should be the discourses that constructed this category (Riley 1988). This appeared at first to remove the idea of women's agency that feminist researchers were keen to identify, but, as Judith Butler has argued, 'construction is not opposed to agency; it is the necessary scene of agency, the very terms in which agency is articulated' (Butler 1990). There is still, then, room to study 'the relationship between cultural constructions and consciousness' (Summerfield 1998: 11). The 'patina of historical postscripts' that rewrite memory can themselves become the focus of study. The oral historian's work is to 'untangle the relationships between discourses and experience' (Canning 1994; see also Bornat 1994, Davies 1992). These relationships can be described as intersubjective: 'personal narratives draw on the generalised subject available in discourse to construct the particular personal subject' (Summerfield 1998: 15). That is, popular and public legends, narratives, stereotypes are made use of by the individual to construct their own story (Chanfrault-Duchet 1991; Thomson 1994).

But there are also two other ways in which oral history accounts are intersubjective: they depend on a relationship between the speaker and the audience (an audience comprising both the interviewer, and the wider audience for the research), and between the speakers and the performance models available to them – for instance, televised interviews, or magazine articles. Different genres influence each other here, while at the same time the researcher must be aware that the oral history account has its own generic features. Kristina Minister sees the oral history interview as taking place between the public and the private, in the intimacy of the subject's own home, but for a wider implied audience (Minister 1991). Marie-Françoise Chanfrault-Duchet in this collection is especially acute in analysing the genre, and also in showing the influence on the oral history account of other discourses and literary patterns.

Feminist researchers have also been concerned about the ethics of the intersubjective encounter that is the oral history interview. They do not want to reproduce the unequal power relationships to which women have always been subjected (Oakley 1981; Reinharz 1992). The ideal is equality between researcher and researched, but this is hard to achieve. They attempt to mitigate the power imbalance 'first, by seeing the interview as a sharing of experience; second, by placing themselves in a subjective position within the interview; and third, by giving the interviewees some responsibility for the project' (Summerfield 1998: 24). These procedures are also seen as necessary to help women voice their interiority, though, as we have seen, that interiority is understood as deeply affected by 'outside' discourses and models. But the argument here is that women's accounts have historically been 'muted', they do not mesh so well with the dominant discourses as do men's, and so they need special encouragement, special listening (Anderson and Jack 1991). Feminist intersubjectivity is not just there, it is something the interviewer tries to create.

Theories of memory are obviously crucial to the practice of oral history (Coleman 1991). Penny Summerfield, in this collection, discusses Graham Dawson's idea of the production of personal memory as 'composure' (Dawson 1994). The subject 'composes' a life-story and a self they feel comfortable with. She asks whether the result of feminist oral history could instead be *discomposure*, as subjects are brought to confront the conflicting discourses of femininity. Mary Chamberlain, another oral historian in our collection, deploys complex theories of memory, and introduces yet another aspect of intersubjectivity, as she learns to interpret the accounts of 'subjects' who conceive of themselves intersubjectively, women who are not separable from their mothers and grandmothers. Magda Michielsens problematises the whole oral history project by investigating the mismatches between past and present cognitive frames, as well as misunderstandings between East and West, when she interviews women from Bulgaria.

Feminism and autobiography

The mutual influences of Feminism and Autobiography which we have been charting in this Introduction have brought about many transformations of both practices. This collection explores the latest of these changes, as they affect autobiographical studies. We focus in particular on an increasing cross-disciplinarity in material and method; a change in the perception of autobiography as not just a literary genre or a collection of texts, but also as a widespread cultural practice, produced as much by social pressures as by an individual inner necessity; and the preoccupation with autobiography as a method.

As we have said, this book originated in a seminar series held by the Institute of Women's Studies at Lancaster University on 'Autobiography and the Social Self'. We hope that our collection will recreate some of the liveliness and excitement of the series. We close with a short section of 'position pieces' from that series, which all address the theme 'Autobiography Matters'. Treva Broughton provides an overview of what the new developments in autobiography studies mean for her particular area, the nineteenth century. Consuelo Rivera-Fuentes and Ruth McElroy both adopt a 'personalist' and experimental approach, one to address the topic of lesbian autobiography, and one to investigate the sometimes contradictory intertwinings of autobiography, academia and nationality. We hope this section will prompt our readers to carry further their own debates on and explorations in the still unfolding issues raised by the conjunction of feminism and autobiography.

Notes

1 The word 'genre' is itself a slippery term with different meanings in different disciplines. For instance, in literary studies it means an established category of written work with similar features and common conventions (established stylistic and thematic practices). 'Autobiography' in a literary sense is sometimes referred to as a 'sub-genre'. But in linguistics, 'genre analysis' can cover forms (spoken, written and visual) as diverse as the academic essay, the talk show, the press photo and the job interview, and the definition of the term starts from the social and practical dimension. Carolyn Miller (1984) defines the term as 'stereotypical social action'.

2 The seminar series 'Autobiography and the Social Self' was funded by the ESRC and took place at the Universities of Lancaster and York from 1996–8. We should like to acknowledge the support of the ESRC, and to record our thanks to the group at the Institute of Women's Studies at Lancaster who planned and organised the six work-

shops, as well as to Janet Hartley, the Institute's Officer. Special thanks go to all the participants in the series.

3 See note 1 above. By using the word 'genre' we are signalling its contested nature – for us it means 'the way autobiography is defined', or 'what can be included under the definition "autobiography"'.

4 Essentialism is the belief that there are basic characteristics that all women share, rather than that 'women' are a historically and culturally specific category. For a good discussion of essentialism, see Fuss 1989.

Bibliography

Ahmed S. (1997) 'It's a Sun-tan, Isn't It?: Auto-biography as an Identificatory Practice', in Mirza, H. (ed), *Black British Feminism. A Reader*, London and New York: Routledge: 153–68.

Anderson, K. and Jack, D. (1991) 'Learning to Listen: Interview Techniques and Analysis', in Gluck, S. and Patai, D. (eds), *Women's Words: The Feminist Practice of Oral History*, London: Routledge.

Anderson, L. (1997) *Women and Autobiography in the Twentieth Century*, London and New York: Prentice Hall/Harvester Wheatsheaf.

Anderson, L. and Broughton, T. (eds) (1997) *Women's Lives/ Women's Times: New Essays on Auto/biography*, New York: State University of New York Press.

Bakhtin, M. (1981) *The Dialogic Imagination*, Austin: University of Texas Press.

Berlant, L. (1997) *Queen of America Goes to Washington City: Essays in Sex and Citizenship*, Durham, NC: Duke University Press.

Bornat, J. (1994) 'Is Oral History Auto/biography?', *Lives and Words, Auto/Biography*, 3, 2.

Brodzki, B. and Schenck, C. (eds) (1988) *Life/Lines: Theorising Women's Autobiography*, Ithaca: Cornell University Press.

Butler, J. (1990) *Gender Trouble: Feminism and the Subversion of Identity*, London: Routledge.

Canning, K. (1994) 'Feminist History After the Linguistic Turn: Historicizing Discourse and Experience', *Signs: Journal of Women In Culture and Society*, 19, 2.

Carroll, B. (ed.) (1976) *Liberating Women's History. Theoretical and Critical Essays*, Chicago: University of Illinois Press.

Caruth, C. (ed.) (1995) *Trauma: Explorations in Memory*, Baltimore: Johns Hopkins University Press.

—— (1996) *Unclaimed Experience: Trauma, Narrative and History*, Baltimore: Johns Hopkins University Press.

Chamberlain, M. (1975) *Fenwomen: A Portrait of Women in an English Village*, London: Virago.

Chanfrault-Duchet, M. (1991) 'Narrative Structures, Social Models, and Symbolic Representations in the Life Story', in Gluck, S. and Patai, D. (eds), *Women's Words: The Feminist Practice of Oral History*, London: Routledge.

Chodorow, N. (1978)*The Reproduction of Mothering: Psychoanalysis and the Sociology of Gender*, Berkeley and London: University of California Press.

Coleman, P. (1991) 'Ageing and Life History: The Meaning of Reminiscence in Later Life', in Dex, S (ed.), *Life and Work History Analyses: Qualitative and Quantitative Developments*, London: Routledge.

Davies, B. (1992) 'Women's Subjectivity and Feminist Stories', in Ellis, C. and Flaherty, M. (eds), *Investigating Subjectivity. Research on Lived Experience*, London: Sage.

Dawson, G. (1994) *Soldier Heroes, British Adventure, Empire and the Imagining of Masculinities*, London: Routledge.

Felman, S. and Laub, D. (1992) *Testimony: Crises of Witnessing in Literature, Psychoanalysis and History*, New York and London: Routledge.

Fonow, M. and Cook, J. (1991) *Beyond Methodology: Feminist Scholarship as Lived Research*, Bloomington: Indiana University Press.

Freedman, D., Frey, O. and Zauhar, F.M. (1993) *The Intimate Critique: Autobiographical Literary Criticism*, Durham, NC: Duke University Press.

Fuss, D. (1989) *Essentially Speaking: Feminism, Nature and Difference*, London: Routledge.

Gagnier, R. (1991) *Subjectivities: A History of Self-Representation in Britain, 1832–1920*, New York and Oxford: Oxford University Press.

Gilmore, L. (1994) *Autobiographics: A Feminist Theory of Women's Self-Representation*, New York and London: Cornell University Press.

Harding, S. (1986) *The Science Question in Feminism*, Milton Keynes: Open University Press.

Heilbrun, C. (1988) *Writing a Woman's Life*, New York: Norton.

Jelinek, E. (ed.) (1980) *Women's Autobiography*, Bloomington: Indiana University Press.

Kenny, M.G. (1999) 'A Place for Memory: The Interface between Individual and Collective History', *Comparative Studies in Society and History*, 41, 3, July.

Kirmayer, L.J. (1996) 'Landscapes of Memory: Trauma, Narrative and Dissociation', in Antze, P. and Lambek, M. (eds), *Tense Past: Cultural Essays in Trauma and Memory*, London and New York: Routledge: 173–99.

▷ Kuhn, A. (1995) *Family Secrets: Acts of Memory and Imagination*, London and New York: Verso.

Lewis, J. (1981) 'Women Lost and Found: The Impact of Feminism on History', in Spender, D. (ed.), *Men's Studies Modified. The Impact of Feminism on the Academic Disciplines*, Oxford: Pergamon Press.

Lorde, A. (1984) *Sister Outsider: Essays and Speeches*, Freedom, CA: The Crossing Press.

Marcus, L. (1994) *Auto/Biographical Discourses*, Manchester and New York: Manchester University Press.

Martin, R. (1991) 'Unwind the Ties that Bind', in Spence, J. and Holland, P. (eds), *Family Snaps*, London: Virago: 209–37.

Maynard, M. and Purvis, J (1994) *Researching Women's Lives from a Feminist Perspective*, London: Taylor and Francis.

Miller, C. (1984) 'Genre as Social Action', *Quarterly Journal of Speech*, 70: 151–67.

Miller, N. (1991) *Getting Personal: Feminist Occasions and Other Autobiographical Acts*, London: Routledge.

—— (1996) *Bequest and Betrayal: Memoirs of a Parent's Death*, Oxford: Oxford University Press.

Minister, K. (1991) 'A Feminist Frame for the Oral History Interview', in Gluck, S. and Patai, D. (eds), *Women's Words: The Feminist Practice of Oral History*, London: Routledge.

Oakley, A. (1981) 'Interviewing Women: A Contradiction in Terms', in Roberts, H. (ed.), *Doing Feminist Research*, London: Routledge and Kegan Paul.

Passerini, L. (1989) 'Women's Personal Narratives: Myths, Experiences and Emotions', in Personal Narratives Group (ed.), *Interpreting Women's Lives: Feminist Theory and Personal Narratives*, Bloomington: Indiana University Press.

Pearce, L. (1994) *Reading Dialogics*, London: Edward Arnold.

Probyn, E. (1993a) *Sexing the Self: Gendered Positions in Cultural Studies*, London and New York: Routledge.

—— (1993b) 'True Voices and Real People: The "Problem" of the Autobiographical in Cultural Studies', in Blundell, V., Shepherd, J. and Taylor, I. (eds), *Relocating Cultural Studies: Developments in Theory and Research*, London: Routledge.

Radstone, S. (1999), 'Social Bonds and Psychical Order', unpublished paper given at the 'Testimonial Culture and Feminist Agendas' Conference, Institute of Women's Studies, Lancaster University.

Ramazanoglu, C. (1993) *Up Against Foucault: Explorations of Some Tensions Between Foucault and Feminism*, London: Routledge.

Reinharz, S. (1992) *Feminist Methods in Social Research*, Oxford: Oxford University Press.

Rich, A. (1977) *Of Women Born: Motherhood as Experience and Institution*, London: Virago

—— (1979) *On Lies, Secrets and Silence: Selected Prose, 1966–78*, New York: W.W. Norton.

—— (1987) *Blood, Bread and Poetry: Selected Prose, 1979–1985*, London: Virago.

Riley, D. (1983) *War in the Nursery, Theories of the Child and Mother*, London: Virago.

—— (1988) *Am I That Name? Feminism and the Category 'Women' in History*, London: Macmillan.

Roberts, E. (1984) *A Woman's Place, An Oral History of Working-class Women 1890–1940*, Oxford: Basil Blackwell.

Showalter, E. (1997) *Hystories: Hysterical Epidemics and Modern Culture*, London: Picador.

Skeggs, B. (1995) *Feminist Cultural Theory: Process and Production*, Manchester and New York: Manchester University Press.

Smith, D. (1987) *The Everyday World as Problematic: A Feminist Sociology*, Boston: Northeastern University Press.

Smith, S. (1987) *A Poetics of Women's Autobiography, Marginality and the Fictions of Self-Representation*, Bloomington: Indiana University Press.

Smith, S. and Watson, J. (eds) (1998) *Women, Autobiography, Theory: A Reader*, Wisconsin: University of Wisconsin Press.

Spence, J. (1986) *Putting Myself in the Picture: A Political, Personal and Photographic Autobiography*, London: Camden Press.

—— (1991) 'Shame-work: Thoughts on Family Snaps and Fractured Identities', in Spence, J. and Holland, P. (eds), *Family Snaps*, London: Virago: 226–37.

Spivak, G. (1986) 'Three Women's Texts and a Critique of Imperialism', in Gates, H. (ed.), *'Race', Writing, and Difference*, Chicago: University of Chicago Press.

Stacey, J. (1997) *Teratologies: A Cultural Study of Cancer*, London: Routledge.

Stanley, L. (1992) *The Auto/Biographical I: Theory and Practice of Feminist Auto/Biography*, Manchester: Manchester University Press.

Stanton, D. (ed.) (1987) *The Female Autograph: Theory and Practice of Autobiography from the Tenth to the Twentieth Century*, Chicago: University of Chicago Press.

Steedman, C. (1995a) 'Inside, Ouside. Other: Accounts of National Identity in the Nineteenth Century', *History of the Human Sciences*, 8, 4: 59–76.

—— (1995b) 'Maps and Polar Regions. A Note on the Presentation of Childhood Subjectivity in Fiction of the Eighteenth and Nineteenth Centuries', in Pile, S. and Thrift, N. (eds), *Mapping the Subject: Geographies of Cultural Transformation*, London, Routledge.

Summerfield, P. (1998) *Reconstructing Women's Wartime Lives: Discourse and Subjectivity in Oral Histories of the Second World War*, Manchester: Manchester University Press.

Thomson, A. (1994) *Anzac Memories, Living with the Legend*, Oxford: Oxford University Press.

Thompson, P. (1988) *The Voice of the Past, Oral History*, Oxford: Oxford University Press.

Tompkins, J. (1991) 'Me and My Shadow', in Warhol, R. and Herndl, D. (eds), *Feminisms*, New Brunswick, NJ: Rutgers University Press.

—— (1996) *My Life in School*, Reading, MA: Addison-Wesley.

Veeser, H. A. (1996) *Confessions of the Critics*, New York and London: Routledge.

Walkerdine, V. (1991) 'Behind the Painted Smile', in Spence, J. and Holland, P. (eds), *Family Snaps*, London: Virago: 26–35.

—— (1997) *Daddy's Girl: Young Girls and Popular Culture*, Basingstoke: Macmillan.

Waugh, P. (1989) *Feminine Fictions: Revisiting the Postmodern*, London and New York: Routledge.

Part I

Genre

1 Enforced narratives

Stories of another self

Carolyn Steedman

Histories of autobiography and histories of the self

If we are interested in autobiography – interested as literary and cultural theorists, as historians and sociologists – then we work with two tacit assumptions. The first is that somehow, in some way, the production of written forms has something to do with the production of subjectivities; and the second is that this process is a voluntary one, that there is an *urge* to tell the self, that it comes from within, and that the impulsion to do so, in spoken or written language, is part of the very process of self construction.

These assumptions, of a connection between self-writing and self-construction, come from two traditions of academic inquiry, the literary and the historical. Over the last twenty years, feminist literary theorists and critics have scrutinised the long-term European project of creating an autobiographical canon and have condemned it for being almost entirely made up of items of masculine self-writing. Naming the problem as the *writing* of normative masculinity actually reinforced the connection between a form of written language and the aetiology of the self. As Sidonie Smith put it in 1993, the difficulty of autobiography (as practised by Augustine, Rousseau and Goethe, or any other male member of the canon you choose to mention) is that it composes a *master* narrative, the 'architecture of the universal subject', a 'hard nut of ... normative (masculine) individuality' (Smith 1993: 3). However, literary criticism has had its effects, and now, at the end of the century, the autobiographical canon has been greatly extended, and the autobiographical *theory* derived from it is more likely to be fashioned out of women's writing than that of men.

The concomitant accusation, that the Western autobiographical canon was constructed from the writings of *élite* men, was more muted, but has brought about an equal shift of attention, from the chronicles of the privileged to the annals of the labouring poor. There are many more writings of women, and of plebeian men *and* women in print and in circulation than there were twenty years ago. In the same period, a vast and proliferating body of postcolonial criticism has directed attention away from the subject of Europe, towards the subaltern and marginalised subjects of the contact zones. But as Pamela Fox noted when she was working on twentieth-century working-class writing (on fiction rather than on autobiography, though the point still holds good), it is a common academic assumption that the written productions of working-class people belong to some realm of 'fact' or 'reality', rather than to 'literature', and are thus the province of the historian rather than the literary critic (Fox 1994: 45). It is certainly the case that whilst modern autobiographical theory has been made out of the published writing of formerly neglected women and some postcolonial subjects, working-class autobiography has not been used in the same way.

During the same period of academic activity, historians of literacy and culture reinforced the connection between the development of modern autobiography and modern selfhood. Any historian of the early modern and modern periods in Europe and the Americas works with the heavy freight of a historiography that charts the rise of individualism and individuality in the West. This insistent 'background' stresses the role of writing and reading in the making of modern social and political persons. From two ends of the twentieth century two examples make the point. In Max Weber's *The Protestant Ethic and the Spirit of Capitalism* (1904–5), spiritual journals, confessional tales, Bunyan's first-person narratives and a whole range of literary texts of the seventeenth and eighteenth centuries are used to inscribe Economic Man or (less figuratively and more prosaically) the relationship between Protestant selfhood and the structures of early capitalist development (Weber 1991). In a major publishing enterprise of the 1980s, *The History of Private Life*, the volume dealing with the seventeenth and eighteenth centuries elaborates, refines and *illustrates*, in charming and compelling detail all the categories of modernity, so that we might see the things and feelings that proliferate around reading and writing (novels, pens, writing manuals, chairs for reading in and *peignoirs* to wear whilst sitting in them, libraries, closets; romantic love and love for children, privacy, intimacy) as the modern subject makes him or herself. Such techniques of feeling, connected to the practices of reading and writing, have been even more recently celebrated in John Brewer's *Pleasures of the Imagination* (Chartier 1989; Brewer 1997).

Outside the fields of literary and historical studies, the question of autobiography has been moved away from exclusive concentration on the written word, and into the more general terrain of narrative. In *Modernity and Self-Identity*, Anthony Giddens describes a 300-year development in the West, by which personhood and self-identity have come to be understood as 'the self … reflexively understood by the person in terms of his or her biography'. He understands 'autobiography' not so much as a form of writing, nor as a literary genre, but rather as a way of thinking and feeling – as a mode of cognition. According to Giddens, the process of actually writing an autobiography, getting it published and having it read is a very minor variant of a much more general 'autobiographical thinking'. He says that in this 'broad sense of an interpretive self-history produced by the individual concerned, [autobiography] whether written down or not … is actually the core of self-identity in modern life' (Giddens 1991: 52–4).

Self-narration (meaning 'interpretive self-history' *and* the formal written autobiography) has come to be emphasised again and again as formative, constitutive and descriptive of the subject of modernity. The understanding is refined by – for example – Charles Taylor, in his *Sources of the Self. The Making of the Modern Identity*. Here he surveys the whole of Western philosophy, and the great sweep of its cultural history (Renaissance humanism, urbanisation, Reformation, Protestantism, capitalism, individualism), in order to claim that *the thing that has happened* since the end of the fifteenth century is the move of the self from outside to inside. He describes the emergence of a 'disengaged, particular self, whose identity is constituted in memory'. This identity is expressed in self-narration: 'the life at any moment is the causal consequence of what has transpired earlier ... [and] since the life to be lived has also to be *told*, its meaning is seen as something that unfolds through the events' (Taylor 1989: 289).

For Taylor the importance of these developments is the questions they force about the *form* of the life-stories people tell. He asks whether the narrated story of the self is simply 'the *result* of the happenings as they accumulate', or whether the form of the life is there already, is somehow 'already latent', waiting to be expressed though an account of what came to pass in any individual life. In these deliberations, the self is conceived of as a remembered thing as well as a narrated thing.

Connections between memory and narrative have led to a recent interest in eighteenth- and nineteenth-century thinking about childhood, and it has become clear that in some autobiographies of the last two centuries the idea of the child was used to both recall and express the past that each individual life embodied; what was turned inside in the course of individual human development was that which was already latent; the child (the child the autobiographer had been) *was* the story waiting to be told. In nineteenth- and twentieth-century autobiographical practice, people's use of the child-figure (their remembering, and sometimes writing, about themselves as child) merged the two perspectives to which Taylor draws our attention (Wolff 1998: 377–401; Coe 1984; Steedman 1990: 62–80; 1995a: 59–76).

One of the many ways in which forms of selfhood have been transmitted and appropriated is through the reading of – or at least knowing about – literary selves.[1] There are even newer conclusions to be reached on this score about the relationship, mediated by writing, of selfhood to social structure and social change. If ways of being a person, and ideas of what a person is, are read, appropriated and learned differently in different historical epochs, then they are also *taught*. The subject of British modernity for example, was made a matter for instruction in the years after the Second World War, in the massive programme of teaching selfhood and self-expression that was in operation in state schools in Britain, from the early 1950s onwards. 'Creative writing' encapsulated beliefs about the psychological benefits of writing the self for children in classrooms and the pedagogical conviction that writing autobiographically allowed a recuperative selfhood to be developed in working-class children (Steedman 1999: 41–54). Creative writing flourished in conjunction with new practices of self-narration outside the school: adult education, the development of the worker-writers' and community publishing movement (and thus an astonishing flowering of working-class autobiography in the 1970s), the rapid growth of community theatre, the folk movement and its deliberate forging of a sense of community between past and present narratives of the poor, the practice of oral histories of the working class, the development of the History Workshop movement, and, towards the end of the 1960s, the practice of consciousness-raising in the emergent women's movement.[2] All these practices operated on the assumption that the subaltern *could* speak; that through self-articulation in spoken or written words, the dispossessed could come to an understanding of their own story.[3] That story – that life – could, by various means, be returned to the people who had struggled to tell or to write it, and be used as basis for political action.[4]

But any conclusions about this development in the period 1945–74 need the perspective of a *longue durée* of taught – perhaps enforced – self-narrative. It is the purpose of this chapter to consider the history of what we may come to call 'the autobiographical injunction': a history of expectations, orders and instructions rather than one of urges and desires.

The autobiographical injunction

The summary above offers an account of the connections that we are able to make now, at the beginning of the twenty-first century, between the making of the modern self and the writing of it. But there is something else to notice, something else to see. The social historian, believing that something like this really has happened over the last three hundred years, starts to ask other questions: Who tells the story of the self? Who does it most, at one time, in one place? Who uses these stories? *How* are they used, and to what ends?

Our autobiographical canon may still be made up of the writings of *élite* men and women, but in England from the seventeenth century onwards, the emerging administrative state demanded that it was in fact the poor who tell their story, in vast proportion to their vast numbers. The major source for Keith Snell's monumental and elegiac account of working-class experience and its expression in rural England between 1660 and 1900 is extant settlement examinations, the many thousands of them that have ended up in county record offices (Snell 1985). Under legislation of 1661, magistrates were required to inquire into the origins of those who might become applicants for poor relief. Determining place of settlement, that is the parish responsible for relief of distress, involved applicants, or potential applicants, in telling a life-story, and having it recorded. Hundreds of thousands of men and women told where they were born, when they were put to work, where they had worked, and crucially, for how long they had worked in any one place, for working consistently in one parish and receiving wages for a calendar year, carried one of the most important entitlements to settlement. A century and a half of this kind of formulaic self-narration preceded Mary Manton's examination in the parish of Astley, Warwickshire, in the autumn of 1815:

Mary Manton says that about September 1813 Mrs Beadman of Market Bosworth in the County of Leicester hired the said Mary Manton to serve her for £7.7.0 but no Time mentioned but when said Mary Manton Came to her Service she hasked her Mistress whether she was hired for 51 week or for 12 months but the Mistress Made answer and Said that was according to her behaviour but about 9 weeks after Christmas 1814 she had some fierce words with his [sic] Mistress whome paid her wages and Left and when to her Father's house for 1 night only which next Morning Returned to fetch her Cloths. She agreed with her Mistress to Serve her Time out and Rcd. her whole Wages, which she did at this Michaelmas 1814.[5]

The most common narrative extracted from women of the labouring poor, after the one framed by work, was the story of seduction and betrayal. Bastardy examinations, again conducted before justices of the peace, were demanded for the same administrative purposes, for an illegitimate child was a potential drain on parish resources. To extract the name of a putative father and charge him with maintenance, or to return an expectant mother to her true place of settlement offered a clear saving against local rates. Elizabeth Wells, examined by Nottinghamshire JP Sir Gervase Clifton in late 1809, was a parish apprentice, that is, a poor child apprenticed out by her home parish, and the legal question here was not who the father of her child might be, but rather, whether or not her home parish or her master had the right to discharge her from her indentures before her time was up:

> The Examination of Eliz. Wells ... Who says she was born in the parish of Ruddington in the County of Nottinghamshire of Parents legally settled there That when she was about nine Years old she was put out parish Apprentice to John Wilkinson of Ruddington Farmer until she was twenty one Years or marriage she was to have her Victuals drink & Cloaths she says she staid there about four years and she getting too big for an under servant her master told her she might go to the Statutes[6] and get hired ... accordingly [she] was hired to George Blount ... Husbandman for one year she staid there two whole years and received her two years wages. ... That in ... June 1809 she went over to Ruddington to ... inquire wether she was out of her time under her Parish Indentures to John Wilkinson he ... said she did not belong there and that he had burnt the Indentures. She says she was then hired to John Butler of Clifton. ... She was hired for this Year but proving to be with Child of a Bastard child he cannot keep her any longer She is now in her twentieth year and is at present with Mr Butler.[7]

The legally required questions that structure these autobiographies can certainly be heard. Like the haunting self-narratives that Henry Mayhew presented to a variety of reading publics in the mid-nineteenth century, they are written accounts produced by questioning, but from which, in transcription, the interlocutor has been removed. By these means, multitudes of labouring men and women surveyed a life from a fixed standpoint, told it in chronological sequence, gave an account of what it was that brought them to this place, this circumstance now, telling the familiar tale for the justice's clerk (who was so very used to the formula that Mary Manton becomes a 'he' by boredom of the pen) to transcribe. Apart from not being written down by the person who lived the life, these brief narratives fulfil the criteria for autobiographical narration (Vincent 1981). And some were written down by the liver of the life presented for scrutiny. The eighteenth-century philanthropic organisation often demanded a story in exchange for its dole. The mid-century London Society for the Encouragement of Honest and Industrious Servants determined that none should join or have entitlement to a handout unless they gave their account *in writing*: 'Every person applying must deliver in a Petition, a Narrative of Information, containing an Account of his or her Service' – 'with whom, when, where, how long, in what quality ...' (Anon. 1752: 10).

There were literary forms, Grub-Street products, that exploited these everyday, enforced narratives of the self. There was the criminal tale, best known through *The Newgate Calendar* but more widely distributed in chapbook form (Rayner 1826; Neuberg 1972). One example plucked from the myriad is *An Account of the Execution of Mary of Shrewsbury for the Murder of Her Bastard Child* of 1775.[8] Mary Saxby's *Memoirs of a Female Vagrant, Written by Herself* (1806) is notable for two reasons. One is that in the massive microfilm publishing venture 'The People's History. Working Class Autobiographies, 1729–1889' of 1986, a series of facsimiles of all such volumes deposited in the British Library, hers is the first woman's story reproduced. It is part of the ongoing project to uncover and circulate the life-stories of the plebeian, the subaltern, the female. In this recovered working-class narrative, Saxby's pain at losing eight of her ten children, and the guilty anguish of coming slowly and creepingly to God, certainly structure a conventional Methodist conversion tale. But a surer and tighter structure for the narrative on the page is the writer's detailing of her contact with the law, and the central and local state. Her bids for settlement, appearances before the justices, encounters with the overseers of the poor (as well as with numerous philanthropic doctors and clergymen, likely to make a cash exchange for her story), dates and places of baptism and burial, as well as births and deaths, but on only one occasion marriage (her cohabitations and fornications provide the book's insistent throb of shame), are listed and recorded, with a detail and precision of recall that the *genre* simply does not demand (Saxby 1806). Mary Saxby's written autobiography was structured by all the other involuntary accounts she had delivered up over the course of fifty years.

The narrative of a life, which when told, explains something of the person, here, now, telling a tale (much more rarely, writing it down) was articulated again and again, by men and women like these, from the seventeenth century onwards. The basic structures of the modern literary character were – perhaps – laid down in these numerous enforced autobiographies. This is a large claim; and as yet, we know very little about the way in which an understanding of what a character was (what an informal theory of 'character' looked like) moved into the emergent novel, and out again, into the wider society, to be taken and used in innumerable acts of self-fashioning and self-perception. There is suggestive work on stage melodrama of the nineteenth century, and the understanding it may have brought into being, that a working-class character was a he or she buffeted by fortune and extraneous events (Booth 1965, 1989: 96–103). And in discussing fictional realism's fixation on 'character' Bruce Robbins has observed that as 'character was the mask that people were expected to don in the face of power', 'it seems more than a coincidence that from the time … when modern criticism took shape, a "character" was a statement in which one employer described to another … the habits and qualities of a servant' (Robbins 1993: 35).

We have not yet moved beyond these tentative suggestions, that the modern literary articulation of selfhood and character had its origins among the poorer sort, in both the literary and the social realm, when their verbal accounts of themselves were recorded by others. But part of the social process involved – the telling of a plebeian narrative; its appropriation and the use of its plot and themes by more genteel others – is enacted and described in two eighteenth-century texts which offer valuable evidence of the ways in which the narrative of the poor might be used by those in other ranks and orders of society for their own purposes of self-articulation.

Moll and Jemima

Extended narratives of the plebeian self were the focus of at least two novels of the eighteenth century (or rather, were used in two fictional texts of the period that we now classify as novels). Mary Wollstonecraft's *Maria, or, The Wrongs of Woman* was published in 1798, and is easier to classify as a novel than is an earlier case in point, Daniel Defoe's *Moll Flanders* of 1722, although in many ways *Maria* displays a weird hybridity more usual in earlier texts. You can for example, read *Maria* as a fictionalising of the arguments of the *Vindication of the Rights of Woman* (1792), embodying the same condemnation of criminal law, common law, poor law and system of police, in the figure of its eponymous heroine, as does the political tract. In the fictional version of these arguments, Maria's baby has been snatched from her breast by a tyrannical husband wishing to gain possession of her marriage portion, and she has been imprisoned by him in a madhouse. You can certainly – for the motifs just adumbrated – read *The Wrongs of Woman* in the Gothic mode; or as an epistolary fiction perhaps, for in her prison cell Maria sits down to pen her tale for her absent baby daughter and it is that narrative that makes up much of the text. You may read the romance in *The Wrongs of Woman* too if you care to, as part of Wollstonecraft's sustained, imagined and – neces-sarily – one-sided exchange with Jean-Jacques Rousseau, when she has us encounter her heroine in her cell, not only with 'her bosom aching with the nutriment for which [her] cherished child might now be pining in vain' (75),[9] but also a little later, deep in a novel, completely engrossed by *La Nouvelle Heloise*, which Darnford, a fellow prisoner has lent her. Maria 'had read this work long since; but now it seemed to open a new world to her – the only world worth inhabiting' (88). Less well-versed in the erotic conventions of the novel than your average eighteenth-century reader, we still know well enough that if an exchange of letters between a man and a woman is almost shockingly warm, then the loan of such a book can only mean that a sexual relationship is on the cards.

Indeed Maria, who has only so far glimpsed the owner of the novel through her prison bars, bestows on Darnford 'the personification of St. Preux', the tutor-hero of Rousseau's text, and 'all St. Preux's sentiments and feelings, culled to gratify her own' (89). So we may also read this novel as a conduct book, and Wollstonecraft in the long line of writers issuing warning against the reading of silly novels by silly women.[10]

A brief survey of the multiplicity of forms in *Maria* is a way of getting a plot-summary in place. Far more interesting – odd and strange – is the structure of the text and the relationship between the two autobiographies it contains: that of Maria, and that of her wardress, Jemima. Wollstonecraft died before *Maria* was finished, and the shape of the posthumous publication owes something to William Godwin's editorial hand. Yet its narrative structure, the timing and placing of the two life-stories that compose it, cannot be altered or reversed. The first story told is Jemima's. Her tale comes before Maria's, and we must read it before we encounter Maria's. It is only after – it is only *because* – Maria has heard Jemima's harrowing record of physical and sexual abuse, rape, abortion, prostitution, starvation, and all the failures of the law to alleviate her suffering, that Maria's 'autobiography' materialises. This point must be emphasised: Wollstonecraft has the bourgeois heroine *only able* to narrate her own childhood and girlhood, *only able* to interpret her own story as one of a woman's suffering under a legal system of extraordinary misogyny, through the previous articulation of Jemima's terrifying tale. As readers *we simply cannot have* Maria's narrative in any shape or form without its framing by Jemima's. The early pages of the novel note that Maria attempts to alleviate the boredom and anxiety of incarceration by writing of 'the events of her past life', which 'might perhaps instruct her daughter' (82). But the autobiography does not materialise textually until Jemima has told hers. Its themes (which we know nothing of, until the memoir appears, seven chapters long, between inverted commas) are explicitly related to Jemima's story by the narrator:

> Thinking of Jemima's peculiar fate and her own, she was led to consider the oppressed state of women, and to lament that she had given birth to a daughter ... she dwelt on the wretchedness of unprotected infancy, till sympathy with Jemima changed to agony, when it seemed probable that her own babe might even now be in the very state she so forcibly described.
>
> (Wollstonecraft 1980: 120)

In textual terms, there is no story of the self for Maria without Jemima's being in place first.

As literary figure, Jemima has precursors, and can be read as one of Moll Flanders' fictional daughters (Faller 1993). Her source, then, may be the very same place of origin as that earlier working-class heroine, for both Wollstonecraft's Jemima and Defoe's Moll originate in Newgate Prison (the character Moll is actually born there), possibly in Defoe's patient transcription of the narrative told him by the actually existing fence and prostitute, Moll King, in her prison cell in 1721.[11] Wollstonecraft was familiar with Defoe's work, though she never mentioned *Moll*.[12] But whether or not their connection is intentional, the stories of Jemima and Moll are resonant. In 1978 Juliet Mitchell observed that Defoe inaugurated a new tradition of writing with *Moll Flanders*, that his Moll starts as a child, and 'what happens to Moll as a mature woman, indeed, who she is as a woman, depends on the conditions of her birth, her infancy, childhood and adolescence'. In this way, claims Mitchell, the first written 'individual' of fictional realism was a woman, or rather, was the 'Capitalist Woman' Moll Flanders (Mitchell 1984: 217). This perception, of childhood experience exercising a shaping force on the adult woman, also profoundly affects Wollstonecraft's writing of Jemima. What holds Moll and Jemima together is their presentation as literary characters who experienced childhood – childhoods that are described at length in the texts, and that are seen as shaping the adult telling the tale. Being *made*, by their social circumstances Moll and Jemima are *individuals* in the modern political and philosophical sense, and are *characters* in the modern literary sense.

At one point in her narrative of childhood, Defoe allows his character to refuse a course of events – the plan that she should become a servant – designed by the adults around her. Wollstonecraft's Jemima on the other hand, is not given the chance to refuse anything, and her bleak tale of a loveless childhood allows for not one moment of the reciprocity and tenderness that Defoe so carefully shows little Moll receiving. Wollstonecraft's intention was indeed to depict a woman who could not love 'her fellow creatures, because she had never been beloved …' (82), whom 'a deadly blight had met … at the very threshold of existence' (79). One of the most interesting aspects of *The Wrongs of Woman* is Maria's determination to waken feeling in Jemima (she needs badly to do this, so that Jemima will attend to the full force of her plight and help her escape the mad-house). Wollstonecraft carefully describes the pedagogy of empathy that Maria exercises, Jemima's 'strange mixture of interest and suspicion' in response to it, the many moves she makes to stop Maria telling her story, 'as if afraid of resigning, by giving way to her sympathy, her dear-bought knowledge of the world' (82).

It is Maria's pathetic maternity, the aching space left by the snatched child, that brings Jemima to full human sympathy – that, and watching the 'animated … accents of tenderness' with which Maria and Darnford converse:

> So animated … were their accents of tenderness … that Jemima felt … a tear of pleasure trickling down her rugged cheeks … the first tear that social enjoyment had ever drawn from her … she felt herself, for once in her life, treated like a fellow creature … and … was so softened by the air of

confidence which breathed around her, that she voluntarily began an account of herself.

(Wollstonecraft 1980: 101)

By telling her story, Jemima is restored to herself and able to empathise with Maria. She helps her escape from the mad-house, and, in the most extensively written of the endings that Wollstonecraft was deciding between when she died, finds Maria's child for her.

Jemima (and Moll before her) would not exist in textual terms were she not a rewritten and reshaped social verisimilitude. But we should not be content to let her existence rest on that point, even though we are left this way, with nothing but questions. Why women as the two first full 'characters' of literary modernity? Jemima possesses a past that 'explains' her – a childhood, and a story of childhood. Why two working-class women?

This retelling of Jemima's tale raises yet more questions about the uses of other people's stories of the self. The first is to do with the late eighteenth-century's most pervasive and protean psychological theory, that is the structures of thought bound up in the terms 'sensibility', 'sentiment', 'sympathy'; what we may call (though the eighteenth century did not) Empathy Theory. Using this theory, a sense of self, of place in the world and identity, was articulated through the use of *someone else's* story of suffering, loss, exile, exploitation, pain. This turn of thought and affectivity was formalised and theorised by the mid-eighteenth-century philosophy that underpinned the social forms of sensibility, sympathy and empathy. Numerous guidebooks, from the philosophical tract to the advice manual, showed how the story of suffering, told by another, could be accessed, and its pathos used for the art of self-construction. Indeed, 'Sensibility' received one of its many hundreds of treatments in the scene from *Maria* just recounted, where Jemima is moved to tell her own story after having been brought to full human sympathy by witnessing the genteel tenderness of Darnford's and Maria's love-making.

This scene from Wollstonecraft's posthumous novel is not, however, typical of the movement of emotion in eighteenth-century fiction: in terms of class, rank and status, the traffic in sentiment mostly goes the other way. In Henry MacKensie's *The Man of Feeling* (1777) the gentry hero wanders the metropolis hearing the stories of abandoned and seduced daughters, poor mad things raving about lost love in Bedlam, the pathetic victims of trickery, sad, exploited soldiers – all in order to feel the fineness of his own empathy. He *must* listen to the victim's tale, to the story of someone who has been made subordinate by disaster.

In those moments of vibrating reception, when the heart throbs in sympathy and we are sublimely aware of the harmony of our reactions with those of the person we are sympathising with, it seems necessary, an absolute rock-bottom line of the exchange, that he or she who tells the harrowing tale, is diminished by *having* that story to tell; and is subordinated in that act of telling. Most of the tellers, in fact, are already inferior, by reason of sex (they are women) or of status (they are of a lower rank than he – it is usually he – who listens, and feels the fineness of his own response).

There are particularly useful philosopher guides to this process. David Hartley, in his *Observations on Man* (1749) (particularly in section IV, 'Of the Pleasures and Pains of Sympathy') and Adam Smith, in *The Theory of the Moral Sentiments* (1759), writing 'Of the Pleasure of Mutual Sympathy', describe in some detail how the process might take place, and allow us to see that the second autobiographical exchange in *The Wrongs of Woman*, when Maria is moved to write her own story *after* hearing Jemima's, follows a more usual route between rank and class of subjects (Hartley 1967: 471–85; Smith 1976: 9–16).

Conclusion: Maria's story

There are some notes to be made, by way of conclusion, towards an alternative history of the modern, Western self. The structure of this alternative history is put in place once full recognition is given to all that can be encompassed by the term 'autobiography': to the understanding that a modern self has been articulated through the processes of personal narration, a narration only rarely written down by the autobiographer. Childhood was told as part of the story, and was later theorised as the well-spring of the self. The first articulation of these points in English literature was probably in two literary figures, both women, both of the poorer sort, both having connection to service. There were contemporary theories of subjectivity and empathy that made necessary the subordinate's tale. And the most consistent, formulaic, the *most* autobiographical action, in the way it has been defined here, in seventeenth- and eighteenth-century England, was probably demanded of the poorer sort, a demand that developed apace in the eighteenth century.

In accounting for people's compliance with their own dispossession and subordination, their continued acceptance of situations that were of no obvious benefit to them and that, in fact, preserved the inequities of the world, Adam Smith suggested in 1759 that we find it easy to identify with those whose conditions we judge to be more fortunate than our own. In *The Theory of the Moral Sentiments* (1759) he suggested that

> when we consider the condition of the great, in those delusive colours in which imagination is apt to paint it, it seems to be almost the abstract idea of a perfect and happy state. It is the very state which, in all our waking dreams and idle reveries, we had sketched out to ourselves as the final object of our desires. We feel therefore, a peculiar sympathy with the satisfaction of those who are in it. Upon this disposition of mankind, to go along with the passions of the rich and powerful, is founded the distinction of ranks, and the order of society.
>
> (Smith 1976: 51–2)

But we have evidence here of the traffic going the other way. Is the possession of a terrible tale, a story of suffering, *desired*, perhaps even envied, as a component of the other self? Wollstonecraft's Maria did not know what the meaning of her story *was* until she heard Jemima's. A late twentieth-century black woman writer contemplates the continued use of other people's stories to make the modern suffering bourgeois self:

> No need to heed your voice when I can talk about you better than you can speak about yourself. No need to hear your voice. Only tell me about your pain. I want to know your story. And then I will tell it back to you in a new way. Tell it back to you in such a way that it has become my own. Re-writing you I rewrite myself anew. I am still author, authority. I am still coloniser, the speaking subject, and you are now at the centre of my tale.
>
> (hooks 1990: 343)

bell hooks's words are made more telling by the uses made of them. This passage is quoted by Robert Berkhofer in *Beyond the Great Story. History as Text and Discourse*, where it is the graphic illustration of his discussion of the problems encountered by feminist history in its appropriation of other people's experience. But Berkhofer uses bell hooks's voice at one remove, by citing the quotation as it appears in Giles Gunn's *Thinking Across the American Grain* of 1992: there is no direct reference to her words (Berkhofer 1995: 184; Gunn 1992: 10). Pursuit of this passage, down through the footnotes, leads only to a dislocation, between hooks and her experience, between this particular woman and her particular story; for, of course, it is entirely to the writer's point that the argument is made in the voice of the appropriator of hooks's tale – who we may call Maria, or indeed, Mary Wollstonecraft – who writes herself, using Jemima.

What we may do with all of this is finally begin to disentangle the history of autobiography from a history of the Western self. An account of the narratives that were demanded of the labouring poor, and the possible expropriation of those narratives by others in different classes and circumstances, may possibly make clear at last that – in the case of those plebeian narrators at least – autobiography was not a straightforward telling of a self. In these cases, a story of the self – told or written – was not the same thing as the life lived. Eighteenth-century enforced narratives and the invented voices of the fictionalised poor from the same period show autobiography to be something that was often demanded: a thing that could be fashioned according to requirement, told and sold, alienated and expropriated. This is nothing new: the discipline of social history has long taught us that the experiences of the labouring poor are probably irretrievable: lost and gone. We are left with a newer and less familiar series of questions, to do with a bourgeois self that was told in terms of a suffering and enduring other, using the themes and items of other, dispossessed and difficult lives.

Notes

1 There are some observations about this process in Steedman 1995b: 77–95.
2 Morley and Worpole (1983); Worpole (1984); Samuel (1981: 22–48); and Dentith (1985: 60–80) for working-class writing. Lovell (1990: 19–67) discusses the relationship between feminism, the women's movement and feminist history in the postwar years. Recently we have had our attention drawn to earlier practices of self-expression and self-narration. Georgie Boyes has discussed the roots of the folk revival in *The Imagined Village*, and Ewan McColl has described the space provided by the BBC for the narration of everyday lives, from the 1930s onwards, in his autobiography *Journeyman*. Boyes (1993); McColl (1992: 311–77).
3 Gayatri Spivak (1988) first asked the question about the possibility of the subaltern woman ever being able or permitted to speak. Spivak's answer to her interrogative title is a (fairly clear) 'No'.
4 There is some discussion of this pedagogical and political practice in Steedman (1999: 17–42). James Vernon (1999) discusses the origins of social history.
5 Warwickshire Country Record Office, DR 19/433493. Parish of Astley. Overseers of the Poor, Removal Orders and Settlement Examinations. DR 19/480, 'Mary Manton's Examination'.
6 The Statute Fair: a hiring fair, at which servants in husbandry and, to a lesser extent, domestic servants, made verbal contracts with employers for a year's employment.
7 Nottinghamshire Record Office, M8051, Notebook of Sir Gervase Clifton, JP, 1805–1810, p. 37. Entry dated 26 October 1809. For the law relating to settlement, and a large number of cases which, unlike that of Elizabeth Wells, made case-law, see Const (1793: 315–515). See the case of Hannah Wright of Derbyshire, pregnant and out of place in 1778, in *ibid.*: 516–18, and in Caldecott (1785: 11–14). Bastardy examinations are a major source for Mark Jackson's *New-born Child Murder* (see Jackson 1996).
8 The British Library's copy of *An Account of the Execution of Mary of Shrewsbury for the Murder of Her Bastard Child – God's Judgement Upon False Witnesses*, Alston, London (1775), is bound with a series of chapbooks, among them *The Merry Life and Mad Exploits of Captain James Hind, the Great Robber of England*, *The Battledore, or, First Book for Children* and *The High German Fortune Teller*. There is some discussion of the relationship of this kind of literature to the criminal biography in Faller (1987). See also the discussion in Gattrell (1994). For the strange dislocations of chronology and voice in a form that allowed the condemned man or woman (like Mary of Shrewsbury) to be publicly hung to the accompaniment of the ballad that recorded their last dying words (which they had not uttered, and would not say), see Davis (1983: 42–84).
9 References in the text are to Wollstonecraft (1980).
10 George Eliot (1856) provided the phrase, in describing their authors.
11 For Defoe's encounter with Moll King, see the Introduction to Defoe (1989: 9).
12 See Kelly (1992: 211). Wollstonecraft reviewed Chalmer's *Life of Defoe* in 1790, but she did not mention *Moll* in it. See Todd and Butler (1989: 305–7).

Bibliography

Anon. (1752) *A Proposal for the Amendment and Encouragement of Servants*, London: J. Shuckburgh.

Berkhofer, R. (1995) *Beyond the Great Story. History as Text and Discourse*, Cambridge, MA: Harvard University Press.

Booth, M.R. (1965) *English Melodrama*, London: Herbert Jenkins.

—— (1989) 'Melodrama and the Working Class', in Carol Hanbery MacKay (ed.), *Dramatic Dickens*, London: Macmillan: 96–109.

Boyes, G. (1993) *The Imagined Village. Culture, Ideology and the English Folk Revival*, Manchester: Manchester University Press.

Brewer, J. (1997) *The Pleasures of the Imagination. English Culture in the Eighteenth Century*, London: HarperCollins.

Caldecott, T. (1785) *Reports of Cases Relative to the Duty and Office of a Justice of the Peace, from Michaelmas Term 1776, Inclusive, to Trinity Term 1785, Inclusive*, London: His Majesty's Law Printer's.

Chartier, R. (ed.) (1989) *A History of Private Life. Volume III. Passions of the Renaissance*, Cambridge, MA: Belknap Press of Harvard University Press.

Coe, R. (1984) *When the Grass Was Taller. Autobiography and the Experience of Childhood*, New Haven: Yale University Press.

Const, F. (1793) *Decisions of the Court of the King's Bench, Upon the Laws Relating to the Poor, Originally Published by Edmund Bott*, vol. 2, 3rd edn, London: Whieldeon and Butterworth.

Davis, L. (1983) *Factual Fictions. The Origins of the English Novel*, New York: Columbia University Press.

Defoe, D. (1989 [1722]) *Moll Flanders*, Harmondsworth: Penguin.

Dentith, S. (1985) 'Contemporary Working Class Autobiography. Politics of Form, Politics of Content', *Prose Studies*, 8: 60–80.

Eliot, G. (1856) 'Silly Novels by Lady Novelists', *Westminster Review*, 66: 442–61.

Faller, L.B. (1987) *Turned to Account. The Forms and Functions of Criminal Biography in Late Seventeenth and Early Eighteenth Century England*, Cambridge: Cambridge University Press.

—— (1993) *Crime and Defoe, A New Kind of Writing*, Cambridge: Cambridge University Press.

Fox, P. (1994) *Class Fictions. Shame and Resistance in the British Working-class Novel, 1890–1945*, Durham, NC: Duke University Press.

Gattrell, V.A.C. (1994) *The Hanging Tree. Execution and the English People, 1770–1868*, Oxford: Oxford University Press.

Giddens, A. (1991) *Modernity and Self Identity. Self and Society in the Late Modern Age*, Cambridge: Polity.

Gunn, G.B. (1992) *Thinking Across the American Grain. Ideology, Intellect, and the New Pragmatism*, Chicago and London: University of Chicago Press.

Hartley, D. (1967[1749]) *Observations on Man. Part the First*, Hildesheim: Georg Olms Verlagsbuchhandlung.

hooks, b. (1990) 'Marginalizing a Site of Resistance', in Ferguson, R., Geves, M., Minhha, T.T. and West, C. (eds), *Out There. Marginalization and Contemporary Culture*, New York and Cambridge, MA: New Museum of Contemporary Art and MIT Press: 341–3.

Jackson, M. (1996) *New-born Child Murder. Women, Children and the Courts in Eighteenth-century England*, Manchester: Manchester University Press.

Kelly, G. (1992) *Revolutionary Feminism. The Mind and Career of Mary Wollstonecraft*, London: Macmillan.

Lovell, T. (1990) *British Feminist Thought. A Reader*, Oxford: Blackwell.

McColl, E. (1992) *Journeyman*, London: Sidgwick and Jackson.

Mitchell, J. (1984 [1978]) '*Moll Flanders* The Rise of Capitalist Woman', in *Woman: The Longest Revolution*, Harmondsworth: Penguin: 195–218.

Morley, D. and Worpole, K. (1983) *The Republic of Letters. Working Class Writing and Local Publishing*, London: Comedia.

Neuberg, V.E. (1972) *Chapbooks*, London: The Woburn Press.

People's History (1986) 'The People's History. Working Class Autobiographies from the British Library, Part I: 1729–1889; Part II: 1890–1920', Brighton: Harvester Press Microform Publications and the British Library.

Rayner, J.L. (1826) *The Complete Newgate Calendar*, 5 vols, London: privately printed.

Robbins, B. (1993 [1986]) *The Servant's Hand. English Fiction from Below*, Durham and London: Duke University Press.

Samuel, R. (ed.) (1981) *People's History and Socialist Theory*, London: Routledge and Kegan Paul.

Saxby, M. (1806) *Memoirs of a Female Vagrant, Written by Herself*, London: J. Burditt.

Smith, A. (1976[1759]) *The Theory of the Moral Sentiments*, Oxford: Oxford University Press.

Smith, S. (1993) *Subjectivity, Identity and the Body. Women's Autobiographical Practices in the Twentieth Century*, Bloomington: Indiana University Press.

Snell, S. (1985) *Annals of the Labouring Poor. Social Change and Agrarian England, 1660–1900*, Cambridge: Cambridge University Press.

Spivak, G. (1988) 'Can the Subaltern Speak? Speculations on Widow Sacrifice', in Nelson, C. and Grossman, L. (eds), *Marxism and the Interpretation of Culture*, Urbana: University of Illinois Press: 271–313.

Steedman, C. (1990) *Childhood, Culture and Class in Britain. Margaret McMillan, 1860–1931*, New Brunswick: Rutgers University Press.

—— (1995a) 'Inside, Outside, Other: Accounts of National Identity in the Nineteenth Century', *History of the Human Sciences*, 8, 4: 59–76.

—— (1995b) 'Maps and Polar Regions. A Note on the Presentation of Childhood Subjectivity in Fiction of the Eighteenth and Nineteenth Centuries', in Pile, S. and Thrift, N. (eds), *Mapping the Subject. Geographies of Cultural Transformation*, London: Routledge: 77–92.

—— (1997) 'A Weekend with Elektra', *History and Literature*, 6, 1: 17–42.

—— (1999) 'State Sponsored Autobiography', in Conekin, B., Mort, F. and Waters, C. (eds), *Moments of Modernity. Reconstructing Britain, 1945–1964*, London: Rivers Oram: 41–54.

Taylor, C. (1989) *Sources of the Self. The Making of the Modern Identity*, Cambridge: Cambridge University Press.

Todd, J. and Butler, M. (1989) *The Works of Mary Wollstonecraft*, vol. 7, London: Pickering.

Vernon, J. (1999) 'Telling the Subaltern to Speak. Mass Observation and the Formation of Social History in Post-War Britain', unpublished paper, University of Manchester.

Vincent, D. (1981) *Bread, Knowledge and Freedom. A Study of Nineteenth-century Working-class Autobiography*, London: Methuen.

Weber, M. (1991 [1904–5, trans. 1930]) *The Protestant Ethic and the Spirit of Capitalism*, London: HarperCollins.

Wolff, L. (1998) 'When I Imagine a Child: the Idea of Childhood and the Philosophy of Memory in the Enlightenment', *Eighteenth Century Studies* 31, 4: 377–401.

Wollstonecraft, M. (1980 [1798]) *Maria; or The Wrongs of Woman*, ed. Gary Kelly, Oxford: Oxford University Press.

Worpole, K. (1984) *Reading by Numbers. Contemporary Publishing and Popular Fiction*, London: Comedia.

2 From 'self-made women' to 'women's made-selves'?

Audit selves, simulation and surveillance in the rise of public woman

Liz Stanley

Introductory

> Thus perhaps at stake has always been the murderous capacity of images: murderers of the real; murderers of their own model as the Byzantine icons could murder the divine identity. To this murderous capacity is opposed the dialectical capacity of representations as a visible and intelligible mediation of the real. All of Western faith and good faith was engaged in this wager on representation: that a sign could refer to the depth of meaning, that a sign could *exchange* for meaning and that something could guarantee this exchange – God, of course. But what if God himself can be simulated, that is to say, reduced to the signs which attest his existence? Then the whole system becomes weightless; it is no longer anything but a gigantic simulacrum: not unreal, but a simulacrum, never again exchanging for what is real, but exchanging in itself, in an uninterrupted circuit without reference or circumference.
>
> (Baudrillard 1988:170)

Auto/biographical practices and the politics of lives

The analytic idea of 'auto/biography' (Stanley 1992a; *Sociology* 1993; Polkey 1999) shares with feminism a focus on the shifting and complex boundaries between self and other, past and present, writing and reading, fact and fiction. 'Auto/biography' in this analytic sense is concerned with basically epistemological matters in relation to a wide range of oral, visual and written accounts of lives. Rather than being preoccupied with the specifically written forms of these – 'autobiographies' and 'biographies' and their sub-groupings – this work has been focused on auto/biographical *practices*, that is the myriad of everyday and frequently fleeting social practices concerned with the articulation of (often competing, sometimes discontinuous) notions of 'selves' and 'lives'.

Auto/biographical practices include the oral and visual and are by no means confined to written accounts, although these are included. They are everyday practices which typically occur as 'moments' within a very wide range of other kinds of activities, rather than as one-off set-piece performances: they are less 'my published autobiography' than they are the routinised and ordinary, such as 'introducing my self to new acquaintances', 'constructing a CV of myself to apply for a job or promotion' and 'describing someone to other people'. The specific auto/biographical practices I am concerned with here are those produced and enacted within organisational contexts, for I am interested in the ways in which selves are recorded and refracted by the regulatory mechanisms of organisational encounters.

Many of these practices occur because of the requirements of organisational regulatory systems and are characterised by constraint or necessity, rather than by any inner felt need to provide an autobiographical account of the self. And most of them occur as aspects of 'other' kinds of behaviour and event, such as applying for a state benefit, making a will or registering a death, rather than being set-piece presentations of the 'here is my life from birth until now' kind.

The development of 'auto/biography' as a specifically analytic tool is something I have been closely involved in, partly through the foundation and subsequent activities of the British Sociological Association's Study Group on Auto/Biography and its journal *Auto/Biography*.[1] I have been particularly engaged by the idea of 'auto/biography' because it is concerned with epistemological matters, that is with issues and claims surrounding what is seen to be knowledge; and consequently it facilitates bringing together my engagement with feminist thinking on epistemological matters and my interest in 'lives' as a means of bringing into focus the relationship between individuals and social structure. The approach of auto/biography proposes that 'what you know is what and who you are', and, correspondingly, that 'you are what is known about you'. It conjoins epistemology and ontology, or rather it refuses the binary here and does so in an explicit and principled way. I can best explain its analytic concerns here by quoting from the Auto/Biography Study Group joining leaflet, which proposes that 'auto/biography' is:

> an epistemologically-orientated concern with the political ramifications of the shifting boundaries between self and other, past and present, writing and reading, fact and fiction, and with an analytical attention to these within the oral, visual, and written texts that are 'biographies and autobiographies'. The writer/speaker, the researcher and author, are certainly not treated as transparent or 'dead', but very much alive as agents actively at work in the textual production process. Auto/biography engages analytically with these epistemological problematics and displaces the referential and foundational claims of writers and researchers by focusing on the writing/speaking of lives and the complexities of reading/hearing them. It thereby unsettles notions of 'science', problematises the claims of research, questions the power issues that most researchers either silence or disclaim.
>
> (Auto/Biography Study Group 1995)

Theoretical and research uses of the idea of 'auto/biography' are consequently directed towards a wide range of social practices which articulate notions (often competing) of selves, identities and lives. These are often fleeting auto/biograph-ical 'moments', occurring through the everyday social processes by which knowledge about lives is made, exchanged and remade in the context of, for example, paid work, domestic life, interpersonal relationships. They are also *polit-ical* processes through and through, for organisational as well as interpersonal reputations, statuses, influences and hierarchies all trade in these currencies of spoken, written and visual lives. One historical example here is that it was no accident of terminology that led to domestic servants needing a 'character' – a written and/or a verbally provided statement about what kind of person they were, as well as what standard of work they did – so as to be able to move from one respectable place of employment to another. The 'character' was not only a moral statement but also a highly constitutive practice that could and did have repercussions for people's places within the labour market, within 'respectable' society' and also as moral beings: it indicated what someone's status and worth should be taken to be, and the giving and withholding of 'characters' was highly consequential for people's positions within class, status and other hierarchies.

Much of the theoretical and analytical running concerned with looking at, 'recovering' and theorising 'lives' over the last fifteen years or so has been made within the frame of Women's Studies scholarship. And of course this is not surprising given, on the one hand, its concern with women's excised selves, women's silenced selves, women's selves seen as 'other' to the real selves of the proper, putatively male, human subject; and, on the other, the almost complete absence of a concern with women's lives during the 1960s and 1970s, when an academic interest in written lives increased (as Jelinek 1980 and Stanton 1987 have both pertinently commented).[2] In this still mushrooming field of feminist work, and with some exceptions (including Stanley 1992a; Polkey 1999; Polkey and Donnell 2001), the idea of 'auto/biography' has been used in a largely descriptive sense to indicate 'both autobiographies and biographies', as in the title of Laura Marcus's *Auto/biographical discourses* (1994). Instead a different set of theoretical and analytical arguments has been developed here, concerned with the changing nature of 'the self' within modernity and the ways in which women's senses of self have been articulated through, particularly, the various written forms of autobiography. This work has been engaged with the conjunc-tion between 'modernity' and 'self-expression' and its focus has been not so much on the articulation as the progressive construction of self as interiority, as a quintessentially 'modern' phenomenon which has enabled but at the same time undermined women's emergent senses of selfhood. This is a concern with 'the interiority project of modernity': at the centre of this approach is a confessional self, where women's interior sense of self is made and remade through the lens, and the means, of 'autography', the writing of self, to use Domna Stanton's (1987) term, in which women's sense of (or lack of, emergent, contested or insis-tent) self has been not only articulated in, but more particularly written into existence through autobiographies, memoirs, diaries and letters.

The emphasis here references an autobiographical confessional 'urge' or 'impulse', a felt need to articulate the self and its interiorities; and this in turn expresses the dominant emphasis in a much wider sweep of feminist work, from the early 1980s on, concerned with the autobiographical self. The background argument (foregrounded in Stanton 1987) is that there has been a conjunction between 'modernity', and notions of interiority and 'self-expression', which has both supported and at the same time undermined women's emergent identities and senses of selfhood. This is not to propose that there is no cognisance in such work of structuring factors which impinge on this – for instance, in the work of feminist Foucauldians writing on 'lives' there is a good deal of interest in discursive practices and the ways in which these impact on lives.[3] However, the concern is very much with the self and its mediation by discursive practices, with the result that 'the social' seems to me collapsed into the interior processes of the self or exterior discursive processes, or else these are read backwards and forwards between each other, and 'the social' as I understand it does not feature as a locus of concern in its own right.

The interest in autobiography in this broad approach comes from the ways in which autobiography – self, life, writing – both shapes and helps enact self-identities; and the locus of analytic attention is on how this takes place within the construction of notions of selfhood and identity. The theoretical argument it is connected with proposes that in the historical period before modernity, selves were understood and experienced through sets of interlocking social and kin-based responsibilities and obligations, with notions of interiority and individuation emerging over an epiphanous period of time and involving a fundamental change to the earlier experience of selfhood. What results is a concern in theorising modernity around the production of selves with interiorities and authenticities locked in a confessional culture. Domna Stanton's twin terms of 'autography' (self writing) and 'autogynography' (writing a woman's self) usefully stand for the emphasis in a wide sweep of feminist work here. More recently, companion terms such as the 'autobiographical impulse' and the 'autobiographical urge' give expression to a similar emphasis on autobiography as the site for articulating an emergent female interiority in a culture seen as preoccupied with testimony and confession.

Much of the work carried out in this analytic frame is thoughtful and insightful, and some of my own work has also been located within it. However, standing back from its interesting specificities to contemplate its broad analytical generalities, there is something of a problem here. This approach, or perhaps the analytic focus on modernity that it has attached itself to, is located in a Whig view of the onward and upward march of the progress and articulation of the modern (female) self; and while there is certainly recognition of differences and fractures within the self, this is still a Bildungsroman, a romance of self-progress and self-actualisation, of impulses and urges to speak self, confess self, make self. Wherever there is romance in the intellectual air, I find myself drawing back, taking stock, and consequently there are a number of caveats I want to make.

First, modernity herein is about as long as a piece of string, for different authors date its origins and then its demise in postmodernity very differently. In part, the problem occurs because 'modernity' as a conjectured period of time is often conflated with 'modernism' as an intellectual formulation composed by sets of ideas, and, in part, it occurs because statements about the origins and inner meaning of both are actually claims being made, and not the announcement of 'facts' demonstrably 'there' at particular temporal junctures. Second, feminist work on women's autobiographical writings in premodern England suggests that many of these developments actually antedate modernity, with their origins more complex and temporally more diffuse than the monocausal explanation covertly present within the 'modernity thesis' implies.[4] Third, the Western European focus of this line of thinking fails to recognise that in many parts of the world women's actual lives have yet to reach the markers taken to be indicative of modernity, but here too women's insistence on self and self-worth erupts into public visibility and is organised and campaigned for, and autobiographically inscribed. And fourth, the emphasis in this body of work is very much on texts and writing and not on 'lives, as such' – Stanton's term of 'autography' is indicative, with its excision of 'bio' as a supposedly naïve referentiality. And yet the intractably inconvenient fact remains that people do indeed have lives in which things happen and the stories which are told about lives come from accounts of these things which happened. A feminist theoretic which denies or despises the necessarily referential basis of autobiography as *life*-writing as well as *self*-writing is in analytical as well as political trouble.

Something of the analytic difference which 'auto/biography' can make to an interest in autobiographies and lives can be indicated by reference to the *Getting a Life* collection edited by the feminist academics Sidonie Smith and Julia Watson (1996). This focuses on a wide range of everyday autobiographical practices by which lives are presented, understood and lived; however, it has no specific analytic edge to its contents, so that, while the editors are concerned with the fragmentations and dispersals of bits of lives as bytes of data and the ways in which identities are invoked and told in stories and other kinds of narratives, these are but two concerns among a good many more which some of the contributors attend to but others do not. The result gathers under a common title some disparate discussions of a wide range of the dimensions of everyday lives in an interesting and suggestive way, but it puts neither an *analytic* edge on, nor puts the *politics* back into, the study of lives. However, the emphasis provided by 'auto/biographical practices' places analytic attention on social organisation and audit as the context in which the speaking and writing and picturing of selves takes place.[5] Recognition of the politics of lives here lies in the attention to organisational encounters and to audit, simulation and surveillance, and the ways in which these produce both exteriority or audit selves and thereby help re/constitute notions of interiority as well.

While both lines of approach – auto/biography and feminist autobiography – are intellectually engaging and produce rich strains of theoretical and substantive work, they also lead to different theoretical, analytical and substantive emphases. 'Auto/biographical practices' are a complex meeting-ground between self-expressions which are the compelled results of acts of audit and surveillance, an approach which might be expressed as a concern with 'the exteriority project of audit'. Work on feminist autobiography conceptualises autobiographies as written articulations of self and identity (again, as Stanton's term 'autography' emphasises); and here autobiography is seen as a central means for constructing a sense of identity, an approach which might be expressed as 'the interiority project of modernity'. The acts and apparatus of confession within Roman Catholicism provide an example which can be 'turned' in both directions: confession can be seen as the expression of an inner sense of selfhood within modernity, but it can also be understood as the product of an external system of surveillance in which regulation and requirement are associated with organisation, power and audit.

So far I have emphasised broad generalities in order to point up some of the significant differences between 'auto/biographical practices' on the one hand, and 'feminist autobiography' on the other. I also want to indicate my recognition that there is a still-developing middle ground between them and I should add that my own recent work concerned with 'lives' has been located in these borderlands (in Stanley 1999, 2000a, 2000b). My interest is in developing a feminist analytical concern with the exteriority project and with what kind of 'self' is constituted by organisation and audit (with 'organisation' here spanning both formal and informal forms). Succinctly, I want to develop a specifically feminist form of auto/biography – 'feminist auto/biography' – and in doing so I want to 'have it all', analytically speaking. That is, I want both to retain a sense of women's articulations of a variety of means to 'speak' and so possess a sense of self and interiority, and also to focus on organisation, regulation and audit in compelling exteriority. Along the way, I am also interested in exploring some interrelated questions about these matters, including: how should gender, class and 'race' be best inscribed within the analytic framework of 'auto/biography'?; what kind of self is constituted by systems of audit?; what are the possible narratives, possible narrative conventions and possible kinds of self that result?; are these audit systems generating consistent or divergent auto/biographical practices?; and what happens to the relationship between the 'exteriority self' of audit and any notions of an interiority?

There are two of these interlinked questions I am particularly interested in thinking about in the rest of this chapter: what kind of self is constituted by systems of audit, and with what consequences for the relationship between the 'exteriority self' of audit and notions of interiority? I shall pursue them first through some ideas about the relationship between interiority and exteriority and appearances and identities, and then some related ideas about 'audit selves', simulation and surveillance, and I will conclude with some thoughts about resistances.

Interiority and exteriority in thinking about selves

As I indicated earlier, while overall the analytic concerns of 'auto/biography' and exteriority, and those of a feminist concern with autobiography and interiority, are parallel but separate intellectual projects, there is a still-expanding borderland between them. For me, a particularly interesting example of feminist work which engages in intellectual border traffic is provided by Carolyn Steedman's (1995) exploration of childhood (and more recently, in this volume, on womanhood) and the idea of human interiority, not least because Steedman's work too 'wants it all', analytically speaking. In her analysis, interiority is taken as a problematic and not as an impulse or urge, and the interiority project of modernity is construed as one in which, from the eighteenth century on, some (bourgeois, male, adult, white) selves were made, constructed, actualised, precisely *realised*, by constraining and indeed often forcing other selves (working-class, female, child, black) to speak, to be articulated. This self was a regulating, collecting, disposing self: by constraining others to speak and to be recorded, this self inscribed and realised and finally possessed its own self to which these others were, or rather became, Other. This is the notion of interiority produced, indeed *externalised*, through the bureaucratic recording, regulating, disposing rationality of the bourgeois male over the period of the emergence of modernity. For Steedman, this was a particularly, and peculiarly, gendered project but one which was articulated within and through class and cultural capital.

Steedman's formulation of notions of interiority as resulting from exteriorising selves through acts of regulation and compulsion makes excellent analytic sense of some of my own past auto/biographical research, in which I was involved in editing and analysing the diaries of the working-class Victorian servant Hannah Cullwick (1833–1909) as these interface with the 'companion' diaries of the upper-class gentleman, Arthur Munby (1828–1910), with whom her life became involved (Stanley 1984). Cullwick's diaries began in the early 1850s soon after she first met Munby, and at his request. Munby insisted Cullwick write her diaries so as to provide the thread of connection between them, often living long distances apart and always at a chasm-wide social distance, not least because of the clandestine nature of their relationship. Cullwick experienced her diary writing as immensely more tiresome and wearying than the relentless hard work of Victorian servitude that her diary mainly inscribes, although it also includes her meetings with and activities engaged in for her 'Massa', as she called Munby.

Munby started to write his diary some time after Cullwick's began, and it records the externalities of his life and not its interiorities. Cullwick's diary was regularly and routinely sent to Munby for collection and its instalments were literally pieced together and made whole by him. Arthur Munby was a man whose 'self' consisted in the spaces between the very different kinds of social milieux within which he moved.[6] His interiority, or such as he had, was one which was literally absent, hidden away in his clandestine involvement with Hannah Cullwick, and, it would seem, articulated predominantly through the injunctions he laid and enforced on her to write her life, and, in doing so, to enable him to write his through his observations of the social spaces around this interiority. But precisely whose self was it that this injunction to write a woman's life most impacted upon? My response is that Munby was able to 'get a life' through some closely and complex interrelated things here: the refraction of his self back to him through its constitution in Cullwick's diary, and 'proof' of his selfhood as indicated by her diary as demonstration of his constitution of 'her' within its pages. And his own diary, it seems to me, served very similar purposes in the making of the bourgeois male self of Arthur Munby: it refracted back to him his self, his existence, his person. But for her, Hannah Cullwick's diaries had both a 'take it or leave it' quality (and just as soon as she felt she could, she left them) and also served more ordinary if no less utilitarian purposes.

Cullwick's diaries and the account they provide of the working life of a woman who was a domestic servant – the kind of life which convention deems too unimportant and trivial to 'count', biographically speaking – were the basis of my initial interest in these 'companion diaries'. Few women of her class, occupation and time have left any individual or personal record, and more typically they are known through whatever traces remain on public record only. As I soon realised, Cullwick's diaries also provide ample demonstration of the very powerful ways in which writing a self autobiographically could and did enable women to gain possession of a sense of self which had earlier been absent from their lives.

Starting in the 1850s, with her marked hesitancy and perfunctory (conventionally stylised) skills as a writer, by the 1870s Hannah Cullwick had become a highly proficient and skilled diarist who recorded her working activities and her observations on her social 'betters' and who also used her diary to engage in a set of inter-textual and then 'inter-public' communications with Munby. Through these textual means she sought to influence, persuade and constrain Munby to particular courses of 'real life' action which she deemed 'correct' and 'proper', in particular with regard to her 'character'. The relationship between Cullwick and Munby by this time had existed for nearly two decades and over this time moved from the entirely clandestine to being 'known about' by some of Cullwick's friends and family but not by Munby's. By the early 1870s and through happenstance, it had also become known to the respectable bourgeois family with whom Cullwick lived and worked as a maid of all work. Questions were then raised concerning the moral and sexual probity of the relationship precisely because it had existed for so many years – could a relationship which failed to eventuate in marriage be respectable, no matter how sexually chaste it might be?

When this first came into the open, Cullwick had settled such questioning by force of moral character; but this settlement was provisional because conditional upon a conventional resolution or denouement to the relationship (marriage, or parting), rather than what Cullwick wanted, the continuation of the relationship and also the continuation of her 'good character' as a working woman. Cullwick recorded these 'debates' in her diary over a period of time, indicating what might happen to the public persona of her 'character' and so her chances of future employment, what was 'due' from Munby in such circumstances, and under what circumstances the relationship would continue. While disliking marriage because it would position her as 'too much like a woman', Cullwick also recognised that external circumstances meant that her continued good character required it, and that Munby should 'of his own free will' offer it to her.

This eventually happened, but only after a lengthy period of her using her diary to record his reactions to the growing knowledge on the part of her employers, his reluctance to face up to the implications for her 'character', and what was due to someone with whom he had had a twenty-year relationship of love and trust.

After their marriage in 1873, the largely clandestine nature of the relationship continued, with Cullwick ostensibly being only Munby's 'servant' and working in his lodgings in the Temple in London. The continuation of secrecy enabled Cullwick to carry on working, for she was extremely proud of her skills and physical strength and prowess, and despised what she perceived as the idle prettiness and enforced weakness of 'ladyhood'. However, Munby seems to have thought that, once she became accustomed to '*appearing like* a lady', then Cullwick would start to '*be a* lady', a lady of his creation, and that her self-identity would change according to the dimensions of the outward life she lived. A number of incidents occurred in which secrecy and openness, dis/guise and transformations, and the relationship between self-appearance and self-identity were at issue. These escalated because Cullwick refused to bend her life and will to Munby's, refused to 'appear to be' a lady on more than a very occasional basis, and they culminated in a major rift in which Cullwick returned to Shifnal in Shropshire, where she had been born and where members of her family still lived. From the middle 1870s to the middle 1880s, there was first a complete estrangement and then the slow establishment of a relationship almost as semi-detached as when they had first met.

As this discussion will have shown, I am interested in bringing the analytical and political ideas involved in exteriority and auto/biographical practices and audit selves, and those involved in interiority and the writing and making of selves and identities, together. For me, the notion of interiority works best when seen as regulated and produced through exteriorities formulated and enacted at different levels within the social structure, including through the organisational as well as interpersonal dynamics involved. An aphorism which can stand for this is that of 'the self outside in and inside out'. Another is that of moving away from the idea of 'self-made women' to that of 'women's made-selves'. However, while I certainly recognise that 'made-selves', 'personae', play a constitutive role, I certainly don't see this as a deterministic one – I'm not convinced by 'it's all compelled' any more than I am by 'it's all self-made'. I now want to look at this idea of 'made-selves' or 'personae' more closely in connection with the idea of 'audit selves' and organisational encounters.

Organisational encounters and audit selves

I'm interested in what kind of self is constituted by monitoring and audit, and what the consequences of this might be for the relationship between the 'exteriority self' of audit and notions of interiority. As my discussion of the Cullwick and Munby diaries will have indicated, these processes of monitoring and audit can occur in interpersonal contexts and by a variety of informal mechanisms, including through the writing and reading of diaries, letters and other 'documents of life'. However, I am also interested in their more formal variants and their use by organisations, and thus with 'organisational encounters' in which people engage in particular auto/biographical practices which are allowed, constrained or sometimes compelled by particular organisational purposes and functions. In discussing this, I begin by looking at some ideas about audit and surveillance in the work of Michael Power (1994, 1997).

Power's influential discussion of the 'audit society' argues that a fairly sharp distinction exists between audit and surveillance with regard to organisational processes. 'Audit' is constituted by the processes which result from the definition and specification of mechanisms to measure and evaluate organisational performance; and it gives rise to notions of accountability and control with regard to the *internal* processes of organisations. For Power, systems of surveillance are separate from this, for these are measures adopted to enable a regulatory 'gaze' on those who are *external* to an organisation. This distinction may be tenable in the abstract but in practice it breaks down, or rather it becomes apparent that 'audit' and 'surveillance' are frequently two sides of the same Janus-faced set of regulatory mechanisms. This is because organisations which adopt internal mechanisms for audit also often require or need some measure of organisational outputs relative to units of input; and while these 'outputs' may be goods produced, items purchased or customers satisfied, they may equally well be children being schooled, students being awarded degrees, claimants given receipt of benefits, patients treated, crimes logged and criminals tried, and deaths named and bodies disposed of. As a consequence, systems of 'internal' audit and systems of 'external' surveillance more often than not involve the same monitoring and regulatory processes, and encompass a range of 'others' who are, formally speaking, external to organisational employment, but whose 'lives', or rather information about particular aspects of these, are in some way necessary for organisational existence or functioning.

A simple example here is that applicants for jobs provide histories not only of their employment lives but also of relevant factors that might impact on these, highlighting those that are deemed to promote employability, and explaining, hiding or rendering invisible those that might decrease it; while job-holders manage their working selves not only in relation to managers and others above them in the organisational hierarchy but also those organisationally beneath them as well; and both groupings shape their employment histories in relation to state agencies concerned with taxation and welfare benefits. And as this example will suggest, the idea of 'auto/biographical practices' includes more than the interpersonal exchange of accounts of 'moments' of lives, for it places at the analytical centre an engagement with 'the social', and it positions selves neither in terms of inner processes, nor in terms of disembodied discursive practices, but instead in the complex in-between.

There are many aspects and dimensions of the 'in-between' that are relevant to a discussion of selves; however, I am particularly interested in some of the effects of the extension of monitoring and audit and bureaucratic control that computerisation of information gathering and storage systems, and means of encoding/decoding this information have occasioned. I discuss this around the idea of 'audit selves', that is, the personae that result from the decoding and analysis of these computerised regulatory mechanisms for accounting for the self and the self being accounted for by others.

My focus here is on the conjunction of 'selves' and the regulating practices of 'audit' around the 'moment' of this that is constituted by organisational encounters. Some of the organisational encounters and accompanying auto/biographical practices and systems of audit I am interested in include: the academic CV, employment evaluations and occupational reviews within educational institutions, the production of student records and educational histories; the taking and recording of medical histories; the completion of tax returns, social security claims, immigration applications; the certification of births, deaths, marriages; and the organisational processes that result in official statistics, in particular criminal, mental health and un/employment statistics. None of these encounters occur because of people's confessional impulses or urges to articulate interiorities. They are instead the sites of organisational activities in which people's lives, or rather particular aspects of them, become connected with and are articulated by means of permitted, constrained or compelled monitoring and regulatory practices. One result is that these encounters eventuate in organisationally created 'personae' which are constructed by producing aggregations of auto/biographical exteriorities, 'personae' which I find it useful to characterise as 'audit selves'.

The relevance of the idea of 'audit selves' to the concerns of feminist auto/biography can be indicated by reference to some of the figures, personae rather than persons, who have stalked public discourse in recent years, for example 'the hyperactive boy', 'the criminal youth', 'the sexually abused girl', 'the mentally ill woman', 'the part-time woman worker', 'the single mother', 'the menopausal woman', 'the homeless man' and 'the HIV-positive man'. Audit selves are composite figures, typically heavily gendered ones, which are artefacts of information collection, retrieval and analysis systems. 'Variables' such as age, gender, class and 'race' are central to the organisation and collection of information, as well as being used as the key means of analysing these. In common with other variable analyses of structured large-scale datasets and 'ends' of data, small sub-sets of the responses of the respondents, are frequently removed or combined with others, while cross-dataset comparisons can create artificial 'relationships' between groupings of people who have no 'real' connection with each other. The result is what William Bogard has described as a shadow order – 'the electronic memory-traces of mass society, or perhaps, as Baudrillard imagines, the very form of the masses today, the medium into which they have "disappeared"' (Bogard 1996: 16).

The temptation is to treat these performative processes of organisations in their monitoring and audit mode as fully intended and directed towards control, and so to emphasise their surveillance consequences. However, the emphasis on surveillance not only confuses effects with causes, and assumes a synonymity between outcomes and intentions, but also misses something equally interesting and potentially considerably more consequential for lives and autobiographies. This is that information technologies collect and process information about 'real people' in highly simplified and schematised ways that produce 'virtual reality' outcomes. While 'old' information technologies did this too, new and particularly electronic forms 'hyperise' it through pushing it to the limits by means of the multiplicity of techniques they make available for schematising and modelling (aspects of) lives. Through such electronic means as modelling information, profiling types of actual or potential users/customers/claimants, telematics as means of processing information and credit flows, and gaming as a means of simulating situations and outcomes, as well as through the more ordinary constructions of typologies of personae through the design and analysis of information datasets, an ersatz or virtual reality comes into being.

This virtualised reality bears the hallmarks of 'the social' and the kinds of people who are found in social life – it derives from 'actual reality' and it is used to manage 'actual aspects' of it and 'actual people' therein. Moreover, these virtualisation processes change not only the *relationship* between what is real and what is false, but, as Baudrillard (1981/3) has pointed out, they also have shared perceptions of what this *is*. Virtual systems dissolve the boundaries of the real, the virtual and the hyperreal, as in the hyperreal versions of actual persons that inhabit credit databases, for example, and which are then used to regulate which 'actual real' persons will and will not obtain credit, are and are not 'creditworthy' kinds of person. And of course simulation and surveillance often overlap and impact upon 'real people' and their lives, whatever the intentions behind the processes involved may be. Here Bogard comments that:

> In the future, perhaps, we will all carry genetic identity markers ... of some sort ... that when scanned (surveilled) supply not just our life histories, but our future biographies, to the relevant authorities, who will then tell us what education we are entitled to, what jobs we are suited for and should prepare for, what special talents we possess and how best to develop them, what illnesses we can expect to encounter and what lifestyles would deter them, how long we are likely to live, how we will probably die. ... To the authorities, at least, they would become in some ways more real than our real selves, because they would stand in for and verify the reality of those selves in ways that are, or have the potential to be, absolutely certain. ...
>
> (Bogard 1996: 20–1)

The paradox is that these 'personae' that Bogard sees as standing for and verifying the reality of actual selves are entirely fictional creations that bear little relationship to existing people but that are also and at the same time fully 'real'. Indeed, they come to be more real than what is 'really' real, for when such datasources are used for profiling purposes, then it is people who are judged against the profile and found wanting or not, and not the other way about. Moreover, the 'accuracy' or otherwise of a profile is irrelevant, belongs to a different mind-set that presumes a 'really real' reality; its purpose is rather to guarantee standard processes for the collection, inspection and evaluation of slices of lives, and to act as a means of verifying or not these slices of lives against particular organisational criteria. One example here is of a profile of a 'type of person' likely to have committed a murder which is used in policing to inspect and assess actual persons; another is of profiles of types of people eligible for particular state-provided benefits used to assess actual claims and claimants; a third is the use of profiles as a means of assessing CVs so as to assign applicants to types of career patterns and to determine who will and will not be shortlisted for interview. And while there are certainly capacities for surveillance here, the concern is in fact not with recording events, but rather with anticipating types of events and then recording instances of what has already been anticipated as happening.

The informated results, in the form of virtual persons or personae or audit selves, become organisationally more real than 'real' or actual selves. Thus when Gertrude Stein visited America in the 1930s she was met everywhere by people who had already conceived and personified a 'Gertrude Stein' that she then had to learn to (appear to) be. As she proposes in *Everybody's Autobiography* (Stein 1938/5), this was actually only an extreme (or hyperised) case of something much more endemic and ordinary about social life and how 'lives' are re/shaped within it. In relation to organisational encounters, there is a stronger process of normalisation involved, for while the organisations 'may not care' as to whether or not actual persons and their lives fit the profiles around which they function, on many occasions the people concerned will.

In relation to three of the audit selves I introduced earlier – 'the part-time woman worker', 'the single mother' and 'the menopausal woman' – I want briefly to suggest that the surveillance and controlling aspects of the organisational encounters involved are by no means certain or absolute, and that resistance occurs most effectively by using simulation against itself. Each of these three audit selves has enormous social as well as organisational resonance, a resonance that can be, and often is, turned back on itself, either by being subverted by someone moulding the required aspects of their self to fit the profile so as to reap the benefits of doing so (for instance, middle-aged women who through their legal representatives successfully use 'menopause' as a defence strategy in criminal cases, or single mothers who manage their sex lives so as not to be – seen to be – attached to and so presumptively financially dependent upon a male 'bread-winner'), or doing so in ways which avoid the disadvantages involved (for instance, women who manage and present their employment histories so as to avoid being seen as a 'typical part-time woman worker'). Of course, a lot more goes on in relation to the intersection of these audit selves and 'women's actual lives', and the costs and benefits involved will vary considerably in different contexts and for different women. Some of the dynamics involved can be shown by looking more closely at the example of an academic CV (Miller and Morgan 1993; Montgomery 1996).

Many UK universities require or suggest that their staff should use the framework for preparing a CV proposed by the Committee of Vice-Chancellors and

Principals (CVCP) of universities for the purposes of the externally imposed periodic Research Assessment Exercise or RAE. These headings are common ones and are on one level even-handed, dispassionate and 'objective' ones; they are apparently ungendered, but they are actually highly so. They add up to a version of academic life which actually presumes a *male subject*, indeed a male subject with a presumptively 'standard' (academic) life, and they in fact encapsulate highly gendered patterns of behaviours and are premised around normative expectations in which particular 'benchmarks' will have been reached at specific points in time in a 'satisfactory' or 'excellent' academic career. Many women, as well as men who also have non-standard 'fractured' academic lives, consequently struggle (or aspire) to fit the actual temporal ordering of their lives, patterns of un/employment, and their actual achievements, into a framework which leads them to being assessed by criteria which are presumptively objective, but which in practice are highly normative and actively discriminatory on gender, age and class grounds (Davies and Holloway 1995).

Moreover, the processes at work here are circular and constitutive: If a job or a change of employment is wanted or if promotion is sought, then organisational requirements (which in this case are also system-wide expectations) necessitate people's actual lives being shaped within the terms proposed by the academic CV. At the same time the requirements of 'fulfilling' the expectations built into a 'good' academic CV are taken into account in the decisions that people make about a wide range of their life choices – how they spend their 'leisure time', the balance of 'work time' and 'non-work time', how much of their legally entitled holiday they actually take, and whether or not they are able to live in the same part of the country as their partner (Wise 1996).

Judgements of people are then put in process by the judgements made about the 'shape' as well as the content of their CV. At faculty level in my university, for instance, a committee pre-reviews cases for promotions around these criteria and advises heads of departments on how best to guide their staff in shaping up their working lives in order to demonstrate in their CVs that they reach the institutional criteria. And this advice is itself shaped by the knowledge that deans and faculty administrators have about the profiles of 'successful career trajectories' used by successive chairs of the university-wide committee which makes the actual decisions about promotions.

There is a further dynamic at work here, one more subterranean but perhaps the most consequential of all. And this is the presumption that the criteria embedded in headings and outputs recorded in the CV do indeed indicate academic merit, professional standing and intellectual worth. That the outcome is a professional world in which the vast majority of its 'names' – its most senior members, its most appointable and promotable members – are white bourgeois males is typically not even seen, let alone viewed as a remarkable demonstration of the endemic nature of *ad hominem* and *ad feminam* discriminatory practices in academia. The effect is that it isn't simply a matter of reaching certain kinds of criteria, it's also a matter of being the kind of person who possesses, and whose personhood is taken to represent their possession of, the attributes of intellectual standing, potential and worth. That these map so closely onto those of gender, class and 'race' is treated as irrelevant.

It might be countered here that I have been discussing a particular case and that these dynamics are peculiar either to that case or just to people who work in the professions. I do not agree. Structurally the same requirements operate in relation to other kinds of (written, but also orally presented) CVs, and not just in the professions either. I observed the same dynamics at work in the 'actual lives' and CVs of women who were skilled manual workers in, and being made redundant from, the Rochdale part of the British cotton industry, while involved in researching this local labour market and the position of household members within it (Stanley 1992b). Indeed, it was thinking about this that eventuated in my present ideas outlined in this chapter. These women too, and from the 1920s on (the period my research was concerned with), looked for and changed jobs in a local labour market structured by pre-existing profiles of types of workers and skills required and around which they shaped their self-presentations, with this then having performative and constitutive effects on how they worked and lived and what future trajectories their working lives were able to take. They and their fellow workers similarly constructed profiles of acceptable and unacceptable workplaces, bosses, managers and co-workers, and these too were part of the dynamics of this labour market.

The outcome of these gendered patterns in the form of 'audit selves' becomes constitutive of the kind of people we need to seem to be in the organisational encounters we find ourselves in. That is, audit gives rise to information requirements which impinge on organisational encounters and produce generalised audit selves that are then accorded the status of truths rather than of mere truisms. In turn, the people who are the objects of organisational encounters shape their self-presentations to organisational information needs, by providing this piece of information and that, the form of which is predetermined as relevant or essential for organisational purposes. In addition, people may feel or may actually be constrained to perform these characteristics of the audit selves with which they are associated because there are surveillance consequences involved (for instance, because knowledge about a 'single mother' cohabiting in the UK context could have consequential effects on a woman's eligibility as a welfare claimant, she is likely to 'perform' her self in public contexts as its audit version – to present herself as the simulated version).

The rise and rise of public woman

As well as having an intellectual interest in these processes of audit, surveillance and simulation, I also have a political engagement with them as well. The crux of Max Weber's argument with Karl Marx's analysis of capitalism lay in his prescient analysis of bureaucracy as the defining trope of modernity, rather than capitalism as such. For Weber, commenting in the 1890s and early 1900s, individuality and escape from the tentacles of the increasingly widespread and effective regulatory systems of bureaucracy lay not in individualism, but rather in the interpersonal 'space' of the interstices between regulatory systems and unregulated aspects of social life. From the viewpoint of the 1990s, there are few interstices which are not themselves subject to parallel 'private' regulatory processes, largely because of the hyperisation of processes of audit, simulation and surveillance that I have been discussing. Consequently, while I am interested in the possibilities of resistance to or rejections of the organisational project, I am most interested in those which are responsive to the organisational processes involved. I find it useful to think of this around the relationship between public and private, a relationship that has theoretically exercised, as well as having been analytically crucial to, feminist analysis for a long time now.

Contra Richard Sennett's (1976) argument in his interesting discussion of 'the fall of public man', what I have been discussing here does *not* evidence the long march of abandonment of the public realm and retreat into the private realm associated with the interiority project of modernity, what Sennett terms as the 'tyranny of intimacy', as a kind of coda to Weber's analysis. Rather, it seems to me there have always been a plethora of different kinds of public as well as private regulatory systems involving mechanisms of audit, from the Roman population census that took Mary and Joseph to Bethlehem, clocking-in in eighteenth-century Lancashire factories, the state auto/biographical records produced through the activities of the East German state police from the 1940s to the later 1980s, to the vast electronic databases constructed through the activities of telematics inter/nationally. Instead of Sennett's proposal that 'the public' is becoming *more pervasive*, electronic forms of audit are instead *shifting its shape*. This is occurring in part through the development of technological, largely electronic means for *extending its remit* as well as the efficiency with which these are being put into operation, and in larger part because these technologies bring with them an increasing requirement for *consistency* in the information provided and so in the self-presentations made in a wide range of different kinds of organisational encounters.

My view, *contra* Weber as well as *contra* Sennett, then, is that what is happening is much less a retreat into the interstices that compose private life, and much more the collapse of the interstices between the different forms of organisational encounters that people engage in, with attendant effects on the public/private distinction. That is, what is said by and to, and what is written by and about, a person in one such encounter has reverberations in many others, so that a person now can be 'caught out' more easily, more quickly, if they are 'not themselves', as this self has been constituted in simulated form. For instance, a woman who is successfully presented, for defence purposes, in a court of law as menopausal and depressed and mentally 'not well' even if not actually 'ill', may not so easily be presented or be able to present herself in the labour market as a potentially full-time employed person, and may instead be seen as either a 'part-time woman' or even as a woman who should spend no time at all in any employment context. And if 'the single mother' is the first or becomes the dominant audit self organisationally associated with an unpartnered woman, then other ways of presenting herself – as a full-time woman worker, a home-owner and so on – not only may be organisationally invisible, but might also be actively denied, withdrawn or made almost impossible to achieve successfully.

Audit selves are quintessentially public selves, publicly created profiles which act as measures and prophecies of what a range of 'types' of selves are and can be. What these witness in the contemporary setting is *the rise of public woman*, the plethora of public versions of what types of woman there are, and what these selves 'are like', accompanied by the new rise of public man, but this time as an object of a public organisational gaze rather than the active agent in the public realm that is Sennett's romanticised view of pre-capitalist and pre-urban man. The rise of public woman – a kind of self set if not determined by the regulatory processes of audit and simulation and enacted through organisational encounters to produce audit selves that are stereotypical versions of what 'a woman' can be and become – has reverberations in feminist analytical terms. The public women of audit selves have been associated with regulation and surveillance rather than enactment and performance, and the organisational context is correspondingly seen as one which effectively denies interiority and individual versions of what the self is.

Analytically speaking, there are two broad choices for feminist analysis. One is to accept the tacit view on which organisational processes and organisational encounters are founded, and to see actual women within these processes of audit in terms of surveillance, as objects who are gazed upon, recorded, measured and disposed of. The other is to question this, indeed to look beyond and within it, to recognise that information collection and analysis and resulting profiling creates simulated selves *which are not perfect simulations*. That is, the tacit assumption in much theoretical writing about simulation is that the created versions of virtual realities are actually *perfect* copies, whereas they aren't: they contain gaps, disjunctures and silences that indicate what is actually only an uneasy fit between actual women and their audit selves. This opens up different possibilities for feminist analysis.

Many women already make use of the gaps, disjunctures and silences which exist between audit selves and actual lives, and this adds up to a pattern of disengagements from or rejections of organisational requirements, some of which are intended as resistant, others of which may not be intentionally resistant but constitute fissures, rifts and failures in organisational functioning nonetheless. Contemporary audit systems make critical use of statements and questions of gender in the construction and use of audit selves; and consequently the intentional or accidental resistances that 'actual women' engender between their simulated audit selves and their real lives are potentially highly consequential for organisational life and functioning.

In addition to making use of this frequent divergence between actual people and the audit selves they are organisationally supposed to be or become, there are two other broad ways of responding to organisational requirements which people already use in organisational encounters, both in face-to-face situations and those involving the completion and/or submission of documents. The first takes the form of what might be called 'disengagements from organisational encounters': not filling in unnecessary (or sometimes even necessary) forms, and other associated strategies that disassociate one's self from organisational audit processes, of which the use of financial privilege to buy the services of proxy persons (such as accountants or barristers) skilled in organisational self-presentations is one example. The second takes the form of 'management of organisational self-presentations': on the one hand, deliberate self-presentations of incomplete fragments, inconsistencies and lies in information given and equally deliberate acts of non-remembrance, accidental failures to keep appointments and so on; and, on the other hand, the maintenance of a self-recording apparatus, the collection and use of personal records constructed to ensure consistency and seamlessness in public self-presentations.[7]

The often observed (from an organisational and audit viewpoint) disorderly nature of many women's lives – feckless sex lives, indigent attitudes towards economic life in general and matters of employment and credit in particular, chaotic relationships, unruly children – demonstrates some of the ways in which the lack of 'fit' between actual women's lives and the audit selves of 'public woman' can and does confound the organisational project. There are also activities which women engage in around the trajectories of organisational disengagement and the management of self-presentation which can result, even if not always intentionally, in patterned divergences from the aims and objectives of the organisational project. These include working across the formal and the informal parts of the economy, being involved in unregulated and short-term sexual relationships, rearing children without a partner being involved, and manipulating the conventions of audit selves to provide excuses for and legitimisation of antisocial or criminal behaviours.

A feminist analytic approach with a political edge to it can and should be built around these resistant relationships between women's audit selves and actual lives. Consequently my discussion has argued for moving beyond the premises upon which much feminist autobiographical work has been tacitly based, and instead recognising that at the heart of the auto/biographical processes involved in organisational encounters are what in organisational terms are perceived as gaps, disjunctures and silences, but which, when conceptualised from the viewpoint of 'actual people' rather than organisational requirements, inject the ideas of performance and resistance into conceptualisations of 'the public'. This analytic tack sees women as agents who are the subjects of their own lives and who are (potentially, actually) performers in organisational encounters by working with, around and through 'women's made-selves', rather than as selves resulting from confessional impulses, which are perhaps 'self-made women' but have no agentive control in relation to the terms, conditions and methods of this making.

My view, then, is that the gulf between 'public woman', the public woman of audit selves and self/surveillances, and actual women and their lives, should become of far more analytic interest to feminist auto/biography. I conclude by briefly sketching out some ways in which future feminist work concerned with auto/biographical practices, organisational encounters and audit selves might usefully and interestingly develop.

Clearly, developing the presently diffuse links between feminist autobiography and feminist auto/biography is one important aspect of this. As I noted earlier, a middle ground already exists which can be built on, and in addition a good deal of interesting relevant empirical work already exists which needs pulling together theoretically and analytically. Within this, there are already interesting examples of historical work that explores the changing relationship between exterior and interior, public and private. However, at the moment this tends to be rather one-off, and charting these developments more precisely in relation to a wider range of historical examples still remains to be done, something which is clearly crucial for the future development of feminist analysis.

With regard to contemporary life, while there is already some interesting work (both theoretical and empirical) concerned with audit and organisation, by and large feminist analysts are not engaged in this and much of the analytic frame is both gender-blinkered and resolutely gazes upon a highly masculinised notion of public life. Clearly, there is the opportunity here for a major feminist initiative concerned with simulation and audit, both theoretically and as this relates to specific organisational encounters.

Finally, I outlined earlier a range of auto/biographical practices connected with simulation and audit, including CVs, employment evaluations and reviews, organisational records; medical histories, birth, marriage and death certifications, taxation and social security claims, and criminal, mental health and unemployment statistics. Focusing in more specific detail on these practices – looking at their development over periods of time, shifts and changes within them, their shaping by organisational processes and requirements, the patterns of responses made to them, and the constructions and reconstructions of the audit selves involved – is important in being able to understand more precisely the dynamics at work. This would also enable a feminist auto/biographical analysis to address some of the other questions that I outlined near the start of my discussion, and specifically those concerned with what the possible narratives, narrative conventions and kinds of self that result are, and whether these audit systems are generating consistent or divergent auto/biographical practices.

Notes

1 For information on the Auto/Biography Study Group (which is open to anyone with an interest in biography and autobiography in all their variants, not just sociologists) and the journal *Auto/Biography*, contact: Michael Erben, School of Education, University of Southampton, Southampton, UK, email m.d.erben@soton.ac.uk

2 Useful collections mapping the ground here include Stanton (1987); Smith (1987); Benstock (1988); Brodzki and Schenk (1988); Personal Narratives Group (1989); Iles (1992); Swindells (1995); Smith and Watson (1996); Polkey (1999); Polkey and Donnell (2001). Interestingly, overwhelmingly the many edited collections that exist focus specifically and almost exclusively on autobiography; there is little other than the contributions to Iles (1992) concerned specifically with biography.

3 Contrast here, for instance, the Foucauldian-influenced approach of Probyn (1993, 1996), with that of Griffiths (1995).
4 See here, for instance, Hinds (1996) and Graham *et al.* 1989.
5 And by 'organisation' I don't mean 'the US Government' or 'ICI' or 'a health group', but social organisation which can exist in formalised structures, such as these examples, or through informally organised patterns of behaviours, persons and practices, such as those that might exist in kin networks or collectivities of friends or people who work in a particular way within a formal organisation. Similarly, while I am interested in formal processes of audit within formal organisations, I am equally interested in the informal variants that audit or monitoring can take in informal settings.
6 Including the bourgeois provincialism of his parents' home, his comfortable professional employment in the Ecclesiastical Commission in London, his social involvement on the fringes of high society (in the circle composed by Victoria's biographer Theodor Martin and his wife the Shakespearian actress Helen Faucit, members of the Severn family who were painters to the haute bourgeoisie and aristocracy, and others), the Christian Socialist circles that cohered around F.D. Maurice and the Working Men's College, and also his activities in 'collecting' Victorian working women's accounts of their lives and recording these in his diaries.
7 Consistency in the sense that the 'same' information, in an exact sense, is kept and given, and seamlessness in the sense that there are no gaps within this information and also no gaps between information given in different organisational encounters.

Bibliography

Auto/Biography Study Group (1995) Auto/Biography Study Group membership leaflet.
Baudrillard, Jean (1981/3) *Simulacra and Simulations*, trans. P. Foss, P. Patton and P. Beitchman, New York: Semiotext(e).
—— (1988) *Selected Writings*, ed. and intro. by Mark Poster, Cambridge: Polity Press.
Benstock, Shari (ed.) (1988) *The Private Self: Theory and Practice of Women's Autobiographical Writings*, London: Routledge.
Bogard, William (1996) *The Simulation of Surveillance: Hypercontrol in Telematic Societies*, Cambridge: Cambridge University Press.
Brodzki, Bella and Schenck, Celeste (eds) (1988) *Life/Lines: Theorising Women's Autobiography*, Ithaca: Cornell University Press.
Davies, Celia and Holloway, Penny (1995) 'Troubling Transformations: Gender Regimes and Organisational Culture in the Academy', in Louise Morley and Val Walsh (eds), *Feminist Academics: Creative Agents for Change*, London: Taylor and Francis: 7–21.
Graham, Elspeth, Hinds, Hilary, Hobby, Elaine and Wilcox, Helen (eds) (1989) *Her Own Life: Autobiographical Writings by Seventeenth-Century Englishwomen*, London: Routledge.
Griffiths, Morwenna (1995) *Feminisms and the Self: The Web of Identity*, London: Routledge.
Hinds, Hilary (1996) *God's Own Englishwoman: Seventeenth-Century Radical Sectarian Writing and Feminist Criticism*, Manchester: Manchester University Press.
Iles, Teresa (ed.) (1992) *All Sides Of The Subject: Women And Biography*, New York: Teachers College Press.
Jelinek, Estelle (ed.) (1980) *Women's Autobiography*, Bloomington: Indiana University Press.
Marcus, Laura (1994) *Auto/biographical discourses: Criticism, Theory, Practice*, Manchester: Manchester University Press.
Miller, Nod and Morgan, David (1993) 'Called to Account: The CV as an Auto/Biographical Practice', *Sociology* 27: 1, 133–43.

Montgomery, Angela (1996) 'In Law and Outlaw? The Tale of a Journey', in Liz Stanley (ed.), *Knowing Feminisms: On Academic Borders, Territories and Tribes*, London: Sage Publications: 58–71.

Personal Narratives Group (ed.) (1989) *Interpreting Women's Lives: Feminist Theory And Personal Narratives*, Bloomington: Indiana University Press.

Polkey, Pauline (ed.) (1999) *Women's Lives Into Print: The Theory, Practice and Writing of Feminist Auto/Biography*, London: Macmillan

Polkey, Pauline and Donnell, Alison (eds) (2001) *Representing Lives: Women and Auto/Biography*, London: Macmillan.

Power, Michael (1994) *The Audit Explosion*, London: Demos.

—— (1997) *The Audit Society: Rituals of Verification*, Oxford: Oxford University Press.

Probyn, Elspeth (1993) *Sexing the Self*, New York: Routledge.

—— (1996) *Outside Belongings*, New York: Routledge.

Sennett, Richard (1976) *The Fall of Public Man*, Cambridge: Cambridge University Press.

Smith, Sidonie (1987) *A Poetics of Women's Autobiography, Marginality and the Fictions of Self-representation*, Bloomington: Indiana University Press.

Smith, Sidonie and Watson, Julia (eds) (1996) *Getting A Life: Everyday Uses of Autobiography*, Minneapolis: University of Minnesota Press.

Sociology (1993) Special issue on 'Auto/Biography in Sociology', 27: 1.

Stanley, Liz (1984) *The Diaries of Hannah Cullwick*, New Brunswick: Rutgers University Press.

—— (1992a) *The Auto/Biographical I: The Theory and Practice of Feminist Auto/Biography*, Manchester: Manchester University Press.

—— (1992b) 'Changing Households? Changing Work?', in Alan Warde and Nick Abercrombie (eds), *Social Change in Britain 1964–1989*, Oxford: Polity Press: 115–38.

—— (1999) 'How Do We Know About Past Lives? Methodological and Epistemological Matters Involving Prince Philip, the Russian Revolution, Emily Wilding Davison, my Mum and the Absent Sue', in Polkey, Pauline (ed.), *Women's Lives Into Print: The Theory, Practice and Writing of Feminist Auto/Biography*, London: Macmillan: 3–21.

—— (2000a, in press) 'On "Knowing About Olive Schreiner": Issues in Representing and Interpreting Past Lives', *Signs, a Journal of Women & Culture*.

—— (2000b, in press) 'Encountering the Imperial and Colonial Past Through Olive Schreiner's "Trooper Peter Halket of Mashonaland" ', *Women's Writing*.

Stanton, Domna (ed.) (1987) *The Female Autograph: Theory and Practice of Autobiography from the Tenth to the Twentieth Century*, Chicago: University of Chicago Press.

Steedman, Carolyn (1995) *Strange Dislocations: Childhood and the Idea of Human Interiority 1780–1930*, London: Virago Press.

Stein, Gertrude (1938/1985) *Everybody's Autobiography*, London: Virago Press.

Swindells, Julia (ed.) (1995) *The Uses of Autobiography*, London: Taylor and Francis.

Wise, Sue (1996) 'What are Social Work Academics for? An Auto/Biographical Journey in Search of Career, Self and Identity', *Auto/Biography* 4: 2/3: 125–38.

3 Textualisation of the self and gender identity in the life-story

Marie-Françoise Chanfrault-Duchet

To the memory of Théoduline, who died in 1997 and to Alice, who celebrated her hundredth birthday in January 1998.

A reader's interest in autobiography usually lies in the promise of unique revelations about a particular individual. But though this may be what draws the reader to the genre, individuality is always a product of social models, and can only be understood through the social. To construct an identity, a subject takes up the models offered by society, as transmitted by culture, and shapes them into his or her own type, bringing into play a system of values. The autobiographical process uses not only facts and events, but also social representations and cultural values. A tension exists between self and society, which is resolved by the narrative presentation of a unique self which can also be recognised by society.

To investigate this issue, I shall refer here to an autobiographical form – the life-story produced within the framework of social sciences – which emphasises the social self, and I shall limit my analysis to the arena of gender identity. How do social models intervene in the construction of gender identity? Where and how do women exploit these models in their life-stories? What are the links between these models and the linguistic and semantic processes, which aim to express a self, an identity? In other words, what is the function of social models in the narrativisation of the self and the construction, through a text, of a meaning for the life experience? These are the questions I shall attempt to answer in this article, borrowing my examples from three life-stories I collected myself.

I shall first draw the outlines of the life-story as a genre, then present the three narratives, retained here as particularly relevant for the question. Then I shall look at the narrativisation of the life experience, the fictionalisation of the self, the textualisation of the identity, and question, in all these processes, the role of gender identity, as marked by social models.

Life-story as a genre

I shall define the 'life-story' as the product of a ritualised speech act, which results from the conjunction, in the 1970s, of a genre, autobiography, with a new medium, the tape recorder, within the institutional framework of social sciences. Life-story is thus at first a methodological tool used to collect information from social categories (among them women) which, although social actors, do not have access to the public stage. But considered as a genre, it can be viewed as an object created by the form and the contents, which produces meaning, just like a literary form (Chanfrault-Duchet 1984).

Drawing upon my former works, and from the perspective of linguistic and literary theory, I shall consider 'autobiography' (as a written and literary genre, whose exemplary model would be Rousseau's *Confessions*) and the 'life-story' as two neighbouring genres, coming from an ordinary discourse (acknowledged as such, in its modern version, since the eighteenth century, among Western civilisations): the autobiographical discourse.

I mean here the ordinary gesture through which a subject accounts for his/her life experience viewed as a whole, by expressing his/her identity in the form of a narrative identity as theorised by Ricoeur, i.e. a form able to express the transformations of the identity as experienced through a lifetime – 'The identity of the subject is supported by a temporal scheme which matches the model of the dynamic identity issued from the fictional construction of a narrative text' (Ricoeur 1985: 355) – and simultaneously the identification with a self (*ipse*), which incorporates and transcends evolutions – 'The narrative identity makes it possible to hold together the two poles of the chain: the permanency of the character in the time and the permanency of the preservation of the self' (Ricoeur 1990: 196, my translation). Viewed from the perspective of pragmatic linguistics, this discourse is based on a form in which author, narrator and character melt into the same pronoun: I. Philippe Lejeune, who defines the literary autobiography as follows – 'Retrospective prose narrative written by a real person concerning his own existence, where the focus is his individual life, in particular the story of his own personality' (Lejeune 1989: 4) – considers this contract through the notion of the 'autobiographical pact'.

On this basis, we can say that the autobiography and the life-story represent two genres, marked by their specific situations of production. Autobiography is determined by the constraints of written communication, which is always deferred, and by particular literary conventions. As for the life-story, it is determined by an oral situation of communication, specified by an interview recorded on tape and by the embedding of the speech act in an institutional framework: social sciences.

The oral situation makes the speech act a narrative interaction demanding the physical presence of a narrator (informant) and a narratee (researcher), so that the narrative is the product of co-enunciation and co-construction processes. The life-story as an object is then at first the interaction as recorded on the tape or its written version: the transcription.

The form and the content of the interaction are specified by the double framework of the interview and the institutional situation (a research project in social sciences). The use of the tape recorder opens up the interaction to a wider audience, the public. This sense of a wider audience produces, in the narrative, an emphasis on the social self, whereas autobiography stresses the inner self (Chanfrault-Duchet 1988, 1991b). Concerning the processes brought into play, autobiography and life-story remain very close. They are the product of

1   A process of narrativisation: events and facts are organised into a dynamic, based on a chronological and causal scheme.
2   A process of fictionalisation: beyond the weight of the referential, of the factual, the subject is presented, in the narrative, as a coherent character within a significant, and thus reconstructed, world.
3   A process of textualisation: the autobiographical discourse tends here to constitute itself as a closed meaning system, i.e. as a text *per se* (Chanfrault-Duchet 1990, 1991a).

This third dimension needs an explanation: speaking of the life-story – an oral genre – as a 'text' could be seen as a paradox. In the frameworks of literary theory, the notion of 'text' has been traditionally reserved for literary productions or at least for written objects (viewed as radically distinct from oral productions). The works of linguists (see, for example, Bakhtin 1984) on the one hand and of theoreticians of the oral literature (see, for example, Zumthor 1983) on the other, allow us now to reconsider the question and to view some oral productions based on genres as 'texts', even as literary texts, a standpoint which makes it possible here to analyse the life-story by means of literary theoretical tools. From this perspective and beyond its referential dimension, it can be seen as a 'literary' text, which possesses its own internal schemes and is thus constituted on the basis of a closed meaning system, which subsumes the narrativisation and fictionalisation processes. It means that the semantic process organises itself, beyond the referential data, within the text, through a complex system of relations among the different constituents brought into play (Chanfrault-Duchet 1987). We consider, on this basis, that autobiography and life-story, as genres, can both be defined as texts.

But the life-story develops specific traits; the orality of the genre produces a system of formal and structural recurrences (Chanfrault-Duchet 1991b,1994), and the interactional system, as well as the stress on the social self, produce reference to socio-symbolic discourse and the social imaginary through which a culture, by means of language, maps and deciphers the world, a dimension also present in autobiography, but heavily marked in the life-story (Chanfrault-Duchet 1990, 1991a).

Finally, I shall posit that all the products of the biographical approach in social sciences cannot be considered as life-stories. As a speech act, the genre requires 'felicity conditions' (Searle 1969):

1   It needs time: one does not collect a life-story on a single cassette, but a 'life history' (i.e. a narrative which emphasises the life course). The life-story as such develops and complexifies the biographical data so as to communicate how events and facts have been experienced and understood by the subject.

2   The researcher has to fade out in order to play the discursive role of narratee (and thus loses control of the interaction).
3   The informant must take up his/her identity (including the contradictions) and possess narrative skills to account for the richness of his/her life experience, of his/her self.

Three women's life-stories

To highlight this definition, in reference to gender identity, I shall borrow my examples from three life-stories that I have collected personally. All the interviews were recorded at the narrators' homes. Concerning the methodology, I always compare the material I personally collect with the material of colleagues working in the same field. These three life-stories belong to two series of interviews. The first series was collected between 1984 and 1990, and deals with the women's perceptions of changes in women's condition since World War I. The second series deals with the women's motivations in becoming teachers. This is a new research project which I started in 1996. My informants are students preparing for the examination to become teachers, student-teachers and older teachers working in secondary schools in Tours. Alice's and Théoduline's narratives belong to the first series, Sophie's to the second.

The three narratives selected present three different life courses and three different modes of representation of women's identities, and are thus appropriate to a comparison aiming to study the role played by gender identity in women's life-stories.

Alice was born in 1898 in Niort in the south-west of France. She grew up in a lower-middle-class family with five brothers and sisters. She went to school until the age of fourteen and began to work in a tobacco shop at the age of fifteen. That same year she studied by correspondence to become a shorthand typist and at the age of sixteen, she began to work in an office as a civil servant. She lived with her parents until the age of twenty. But as she had to give them her wages and did not feel independent, she decided to live on her own and came to Tours, where she worked as a secretary for a deputy. After six years and a nervous breakdown, she had to resign her job and went to live with her brother, who had lost an eye and his two forearms during the First World War. The brother had prostheses so that they could work at home as independent typists until 1967. The brother died in 1972. Alice, now 101, lives in a pensioners' home near Tours.

Théoduline was born in 1909, the first child of a very poor family, in a rural area near Orléans. She had one brother and one sister. Her father fell on the front at the beginning of the First World War. But as the body could not be found, the mother could not get a war pension. So Théoduline had to leave her mother and was brought up by her grandparents who were also very poor. She began to work at the age of six, herding cows, and could not then go regularly to school. As a teenager, she was hired as a maid by ruined aristocrats in the country, then by different families in town. She married a labourer at the age of twenty and had ten children. But as her husband had very low wages, she had to work too as a gatekeeper for the French railways and as a charwoman in town, where she went by bicycle. Retired and a widow, Théoduline lived, by the time of the interviews, in the very small house that the couple had managed to buy in the 1950s and where she died in 1997.

Sophie was, by the time of the interviews, my student at university. Born in 1961 in a modest family, she grew up as a divorcee's daughter and was brought up by her grandparents (a charwoman and a manual worker) in a Parisian suburb until the age of seven. Her mother, an employee at a beautician's, married for a second time and took her back to Tours. Sophie has a step-brother. Although a brilliant pupil at school, Sophie had a broken academic career. In order to live with a friend, she ran away from home at the age of seventeen, just before her examinations and scraped through the examinations as a result. Later, a grant-holder at university, she began to study economics, sociology and then finally French literature. But as she attended lectures irregularly, it took her an extended time to graduate.

Unmarried, she still lives with her friend. The couple have two children (aged five and three), who are disabled (they cannot move their fingers). Sophie was aware of this genetic disability running in her friend's family, but took the risk. As the father is slightly disabled too and works part-time as a primary teacher, Sophie had to work as an auxiliary teacher for several years. In 1996 she returned to university, with a training allowance to become a teacher in 'Lettres classiques' (French, Latin and Greek), a discipline viewed in France as prestigious.

The narrativisation of the life experience

The main process in the life-story is the narrativisation of the life experience, which accounts for one of the two dimensions of the 'narrative identity' as described by Ricoeur (1985): the evolution of the self.

In the life-story, the narrativisation always takes the form of a life course – facts and events selected as relevant are organised within a path, marked out by rites of passage: birth, school, first communion, first love, examinations, first job, marriage, birth of children and so on. The construction of the life course scheme refers, in the interaction with the audience, to a shared knowledge: the models of life experience taken for granted in a socio-historical context.

As the German historian and sociologist Kohli (1989) says, the standard model, taken for granted at the present, remains the 'modern' life course institutionalised at the end of the eighteenth century. This model supposes a social and political context, which allows individual social promotion and personal development, explaining the emergence of Rousseau's *Confessions* at the end of the eighteenth century (Goulemot 1981).

This model of the life course, based on social representations and conveyed by institutions (about the role of school in this diffusion, see Chanfrault-Duchet 1997), is at first a masculine model and can thus include women's roles only as traditionally defined by society. In France, the possibility of a particular life course model for women, based on autonomy, was opened in the nineteenth century by the feminists (see Flora Tristan's 1833 and Louise Michel's 1886 memoirs). Beyond the positions of politically engaged feminists in the 1950s (see De Beauvoir 1949 and her slogan 'one is not born a woman, one becomes a woman'), it has been possible since the 1970s, for ordinary women to see their life-stories, and thus their aspirations for personal development, acknowledged by society as a consequence of the women's liberation movement within the social representations in Western civilisations. The diffusion of the new models in France took place principally within radio programmes dedicated to women, which discussed such issues as contraception, family, divorce, financial autonomy, household and wage-earning work etc., and contributed to spreading the new female representations and thus new female life course models among all social classes (see Chanfrault-Duchet 1995).

To be relevant, a life-story must refer to the expected features of life course as viewed through the current social representations. The questions here then are the following: how do life-stories collected in the late 1980s and the 1990s integrate the changes in woman's condition since the First World War and especially the new models, which appeared in the 1970s, and how, in terms of genre, do narrators, as women, bring into play the new models to express the singularity of their life courses? My three narratives provide examples of different possibilities.

Although the oldest of my informants, Alice organises her life course so as to make work the principle which allowed her to conquer autonomy. She thus presents herself as a pioneer of the new models:

> The injuries of my brother changed my life but ... I am an old spinster, as people used to say (she laughs) but I always had modern ideas. So when I came to live with my brother, I told him: 'I do not want to be a kept woman. You are my brother, but I do not want to have to ask you for money to buy a new dress' [...] And when we decided to work at home, I told him: 'You will not be my boss. We will be associates. I shall be a craftswoman [sic] and I shall be my own boss'.

Reconsidering her life on the basis of the new models of a woman's life course, which imply the right to birth control, Théoduline focuses on the difficulties she had to overcome and which refer to the traditional representation of motherhood:

> Well, I had ten children. It was very difficult to feed them, to educate them. But anyway, I managed to do it. Now I would have only three. But, you know, in those days, we did not have the pill.

As for Sophie, in conformity with the new standards, she does not view marriage as a rite of passage and claims her right to refuse this institution, focusing thus on the idea that she has always been able to manage her life:

We did not marry. We do not want to. You need not be married to live together and have children. In fact, our 'marriage' took place when we were seventeen and decided to live together. It was a decision, not a ceremony.

These extracts could give the impression that the facts and events evoked in the life-story lead to the narrator's references to current social models, but the analysis of the narratives shows that the reverse is true: the current representations of female roles are constituents of the meaning system which organises facts and events of the life experience into the narrative of a life course. But, as we shall see, these representations intervene as well in the processes of fictionalisation and textualisation.

The fictionalisation of the self

As a product of the narrativisation, the life course represents in the life-story a basic scheme which is made specific by the fictionalisation of the self, i.e. the construction of a character. But although we can speak here of the creation of a fictional character, and thus refer to a written form, the novel, we must make it clear that in the life-story the process is marked out by formal and structural features, which have to do with repetitions, related to the orality of the genre.

The process of fictionalisation, which creates the second dimension of the 'narrative identity' – the permanence of the self as described by Ricoeur (1990) – is marked out in the life-story by the recurrence of what I call 'key phrases' and 'key patterns'.

'Key phrases' are phrases such as 'It was regular', 'I had to', 'I refused', 'I did not want, but what could I do?' etc., which catch the attention of the listener-reader by the regularity of their recurrence. Functioning as refrains, they constitute formal markers that accent the narrative, within the phases of evaluation of the life experience. Reactivating the meaning's co-construction, they designate a type of relation between the self and the social sphere (the community which contributed to the formation of the self) and, more broadly, society as a whole. So doing, they express a steady position towards the world, which maintains, beyond the evolution of the subject, the permanence of the self. This position takes the form of an attitude marking the relation between self and society: harmony, indifference, submission, ambiguity, conflict etc. (Chanfrault-Duchet 1991a, 1991b, 1994). The question is then: are the key phrases marked by gender identity? In fact, insofar as the key phrases refer to abstract models of relation, they are not marked by gender identity, a dimension confirmed by my three narratives.

Alice's key phrase, 'I always respected norms, but I always followed my idea', expresses a form of ambiguity, in which the subject is presented as keeping within social norms but also autonomous, a pattern which makes every turning point in the life course the result of a decision.

Théoduline's key phrase, 'It was like that, but I managed to cope with it', expresses another form of ambiguity: the conflictual relation with society is mastered by the obstinacy of the subject.

As for Sophie's key phrase, 'I have always been outside the norms. It is my fate, but I claim it', it expresses a conflict, which paradoxically reveals, beyond defiance, a shutting up in another closed system of norms: marginality.

But if gender identity is not present in the key phrases, it appears in the 'key patterns'. Directly linked to the key phrases, the 'key patterns' transpose the steady position expressed in the key phrases into behaviours which contribute, in the narrative, to the construction of the self as a character. Exemplifying the attitude expressed in the particular key phrase of the life-story, they are brought into play within the frameworks of the anecdotes which dramatise the self. Their recurrence, which reactivates regularly in the narration the meaning's co-construction process, refers, beyond the diversity of the scenes, to a matrix of behaviour which aims to construct, in relation with social models, the coherence of the fictionalised self as a character. The key patterns thus govern, in the narration, the tension between the evolution and the permanency of the self as 'narrative identity', and simultaneously the tension between self and society (Chanfrault-Duchet 1991a). Since this process brings into play, in the woman's life-story, the different female roles as defined by society, the marks of gender identity tend to be concentrated within the anecdotes which actualise the key patterns. This feature can be shown through significant examples from my three narratives.

Shaping her identity on the basis of an ambiguous relation to society, and aiming to argue about her status as woman, Alice calls up, through a dramatised dialogue, the social role of spouse:

> One day, I was invited to a reception and a woman I knew came to me and whispered: 'You are so beautiful, tonight. I do not understand you. Why do you stay with your brother? You make an odd couple!' I retorted, wild with rage: 'Yes we are an odd couple: we do not have sexual intercourse!'. She could not understand!

Théoduline refers in the same way to the social representations of motherhood:

> One day, I had to take my turn at the gate by the railway. It was a few miles away and I always went on my bicycle. It was pouring with rain that day, I was pregnant and I had nobody to look after my last child. So I wrapped my son in a big macintosh, and I put him in a basket, that I secured on the back of the bicycle. And on we went. On the road, we met a neighbour under her umbrella. She shouted at me: 'How dare you go out in the rain?' She knew I was pregnant, she said: 'You will kill your child and the one you are awaiting!' I did not answer. I looked straight ahead and pedalled.

As for Sophie, she dramatises the representations of femininity:

> When I was an auxiliary teacher, I did not want to change my style and I went teaching with my long hippie skirts. So when I was teaching in this

technical school, one day I was called in by the head. He told me: 'You have to dress differently. You cannot have any authority over those boys if you keep wearing those skirts with flowers!' I decided to remain cool and I said: 'Show me the ban in the school rules!'. He did not answer, but the next year, I did not get the job.

But if I use these examples as significant for each narrative, I must make clear that in the woman's life-story, so as to account for her female identity as a whole, the narrator has to mention in the course of the narrative all the female roles which determine, in social representations, a female identity. So that the work on social representations – whether acknowledged, kept at a distance or reorganised through values – constitutes the basis of the work of the meaning which aims to express the singularity of the female identity.

The textualisation of identity

The double process of narrativisation and fictionalisation which takes charge of the organisation and interpretation of biographical data is specified and complexified by a process of textualisation, which aims to express the singular identity through a closed meaning system, bringing into play symbolic structures.

Narrativisation (life course) and fictionalisation (self as character) both lead to the elaboration of narratives marked by biographical and psychosocial types, a dimension related to the constant implicit reference to current biographical standards, with the result that reading numerous life narratives gives the odd impression of reading stories which form series and only modulate, through individual details, a standard matrix induced by the socio-historical context. To avoid being a simple informant, a number in social sciences data, the narrator must communicate the uniqueness and the richness of his/her self through the richness and the originality of the text he/she produces, i.e. he/she must enter the textualisation process. This situation is relatively rare, so that in the narratives produced within social sciences, we find more life histories (see above) than life-stories as such. When engaged, the textualisation process works on two levels: the thematic configuration and the connotation system, as related to the 'key words'.

The life-story thus implies the elaboration of a particular thematic configuration which connects facts, events and scenes, so as to cross the basic thematic organisation induced by the standard life course scheme. Contributing to the expression of the uniqueness of the self, this configuration brings into play gender identity as a constituent of the self, a process which can be shown here through my three narratives.

Théoduline organises the themes into a configuration based on oppositions: cow-herdess vs school pupil, domestics vs aristocrats, behind-the-times mentality vs modernity, poverty vs wealth and so on. These oppositions are integrated into a binary system ultimately opposing country and town. This system plays simultaneously on different levels, a feature which introduces polysemia into the narrative and thus a literary dimension to the text produced. The opposition works on the geographical level (marking the geographical distance between the village and the town, and the difference between two landscapes, two environments), on the social level (expressing the distance between poverty and wealth, home and work, the role of a mother and of a maid), on the cultural level (underlining the differences between rural and urban culture, tradition and modernity) and finally on the symbolic level – beyond her love of her region, Théoduline invests country with negative values and town with positive ones. But, in this configuration, the two worlds do not remain isolated, they are connected by the bicycle, by Théoduline's daily rides to and from town. These rides are not just movement, they cost Théoduline an effort, which represents in the narrative the translation of a moral position (her tenacity to master her personal and social condition) into physical marks. In the meaning system built by this configuration, the resolution of the tension between these two universes is presented as the ultimate significance to be given to the lived experience. In this closed meaning system, the female roles play a functional part, whereas the bicycle assumes a symbolic role, that could not be taken over by a car or even a moped. Pedalling on her bike, Théoduline, as a mother, goes to town and comes back to the country with money earned by the sweat of her brow. But this experience goes beyond motherhood to designate a personal achievement, which refers to another woman's role, that of the housekeeper. In the form of modern conveniences, Théoduline could bring into her home in the country a symbolic piece of wealth and modernity from town.

Alice builds a binary configuration too. She opposes indoors and outdoors, and thus inverts the social image of the woman working outside and suspected of neglecting her family and home. The meaning system presents the home as the universe of the accepted duty (she cares for her brother, looks after the house, and types to military schedules) and outdoors as the universe of leisure, pleasure and freedom: she goes to the restaurant, to receptions and to the beautician, so as to preserve her femininity. In so doing, she builds for herself a new definition of the unmarried woman, taken for granted by society. She refuses the image of the old spinster and the traditional role of 'maid of the parish priest' to take on indoors and outdoors the apparent role of a 'married woman'. But this first level of meaning is crossed by another one based on values, which subsume, in the idea of gain, an axiological configuration referring to money, morality and freedom. The identity conveyed here finds its balance between Alice's duty to the family and society on the one hand and freedom, femininity and intellectual development as a duty to herself on the other. The personal achievement lies in the balance between the 'losses' (husband, sexuality, children, 'normal' life course) and the gains (wealth, relative autonomy and social acknowledgement for the 'fulfilled duty').

Sophie organises her themes in a complex configuration within two fields which never join together: a mythic world marked out by literature and ancient civilisations on the one hand, and the world of reality on the other. This second universe is grasped through social roles (daughter, 'spouse', mother, student and militant ecologist) given coherence through the status of an outsider. The meaning system consequently combines three axes: a reality transformed by literature, a refused social reality and a personal reality built against social norms. The tension that arises between the three axes is increased by the axiological system: whereas Sophie fetishises the world of literature, she systematically invests social representations with negative values so as to justify their inversion and thus legitimate her identification with the model of the outsider. But this first meaning system is crossed by another one, based on an idealised view of the social models, which organises the life experience into a dynamics marked by desire, deception and refusal, a position which reveals, beyond the affirmation of marginality, the implicit avowal of aspirations that could only be fulfilled – magically – by a success in the exam, which would reconcile the mythic world and reality. The singular identity conveyed in the life-story thus presents a split self which overcomes failures through the claiming of difference. But we must notice that if gender is here part of the identity, it is not presented as the core of the self, as in both other narratives. We shall retain two hypotheses: (1) Sophie's actual status as student obliterates the dimension of gender, and (2) Théoduline and Alice belong to generations which had to struggle to see their woman's rights acknowledged, whereas Sophie, born in the 1960s, belongs to the new generation which received the benefits of the women's liberation movement, – a situation which allows the subject to integrate gender identity without making it the centre of the self.

In the life-story, the closed meaning system built by the particular thematic configuration is reinforced in its coherence by a particular connotation system. From the linguistic perspective, 'connotation' means a semantic process induced by the existence of suggested values, beyond the referential meaning of words. Related to the discursive use of lexicon, this dimension loads the words with symbolic meaning and ideology (Kerbrat-Orecchioni 1977: 18). Beyond the first level of significance conveyed by words, symbolic meanings are thus called to mind on a second level. As intended meanings, the connotations tend to organise themselves into systems which introduce polysemia and so give access to the deep significance present in texts and discourses. And if Kerbrat-Orecchioni (1977: 201) notes that 'connotation is omnipresent in the everyday language, which is deeply affective, axiological and stylistically marked' (my translation), we shall recall that the literarity is generally defined on the basis of polysemia and thus connotations, – a double perspective which can account for the specificity of the textualisation in the life-story.

In this genre, the connotations which complexify the particular thematic configuration are produced by the 'key words' (i.e. words which are related to thematic axes and which, loaded with symbolic meanings, recur in the narrative) and organised into a system. Proceeding as a semantic network, this connotation system crosses the whole narrative and is related, through the axiological system, to the social imaginary and the cultural symbolic system, thus integrating gender representations.

I shall limit my presentation of the meaning system, as developed through connotations, to the key word 'school'. This choice is not made by chance: school refers to an inevitable theme in current life course models, and, as an institution, represents for women a way of escaping the fate imposed by gender condition.

This key word as used in my narratives calls up shared representations which remain very vivid in France, since they belong to a republican myth. Loaded with ideology, the term conveys in French culture the idea of social promotion (we could even say salvation) through education and the principle of the 'equality of opportunities' beyond social and gender condition. And as it refers to a common experience it appeals in the narrative to a shared imaginary which is unfailingly related to childhood. My three narrators exploit these elements, through different meaning systems, to account for their identity.

In the three narratives, the word is invested with positive connotations, but it is in Théoduline's narrative that it has the most strength. The word 'school' evokes the imaginary linked to education in the rural districts, i.e. old images still vivid in the French collective memory: a long walk with comrades along country paths to reach the school, and episodes of playing truant. But this collective imaginary is here worked out so as to express an individual imaginary and supports, in the narrative, a particular significance. In Théoduline's text, the word, with its constellation of connotations, evokes a social and personal experience, something painful – an incomplete education – and is thus loaded with frustration:

> I only went to school in winter time, because the rest of the year I had to herd the cows. The others ... they could go on, whereas for me ... I had to herd the cows to earn some money to send to my mother. ... So that ... I was not entered by the school master for the 'certificat d'études'. I remember the day when the others took a cart to go to town and take the exam. I was in the field. ... As they passed by, they smiled at me and waved in my direction ... kindly. ... But I ... I had a heavy heart! I learned easily though. ... But as I was absent most of the year I could not make up. ... What a pity!

The word crystallises, then, Théoduline's resentment against a traditional mentality which remains alien to republican ideology and does not consider the education of girls as a priority:

> My brother was very lucky. ... He could take the exam. ... And he passed it! I loved him but sometimes I was envious. ... I often said to myself: why could not I take the exam? My brother did! But, you know, I was the eldest, he was the youngest. ... He was a boy and I was ... a girl! And in those times people thought that girls did not need education ...

But in the meaning system of Théoduline's text, this resentment is overcome within the framework of gender identity. Redefining motherhood on the basis of the republican ideology, Théoduline assumes the new mentality: she brought up her ten children so that, thanks to school, they could all escape their class condition:

> I have always been severe with my children about school. I even paid for them to have particular lessons when it was necessary. I wanted them to succeed, because as I could not have a real education, I absolutely wanted them to get one. I wanted them to have diplomas. ... For example one of my daughters already had two diplomas at the age of sixteen!

In Alice's narrative, the word is loaded with gratitude: instruction allows autonomy through work and access to philosophical and literary texts, which help her to understand the world, a dimension perceived as a personal achievement. School is thus presented as a means of escaping class condition and, above all, gender condition. The ideological connotations of the term echo the axiological system brought into play in the text: they are given as constituents of an individual identity. Pointing out her choice to continue to learn by correspondence while working for a tobacconist, and then, year after year, her tenacity in improving her education and enlarging her culture by reading books, Alice implicitly presents her adhesion to the ideology of school as a decisive turning point in her life, one which made it possible to get her autonomy despite various family constraints.

As for Sophie's narrative, the word does not call up the connotations related to gender: she belongs to a generation which did not have to struggle to go to school. According to the meaning system brought into play, the word is loaded both with desire and resentment and refers to an insitution which creates conformity, and thus contributed to reinforce her propensity to marginality. But simultaneously the word and its ideological contents are so over-invested that they become an essential constituent of the self in the form of a vocation, in the religious meaning of the term (a situation possible in France where education, as secularised by the Republic, stands for religion). Her narrative thus presents her relation to literature and ancient civilisations on the one hand, to the republican myth on the other, as two 'religions', which can melt in the framework of a double salvation. She wishes to pass the examination and become a teacher to save the pupils (to help them to escape their class condition through access to higher culture), as well as to save herself (to fulfil by her own means the republican promise, made by school, of a social promotion). This double salvation refers to a situation which would allow, within a new identity that remains a dream, the reconstruction, beyond gender and through an identification to a republican heroine of the split self.

Gender as a constituent of the self

Gender identity is, then, an important constituent of the woman's life-story in many ways. It intervenes in the main structures of the narrative: the life course, the key patterns and the anecdotes, and, finally, the closed meaning system (shaped by the thematic configuration and the connotation system), as part of the identity conveyed and taken up by the subject, in reference to accepted models of female identity. But it must be noted that, in the life-story, gender identity cannot be isolated as such. It is integrated within the social discourse, within the social imaginary, which function here as shared knowledge, to communicate, through a complex process of construction, the meaning of the life experience, the singularity of the self.

To conclude, I would like here to stress the making of meaning in the life-story, which seems to me the most interesting – the most fascinating – dimension of the genre. This quality has usually only been recognised and analysed in literary texts. But we must question here the fetishisation of the literary text that such a position reveals. What life-stories and their analyses tend to show is the remarkable ability of ordinary people to construct complex meaning systems which are as complex as and similar to literary productions. And I would say that if life-stories are to convey information within the field of social sciences, it is primarily about the very means by which individuals attempt to give a meaning to their life experience, to their identity and to the world.

Bibliography

Bakhtin, M. (1984) *Esthétique de la création verbale*, Paris: Gallimard. First edition: 1979, *Estetika slovesnogo tsortchestva*, Moscow: Iskoustvo.

Chanfrault-Duchet, M.-F. (1984) 'La Littérature de témoignage en langue française: structures et formes linguistiques', unpublished PhD thesis, University of Tours, France.

—— (1987) 'Le récit de vie, données ou texte?', *Cahiers de Recherches sociologiques, Montréal: Université du Quebec à Montréal*, 5: 2: 116–28.

—— (1988) 'Le Système interactionnel du récit de vie oral', *Sociétés* 18: 26–31.

—— (1990) 'Mytos y structuras narrativas en la historia de vida', *Historia y fuente oral*, 4: 11–21

—— (1991a) 'Narrative Structures, Social Models and Symbolic Representations in the Life-story', in S. Gluck and D. Pataï (eds), *Women's Words*, New York: Routledge: 77–92.

—— (1991b) 'Oralité, choralité du récit de vie', in M. Margarito (ed.), *Parole ai margini*, Torino: Tirrenia stampatori: 129–56.

—— (1994) 'Les Refrains du récit de vie oral', in *Rocznik-Etudes romanes*, 171: 41–9.

—— (1995) 'Faire le point: lettres à Ménie Grégoire', in Ph. Lejeune (ed.), 'Le Tournant d'une vie', *Cahiers RITM*, 10: 129–39.

—— (1997) 'L'Ecole et les discours autobiographiques', in Ph. Lejeune (ed.), 'L'autobiographie en procès', *Cahiers RITM*, 14: 79–94.

De Beauvoir, S. (1949) *Le deuxième sexe*, Paris: Gallimard.

Goulemot, J.-M. (1981) Introduction to *V. Jammerey-Duval, Mémoires*, Paris: Le Sycomore.

Kerbrat-Orecchioni, C. (1977) *La Connotation*, Lyon: Presses universitaires de Lyon.

Kohli, M. (1989) 'Le Cours de vie comme institution sociale', *Enquête, 'Biographie et cycle de vie'*, 5: 37–43.

Lejeune, P. (1989) *On Autobiography*, Minneapolis: Minnesota University Press. First edition: 1975, *Le Pacte autobiographique*, Paris: Seuil.

Michel, L. (1886) *Mémoires*, Paris.

Ricoeur, P. (1985) *Temps et récit III: le temps raconté*, Paris: Seuil.

——— (1990) *Soi-même comme un autre*, Paris: Seuil.
Searle, J.R. (1969) *Speech Acts*, Cambridge: Cambridge University Press.
Tristan, F. (1833) *Pérégrinations d' une paria*, Paris.
Zumthor, P. (1983) *Introduction à la poésie orale*, Paris: Seuil.

4   Extending autobiography

A discussion of Sylvia Plath's
The Bell Jar

Mary Evans

In a recent essay on postmodernity, Perry Anderson situates the emergence of postmodernity in Hispanic America, and describes its emergence in terms of a new voice within modernism: 'a muted perfectionism of detail and ironic humour, whose most original feature was the newly authentic expression it afforded women' (Anderson 1998: 4). That voice – of irony and humour – is predominant in Sylvia Plath's *The Bell Jar*. It is a voice of resistance, of resistance to the organising and authoritarian limitations of conventional autobiography that at the same time proposes a realisation of the limits of the self. *The Bell Jar*, in its many fictional selves, avoids the controlling form of the conventional autobiographical self, yet suggests to its readers that the self is only possible through contradiction and ambiguity. In terms of the moral and social agenda of the USA (and indeed the accepted conventions of autobiography), it is a deeply disturbing (and heretical) thesis. For all its apparent simplicity, and tone of *faux-naïvete*, I will argue that *The Bell Jar* opens up possibilities within the autobiographical form which still demand recognition and development.

The Bell Jar was originally published under the pseudonym Victoria Lucas and presented as a novel. However, the use of the term 'novel' for what is transparently an autobiographical discussion opens up questions about the boundaries between *genres* and Sylvia Plath's entirely knowing and self-conscious wish to subvert them. *The Bell Jar* (which was published in January 1963 only a few weeks before the author's suicide) challenges the idea (now widely discredited) that novels and autobiography are different, and that what can be said in fiction would not be acceptable in autobiography. Clearly, in choosing to publish under a pseudonym Plath was well aware of the complicated relationship which she was establishing between herself and her account of her life. By choosing to be 'Victoria Lucas' she draws attention to the *fiction* of the fiction: the exercise of writing an autobiography as fiction becomes a double take on our expectation of fiction. Since we expect fiction to be fiction, we do not expect authors to need to hide themselves. Implicit in this belief is our taken-for-granted assumption that we can distinguish between fiction, what is made up and imagined, and autobiography, the truthful – if limited – account of a life. Secure in the distinction between these two genres, we then need not ask questions about the extent to which autobiography is, or can be, as much a work of fiction as any conventional fictional work. Conversely, our assumptions about fiction are secured by the boundaries established by autobiography.

As readers of *The Bell Jar* will know, the novel/autobiography is an account of the breakdown, and subsequent recovery of Esther Greenwood, a white, middle-class late adolescent of Eisenhower's USA. Esther, like Sylvia Plath (indeed *as* Sylvia Plath) had to negotiate the sexual and social contract of the 1950s: a contract which in the early pages of the novel seems hopelessly weighted in terms of male agendas and interests but gradually shifts towards the possibility of female autonomy and agency. The context of Esther's struggles for self-determination is a culture which is obsessively domestic in terms of its national identity and sexual politics (Macpherson 1991). 'Abroad' is associated with strangeness, with the dangerous if not the positively subversive, and with all those moral ambiguities and complexities which had long presented a problem for the USA. In this cultural sense, the understanding of the world which is ascribed to the USA by Esther Greenwood is that of the simple-minded Americans presented by Henry James (Bradbury 1996, esp. chaps 5 and 6). Incompetent and muddled in the face of European cynicism and worldliness, Americans in James's fiction were endlessly outmanoeuvred by the subtle machinations of the characters of old civilisations.[1] For Esther, Europe is implicitly a seductive presence and a deeply attractive one.

As is widely known, Sylvia Plath's own history involved a complex rejection of the USA. She condemned the dirt and the decay of Great Britain in the 1950s and was appalled, as generations of visitors from the USA have been, by the absence of domestic comfort and ease. Plath's flight from the USA (and her refusal at the end of her life to return there) was obviously related to the difficult relationship which she had with her mother as much as any more explicit politics, but that flight – fuelled as it probably was by personal circumstance – was also articulated through a critique of the cultural and political values of the USA (Aurelia Plath 1975: 437–8). Plath emerged from a generation, on both sides of the Atlantic, which did not grow up in either a permissive or an affluent society. 'Plenty', in the sense of both sexual activity as a widely available right and the extensive availability of material goods, had not yet become a characteristic of either Britain or the USA. Even though there were obvious material differences between the societies, of which Plath remained aware throughout her life, both societies could still recognise scarcity and material limitation as social possibilities. But out of postwar reconstruction a consumer society was emerging, and *The Bell Jar* is particularly acute in its presentation of the part which the USA is beginning to play as the dominant culture – and certainly the dominant mass culture – of the second half of the twentieth century. In this sense, *The Bell Jar* is situated at that point where the mass culture uniquely produced by capitalism in the USA is beginning to subvert tradition, and particularly sexual tradition. Esther Greenwood realises that she is taking part in a world dominated by the construction and the marketing of fantasy; Sylvia Plath (as Victoria Lucas) demonstrates that her fantasy selves, both Esther and Victoria, attempt to find order in this world but cannot do so because the boundaries between fantasy and reality, between fact and fiction, between fiction and autobiography are neither distinct nor intact. Sylvia, Esther and Victoria – the three constituent female selves of *The Bell Jar* – all exist in different relationships to the world of the postwar West. As women in this world, they have to try and achieve a concordat with it which does not reproduce the domestic oppression of the suburbs of east-coast America or the life of the corporate woman, both of which so frighten Esther.

Throughout the nineteenth century, women novelists in Britain had outlined the possible forms of the achievement of domestic harmony and argued (with varying degrees of determination and ruthlessness) an agenda for the domestication of men. Charlotte Brontë's virtual castration of Rochester in *Jane Eyre* is probably the most extreme case of a man being brought to domestic heel by a woman writer, and having to suffer extraordinary physical injuries in order to achieve the marriage he so desires. Even though those injuries are acquired through an attempt to save the woman (the 'mad' Mrs Rochester) who represents 'bad' sex, Charlotte Brontë does not suggest that there is any wish to return to transgressive sexuality in the novel's final pages of reconciliation. Indeed, through the virtues of self-reliance, endeavour and hard work Jane Eyre has achieved a considerable inheritance of domestic peace and prosperity, and defeated the forces of male grandiosity and unprincipled desire. In the same way as other heroines of other female authors (for example, Dorothea in George Eliot's *Middlemarch* and Margaret Hale in Elizabeth Gaskell's *North and South*), Jane Eyre has, almost literally, cut a hero down to size in order to fit him into a domestic space. These fictional endings suggest a pattern of female agency which involves women remaining determined guardians of both their own sexuality and the domestic world. As helpmeets to men, they offer a consistent nineteenth-century model of mutual and complementary relationships between women and men.[2]

But this model of complementarity, while it was entirely consistent with the social reality of much of the Victorian middle class (and a goal for sections of the working class), became increasingly untenable as the twentieth century progressed. For numerous reasons, relations between the sexes changed, and the idea of the unity of the household (even if enforced by patriarchal authority) was increasingly translated into a model of autonomous individuals, bound by individual contracts rather than constraint. This shift towards autonomy and individuality for women, as much as for men, undermined what Patricia Meyer Spacks has described as the combination of 'assertion and concealment' in the 'feminine ideal' (Spacks 1975). Thus women in the twentieth century have been increasingly expected to write of their own experiences as the record of the actions of autonomous individuals, and claim for themselves characters with the self-determination which had hitherto been largely the preserve of men. Yet just as women were able to do this (and middle-class women such as Vera Brittain and Naomi Mitchison very rapidly claimed the right to speak for, and of, themselves and their interpretation of public events), it would be incorrect to assume that women found the autobiographical voice to be unproblematic (Stanley 1992). Brittain and Mitchison could speak for difference, and for the particular views of women about politics, but convention still demanded that women (and to a large extent men) did not speak of their sexuality in anything other than a conventional way. What was not allowed was ambiguity and doubt around the issue of gender. For women, autobiography has always demanded a secure, determined self, in which an individual confronts specific forms of difficulty and difference but nevertheless suggests a self which is clearly defined.

It is in this context that Sylvia Plath's *The Bell Jar* is such an important, indeed undervalued text, precisely because it is through this text that Sylvia Plath explores the limits of women's autonomy and the secure first-person singular. Sylvia Plath originally chose to publish *The Bell Jar* under the pseudonym of Victoria Lucas in order, it is generally assumed, to protect her mother (and others). Yet so little does Sylvia Plath attempt to disguise herself, or the actual circumstances of her life, that this intention has to be received with some scepticism. Even if Sylvia Plath assumed that some readers would not connect her with Victoria Lucas, she was too sophisticated an author not to recognise the diversity of readerships for any texts, and know that for many readers recognition of real people (herself included) was inevitable. The story of Esther Greenwood is presented by Plath as fiction, but from the first pages, Plath adopts a mocking and ironic tone towards her fictional self, which raises questions about the identity of author and subject. In this disguise what emerges is a vivid piece of writing, which both subverts expectations about the novel and autobiography and yet extends the possibilities of both. Indeed, what Sylvia Plath achieves in *The Bell Jar* is a demonstration of the limitations of the factual and the literal, and the degree to which the containment of fantasy undermines the accurate portrayal of the person. In allowing herself (and of course the 'self' in *The Bell Jar* is the three selves of Esther Greenwood, Sylvia Plath and Victoria Lucas) to abandon the idea of the unitary self, Sylvia Plath shows first, how conventional autobiography is organised around a rigid set of expectations about character and experience and second, how individuals not only construct themselves but are constructed by others. The various personae that Esther Greenwood tries out in *The Bell Jar* are all, in their various way, perfectly authentic selves, even if none of them is the person that Esther identifies with and wishes to become.

The instability of the self in the twentieth century is therefore presented in *The Bell Jar* as an *inevitable* consequence of the increasing choice of 'person' which is open to women in the latter part of the twentieth century. The human tragedies which *The Bell Jar* describes are three-fold: the execution of the Rosenbergs with which the novel opens, the horrific medical treatment given to Esther Greenwood and the more general, if less final, situation of many women who are expected to conform to one of two rigid models about women – either the childless executives who terrify (and are satirised by) Esther or the domesticated mothers of the suburbs. When *The Bell Jar* was first published the changes were only just beginning which suggested that women could be both mothers and independent wage earners. The excitement of that idea – and the expectations which it led to – has now given way to a degree of scepticism about the terms and conditions of combining motherhood and paid work. *The Bell Jar* achieves an extraordinary degree of engagement with all the issues relating to women and both the public and the private worlds: critical of the exaggerations of the models of women with careers and women as mothers, it demonstrates the loss of self which is involved in both these choices. At the same time it shows an awareness of the difficulty of achieving the real, ambiguous self, which suggests that, long before Judith Butler *et al.*, Sylvia Plath had recognised the loss, rather than the gain, implicit in rigidly imposed sexual categorisation (Butler 1990).

The famous opening lines of *The Bell Jar*, in which Esther introduces herself as a person who is – apparently uniquely – 'stupid about executions', allows Esther to place herself as immediately outside the conventional world. In that first paragraph Esther both claims distance from the executions ('It had nothing to do with me') and yet demonstrates in the same sentence her intense engagement with these events. This pattern – of the denial of evident commitment – is one which is to recur throughout *The Bell Jar*. For example, in the first pages Esther undermines both herself, the character she is 'playing' and the beloved mores of North American society. As she says:

> Look what can happen in this country, they'd say. A girl lives in some out-of-the-way town for nineteen years, so poor she can't afford a magazine, and then she gets a scholarship to college and wins a prize there and ends up steering New York like her own private car.
>
> (Plath 1963: 2)

As we are to learn in a few pages, these sentences contain considerable misrepresentation: Esther was far from being too poor to afford a magazine and the 'out-of-the-way town' was in fact the home of a major, and prestigious, college. But the tone is set: one in which interpretation is all, and what is assumed to be a 'fact' (that is the North American belief in the endless possibilities of upward social mobility) is made ridiculous precisely by being presented as literally true.

Of the many 'facts' which are undermined in *The Bell Jar*, two are more central than others. The first is the 'fact' that the way of life of the suburbs of the USA represents the pinnacle of human achievement, whilst the second theme is the apparent agreement of women with the domestic settlement and contract of that society. In Esther's world, the maintenance of normality depends upon the uncritical acceptance of the idea that the way of life of the suburbs is the definitive way of life of the world and second, that women have endorsed this suburban ideal despite its limitations and distinctions. In order to maintain this society, women are expected to maintain a precarious balance between the appropriate appearance of 'normal' heterosexuality and rigidly policed boundaries about sexual availability. Little wonder, as Esther Greenwood points out more than once, that these contradictions make people (and particularly women) go mad. In a society which refuses ambiguity and diversity, the only way to articulate difference is through refusal and the explicit rejection of the models of success which are conventionally available.

In order to tell the story of her breakdown and attempted suicide – in order, in fact, to offer her own conventional autobiography – Sylvia Plath would have had to establish herself as the first person of the narrative. In choosing to become both Victoria Lucas and Esther Greenwood, she allows herself both distance from herself (which is impossible in conventional autobiography) and a degree of control over the narrative. The relationship between self and events has always been problematic in autobiography, in that for most people events outside their own immediate control have considerable impact – and an impact which is generally shared with others. Authors then become involved in explaining particular reasons why events affect them: the point at which they inevitably lose control of the narrative. Other than the execution of the Rosenbergs there are no 'events' as such in *The Bell Jar*, but what there is, because Sylvia Plath is firmly in control of the narrative, is the final major event of Esther's renegotiated relationship with society. That renegotiation has involved the loss of innocence and a growing scepticism about the sincerity of others. As readers we are allowed to see Esther progressing towards a self which is identifiably the same as her original self, but standing in a different relationship to the social world. What has been managed, therefore, is an evocation of personal change in which Esther has acquired a new, *additional* identity of a sexually active adult woman, in order to sustain and enhance her sense of self.

Of the many aspects of the conventional world which are undermined and lampooned in *The Bell Jar* there are several which relate specifically to what has been seen as the struggle by women in the twentieth century for equality. One of Sylvia Plath's first targets is academic achievement. As she well knows, the higher education of women has always been (and is still) held as a central plank in the emancipation of women. As she equally well knows, this aspiration implicitly endorses a system of higher education largely organised by and for men. Thus women in 1963 (or 1953 which was the year of the execution of the Rosenbergs) were asked to emulate the achievements of men. That they might, in this, *lose* a voice rather than gain one is suggested in the contrast between the characters of Buddy Willard and Doreen:

> Buddy Willard went to New York, but now I thought of it, what was wrong with him was that he was stupid. Oh he'd managed to get good marks all right, and to have an affair with some awful waitress on the Cape by the name of Gladys, but he didn't have one speck of intuition. Doreen had intuition. Everything she said was like a secret voice speaking straight out of my own bones.
>
> (Plath 1963: 7)

The 'secret voice' which Doreen has is one which cuts across and questions all the virtues and values which Esther has so painfully acquired. Doreen's worldly cynicism questions Esther's acceptance of conventional agendas and encourages

Esther to entertain the rebellion which we are allowed to know she is considering. For example, describing her relationship with her benefactor at college Esther writes:

> So I wrote to Philomena Guinea a long letter in coal-black ink on grey paper with the name of the college embossed on it in red. I wrote what the leaves looked like in autumn when I bicycled out onto the hills, and how wonderful it was to live on a campus instead of commuting by bus to a city college and having to live at home, and how all knowledge was opening up before me and perhaps one day I would be able to write great books the way she did.
>
> (Plath 1963: 42)

However, what follows this *apparently* sincere letter of thanks is a rapid disavowal of any shared ground between the author and Philomena Guinea. Philomena's novels are lampooned as romantic and illiterate, and her performance (and presumably her participation) in college life described as 'very stupid', a performance which made absolutely no difference to her considerable success in later life. Hence what the passage does is both to subvert Philomena Guinea and Esther herself: the former ridiculed for her trite work, whilst Esther makes fun of herself for her relentless pursuit of academic achievement. This pattern of self-criticism and self-mockery is one which continues throughout *The Bell Jar*. Time and again Esther allows herself distance from herself and mocks the pattern of relentless self-improvement which she has been following throughout her life. Yet it is not so much the assiduous attention to her school work (and the other agendas of the white, middle class USA) that Esther questions, it is the part that these achievements play in heterosexual relationships:

> I tried to imagine what it would be like if Constantin were my husband. It would mean getting up at seven and cooking him eggs and bacon and toast and coffee and dawdling about in my night-gown and curlers after he'd left for work to wash up the dirty plates and make the bed, and then when he came home after a lively, fascinating day he'd expect a big dinner, and I'd spend the evening washing up even more dirty plates till I fell into bed, utterly exhausted.
>
> This seemed a dreary and wasted life for a girl with fifteen years of straight As, but I know that's what marriage was like, because cook and clean and wash was just what Buddy Willard's mother did from morning till night, and she was the wife of a university professor and had been a private school teacher herself.
>
> (Plath 1963: 88)

Esther Greenwood/Sylvia Plath recognises that for women the path from 'straight As' does not necessarily lead to professional success; the price of that success is, if not a complete refusal of heterosexual activity, then at least a refusal of maternity. The postwar settlement of gender relations allowed for the higher education of women, but it did not entertain (as Betty Friedan was to point out in *The Feminine Mystique*) the idea that women with children would actually use this education in employment. Betty Friedan discovered in the suburbs of the USA legions of married women, largely white and middle class, becoming increasingly depressed as they became domestic drudges (Friedan 1963). Once hopeful, these women were turned by a particular form of marriage into door-mats:

> And I knew that in spite of all the roses and kisses and restaurant dinners a man showered on a woman before he married her, what he secretly wanted when the wedding service ended was for her to flatten out underneath his feet like Mrs Willard's kitchen mat.
>
> (Plath 1963: 88)

In *The Bell Jar* Sylvia Plath provides, in passages such as the above, a searing attack on the values and expectations of the USA of the 1950s. But the novel is very much more than a passionate critique of the constraint and the cost to women of this particular form of domestic life. It is also an argument and a discussion about how the self is to be maintained by women, in the face of what seem to be (and is certainly presented by Plath as such) overwhelming attempts to disestablish and undermine any sense of secure identity in women. What *The Bell Jar* thus offers to us is a thesis about the virtual impossibility – for women – of articulating a self which is not formed, affected and distorted by immensely influential pressures. These include both pressures from given significant others (in the case of Esther/Sylvia this person is Esther's mother), peer groups, institutions and above all else a normative culture. Sylvia Plath writes of a decade in which many of the pressures of conformity were recognised by male sociologists writing about men in organisations (William H. Whyte on *The Organisation Man* and David Riesman on *The Lonely Crowd* are notable examples). But for these men there was no problem about the impact of a public culture on women, since women did not belong to it. What Sylvia Plath does in *The Bell Jar* is to show exactly how much women do not just to make and sustain the public culture but also the costs to them of doing so.

The outward symbols of conformity which Esther Greenwood first identifies (and rejects) are those of dress and appearance. Her discomfort in the early pages of *The Bell Jar* is described in terms of the clothes she wears in New York and what she presents to the reader as a series of disguises. The relationship between women and clothes has now been discussed by writers such as Marjorie Garber and Elizabeth Wilson; what these writers recognise is that it is impossible simply to 'get dressed': what we wear is a matter of choice and a deliberate deci-sion to appear as a particular kind of person (Garber 1993; Wilson 1985). But in the 1950s in the USA this perception of the deeply self-conscious process of getting dressed was not available to suburban teenagers: getting dressed involved the acceptance of getting dressed both as a natural process and as the social process of demonstrating the successful internalisation of a series of codes and rules about appearance. What was to become possible for urban youth in the 1970s and 1980s (underwear as outerwear, the mixing of genres of clothing, body piercing and other forms of highly deliberate dressing) was not possible in a society which rigorously policed clothing and through this imposition assumed that the correctly dressed person can be interpreted literally as the sum total of their appearance. The disintegration of Esther's ability to function in the world is replicated by her inability to get dressed, her revived competence as a social actor is marked by her revived interest in dress.

The outward self which is expected (of Esther and other characters in *The Bell Jar*) is an outward self which is conventionally dressed and presented: 'sane', 'ordinary' and 'normal' people do not question the limits of the appearance of normality nor offer to the social world confusing juxtapositions of styles, whether of dress or behaviour. This self, organised in ways appropriate to the culture, is equally rigorously organised in terms of the language and the manners which it recognises. For Esther/Sylvia this self is impossible to maintain and what runs through every page of the narrative of *The Bell Jar* is an intense sense of both the need and desire to subvert the reality of the taken-for-granted world. Indeed, what Plath offers in *The Bell Jar* is a fictional account of what Goffman was to describe in *The Presentation of the Self in Everyday Life*. In that text (and in *Asylums*) Goffman theorised what Plath described and illustrated: that our sense of ourselves is dependent on the reaction of others, and that their reaction can be controlled and manipulated by our own self-presentation (Goffman 1969, 1968). But the costs of maintaining an appropriate self can be overwhelming and – as they are for Esther – debilitating. These costs are made greater since the self to be maintained is not one which is voluntarily chosen, but at least in part imposed by an external culture.

The elements of that culture which make the greatest demands of Esther are expectations of conformity to an ideal of female selfhood and the acceptance of external authority. In the first case, the conformity expected of women is to a model of heterosexuality which limits women's sexual activity to marriage and to the recognition of male sexual needs. The sexual 'line' which women have to walk is one which assumes the importance of attracting male sexual attraction but then effectively organises it into marriage. Esther Greenwood, like millions of other women of her generation, is burdened with expectations about sexuality which effectively encourage both disguise and deceit about sexuality, the sense that women were expected to conceal the possibility of female sexual desire and yet at the same time endorse its recognition by men. Nevertheless, what Esther also recognises is that sexual emancipation for women is far from an issue about greater clarity and openness in sexual relations; the very idea of sexual emancipation and liberation is itself complicated by questions about maintaining a single sexual identity. Hence, the importance of the character of Joan in *The Bell Jar* – the co-patient of Esther's in the mental hospital whose illness, like that of Esther, originally manifests itself through the wearing of bizarre and unsuitable clothes. Joan, like Esther, has been unable to find for herself a secure and stable

self; part of that instability is manifested in her attitude to Esther and in particular her replication of and involvement in many of the same experiences as
Esther:

> I looked at Joan. In spite of the creepy feeling, and in spite of my old,
> ingrained dislike, Joan fascinated me. It was like observing a Martian, or a
> particularly warty toad. Her thoughts were not my thoughts, nor her feelings
> my feelings, but we were close enough so that her thoughts and feelings
> seemed a wry, black image of my own.
>
> (Plath 1963: 231)

Esther Greenwood goes on to tell us that 'sometimes I wondered if I had made
Joan up'. This remark illustrates a great deal of the interest of *The Bell Jar*: the
way in which Sylvia Plath constantly shows how character is constructed through
the perception and recollection of others. For example, in the discussion immediately following the passage quoted above Esther Greenwood comments critically
on Joan's 'silly smile'. This remark is then abandoned, whilst the narrative turns
to a description of a lesbian relationship. As readers we are left to make the
connection for ourselves: Joan's 'silly smile' is part of a suspect world, but also
part of a world which can offer the tenderness which is identified as absent from
heterosexual relations. We see, in what amounts to barely a page of *The Bell Jar*,
Esther turning to the various possibilities of adult sexuality and expressing her
confusion about them all. In terms which are derived less from narrative than
from psychoanalytical theory, we also see Esther attempting to construct her
fragile sense of self by the integration of a perception of another's sexual desire.
This process of acquiring identity through the perceptions of others is, in social
terms, the way in which individuals acquire cultural identity, but in emotional
and sexual terms it is what Lacan has described as the 'mirror stage' of human
development, and a process which has been summarised by Juliet Mitchell as:
'Lacan's human subject is a being that can only conceptualise itself when it is
mirrored back to itself from the position of another's desire' (Mitchell 1984:
254).

These words might have been written to describe Esther Greenwood and her
history. Esther longs to become the object of male desire, but what makes this
impossible is cultural intervention. The manners, mores and morality of the
USA in the 1950s (and even to a significant extent in Europe at the end of the
twentieth century) police the sexual behaviour of women in a way which Freud
recognised as both suppressing *and* exaggerating women's sexuality. Thus Esther
is intensely aware of her sexuality, but beset by the conflicting ideas and pressures which surround her. Her mother, her teachers and her peer group all
endorse a version of heterosexual morality which strictly controls female sexuality and tacitly accepts a sexual double standard. Little wonder that Esther
Greenwood becomes suicidal, and can only reconstruct herself by accepting her
female doctor's permission for heterosexual activity. Significant female characters
in *The Bell Jar* deny Esther the right to sexual relationships, but it is finally a

female doctor who allows Esther to begin a life of sexual activity. When Doctor Nolan 'allows' Esther Greenwood to hate her mother, she also allows her to escape from her mother's control. Achieving this separation is part of Esther's emancipation from her mother's expectations, even if part of that emancipation is achieved through the electrotherapy which Dr Nolan persuades Esther to accept. This experience of the medicinal use of science is the novel's juxtaposition to the destructive use of science (the electrocution of the Rosenbergs) with which the novel opens.

In raising these issues about Esther Greenwood's passage to adult sexuality I wish to emphasise how the narrative of *The Bell Jar* systematically demonstrates the ways in which it is impossible for Esther to speak confidently of 'herself'. In her case (as perhaps in many others) the social pressure to emerge as a coherent self is in fact deeply destructive and undermining. Esther is beset on all sides by individuals who wish to influence her in one way or another: she is surrounded by powerful people whose agendas are projections of themselves. Inevitably, Esther cannot meet these expectations and her failure to find a secure 'I' in which to locate herself becomes a mark of failure. No doubt there is a convincing psychoanalytic explanation for this failure or inadequacy of the superego; no-one who has read the biographies of Sylvia Plath and the plethora of material relating to them could doubt that Sylvia herself had significant reasons to fear the onslaught of well-defined individuals onto her fragile sense of self. But this is not an account of an individual pathology, rather of both the impact of a particular form of narrative on an individual, and the strength of social pressures on a particular person. Esther, as we first meet her, is a hard-working schoolgirl. She has done, as she knows, exactly what she is told, and she has the certificates to prove it. But as she begins to suspect, this conformity and obedience has robbed her of part of herself and she is left with a sense of herself which is inadequate to sustain the problems of an existence which is more complex than that of the school-room.

At the conclusion to *The Bell Jar* Esther Greenwood is pulled back to life by a 'magical thread', a metaphor which emphasises the maze-like nature of social existence. With the help of a sympathetic doctor, Esther has put together a self which can become sexually independent and assume a capacity for action which is apparently free of the control of others. It is a conclusion which suggests a triumphant passage to heterosexuality. We know, however, that this triumph is far from simple: Esther has already voiced considerable reservations about the social order of heterosexuality and if there is any triumph in her newly found sexual sophistication it is surely only limited. 'The magical thread' which takes Esther to freedom takes her to a compromised freedom: she has learned two harsh lessons in her breakdown. The first is that she followed too literally the demands made of her: the imperatives she took so much to heart were more closely related to maintaining social structures than supporting or developing individual people. Esther comes to realise that her scholastic achievements, however remarkable, had only a marginal utility in the 'real' world of relations between women and men and women and employment. Recognising this forces Esther to recognise the fantasy she has pursued, and indeed the false promise of taking seriously the agendas offered to her. Inevitably, realising this is deeply undermining for the self, and Esther's fragile stability is deeply disturbed by her growing realisation that she has, in the words of the song, 'followed a dream'.

If this realisation is not enough, Esther also has to confront the demands made on her by the social world at the same time as she is coming to realise that these demands are themselves in part fictitious. The extraordinary strength of *The Bell Jar* is that Sylvia Plath manages to show us that achieving the 'real' self, the kind of self which is deemed secure and stable, involves a degree of distance from society. At precisely the point in its history when the USA was proposing a life script to the entire world, the character of Esther Greenwood suggests to us ways in which this authoritarian, and indeed simple-minded, script is impossible to fulfil. In doing this, Esther obviously subverts the entire ideological project of the USA: she shows the limits of its domestic contract, the internal compromises of its educational system and, above all else, the refusal of debate which characterised its politics. But in terms of the genre of autobiography *The Bell Jar* does something more: it poses questions about the boundaries between the self and society. In particular, it raises the essential issue about whether or not there actually *is* a self which is separate from the pressures and the forms of the social world. The characters of *The Bell Jar* who intrude upon, and menace, Esther Greenwood are formed from the ideological premises of the USA in the 1950s. Mrs Greenwood, Buddy Willard, Philomena Guinea and Dodo Conway are all, in a very literal sense, *social* actors who have taken to heart the demands and strictures of their social world and fully internalised them. The challenge to this world of dissenting ideas and experiences comes from Esther's commitment to the world of the imagination; although she has taken literally the educational agenda of her time it has been impossible for that education to conceal entirely the ambiguities and complexities which are contained in literature and the arts. Hence, however much what Ted Hughes describes as 'college America' attempts to avoid this tradition, it remains unavoidable (Hughes 1998: 39). Significantly, its first literal manifestation was to be, for Sylvia Plath, Spain. To quote Ted Hughes again:

> Spain frightened you. Spain
> Where I felt at home. The blood raw light,
> The oiled anchovy faces, the African
> Black edges to everything, frightened you.
> Your schooling had somehow neglected Spain.
>
>   (Hughes 1998: 39)

The 'somehow' in the description of the neglect is, of course, disingenuous. As Hughes is well aware, the contrast between Spain and the USA of Esther Greenwood is a contrast between Catholic and Protestant, between the symbolic and the literal, between a culture of disguise (in the case of the USA) and one of fierce recognition (in the case of Spain). The very ideas which are transparent in

Spain, of death and human limitation, are essentially ideas which are alien to the world of *The Bell Jar*, which takes for granted the congruence of a simple, coherent, ideology and equally simple, and straightforward, human beings. In this culture, autobiography, in the sense of the revelation of the person and the internal self, is near impossible since the invasion of the person by the culture (the boundary which Esther Greenwood has so much difficulty in maintaining) is systematic and total. On the other hand, the need to *acquire* an autobiography, to become a socially realised self, is a paradigmatic and normative part of the culture, albeit a culture which is hostile to a fully realised self.

Acknowledgements

I would like to thank Pat Macpherson for the many fascinating conversations about *The Bell Jar*, and Celia Lury, Tess Cosslett and Penny Summerfield for their helpful and insightful comments on this paper.

Notes

1 The most striking example is to be found in James's *The Europeans*, but Henry James's own career was informed by what he described as the essential 'European Standpoint'.
2 The politics of 'domesticating culture' are discussed by Nancy Armstrong (1987).

Bibliography

Anderson, P. (1998) *The Origins of Postmodernity*, London: Verso.
Armstrong, N. (1987) *Desire and Domestic Fiction*, Oxford: Oxford University Press.
Bradbury, M. (1996) *Dangerous Pilgrimages*, London: Penguin.
Butler, J. (1990) *Gender Trouble*, London: Routledge.
Friedan, B. (1963) *The Feminine Mystique*, New York: Norton.
Garber, M. (1993) *Vested Interests*, London: Penguin.
Goffman, E. (1968) *Asylums*, Harmondsworth: Penguin.
—— (1969) *The Presentation of Self in Everyday Life*, Harmondsworth: Penguin
Hughes, T. (1998) *Birthday Letters*, London: Faber.
Macpherson, P. (1991) *Reflecting on The Bell Jar*, London: Routledge.
Mitchell, J. (1984) *Women: The Longest Revolution*, London: Virago.
Plath, A. (ed.) (1975) *Letters Home*, New York: Harper.
Plath, S. (1963) *The Bell Jar*, London: Faber and Faber.
Spacks, P.M. (1975) *The Female Imagination*, New York: Alfred Knopf.
Stanley, L. (1992) *The Auto/biographical I: The Theory and Practice of Feminist Auto/biography*, Manchester: Manchester University Press.
Wilson, E. (1985) *Adorned in Dreams*, London: Virago.

Part II

Intersubjectivity

5 Dis/composing the subject

Intersubjectivities in oral history

Penny Summerfield

In a recently published biography, Helen Bamber, the human rights activist, is quoted as saying of the Holocaust survivors with whom she worked at Belsen in 1945–6,

> Above all else ... there was the need to tell you everything, over and over and over again ... it wasn't so much grief as a pouring out of some ghastly vomit like a kind of horror, it just came out in all directions.
>
> (Cassidy 1999:22)

Bamber's analogy between this remembering and retelling, and repeated vomiting, is striking. Vomiting is a painful process which can make you feel humiliated and debased. Bamber the therapist was confident of the eventual healing effects of encouraging verbal vomiting to happen. Oral historians also subscribe, usually inexplicitly, to the idea that the recall and retelling of past experience is beneficial to the teller, as well as useful for the listener. But most oral historians' ideas about what happens when subjects tell stories about themselves are quite different from Bamber's. Perhaps the most common is the idea that reminiscence is good for people because of its similarity to the 'talking cure', the kind of therapy that involves working through past experience with someone else, so that past and present, memory and the self, can be integrated. Bamber's metaphor is shocking because it suggests the rejection of the attempt at reintegration of experience suggested by the talking cure, and, as a result, the imperative of expulsion.

Composure, discomposure and the life-story

The concept of 'composure' usefully encapsulates the purpose of life-story telling as it is currently understood in oral-history theory and practice. The term was developed by popular memory theorists in the 1980s and 1990s in relation to everyday life-story telling. Graham Dawson, its main exponent, draws on the double meaning of the verb 'to compose' to suggest that in telling life-stories we engage both in the cultural activity of constructing narratives about ourselves, and in the psychic one of striving for an 'orientation of the self within the social relations of its world', which allows us a sense of self with which we can live and thus enables us to achieve 'subjective composure' (Dawson 1994: 22–3).

Other theorists of the life-story refer to the process of composure in terms of the achievement of coherence. The gerontologist Peter Coleman writes of achieving 'a sense of meaning and coherence' through reminiscence and suggests that it is abnormal for a narrator to be 'unable to gain comfort from his/her memories' (Coleman 1991: 134–5). The socio-linguist Charlotte Linde states: 'In order to exist in the social world with a comfortable sense of being a good, socially proper and stable person, an individual needs to have a coherent, acceptable and constantly revised life-story' (Linde 1993: 3). The link which Linde makes between the notion of constant revision of the life-story and coherence, is commonly made by life-story theorists. Coleman insists that 'there can be no such thing as a final account of a person's life. Any coherent account is shaped by an underlying and continuing search for meaning' (Coleman 1991: 122). Composure, this suggests, is never completely accomplished but is always provisional, for life-stories are similar to history itself. The process of interpretation and reinterpretation never stops. It cannot stop, because the social world is always in flux and we are constantly seeking ways of understanding both it and ourselves within it.

Life-stories are understood as taking a range of forms and relatively rarely being delivered as a whole, but rather as fragments. Dawson gives the examples on the one hand of any of us 'composing a story of the day's events' and on the other of a returning soldier narrating his experiences of war (Dawson 1994: 22–3). Linde suggests as a general definition that life-stories are discontinuously told accounts which 'express our sense of self: who we are and how we got that way' (Linde 1993: 3).

Oral historians enter the world of the life-story in search of personal accounts of historical processes. British oral history of the 1970s and 1980s was inspired by a commitment to giving a voice to the voiceless, so that they might 'tell it as it was', and it developed in academia within a social science framework. These two aspects of its recent origins contributed to an emphasis on truth rather than meaning, that is to say on discovering the hidden past through oral history and proving that this revelatory data was valid, rather than on exploring the complexities of its shifting meanings (Thompson 1978, 1988). More recently, following the Italian scholars Luisa Passerini and Alessandro Portelli, British oral historians have become less concerned with validity and authenticity as such, and more interested in the processes that go into the construction and telling of such accounts (Thomson 1994; Summerfield 1998). This development is marked by greater awareness of the psychic dimensions of the oral-history account, including, for example, the personal and collective meanings of silences concerning certain subjects, of defensiveness and denial of others, and of repeated emphasis upon some aspects of the past at the expense of others.

But however interested they may have become in psychic processes, oral historians, myself included, do not think of themselves as therapists. We need to believe that the process of telling a life-story has a beneficial effect on the tellers as such, and that, without therapeutic intervention, it helps them to integrate their pasts rather than initiating a process of expulsion. Otherwise we could hardly impose ourselves as researchers upon our respondents. We need the presence of a 'feel-good factor' in the oral-history interview, both for our own job satisfaction, and in terms of research ethics, and we are therefore committed to the dual meanings of the concept of composure. On the one hand, oral historians expect to offer respondents the chance to reflect on the past, review their lives and produce a version with which they can live in comfort, in short to compose themselves. And on the other, oral historians expect to facilitate the process of narration. The analogy an oral historian might use to describe their work of eliciting stories from narrators is of helping them to paint a picture of their life, to weave it into a tapestry, to construct a collage of it, or put it to music – in short to compose it – rather than helping them to vomit.

Narrators, too, have an idea of the purpose of an oral-history interview. The practice of oral history is sufficiently well understood in popular culture for it not to be an exaggeration to talk of an oral-history contract. In this unspoken deal the interviewee agrees to become a narrative subject, that is to place themselves at the centre of 'a narrative focused upon the inner self' and 'to organise her (or his) memory in such a way as to give it coherence and significance' and so produce for public consumption, stories based in their own interiority (Chanfrault-Duchet 1991: 78, 91). British TV documentaries such as *People's Century, Hidden Lives* and those produced by Stephen Humphries' Domino Films, such as *The Secret World of Sex* and *Labour and Love* show ordinary people giving this kind of testimony. Mass release films, from *Fried Green Tomatoes* (1991) to *Titanic* (1998) are framed by oral reminiscence. Oral histories form the basis of numerous books and magazine features. The technique is used in old people's homes and schools, by museums and within families. The model and the responsibilities of composition it imposes on the narrator are widely understood.

So oral history made a particular contribution to 1990s confessional culture. It is a popular genre for the public telling of private memories, the results of which are expected to be benign, however shocking or painful the interviewees' stories about the past may be. Yet in spite of widespread confidence that the method is 'for the good', I am going to argue here that oral-history practice may contradict the commitment to composure, and that oral history is inherently more likely to produce instabilities in the telling of life-stories than other, more casual, ways of encouraging reminiscence. (I am separating it now from the methods used by counsellors, psychotherapists and psychoanalysts, who, like Bamber, are engaged in helping people to cope with personally devastating experiences by recalling and reliving them.) My purpose is not to suggest that oral history is or is not ethical or a good research method. But I want to draw attention to some of its complexities, notably the relational qualities of the oral-history interview which may give rise not to composure, but to the *dis*composure of both the narrator and their life-story narrative. The discussion here addresses these relationships as aspects of intersubjectivity stimulated by the contact between interviewer and interviewee, but reaching beyond what is obvious and ostensible in the interactions between them. The first part of what follows explores the relationship between the interviewer's research frame and the narrator's memory frame. The second part discusses the implications of the relation between public stories and interviewees' parallel more private stories for interviewing for interiority. The third considers the results of non-verbal inter-personal dynamics between interviewer and narrator. I shall draw for examples of these different types of intersubjectivity on the interviews undertaken by myself and two researchers for a project on women's memories of the Second World War, published recently as *Reconstructing Women's Wartime Lives* (Summerfield 1998).

The research frame and the memory frame

The process of life review which occurs within reminiscence, whatever form it takes, is structured in some way or other, at the very least by the assumptions of the narrator about the audience. As Coleman argues, 'older people in part tell us what they want to say, in part what they think we want to hear' (Coleman 1991: 135), and, as Dawson argues, the recognition that different types of audience offer to the teller 'exercises a determining influence upon the way a narrative may be told, and therefore, upon the kind of composure that it makes possible' (Dawson 1994: 23). Oral historians make a special contribution to this process.

It is common for oral historians to follow a social science typology of inter-view techniques in talking about what they do, in which interviews are structured, semi-structured or unstructured (Hitchcock and Hughes 1989). The use of structured interviews, in which the interviewer works systematically through a list of questions ticking boxes, is rejected by oral historians because it does little to tap the unique experience of the subject, who is never given the chance to become the narrator of their life-story. But the unstructured interview is rarely used either. Oral historians have a project to complete, and limited resources of time and money. The conversations they have with those they have recruited to take part cannot be about simply any topic which is on the subject's mind that day. They must relate to the aspects of the past in which the oral histo-rian is interested, and which constitute their research frame, that is the parameters within which their historical enquiry is taking place. These may be set by concerns which are specific to a period and substantive, about, for example, women's experiences of work in the Second World War (Summerfield 1998), or by more general and abstract lines of investigation, like the use made by women of narrative forms and popular myths in constructing accounts of their lives (Passerini 1989; Chanfrault-Duchet 1991). The frame may expand or contract in the course of the research, and the researcher's expectations of what might fill it may be flexible. But I cannot be the only oral historian who has been afflicted by anxiety and frustration as a result of lots of talk about, for example, my subject's pets to the exclusion of her past, after a cold, wet three-hour journey, during an hour and a half's interview. The oral historian is, on the one hand engaged in the creation of knowledge with academic, social and political objectives. On the other hand they are a representative of an arm of society which will spend funds (public, charitable or personal) on finding out more about itself (even though critics may not always agree that the funds are well spent). Semi-structuring is an inevitable part of oral history interviewing. It can be consciously modified by the oral historian according to the balance in the desired outcomes between gaining data for the project and discovering what this particular interviewee most wanted to talk to the interviewer about. It can be resisted or subverted by an interviewee unwilling or unable to compose their memories within the researcher's frame. But nevertheless the oral historian's research frame influences the path through the past which the narrator takes, and requires the narrator to remember where they have been. This means for the narrator that they may find themselves pursuing parts of their past that they were not expecting to confront and for which they had not prepared their memory frame.

A memory frame is the locus for remembering which makes possible the process of reminiscence. It is created by means of what some popular memory theorists refer to as the cultural circuit (Dawson 1994: 24–6), that is the feedback loop between personal accounts and public discourse. The way a topic is related in a personal narrative is not crudely determined by the public treatment of that topic, and personal and local renderings influence public cultural productions. But the generalised discursive versions, in Dawson's words, 'have an apparent life of their own ... constituting a tradition of recognizable public forms that tends both to define and to limit imaginative possibilities' (Dawson 1994: 25). Personal narratives draw on the generalised subject available in discourse to construct the particular personal subject. They may contest as well as accept the public rendering but must relate to it and negotiate it. Memory is framed within the repertoire of concepts and definitions available in popular culture, which themselves may not be unified or free from contradiction.

An interview with a woman born in 1920, whom I shall call Ann Tomlinson, provides an example of discomposure produced by the movement from the point at which the research and memory frames of the participants in an interview coincided to one where they did not. When talking about her wartime work, Ann Tomlinson told an epic story of battling against stereotypical understandings of the kind of war work a person like herself should do. She had been trained as a secretary and although she joined the WRNS in 1943 with the express intention of becoming an air mechanic, she was dismayed to find that she had been sent for initial training to a centre for secretarial work. She told a vivid account of challenging the authorities and of being warned by an officer about the unsuitability of the work she wanted to do:

> She said, 'This job ... is dirty, difficult, out of doors in the most appalling weather ... you are working all the time with men ... you would have to carry heavy things. You might have to go up in the aeroplane. ... You have a very arduous training course ahead of you'.

> (Tomlinson 1992: text unit 99)

Figure 1   Ann Tomlinson testing an aircraft in the WRNS *c.*1944

Ann described sticking it out and becoming a qualified aircraft electrician, ending her proud and defiant account with the insistence that her job put her 'in almost what I would consider a fighting capacity, or at least enabling the fighting to go on' (Tomlinson 1992: 106). Ann was drawing here on a public wartime discourse of the heroic woman war worker who left feminine norms behind her in order to take the place of a man in war work. Ann's final statement in this part of her narrative, 'at least enabling the fighting to go on', indicates her recognition of the limitations within this discourse: women were not allowed at the front line, they were not supposed to do the fighting themselves. And of course – as she experienced – within the discourse of wartime femininity, the heroic version was contradicted by another rendering: that of the woman fulfilling conventional feminine tasks both at work (as, for example, secretaries) and at home (keeping the home fires burning, watching and waiting for the men to return). Nevertheless, in reconstructing her wartime self, Ann was able to draw on well-defined and publicly proclaimed concepts of feminine patriotism expressed in numerous wartime recruitment posters, such as Jonathan Foss's 'Serve in the WAAF With the Men who Fly' or Beverley Pick's 'ATS at the Wheel'. Ann found what she needed within the repertoire of cultural representations of the woman war worker to compose a narrative about herself which felt right – which was socially acceptable and gave her psychic comfort.

The main focus of the research frame that I was using, as interviewer, was on the war years, but its parameters extended from my subjects' childhood to the years after the war. Thus later in the interview I moved Ann from her wartime to her postwar life. Her narrative now concerned a succession of new identities. She exchanged that of air mechanic for that of economics student, and soon combined being a student with being a wife. These transitions were not problematic in her account. Each one was told as a successful struggle: to get a government grant; to complete in six months what should have been a twelve-month course; to get a financial supplement to her lower level grant which was cut when she married. Then, in 1949 in the middle of a postgraduate course in psychology, she exchanged the identity of student for that of mother.

She did not present her withdrawal from training and employment to become a full-time mother, as such, as a problem. Ann drew on the language of postwar psychology about the salience of the mother to her young children's wellbeing, to indicate her personal investment in the role. But when she came to the part of her narrative when, in 1959, she re-entered the labour market full-time, and after a few years resumed her training, her account shifted from one of maintained self-esteem to a more anxious review of her life within which her achievement of composure was more fragile. As she reconstructed her subject position as a mother in the 1950s she had to negotiate the repertoire of concepts and definitions available to her within the 1950s discourse of motherhood.

The concept of maternal deprivation was a strong element to which she subscribed in her account of her commitment to mothering:

Figure 2   Ann Tomlinson with her children 1952

I wanted positively to be there to feel responsible perhaps for them in a way that I wouldn't have been happy to delegate to anybody else. ... I just felt a tremendous motivation to be the one who was looking after them, to be there, perhaps influencing their development.

(Tomlinson 1992: 374)

The reiteration 'to be there ... to be there' established it as the central motif of this account. However it was contradicted by the ensuing story of resuming a career. This drew on a different element in the discourse, that of the 1950s working mother who undertook a 'dual role' that harmoniously combined women's work and family duties, assisted by a companionate marriage.

In such a marriage, according to 1950s constructions, *she* helped solve the problem of the national labour shortage and contributed extra cash from her earnings to the home, and *he* tolerated the erosion of his role as breadwinner and assisted her with a limited amount of child-care, if not housework (Myrdal and Klein 1956). Ann said that when both children were at school she 'knew that that was all right ... I could go off and teach which was a preparation for the future work I was going to do' (Tomlinson 1992: 374). She emphasised that she not only made practical arrangements with her husband (who sometimes took the children to school) but also managed her emotional economy to accommodate her depar-

Figure 3   Ann Tomlinson with her husband and children 1959

ture: the work would not deprive her of 'emotional energy to look after the children'.

But in spite of the apparent confidence of the account, there were indications of the difficulties she had in reconciling its contradictory elements. Her testimony as a whole, particularly her account of her wartime self, was of someone who pursued opportunities and overcame every obstacle – who never gave up. But when she spoke of her life as a working mother this construction slipped. She introduced the possibility of quitting. She said of her salary, it was 'a tremendous help. An incentive to go on of course, not just give up. Not that I wanted to give up. I wanted to work and do what I had set out to do' (Tomlinson 1992: 382).

In addition there were elements within the later discourse of motherhood, from the 1970s to the 1990s, that were strongly critical of the notion of full-time maternal care, in terms of child welfare as well as of the rights of women as mothers. These were also available to Ann, and they were represented in the interview by the interviewer – myself. I became a mother in 1978 and have worked full-time throughout my three children's lives, 'delegating', in Ann's words, some of their care to others. Ann's account became particularly questioning when I invited her to reflect on her feelings about mothering in the 1950s:

> I was ... very very happy looking after the children, very, exceptionally happy I think. I never felt bored. I loved reading to them, I loved playing

with them, I loved taking them out. I hope that I did let them be, and wasn't a smothering mother. ... I maybe sat and knitted and sewed and read and that kind of thing, and was just there, but didn't perhaps overdo the mothering. I hope not. ... I do remember feeling a great love for them and wanting to be with them and look after them as long as I felt they needed to be looked after, with my presence there all the time.

(Tomlinson 1992: 374)

'I was very happy looking after the children ... I hope I wasn't a smothering mother', 'I never felt bored ... I was just there'. Ann's dilemma, that is her relative discomposure, resulted from being moved away – by the interviewer – from her wartime life, which she could represent confidently in relation to a discourse of feminine patriotism and opportunity, to her life in the 1950s, when discourses concerning motherhood and femininity were particularly contradictory, and which was outside the wartime memory frame she had prepared. In remembering the 1950s she confronted the validity of her two-phase life as a mother, when she was 'there all the time' and when she was not, and wrestled with the confusing discursive repertoire available to her, both to express who she was in these phases of her past, and to achieve composure.

Interviewing for interiority

The feminist oral historians Anderson and Jack comment on the preference of interviewers for relatively 'safe' questions about doing, rather than 'unsafe' ones about feeling (Anderson and Jack 1991). They attribute the bias of interviewers towards 'doing' rather than 'feeling' to schooling in social science which prioritises the collection of data about external activity over interiority. Interviewers are certainly often inhibited about asking about inner lives.[1] The cultural construction of privacy within Western societies means that they may be thought to be prying; popular understandings of psychotherapy suggest that intimate questions may be emotionally disturbing – indeed that they may discompose the subject and remove the feel-good factor from the interview. However, the very prohibitions on asking about it make private life all the more intriguing. The result is a guilty sense among oral historians that it is interiority that we find really interesting – guilty because beneath the feminist researcher we thought we were, we may detect the prurient voyeur.

However, there are feminist theoretical approaches that claim that as far as women are concerned, interior, private accounts are more true or more valid than public ones (Chanfrault-Duchet 1991: 78; Anderson and Jack 1991: 16–17; Minister 1991: 31). The argument is that women as a social group are not perceived by those in control of socio-linguistic processes as having the same legitimacy or authority as men. From a popular memory perspective, one could suggest that this means that women's personal and local memory stories are not returned via the cultural circuit as readily as those of men, and are likely to be altered to conform with generalised perceptions of femininity if they are. Furthermore (as we have seen in the case of Ann Tomlinson) the construction of feminine subjectivity takes place under special duress. Everyone is confronted by a multiplicity of discursive options when framing their memories, but these are arguably more contradictory in the case of women than men, and the contradictions contribute to the constitution of women's subject position as subordinate (Davies 1992). Anderson and Jack argue that revelations of inner feelings expose the contradictions in a woman's life between the pleasures and pains of conforming to gender norms, for example those of daughterly and wifely submission and motherly duty. Expression of inner feelings reveals the capacity of women to accommodate these constraints, to negotiate themselves some space within them, or to resist them altogether. Shirley Ardener's theory of muting (Ardener 1975) has been popular among feminist oral historians as a way of conceptualising the dual consciousness a woman may have. A woman may present expressions of conformity to norms first, and these may silence her other voice, the one which tells about her difficulties with conformity. Anderson and Jack argue that sensitive questioning by oral historians, particularly about how a woman *felt* about the things she did and that happened to her, enable them to bring out women's muted voices (Anderson and Jack 1991: 16–17). It follows, however, that the feminist oral historian's mission to 'give women a voice', and so to rescue them from the generalising force of discursive stereotypes, is conducive to discomposure rather than composure, if it is actually accomplished.

The simple division between doing and feeling, exteriority and interiority, which is central to Anderson and Jack's approach to oral history, needs further exploration. The theory of the muting of women's voices was developed in the 1970s. By the 1990s many more specifically feminine models for personal telling in the public arena were available, from the confession spreads in women's magazines, to radio phone-ins and TV chat shows on Oprah Winfrey lines. So although women (especially black and working-class women) were still in the 1990s relatively excluded from formal opportunities for public address, there were by now numerous routes by which their testimony, about how they felt as well as what they did, might reach the public domain, of which oral history was but one. It therefore no longer had the unique role that Anderson and Jack attributed to it. Oral history might nevertheless have a special place in eliciting an account of the contradictions in women's lives, because of its interactive characteristics, that is the opportunities it offers for interrogation. One of the implications of the theory of muting (which ties in with the conceptualisation of feminine subjectivity reviewed above) is the idea that there is a tension in women's testimony between different versions of feminine identity. Because multiple subjectivities are offered discursively, constructing a singular consistent narrative of the self from them may be virtually impossible. Asking women narrators how they felt (or feel now) about the past may facilitate reflection and hence interpretation, which is a vital part of life review. But exploration of contradictions may need to focus not so much on feelings as such, but rather on who a woman says she is, how she represents – or composes – herself. The challenge to the interviewer, then, is to use the opportunities offered by answers to questions about feeling, to find out more about the way a narrator is representing herself. There are examples from my own project, of interviewers accepting without further enquiry 'feeling statements' such as 'I wasn't keen on that' and passing on to 'doing questions' like 'where did you go next'. There are also examples of missed opportunities of asking someone to elaborate on why she thinks of herself in a particular way, as in the following interchange:

> *NC:* So did you have any brothers and sisters?
> *HM:* Yes, I had an older brother and a younger sister.
> *NC:* So you were in the middle.
> *HM:* I was in the middle, I was the black sheep.
> *NC:* And when were you born?
>
> (McLaren 1991: 19–22)

Why did Heather McLaren speak of herself as a 'black sheep'? The issue remained ambiguous, clouded. There were hints later in the interview that Heather felt herself to be disapproved of by her parents, a misfit at school and in the work as a grocer's assistant to which she went on leaving school. She depicted herself as wilful in leaving the job against her parents' wishes to go into the Women's Auxiliary Air Force when she was twenty-three (McLaren 1991: 92, 98). A story of gradual reconciliation with her parents, particularly her father, runs through the narrative (the lost sheep returning to the fold). But while the black sheep identity is implied, the interviewer never invites a recapitulation. Such self-representation is an invitation to probe further the relationship between interior constructions of the self and exterior, publicly imposed identities. It provides important clues as to how a narrator understands themselves to have interacted with their social world. It is a key to their relationship to the identities bestowed upon them by cultural norms, discursive forms and social institutions with which they have conformed or compromised, or against which they have rebelled.

Interpersonal dynamics

Simultaneously there are interpersonal dynamics at work in an oral-history interview which are even more difficult for the interviewer to be aware of and respond to. They are the result of intersubjective exchanges at a barely conscious level between narrator and interviewer. The interviewer's style of dress, accent, tone of voice, demeanour, body language, spoken and unspoken attitudes give clues to the interviewee not just about the interviewer's research frame, but also what else might be preoccupying them, and whether narrator and interviewer hold shared values. The narrator sends out similar signals. Some of the most noticeable to the interviewer are those communicated by the preparations interviewees have or have not made for the interview. Interviewees may prepare themselves and their environment by dressing smartly, tidying and cleaning the parts of their home where the interview is to take place, and getting refreshments ready (Minister 1991: 28–9; Summerfield 1998: 22). They may also prepare their memory frame, for example by finding relevant documents and photographs, calling in a friend from the time, or simply putting their thoughts

about their past in order. The degree to which any of these have been undertaken tells the interviewer something about the willingness of the interviewee to
enter the oral-history contract, that is their readiness to share their memories
and to become a narrative subject. These aspects of the performance which both
participants in the interview stage for the other themselves trigger responses of
empathy and antipathy, expansiveness and defensiveness, trust and mistrust,
remembering and forgetting, and shape the stories told.

One example of how my own physical state may have produced an interpersonal dynamic which influenced the content of the narrative told me, comes
from an interview I did in 1991 with a woman called Greta Lewis, who worked
on an anti-aircraft gun-site as a member of the Auxiliary Territorial Service in
the Second World War. I was eight months pregnant and drew attention to my
very evident condition by sitting on the floor of Greta's sitting room because I
didn't feel comfortable anywhere else. Greta introduced the fact that she left the
ATS in 1943 because she was pregnant, early in the interview, and narrated this
event no less than four times, the second of which was different from the other
accounts to the point of contradiction. In the first iteration, Greta cast her
departure from the army camp in terms of regret: 'they all came to the gate to
me and they all sang "Will ye no' come back again" and I cried all the way to the
bus station. Well I didn't want to go home' (Lewis 1991: 191). Her second
account was quite different. In this she was impatient to leave and attempted to
run away from the camp before she was given her official discharge. In this
fluently told story she scrambled through barbed wire and into a frosty cemetery,
but as the clock struck midnight she took fright and returned to the camp where
she could see lights flashing and hear her name being called. She crept to her
hut to be greeted with cocoa and a welcome from her friends, but was repri-
manded by her officer next day. She concluded 'I didn't care, but I came home
the week after. So I did something good' (348). Picking up on Greta's apparent
satisfaction with her agency in obtaining her release, I asked her if she was
'pleased that the waiting around was over', but in her third account Greta
reverted to her previous negative version:

G: No, I didn't want to come home at all. I didn't want to be pregnant.
P: Did you not? It was an accident?
G: Well, he wanted me out. It were him that wanted me to come out, you see.
P: Did he want you at home?
G: Yes, he didn't want me in the Army.
P: Why not?
G: I don't know.
P: Too much freedom?
G: Happen so. Might have thought I'd got off with somebody else. I don't
know, love.

(Lewis 1991: 356)

In the fourth and final version, offered in response to my question about whether she felt a sense of personal change as a result of her war work, Greta reiterated the negative story of leaving the ATS.

> G: I didn't want to come home.
> P: Did you feel differently once the baby was born? Did you feel better about it or worse about it?
> G: I used to cry every morning at 10 o'clock when I used to imagine them all going in the NAAFI. I did.
> P: Was it more lonely?
> G: Being at home it was, yes. I used to just sit wondering what they were all doing you see. Of course you slept together like, well there were a lot of Nissan huts but there were a lot of us in each Nissan hut, which you didn't bother about. So you missed all that because you were on your own when you came home, weren't you?
>
> (Lewis 1991: 416)

Greta was not literally on her own, as she was living with her baby, her mother and her husband when he was home on leave and then demobilised. But was my very evident pregnancy a reminder to her of the deeply mixed feelings she had about her own pregnancy, which required her to exchange the identity of ATS gunner for that of mother? The tension between the story of wanting to leave the ATS, and the other three accounts of deep regrets about leaving, suggest that she was actively reviewing, in the interview, the meaning for her of being in the state in which I arrived on her doorstep. The story which apparently afforded her the most psychic comfort was the one in which she 'did something good', that is obtained her release by her attempt to escape. This was the one which was both best composed and appeared to offer her the most composure. It conformed most closely to the dominant public construction of women's role at the end of the Second World War, which was that they should exchange war work for motherhood. Yet Greta explicitly rejected the positive meaning of this account, and hence the composure it offered, three times over.

Conclusion

I have argued here that oral history is committed to composure and yet contributes to discomposure – that in the name of returning to women their 'honest voices', feminist oral history is particularly likely to produce discomposure, if not vomiting. Discomposure results from a variety of intersubjective processes. One of them involves the relationship between the research frame and the memory frame, which may well not fit. Another arises from the difficulties for a narrator of selecting from the discursive repertoire a set of concepts and definitions which allows them psychic comfort when telling their pasts. Discomposure is a likely product of the interiority project of feminist oral history, conceptualised by some feminist oral historians as the removal of the mute from the trumpet of testimony. It may arise from probing the self-representation which a woman offers, whether it is that of the black sheep or that of the mother hen. And it can be the product of silent intersubjectivity – the unspoken and unwitting messages of one female body to another.

Acknowledgements

I should like to acknowledge and thank the other two interviewers, Hilary Arksey and Nicole Crockett, involved in the project from which the examples of discomposure given here are drawn, and also the Economic and Social Research Council for its funding (Research Grant Number R000 23 2048, Gender, Training and Employment 1939–1950, held at Lancaster University). Above all thanks are due to the forty-two women who agreed to be interviewed. To protect the identities of those quoted here I have used pseudonyms. In referring to them I have given the year in which they were interviewed and the relevant text unit number on their transcript, used for retrieval. Discussions of earlier versions of this paper at the Universities of Lancaster, Galway, Staffordshire and Strathclyde, and the comments of my co-editors have been invaluable in preparing it for publication.

Notes

1 For example, the well-known oral historian Elizabeth Roberts has spoken publicly of feeling unable to ask women in their eighties about birth control and abortion; my project workers and I felt inhibited about asking women war workers about lesbianism; a colleague in the Lancaster University Management School has spoken about finding it difficult to ask higher-education managers about their personal lives.

Bibliography

Anderson, K. and Jack, D.C. (1991) 'Learning to Listen: Interview Techniques and Analyses', in S.B. Gluck and D. Patai (eds), *Women's Words. The Feminist Practice of Oral History*, London: Routledge.

Ardener, S. (1975) 'Introduction', in *Perceiving Women*, London: Dent.

Cassidy, S. (1999) Review of 'The Good Listener: Helen Bamber: A Life Against cruelty' by Neil Belton, *Times Higher Educational Supplement*, 23 April.

Chanfrault-Duchet, M.-F. (1991) 'Narrative Structures, Social Models and Symbolic Representation in the Life-story', in S.B. Gluck and D. Patai (eds), *Women's Words. The Feminist Practice of Oral History*, London: Routledge.

Coleman, P. (1991) 'Ageing and Life History: The Meaning of Reminiscence in Late Life', in S. Dex (ed.), *Life and Work History Analyses: Qualitative and Quantitative Developments*, London: Routledge.

Davies, B. (1992) 'Women's Subjectivity and Feminist Stories', in C. Ellis and M.G. Flaherty, *Investigating Subjectivity. Research on Lived Experience*, London: Sage.

Dawson, G. (1994) *Soldier Heroes. British Adventure, Empire and the Imagining of Masculinities*, London: Routledge.

Hitchcock, G. and Hughes, D. (1989) *Research and the Teacher. A Qualitative Introduction to School-based Research*, London: Routledge.

Lewis, G. (1991) Transcript, ESRC Gender, Training and Employment Project, Lancaster University.

Linde, C. (1993) *Life-stories: The Creation of Coherence*, Oxford University Press.

McLaren, H. (1991) Transcript, ESRC Gender, Training and Employment Project, Lancaster University.

Minister, K. (1991) 'A Feminist Frame for the Oral History Interview', in S.B. Gluck and D. Patai (eds), *Women's Words. The Feminist Practice of Oral History*, London: Routledge.

Myrdal, A. and Klein, V. (1956) *Women's Two Roles. Home and Work*, Routledge and Kegan Paul.

Passerini, L. (1989) 'Women's Personal Narratives: Myths, Experiences and Emotions', in Personal Narratives Group (ed.), *Interpreting Women's Lives: Feminist Theory and Personal Narratives*, Bloomington: Indiana University Press.

Sieder, R. (1993) 'A Hitler Youth from a Respectable Family: The Narrative Composition and Deconstruction of a Life Story', in D. Bertaux and P. Thompson, *Between Generations: Family Models, Myths, and Memories*, Oxford: Oxford University Press, 99–119.

Summerfield, P. (1998) *Reconstructing Women's Wartime Lives: Discourse and Subjectivity in Oral Histories of the Second World War*, Manchester: Manchester University Press.

Thomson, A. (1994) *Anzac Memories. Living with the Legend*, Oxford: Oxford University Press.

Thompson, P. (1978) *The Voice of the Past: Oral History*, Oxford: Oxford University Press.

—— (1988) *The Voice of the Past: Oral History*, Oxford: Oxford University Press.

Tomlinson, A. (1992) Transcript, ESRC Gender, Training and Employment Project, Lancaster University.

6 Spellbound

Audience, identity and self in black women's narrative discourse

Gwendolyn Etter-Lewis

The great night is over and it was the finest commencement in the history of the school. Every body seemed to be more than glad. I don't believe I ever spoke as well as I did on that occasion. Everyone was spellbound and it set the city to talking. It was a grand affair.

(Attorney Evva Kenney Heath, 31 June 1904)

Using the preceding words to describe commencement in a letter to her mother, Evva Kenney Heath announced that she had indeed completed her postgraduate education. At a time in the USA when few women of any colour entered colleges or universities, Evva had completed a JD degree at Howard University in 1904. In the years between 1897 and 1909 Attorney Evva K. Heath wrote over 101 letters to her family, especially to her mother, describing both the exciting and mundane events in her life.[1] This chapter examines these personal letters as a collection of individual texts that build a larger autobiographical narrative. The central focus is the intersubjective construction of the female 'self' in relation to an audience. The chapter pays special attention to ways in which the narrator situates her 'self' within shifting positions of narrative authority.

Personal letters as autobiography: expanding the genre

Writers of personal letters usually do not undertake their task with the same purpose as someone penning an autobiography. However, the personal letter writer inadvertently creates an autobiographical text, especially if letters have been written to the same person/audience over a prolonged period of time. This text is created piece by piece, letter by letter and ultimately reveals various facets of the writer's life. The parts may not necessarily add up to a seamless whole, but to a large extent will reflect a life-story from an intimate first-person viewpoint. According to Margaretta Jolly, who analysed the letters of Maimie Pinzer (1885–1922), a Jewish working woman and ex-prostitute with a disability, '*The Maimie Papers* require us to re-evaluate letters, and more specifically, letter-collections, as a form that has been unduly neglected in the study of autobiographical writings' (Jolly 1997: 10).

Arguing whether or not a series of letters fits the mould of 'traditional' autobiography may not be as useful as questioning restrictions of the autobiographical 'canon'. Schenck has contended that 'Western genre theory ... remains for the most part prescriptive, legislative, even metaphysical: its traditional preoccupations have been the establishment of limits, the drawing of exclusionary lines, the fierce protection of idealized generic (and implicitly sexual and racial) purity' (Schenck 1988: 285). Thus, strict adherence to arbitrary boundaries imposed by taxonomical hierarchies within the canon guarantees that some voices will not be heard. On the other hand, it is not practical or advisable to approach every story as autobiography. So rather than perpetuate patterns of silence fostered by either extreme, scholars' consideration of women's life writings makes possible the creation of more effective theories of autobiography (written or spoken) as practised in real life. Setting aside a preordained set of culturally exclusive meanings that may not apply to all, exploration of women's life writings in a variety of forms (such as formal autobiographies, diaries, journals and letters) allows us to understand more fully authentic aspects of self as perceived by the writer/creator.

A broad-based definition of autobiography not only frees us from the artificiality of canonical restraints, but it also helps us to recognise specific strategies women used in order to tell their own life-stories in ways radically different from those of their male counterparts. Most women did not write autobiographies, but many more wrote letters. Thus a collection of letters can be regarded as a valuable source of cultural and historical data from a first-person point of view that 'is rooted in a tangible reality, since it normally contains a date, an address, and a signature. All of these elements locate it in time and space' (Zaczek 1997: 12). Furthermore, a signature verifies the identity of the writer and confirms her authority. In an age when exerting authority was not a woman's place, written correspondence sometimes provided the only safe environment in which a woman, particularly a woman of colour, could freely express her 'self'.

The issue of whether the written 'I'/'self' of an autobiographical narrative is unitary needs to be considered. Bloom suggests that postmodern feminism rejects the idea of a unified self in favour of a subjectivity that is non-unitary and fragmented. She explains that 'subjectivity is also thought to be produced through contradiction and conflict, which cause subjectivity to fragment' (Bloom 1998: 2–6). Certainly, there are conflicts and contradictions in the lives of African-American women, however the extent to which these issues are manifested in their autobiographical narratives is open to question. In fact, Bloom warns that 'we must not fall into the fallacy of assuming the transparency of narratives' (Bloom 1998: 146). Given the covert ways in which black people learned to communicate in English during the slavery era (for example, through the double and hidden meanings in so-called Negro spirituals, and through escape codes sewn into the patterns of quilts), and the discrimination that has continued to exist, what we perceive as a fragmented subject may in fact be a veiled or cloaked subject. Fragmentation implies a splitting from something that was whole/unified. Yet, the postmodern feminist argument regarding subjectivity is that there is no whole, there is no 'seamless I'. Questioning this idea does not insinuate that a single narrator cannot speak with many voices but a more useful concept might be the description of subjectivity offered by Clifford and Marcus: 'Subjective experience … is spoken from a moving position already within or down in the middle of things, looking and being looked at, talking and being talked at' (Clifford and Marcus 1986: 32).

The 'moving position' they refer to could be found in the memory of significant events in a narrator's life as well as in the present situation in which the narrator is writing or speaking her life. These two components of autobiography, remembering and (re)telling (either through written or spoken language) take place simultaneously, thus establishing a constantly moving or shifting subject position. It is within, across and through these changing sites that scholars of autobiography seek to understand the narrated 'I'.

Historical context

Reconstructing the lives of early African-American women through their personal letters is a difficult task complicated by a variety of factors including accessibility and public recognition of the importance of such primary sources in understanding women's history. Research that focuses exclusively on the letters of African-American women is rare. Thus, the recent publication of *Beloved Sisters and Loving Friends: Letters from Rebecca Primus of Royal Oak Maryland, and Addie Brown of Hartford, Connecticut, 1854–1868* by Farah Jasmine Griffin is a marked departure from traditional approaches that presumed the non-existence of primary materials by black women. 'For years, we have been led to believe that ordinary black women left no evidence of their historical existence. We were told that they did not keep diaries or journals and that they did not write letters' (Griffin 1999: 3). Even though Evva Kenney Heath was no ordinary woman, she was not well known, and except for her letters, probably would have been forgotten. The paper trail that she left behind has expanded our knowledge of African-American women's historical presence, and has simultaneously offered glimpses of her private life that otherwise would have been unknown.

Evva Kenney Heath (1880–1909)[2] graduated from Howard University School of Law in 1904 (the only female in a class of twenty-two).[3] Evva and her husband Henry, also an attorney, opened their own practice in Washington, DC. Evva was one of a handful of black women attorneys and concentrated on women's legal rights. She was successful in establishing the legal status of women's property rights in a test case in Washington, DC.[4] Also a popular speaker, she was noted for insightful lectures on women's issues. She died in 1909 of an undetermined illness.[5] Fortunately, Evva left behind approximately 101 personal letters handwritten in beautiful cursive script (averaging two to four pages per letter) and addressed primarily to her mother. It is remarkable to find such a large number of intact letters from an African-American woman who lived during this time period. Her comments about the events of that era are informative, but what she tells us about her life is valuable beyond the pages of history.

Figure 4   Evva Kenney Heath

Reconstructing the gendered 'I'

Autobiography implicit in a collection of personal letters is shaped by a variety of factors. The letter writer usually knows the 'audience' intimately, whereas the traditional autobiographer tends to write for a remote or even unknown audience. Evva wrote the majority of her letters to her mother, Louisa. Regardless of whether or not mother and daughter were close, the asymmetry inherent in the mother/child relationship implies that Evva had a vested interest in presenting a positive self-image as opposed to a realistic concept of self. Except for intermittent financial difficulties and the incorrectly diagnosed illness that eventually claimed her life, Evva did not share with her mother her disappointments or shortcomings. Jolly has pointed out that such a discrepancy is the natural outcome of the tension between 'structure and anti-structure', the 'projected "self-written"', and the 'I' (Jolly 1997: 26). In other words, the autobiographical self transcends the self of actual lived experiences.

Evva Kenney began corresponding with her mother when she left home after graduating from high school in 1897. She moved to Bramwell, West Virginia, where she taught school for a short period of time. In her letters she constructed and reconstructed her status and privilege as an educated black woman for her mother, playing on the interrelation between colour and social standing. In a letter dated 12 August 1897 she said of her landlady:

> Mrs. Wheeler, with who I board, is a woman of excellent quality and culture. Although a southern woman she is fine in her manners and precise in her ways. Her home is common but neat. ... Mrs. Wheeler has not introduced me to any colored girls yet nor boys. She says she don't want me to mix. Color takes you a great ways here. Dark colored people don't stand far in school.[6]
>
> (12 August 1897)

Evva recognised without apology or guilt the role that skin colour played in the upward mobility of African-Americans. Achievement could be won through hard work, but it was also contingent on being the right/correct shade of brown. Sometimes Evva mentioned colour without comment. In her description of Henry Heath, her future husband, she merely noted that particular aspect of his physical appearance: 'Heath wanted me to go to Bluefield with him, and I hadn't been here 3 days I guess. He looks like a white man' (25 August 1897). She may have called attention to his skin colour as a way of tantalising her mother, who apparently had urged Evva to seek out eligible men as marriage prospects. Henry Heath possessed many qualities that would in theory make him 'a good catch': he was educated, already a teacher and light skinned.

As for her own appearance, Evva was pleased by what others had observed. Being lighter meant greater opportunities in general: 'You won't know me when I come back, scarcely. The people all say I have bleached out wonderfully since I have been here' (28 December 1897). 'Bleaching out' meant that she was several shades lighter than when she had first arrived in Bramwell. Of course, this was perceived as making Evva more desirable professionally and socially.

Explicit comments on social standing were another interesting feature of her correspondence. As the first letter from her lodgings with Mrs Wheeler indicated (12 August 1897), Evva and her close associates were critically conscious of social status. Even her subtle wording suggested covert prejudices against southerners ('Although a southern woman she is fine in her manners') and 'common' people ('She says she don't want me to mix'). Upon Mrs Wheeler's advice Evva did not socialise with her peers, thereby separating herself from others while preserving her high social status as a teacher:

> People think its funny I don't go out much, and cling to Mrs. Wheeler. But the truth is, I have no company, no fit girls to go with. I haven't been with any girls of my equals yet. There are only a few decent old girls.
>
> (4 December 1897)

Instead of associating with local girls her age, Evva cautiously arranged her social life to include a select few: other teachers, her landlady/adopted mother

Mrs Wheeler, and on rare occasions one or two couples who were parents of some of her students. Evva communicated to her mother that she managed to enjoy life within this limited social circle, and otherwise immersed herself in teaching and in her plans to continue on to college.

I vs we

Even though Evva may have been comfortable with the stratification inside the black community, she was not blind to racial differences outside. She was disturbed by the obvious segregation of the black and white citizens of Bramwell, a situation she was not accustomed to back home. In a letter of 25 August 1897 Evva observed that: 'White people here don't mix much with colored. The old principles have not yet died out. But they all respect me.' Evva's bottom line was based on respect, her minimum requirement for civil relations with others, especially whites. Even so, she was not anxious to break the barriers of segregation historically entrenched in her adopted community. On 1 November 1897 she wrote: 'A white girl came over and invited me to call on her folks. I am going out to call in a few minutes, but not there.' Evva's hint that she did not accept the girl's invitation seems to be a contradiction of her previous social practices. On the one hand, she was uncomfortable with the segregation she found in the town, but on the other hand, Evva did not offer herself as a token or martyr for the cause of racial integration.

Regardless of her own personal success, Evva never lost sight of the position of black people in the USA. Although individuals were able to achieve some degree of success, on the whole, African-Americans were usually at a disadvantage in comparison to white Americans. In a later letter, of 10 September 1906, she said as much: 'All our people ask for is equal opportunities in life. We started 41 years ago with nothing and we have proved our right to a "square deal".' The 'square deal' is an oblique reference to US President Roosevelt. He had promised a 'square deal', that is fair shares for all US citizens. However, Evva was not fooled by words unsupported by deeds. 'All' did not include African-Americans. She expressed her disappointment with the racial attitude of the president:

> We have the president's message to congress and it is quite full of food for thought. I see he deals with the colored man too, but his attitude toward the colored soldiers of the 25th has lowered him much among our people, and not a little among his own, here and elsewhere. I don't understand to what end such action should be taken.
>
> (4 December 1906)

Evva's shift from privileged 'I' to 'our people', or the self that was part of a collective whole, suggests that she indeed had a sense of racial identity that transcended social class distinctions. This situation reflected the kind of dilemma/challenge that upwardly mobile African-Americans faced on a daily basis: that is, how can the benefits of success be effectively utilised without rejecting one's own race and culture? Throughout her letters, the thread that connected Evva to other African-Americans was the racial injustice that she witnessed living in the nation's capital. She was never so comfortable or preoccupied with her own life that she could ignore the deplorable conditions of other black people.

Multiple roles/multiple selves

As a teacher Evva, like others of her own generation, regarded education as the key to rising above prejudice and discrimination. In order to create a positive learning environment and to elevate the expectations and hopes of her young charges, she referred to her elementary school students as scholars. In a letter of to her mother, sister and brother she described the poor condition of the school:

> I found the school in bad shape. There are scholars of all ages from 6 to 18, and in all classes. ... The scholars have many habits I will have to break them of or give them the 'Hammer of Jeremiah' [corporal punishment]. ... I was telling you about my school. My scholars are colored, all of them, some are light and some are dark. I am going to try to make such a raise in the school that everyone will be satisfied.
>
> (2 September 1897)

In spite of the difficult work that she faced, Evva was fully committed to teaching school, even at the cost of furthering her own education. In that same letter of 2 September 1897 she mentioned briefly: 'I have not been able to start a class yet. You see my school work comes first and everything else after.' Evva recognised the importance of developing a good teaching record not only for her future employment, but also for her students. She could give back to the community by ensuring that black children were educated to the highest level circumstances allowed.

Another indication that Evva still was connected to her roots was her relationship with her mother. As a dutiful daughter, Evva wanted to share the fruits of her career with the most important person in her life at that time:

> Ma, don't work yourself to death and then be able to enjoy nothing with me. You know I always said I would make a good living for you & I. I think that time is coming. I think I see a bright future before me and it awaits my arrival. I feel too, that I am nearing it step by step. I wish you had all your debts payed up at Cardington and was free, but do not worry, for we will be straight by and by, and I hope soon too for as I have said all the time, 'Tomorrow may bring a rose.' I did not know when I sat on the stage the 28th of May that today I would be demanding $32 per month. And I did not know how soon I would step from Spear's kitchen, nor do I know what the next step will be. I have to wait and watch.
>
> (8 September 1897)

Spear's kitchen may have been a menial job Evva held prior to her acquiring work as a teacher. The important aspect of this particular letter was her promise to her mother that she would share whatever good fortune she received. Again, she uses inclusive pronouns and phrases – 'you and I', 'we' – to indicate her close bond with her mother.

In spite of Evva's desire to maintain this close connection with her mother, by 8 December 1897 the relationship between daughter and mother had become strained. In very strong terms Evva addressed some sensitive issues apparently raised in her mother's previous letter:

> It is hard for me to leave home and come out here alone and unknown; the place is lonely, no society, no girl that I can speak to. Do you expect me to live in solitude? The mountains are solitude enough for the people. I know what you have been to me, what you have suffered and what your present condition is. You have no clothes and no difference how much I send you, you will use it for other things and then say, you have no clothes. You borrowed the money from me, but you will never say you paid the debt; *no*, a *thousand* times *no*. I don't feel that because I am making a little that I am ungrateful for past favors because I know not how soon I may stand still. You chastise & rebuke me for one who I owe my present situation to; one who started my life after I stepped from the stage; one who opened my future if it can be so called. If I had one thought of marrying him, do you think chastisement would heal it? Never. You did not advise me for advice is loving and tender but you rebuked me as I never have been by strangers. Through God I received my situation and now I implore Him to help me keep it, for now that I am excluded from home, I live in hopes to make one here.
>
> P.S. You did not tell me to answer, but I wish to hear from you, and if you don't want me to write any more I will read your letters, think over them and lay them down in silence.
>
> (7 December 1897)

Borrowed money and unsolicited advice seem to be the cause of the disharmony between Evva and her mother. Without more details we can only speculate about the exact nature of this rift. It is possible that Evva's education after high school and before her marriage could have been financed by a man known to her family. This may have been his investment in a future wife or simply a good deed, but Evva vehemently rejected the idea of marrying her benefactor, whose identity was not disclosed.

Furthermore, in writing that God helped her and not man, Evva disavowed any obligation to the mystery benefactor and simultaneously asserted her right to choose. It is clear that the mother/daughter relationship suffered because of the divergent goals of both. Apparently they reconciled quickly because in a letter of 9 December 1897 Evva acknowledged a letter from her mother. She promised to send her mother money for a new roof and indicated that she would not be coming home for Christmas. The disagreement is not mentioned again in any of her subsequent letters.

Remaking self

As Evva's life progressed, she constantly revised her self-image to reflect the change in her outlook and/or personal status. This did not manifest itself in her letters as an identity crisis, but rather as a situating of self in the shifting contexts of day-to-day living. She constantly remade herself according to the demands of her life.

Evva's marriage to Henry Heath, for example, was a significant life change that seemed abrupt. Yet, what appeared to be sudden in Evva's life may actually have been merely a matter of discretion on Evva's part, especially given the previous misunderstanding with her mother regarding prospects for a future husband.

Henry Heath was a seasoned teacher at Bramwell when Evva arrived at the same teaching post. She did not indicate in any of her letters that she was interested in him, but hinted that he was interested in her. In the collection of family correspondence, Mother Kenney began receiving letters from Henry Heath in early 1899. This may have been the beginning of his official courtship of Evva, which included establishing a relationship with her mother. By June 1899 Evva and Henry were married and had moved to Washington, DC. Evva wrote five letters to her mother in January of 1899 and then there was no further correspondence until her letter of 11 June 1899, which informed her mother that they had arrived safely in Washington, DC, Evva's new home. She wanted her mother to know that even though she now was married, she intended to maintain their close ties:

> I want you should think of me as being near you & not as being gone forever, and though a change has come over us, but you have the kind remembrance and tender thought & where once was *one*, now two hearts, that love thee still.
>
> (11 June 1899)

Evva may have been torn by a sense of guilt for moving so far away from home, as well as a divided allegiance between her mother and her husband. She seemed to want to reassure her mother that the addition of Henry to the family equation simply increased the amount of affection that Mother Kenney would receive. Otherwise, their daughter/mother relationship would not really change.

Evva described her union with Henry in ideal terms. She constructed a flawless image of her married life. She never wrote about their relationship except in the most positive terms:

> We get along splendidly, in perfect harmony, and if ever a woman had a loving, kind husband, it is Evva. He will do anything in his power for me. He laughs when I laugh and weeps when I weep. A better man is not on earth.
>
> (12 December 1899)

Evva's idealisation of her marriage may have been an attempt to win over her mother since she had married a man who was not Mother Kenney's first choice. She always portrayed herself as a happily married woman even though there was a slight crack in the façade some years later: 'I am pleased to say Henry has stopped using tobacco in any form. He just naturally got disgusted with himself: and I quarreled so much, too' (26 February 1902). This instance of marital disagreement suggests that over time Evva relinquished the idea of representing herself in a perfect marriage. Instead, in her later letters, we find a more believable view of married life.

Upon the celebration of their eighth wedding anniversary, Evva implied that all was not well. There was no particular sadness in her words, but the fact that she mentioned the situation to her mother suggested that it weighed on her mind: 'Saturday was our anniversary. It rained here just as it did on that Thursday night. Did you think about it? It has been eight years and no babies. How's that?' (3 June 1907). Evva could claim a successful career and marriage, but her childlessness was probably viewed as a sign of failure. She did not lament or speculate to her mother, but simply made an observation as if she were a disinterested party. Undoubtedly the lack of expressed emotion was not an accurate measure of her distress.

Domesticity

Unlike 'standard' autobiographies, Evva mentioned the particulars of her daily domestic life in almost every letter. She may have been trying to prove to her mother that she was a good homemaker or this may simply have been a characteristic of her writing style. One way or the other, domestic duties were described frequently:

> Henry is gone now from 8:00am to 3:30pm so I have considerable time to myself. But I cook for us and it keeps me busy studying for each meal. He asked me if I would rather take my meals at the restaurant or hotel, but I preferred cooking myself. We use the ladies kitchen and all.
>
> (20 June 1899)

Early in her marriage Evva decided that she would assume household chores as a way of keeping herself busy. She was not in school at the time and did not teach. However, a month later she was bored: 'Tell her I sleep nearly all the afternoon & sometimes before noon as I have nothing else to do' (13 July 1899). Unfortunately, the boredom did not last. Her household duties increased significantly: 'I washed Monday. I hadn't washed for two weeks. I never got done until half past one. But my clothes looked well, for the water is clear as a crystal nearly' (26 February 1902).

Washing, cooking and cleaning were a part of domestic life that Evva shouldered with quiet reserve. She usually shared with her mother the details of her work: 'I have my cleaning done for the holidays and will put up my curtains this week or next. Everything looks fine' (21 November 1905). The emphasis seemed to be on appearance. Evva mentioned to her mother several times that she wished Mother Kenney could 'see' the excellent condition of her home. Again, this may have been an offer of proof that she was a good housekeeper or a way of further establishing her middle-class status. Even during the last months of her life, when she was physically incapacitated by illness, Evva was concerned about housework: 'My house is not cleaned yet, but I am to have a woman next week to come and put everything in shape. I am going to get some new pieces too and some new carpets' (21 May 1908).

Every year, in almost every letter, Evva mentioned some kind of housework that had to be done. These seemingly trivial details may have served a very useful purpose. They may have represented the standard by which women judged one another. During Mother Kenney's visit to Evva and Henry in Washington, DC, for example, the older sister Bessie sent a letter that admonished them, especially Evva, for not doing an appropriate amount of housework:

> We are agoing to butcher before long so I shall not put down the carpet until I do that. You all don't clean house. I guess I never hear you speak of it. I guess Henry aught to tie you to the bedpost and not let you go on the street car so much. You all are ruined darkeys and I feel that he [Henry] has a hard life of it.
>
> (19 November 1900)

It is ironic that in the few existing letters from Evva to Bessie, Evva rarely mentioned housekeeping, in spite of the stress she gave it in her letters to her mother. So it was easy for Bessie to believe that Evva's husband suffered because his wife did not do household chores. The phrase 'ruined darkeys' implies that Bessie believed that the privileges of education spoiled Evva and Henry to the point that they did not know the importance of hard work, especially in the home.

Surrogate motherhood

In the midst of her many household and professional responsibilities Evva temporarily took in a child. There were no letters leading up to this event or, if so, they were lost or destroyed. It appears that suddenly there was a child in Evva's life. She did not explain in her letters to Mother Kenney exactly who the child was, his age, or how he came to be in their care: 'I have much trouble with Harry, trying to break him from mussing his clothes. I have done everything and whipped him good but he still keeps on' (22 October 1902).

She responded to caring for a child with the same confidence that she brought to other challenges in her life. Although she was still in law school at the time, she accepted the added responsibility of looking after this boy. But by the following year it was apparent that Evva and Henry would not adopt Harry permanently: 'Harry is not a strong child. He is nervous and excitable. I don't think we will raise him. Poor little fellow has had an awful hard time' (9 February 1903). 'Nervous' and 'excitable' may have been euphemistic terms for a 'problem' child. Ultimately, this may have influenced Evva's decision not to keep him. Even so, she gave it her best effort. In 1905 Harry was still with Henry and Evva and had entered school: 'Harry takes up first reader Monday. It is a very hard book. He is doing well in school' (5 January 1905).

In spite of his progress in school, Evva did not renege on her decision not to keep him and returned Harry to his family of origin. Evva had discovered that she wound up doing all the work and it took a precious toll. Unlike most other women of her generation, she eventually resisted sacrificing herself for the sake of the family: 'I have been quite busy this spring. The little boy has gone home and it is quite a bit of rest for me. I was worn out worrying with him, and it seemed, in vain. He has been away about three weeks' (26 March 1906).

After four years of being a surrogate mother Evva decided that she could no longer bear the strain of caring 'in vain' for a child. She did not share in her letters any insights she may have gained in her role as a mother. Her factual, emotionless account leaves little data for speculation. She evidently missed Harry, but the oddness of his absence and the reduction in her workload were all that she shared regarding his not unexpected departure: 'Henry has gone to church but I remained at home. It seems strange for us without Harry, but there is less work to do' (3 June 1906).

The last mention of Harry is in a 1907 letter in which Evva expressed the desire to have some kind of relationship with the child even after he left her home. She may have been prompted by guilt or loneliness, but did not say so directly. 'I want to write to Harry. I have started several times, but I don't know what to say' (3 June 1907). There is no evidence that Evva maintained contact with Harry. She resumed her childless status without comment.

In remaking herself over time, we see Evva assume several roles simultaneously. As she moves from wife to homemaker to surrogate mother, readers witness Evva's descriptions of her experiences as if she were an onlooker instead of a participant in her own life. The lack of emotional content, intimate details or personal reflection may be attributed to a variety of variables including the fact that she was writing to her mother. Mother-as-audience may have suppressed some of the more 'sensitive' information that Evva otherwise could have revealed. Certainly Evva was a caring individual, but this aspect of her character was not entirely transparent in her personal letters. In fact, her vulnerability as a human being does not surface until the last two years of her correspondence when she was ill with a misdiagnosed disease.

'Always after something': being and becoming an educated woman

In spite of her success as an educator and attorney, Evva tended to write more about her husband's education and career aspirations than her own. However, when she entered law school, Evva found that she could no longer maintain a stoic silence:

> I have to cook something quickly on Mondays and Tuesdays and Thursdays because I go to the University on those days. ... Well, I get along right well in school. I am still at the head. Mr. Heath is doing nicely in school also ...
>
> (19 October 1899)

While in law school Evva realised that she could not do all of the housework herself and be successful in school, so she explored some alternatives:

> Well, I am glad you are able to do your work, as you say. It is a good thing to be able to say: but though I am physically able I would like to be financially able to employ some one all the time and thus give myself more time to study; though Henry wants me to get Aunt Sophie whenever I want her. I guess I will get her next week to wash and clean up. For I want to prepare for the examination ...
>
> Tonight I have to go to school. We have two lectures. I have one lesson and have another yet to get. It is noon now. Tomorrow Mr. Barcus is coming over to look up criminal law questions with me. He is a good scholar but they all give up to *me*.
>
> (9 January 1902)

Evva's letters during the time she was in law school were the most detailed of all. She thrived on the attention she attracted by being the only woman in the class, and she was energised by the prospect of competing with her male counterparts:

> Last night our grades in Real Estate were turned over to the Dean and mine was 100%, the first grade of that rank in the school. A great many were disturbed. Spaniard ran me close and made 99%. Some made 55, 40, 31, etc. I received congratulations and good wishes.
>
> (26 February 1902)

Each year of law school Evva rose to new heights academically. She was eager to demonstrate her knowledge and proud of her high standing in the class:

> I must hurry. We have a case tonight. I have the tough side of it and I have to, as the students say, 'paw air.' I make speeches around here and Harry asks me who I am talking to. I have to get ready for there is a warm member

opposed to me. I had one of the faculty tell me that I was leading right along and that he wanted to see me leave a record. He is a prominent man of color. Is said to possess more legal knowledge than any other lawyer in the district, white or colored. I asked my grade in constitutional Law and the dean, a white man, told me he could not tell me, but my paper was fine. It was alright!

(27 March 1903)

In preparing for her graduation from law school in 1904, Evva decided that her focus would be on helping other women. She used commencement as a springboard for launching her ideas about women and the law:

On the 30th of this month our commencement comes off and I have to speak. I am getting ready for it. I haven't fixed up my subject yet, but I will speak about the rights of women under the law.

(8 May 1904)

Evva's commencement apparently measured up to her expectations. It represented the beginning of a productive career in law. Interestingly, Evva seemed to view her achievements through a kind of record-keeping perspective 'it was the finest commencement in the history of the school'. This kind of viewpoint may have been inspired by Evva's position as the only African-American woman in the majority of both her high school and university courses or it may have been due to her sense of history. In the same letter about commencement Evva casually mentioned she planned to take the bar exam soon:

I got three fine bouquets of flowers, a white lace collar, a set of white linen doilies & a book. I only wished for you all to be there. I am preparing for the bar examination. It will come off the last of this month.

(30 June 1904)

Evva's seeming lack of excitement about the bar exam may have been a sign of wariness or anxiety. She did not write much more about the exam.

Even though her professional life had changed, Evva discovered that her domestic life remained much the same. She was the one responsible for the household and all of those therein: 'Henry took the examination for Law Clerk. He has not heard from it. I did not take it as I had company and could not prepare' (31 March 1905). Without anger or bitterness, Evva simply stated the facts – she could not prepare for the exam because they had visitors. The identity of the 'company' was not revealed, but the burden of the work fell on Evva.

Evva was not dismayed, and continued to plan for practising law. She looked forward to the possibility, but was realistic about the barriers she had to face:

Of course all the rebels are not dead and Washington has a share of them right here bossing some of the best departments. But I don't stand back for prejudices or anything. God is sufficiently able to remove all stumbling blocks and our people who are industrious and upright, *will rise*, though it be over the rebel's grave. ... I won't be discouraged if I don't get the place [job] I want, but I will keep trying. I am not satisfied to sit still. There is so much to be done.

(20 February 1906)

Evva refused to surrender to the bigotry rampant in her profession. So the process of reinventing/remaking herself was driven, in part, by the discrimination of the time. If one position did not open up, she tried for another: 'I want to take an examination for Law Clerk. I am always after something. I have not heard from my other movement [job application] as yet. Perhaps I will not' (19 April 1906). Opportunities for an African-American woman lawyer were few, but even so, Evva was persistent. She did not reveal her frustration in her letters to her mother, but focused on her goals instead.

Following 1906, two years after graduating from Howard University Law School, Evva rarely mentioned her career. She noted that the law office that she and Henry had established together was in operation, but did not provide any details:

I was glad to read the news of the old friends. I wrote to Henrietta a few days ago. I don't get an opportunity to write so much. Some one comes in or I have legal work to do or something.

(10 February 1907)

The excitement that Evva had expressed during her time in law school had faded. She did not complain or analyse her situation in her letters. She merely described events directly related to their law practice in an objective manner: 'I have had much law business. Four came in Saturday after 7 o'clock. One this morning before nine' (9 December 1907).

The fact that Evva and Henry had applied for other jobs (for example, law clerk, government work) may mean that they did not earn enough money to sustain themselves exclusively through their practice. She remarked in many of her letters that Washington, DC was an expensive place to live and that many African-Americans found much prejudice in the city. Whatever may be the case, the silence that Evva maintained with regard to her career, a goal that she had long aspired to attain, is at best suspicious.

In the process of becoming an educated woman Evva's discussion of her professional life switched from enthusiasm to realism to silence. Evva the achiever was optimistic and fearless. However, the voice of exuberance during her years in law school gave way to an 'objective' stance that had neither the feeling nor warmth of personal experience. She 'reported' only good news and remained mute on other issues.

Text and subtext: what is hidden in the language?

Learning about an individual through her personal letters requires close scrutiny of the language as well as skill in reading between the lines. The resulting information may not read like a novel, or indeed an autobiography, but it does provide scaffolding for understanding the articulated segments of a life once lived. Hymes referred to this kind of support structure as 'textual architecture' (Hymes 1996: viii). It has the potential to reveal aspects of culture embedded in a narrative. Evva's use of 'textual architecture' is interesting and revealing beyond what she actually wrote in her letters.

One of the most noticeable aspects of Evva's letters is their formality. She frequently referred to her husband as Mr Heath and used titles when mentioning her friends and guests instead of their first names: Mrs Wheeler, Mr and Mrs Kitchen, etc. This may have been a symbol of middle-class manners or, better yet, a way of preserving the dignity of African-Americans whose good names were routinely assaulted, literally and metaphorically, by a racist society.

In contrast to Evva's formal style, her mother's letters expressed a more basic use of the language. Part of this discrepancy between mother and daughter was due to Mother Kenney's educational background. She was neither a strong reader or writer and Evva recognised the situation in many of her letters: 'I wish you could read better. I hope you will take an interest in trying to improve yourself. You can do this by reading' (15 January 1905).

Evva regularly encouraged her mother to improve her literacy skills. In a letter dated 18 October 1906 she made a joke about her mother's writing habits: 'Since Roosevelt authorized Phonetic Spelling you will have no trouble. You spell by sound. Ha! Ha!' This did not appear to be a malicious teasing, but rather a humorous observation that would not offend her mother. In spite of Mother Kenney's inability to read or write well, Evva always asked for letters even when she first left home: 'Tell ma to write me, and not to be so distant when I am so distant' (25 August 1897). Her play on language implied an emotional as well as a physical separation. Yet, whatever course their relationship took, Evva faithfully wrote to her mother, sometimes weekly.

From a different perspective readers will notice that Evva's language was coded. She made up nicknames for some people or simply used the initial of their first names: 'I was down Southwest yesterday. The old house is the same. Mrs. three-child has moved. Old lady legs is still there' (15 January 1906). 'Sunday I am going to Spica to take dinner with Mrs. King. I am looking for D. to come in now. He is gay [happy]. He makes the coin $2 a trip' (1 November 1897). This coding may have been a precaution against the prying eyes and ears of others. Evva frequently asked her mother to have someone else read or write a letter on Mother Kenney's behalf.

Another kind of coding included indirect references to Henry Heath, her future husband. Later when the relationship became serious, she still would not refer to Henry directly:

I got a letter but have not answered it yet. It has been nearly a week now. …
I guess you must have *received* a nice little letter. I guess it would be well not
to answer it as it was only meant for a response to the gift. See! Do as you
like.

(10 January 1899)

The 'nice little' letters Evva wrote about were both from Henry Heath, one to
her and one to her mother. The fact that she waited at least a week to answer his
letter and requested her mother not to reply to him indicated that she may have
been unsure of her feelings for Heath or just playing the role of a coy, unmarried
lady.

A last kind of coding found in Evva's correspondence was coding by omis-
sion. In many of her letters Evva referred to certain events without actually
naming them: 'Time passes so rapidly. It was but yesterday I saw you, but
yesterday is four long years, hardly possible. And thus life goes' (19 April 1906).
The event that united Evva with her mother and the rest of her family was the
death of her oldest sister in 1902. Evva's sister Bessie died unexpectedly and was
survived by her husband and infant daughter. After that point in time Evva
usually referred to her sister's death in covert language and she rarely used her
niece's name, Florence. Instead, she called her 'baby.' Almost every year on or
about the date of the anniversary of Bessie's death, Evva found time for reflection. Often it seemed to be fuelled by something her mother had written in a
previous letter:

Yes, it is sad to think of Bessie! Very sad indeed. Sometimes I feel very sad
and at other times a feeling of relief comes over me, for she never was and
never could have been happy as long as she would live with him [husband,
Will Brimbe]. Do you ever hear of him or the baby? Poor little thing! I hate
to think of it being down there. If she could only speak.

(24 May 1903)

The pain of her sister's untimely death may have been too great for Evva to
discuss. However, her established pattern of discourse was never to write about
unpleasant events. Evva's extensive use of euphemism and coded language
further supports the idea that she edited out of her letters some of life's
tragedies. Her practice of portraying herself as a successful person may not have
extended to including the difficult periods of her life in her writing.

On a lighter note, another contrast to the formal register of her letters was
Evva's occasional use of dialect. She inserted the following story in one of her
early letters:

The snow is lying in drifts on the ground. Old crimp lingers whenever he
finds a thinly clad 'critter.' He howls and roars like a lion. And he will 'cut
you to the red.' Old Mr. Nig runs now when he goes out. But he don't
venture out often because Old Crimp says by his moan, 'If you come out

I'se gwine tur smack the bref out of yer.' So old Mr. Nig stays close. I hates the climb out of mornings it is so keen. This mornin was a hustler from Kilkenny. I ran mighty nigh all de way to keep Old Crimp from catchin me, but he caught me whether or not. Tain no use to run when he gets after you because when he catches yer he'll shake yer head off. So I'se gwine ter tend to takes it aisy. I'se in schule now and Old Crimp might nigh shakes the house down. I ain't gwine to keep long. I'se gwine home. ... Old Dessie, as you call her, will be there in de mornin by the bright light.

(1 February 1898)

This long segment took up several pages and may have been Evva's attempt at telling a humorous story about the cold weather she experienced in West Virginia. 'Old Crimp' appears to be a figurative African-American term for winter or 'old man winter'. Her personification of the bitterly cold weather was in the tradition of Charles Chesnutt's and Paul Lawrence Dunbar's dialect tales (Donalson 1996). Other uses of dialect meagrely sprinkled throughout her letters included emphasis or highlighting a particular idea:

Old E.G.B. has took the hint Mr. Heath says for he hasn't been here since Ma raked him. Ha! Ha! I guess he is mad because I didn't ring in with his gang. Well, its alright, 'For da Spirit and de bride say come,' etc.

(24 January 1900)

Glad to know you were coming and will be right da, right den.

(8 March 1900)

Use of dialect created a humorous backdrop for some of the topics Evva discussed. It offered yet another way to identify with the folk ways and wisdom of the African-American community.

One other instance of Evva's deviation from a formal writing style was her incorporation of racial slurs in a few of her descriptions of the African-Americans who populated her world. She was blunt and unapologetic:

That darky who wanted doilies would not pay & so I am going up to his room & take every one down.

(26 January 1899)

How do all the coons come? Do you abound in nig news or do you 'record deeds,' yet?

(13 July 1899)

We could give Johnny more nig news than he could give us. Wasn't that odd?

(9 October 1900)

This kind of language served many functions. It marked inappropriate behaviour as well as establishing a dividing line between those African-Americans with cultured/educated manners and those without.

The 'textual architecture' in Evva's letters reveals an aspect of her personality that might otherwise be overlooked. Through this 'scaffolding' she expressed her sense of humour and simultaneously concealed her pain. Her manipulation of language to these ends implies a special intelligence and wit.

Black womanhood and the 'situated' self

> For twentieth-century black women identity is grounded in models of nineteenth-century black women who passed on to their generations the most vital lesson of their experiences: black womanhood was not static or a single ideal. The selves in the stories of the early foremothers reveal black female identity as a process of on-going invention of self under the pressures of race, class, and gender oppression.
>
> (Smith and Watson 1998: 100)

So the question of invented selves in black women's autobiographies does not conform to a particular norm, but rather uniquely varies according to the many ways in which the narrator chooses to configure aspects of 'self' in the context of her immediate environment. For Evva specifically this meant creating an identity steeped in the values of her family, but accentuated by education and social class. The 'self' revealed in her letters is anchored in family relationships and simultaneously reoriented as her social standing shifts. She wanted to remain a part of her birth family and regularly communicated with them, even as her circumstances changed her from an uneducated to an educated person, from a single to a married woman, from an attorney's wife to an attorney. The reinvention of the black female self is in part a consequence of changing personal landscapes within an unchanging social order based on race and gender bias. It is also due to a deliberate manipulation of narrative structures in order to reflect qualities and images important to the intersubjective relationship at stake.

Evva's 'multiple selves' were perpetually evolving in response to the external pressures of race, class and gender oppression, which forced her constantly to recreate herself or, in her words, to 'always be after something'. But her internalised mother-as-audience motivated Evva to shape her 'projected self' in narratives that filtered out the usual patterns of life's sorrows and disappointments. Evva's tendency to represent herself as a 'detached' narrator, reporting without comment or emotion the events of her life, indicates that (with the exception of her self-affirming law school years) she positioned herself in her narratives mainly as an observer rather than as a participant. This distancing between the narrator and audience creates a dissonance that cannot always be overcome, but at the same time core meanings within the narrative text are largely preserved. Even though Evva chose not to disclose the truly intimate details of her life, readers will still be interested in her as a narrator constructing herself as a moving subject.

Notwithstanding the enigmas in the letters of Attorney Evva Kenney Heath, the historical significance of this African-American trailblazer should not be ignored. Her life-story as revealed through her letters expands the corpus of primary materials on African-American women and adds to our knowledge about women's lives in historical and cultural context. The academy may not place black women at the core of its curricula, but it will become more difficult for it to sustain this neglect as we make visible, for discussion and analysis, the remarkable legacy of our foremothers.

Acknowledgements

I wish to express my gratitude to Mrs Alfreda Bonner, relative of Evva Kenney Heath, for making this research possible, and for kindly giving permission for publication of the photograph of Evva.

Notes

1   Mrs Alfreda Bonner, Personal Family Collection. The family saved approximately 283 letters: 101 written by Evva, 150 letters by her brother John, twenty letters by her sister Bessie, ten by her mother Louisa and the remainder by miscellaneous friends.
2   Dates can be found in the family Bible and in Evva's obituary published by a local paper in Washington, DC in July, 1909.
3   Correspondence to Mrs Alfreda Bonner from Howard University School of Law, 27 January 1972.
4   Obituary, n.d.
5   Evva was the youngest of the three children (John, Bessie, Evva) of Louisa and David Kenney. All three children died before they were forty (first Bessie, then Evva and John). Their father died when Evva was a young child and their mother died on 26 May 1948 at the age of ninety-three (obituary, n.d.).
6   All of Evva's letters are in the family collection owned by Mrs Alfreda Bonner of Delaware, OH. Quotes from the letters will not be footnoted after this point.

Bibliography

Bloom, L.B. (1998) *Under the Sign of Hope: Feminist Methodology and Narrative Interpretation*, Albany: State University of New York Press.
Clifford, J. and Marcus, G. (1986) *Writing Culture: The Poetics and Politics of Ethnography*, Berkeley: University of California Press.
Donalson, M. (1996) *Cornerstones: An Anthology of African-American Literature*, New York: St. Martin's Press.
Griffin, F.J. (1999) *Beloved Sisters and Loving Friends: Letters from Rebecca Primus of Royal Oak Maryland, and Addie Brown of Hartford, Connecticut, 1854–1868*, New York: Alfred A. Knopf.
Hymes, D. (1996) *Ethnography, Linguistics, Narrative Inequality: Toward an Understanding of Voice*, Bristol, PA: Taylor and Francis.

Jolly, M. (1997) ' "Life Has Done Almost as Well as Art": Deconstructing the Maimie Papers', in T.L. Broughton and L. Anderson (eds), *Women's Lives/Women's Times: New Essays on Auto/biography*, Albany: State University of New York Press.

Schenck, C. (1988) 'All of a Piece: Women's Poetry and Autobiography', in B. Brodzki and C. Schenck, (eds), *Life/Lines: Theorizing Women's Autobiography*, Ithaca: Cornell University Press.

Smith, S. and Watson, J. (eds) (1998) *Women, Autobiography, Theory: A Reader*, Madison: University of Wisconsin Press.

Zaczek, B.M. (1997) *Censored Sentiments: Letters and Censorship in Epistolary Novels and Conduct Material*, Newark: University of Delaware Press.

7 Our mother's daughters

Autobiographical inheritance through stories of gender and class

Sara Scott and Sue Scott

Introduction

> What are the links between stories and the wider social world – the contextual conditions for stories to be told and for stories to be received? What brings people to give voice to a story at a particular historical moment? ... Once told, what functions might such stories serve in the lives of people and societies? How might stories work to perform conservative functions maintaining dominant orders? And how might they be used to resist or transform lives and cultures?
>
> (Plummer 1995: 25)

It is questions such as these – expressing sociology's recognition of the centrality of 'stories' to social life – which have encouraged the analysis and writing of this chapter. In the past decade such questions about 'other peoples' stories have been accompanied by a reflexive awareness that 'stories' are also central to what sociology itself does: collecting them as data and telling them as theory. At the same time it is widely held that the more general production and interrogation of auto-biographical stories constitutes a self-reflexive turn in the constitution of identity and is a particular feature of late modernity (Giddens 1991, 1992). Some commentators have dubbed this a 'confessional culture' and warn of hysterical epidemics (Showalter 1997) or the dangers of narcissistic societies (Lasch 1980).

As feminist sociologists, our work has been influenced by 'the narrative turn', while as sisters with a ten-year age gap we have exchanged and compared stories about our lives, seeking both entertainment and insight. This chapter is part of our ongoing projects of making sense of who we are, of the relationship between childhood experience and adult identity, and of the specific impact of our mother on the women we have become.

The issues which we raise in this chapter arise from our joint exploration of the function of our mother's stories in relation to her identity, our identities and the constitution of the entity called 'our family'. However, these issues also relate to the sociological concerns identified above – as we see them raising questions about the lack of attention to 'family stories' in the sociology of the family, suggesting the ways in which biographical narratives produce class as an aspect of personal identity, and querying whether the reflexive production of person-hood should really be identified as a specifically late- modern phenomenon at all.

The role of 'family stories' in families has rarely been discussed except perhaps by family and narrative therapists (White 1995). Despite the huge popu-larity of tracing family trees, or the pictorial histories represented by a century of family albums, the role of narratives in families has attracted little sociological attention. Family 'practices' get discussed in sociology, as do public 'stories' about 'latch-key kids' and 'single mothers', but the stories people tell within families, or about their families, have not been subject to much interest. Yet, as Lynn Jamieson has recently pointed out: 'If private lives are affected by public stories, then so also are public stories dependent on being heard and retold in everyday life. Practices, private stories and public stories are not neatly separate but inter-connected and mutually creating' (Jamieson 1998: 158–9).

This chapter takes the private autobiographical stories told to us by our mother and explores their role in the intersubjective production of identities – hers and ours – while simultaneously acknowledging their relationship to the public stories about families, motherhood, gender and class in Britain in the middle decades of the twentieth century. Our particular focus is on the way in which our mother's stories, told to each of us in the context of different geograph-ical, temporal and social locations, mediated our different experiences of class.

Some theoretical antecedents

We are sisters who were told stories of our mother's childhood and young womanhood throughout our own childhoods. Our interest is in the function of these stories in our family, and the particular role that they played in our devel-oping senses of ourselves as Susan and Sara, Olive's daughters. As both the consumers of these family stories, and the producers of this account we are inevitably active readers. Versions of ourselves were present in our mother's stories: as the longed for baby preceded by four miscarriages; or the robust, happy child contrasted with her own sickly, miserable younger self. These versions called forth both resistance and capitulation to the 'preferred reading' set up in Olive's 'writing'/telling, which worked not simply to 'persuade and cajole' but to 'recruit' us as co-authors extending and continuing the same narra-tive. Our understanding of the social operation of texts is much informed by the work of Dorothy Smith (Smith 1983, 1990). As Liz Stanley, also drawing on Smith, puts it:

> Reading is both active and a process; it also relies heavily on intertextuality. Texts are certainly not inert and how they are structured certainly intends a preferred reading. ... However, readers are also *active* readers. ... We may be textually persuaded, cajoled, led and misled; but we can, and we do, also scrutinise and analyse, puzzle and ponder, resist and reject.
>
> (Stanley 1992: 131)

Figure 5   The sisters

Here we are concerned with a particular form of intertextuality – not so much with our mother's borrowings from other 'texts' but with the construction of her narratives with the intention of their entering other narratives (ours); that is to say, with an eye to the future of their intertextual influence. Whether on an inter-personal or international stage, the ways in which stories are told, received and passed on is central to their sociological interest:

> Story telling can be placed at the heart of our symbolic interactions. The focus here is neither on the solitary individual life (which is in principle unknown and unknowable), nor on the text (which means nothing standing on its own), but on *the interactions which emerge around story telling*.
>
> (Plummer 1995: 20)

In this chapter we assume that identities are first of all formed within – although not entirely determined by – carer–child relationships, but, by contrast with the psychoanalytic accounts of Karen Horney (Horney 1967) or Nancy Chodorow (Chodorow 1978), we focus not on consistency of treatment or emotional avail-ability, but on maternal stories. While we make no claim to the recovery of our mother's subjectivity through our consideration of her stories, we try to place her as an active producer of meaning, rather than as the cipher-mother existing only through the experience of her child commonly portrayed in psychoanalysis (Suleiman 1994).

The universality of autobiographical stories told by parents to children cannot be assumed. They may be a particular feature of fast-changing societies where the theme of 'when I was a little girl' involves visiting 'another country' of dray-horses and ha'penny liquorice. Even within modern societies such stories may be particularly a feature of families where social location and identity are problematic or in transition. Such stories are therefore frequently concerned with changes of class and status, with identities as they make transition from 'nobody' to 'somebody' (or in their d'Urbervillesque reversals from 'somebody' to 'nobody'). It may well be that the narrative structure of the spoken life-story is perfectly adapted to capturing the inherent ambiguity of class and status. Certainly life-stories are much more complex than accounts of the self made up of identity labels, for example 'working class', 'lesbian'. Life-stories couple the individual and the social through a nexus of roles and make possible the exposure and exploration of contradictions within the self. They incorporate aspiration and desire as well as actuality, and therefore include the 'colonisation of the future' which Giddens associates specifically with the management of risk in late modern societies (Giddens 1991).

The problematic

We have often talked about having grown up in 'different families'. Ten years apart, our teens were lived in rather different decades and at different points in our parents' life course (they were in their mid-60s by the time Sara left home). We also grew up in very different places both geographically and socially: Sue spent her childhood in Inverness, when the family was upwardly mobile into the lower middle class; Sara spent hers in Middlesbrough when they returned abruptly to the extended working-class family previously left behind.[1] Despite this we have ended up in similar places. This would probably not have struck us as a sociological puzzle if it were not that our achievements of the 'necessary conditions' for class mobility followed rather different paths. Counter-intuitively, given our childhood locations and conventional notions of educational opportunity, it was Sara who did particularly well at school, heading from her comprehensive school to Oxford University, and Sue who did relatively badly, escaping her girls' grammar for Newcastle Polytechnic.

It was our interest in explaining to our own satisfaction how this occurred and how we went on to arrive at similar places by different routes, that led us to think more generally about 'consciousness of class', the desire for social mobility, and differentiating both of these from more content-focused ideas of class *reproduction* through the transmission of 'cultural capital' from one generation to the next. Bourdieu's concept of 'cultural capital' is multifaceted, it includes not just piano lessons and knowing that Puccini wrote *Turandot* (and how to pronounce it!) but embodied values 'capable of instilling a whole cosmology ... through injunctions as insignificant as "stand up straight" or "don't hold your knife in your left hand"' (Bourdieu 1977:121). However, we felt that something else facilitated our class *mobility* that could not be straightforwardly captured in terms of 'know-ledge' and 'skills' taught or 'injunctions' given. Our inheritance seems to have been 'cultural ambition' as a sense of direction, rather than cultural capital as useful baggage for the journey.

'Mother's aspirations' have been identified as key variables influencing upward mobility in their children (Jackson 1968). However, in psychoanalytic and feminist accounts mothers are often seen as holding their daughters back:

> In stories that explore strategies of separation, mothers play an ambivalent role for both cultural and developmental reasons. From a developmental point of view, the mother's power as a conduit of both ethnic and gender identity appears to limit the benefit to her daughter of separating from her. But from a cultural point of view, disconnection appears to offer certain advantages.
>
> (Burstein 1996: 49)

Although there were times when our mother attempted to 'police our femininity' in conventional ways, she generally encouraged our movement beyond her experience in both class and gender terms. How then were her aspirations passed on in such a way that they became part of her daughters' subjectivity? We believe this occurred primarily through the telling of stories about her life, and that these stories conveyed not just 'aspiration', i.e. *her* desire, but class awareness, specific social skills and a narrative of upwards movement in which we were 'always already' placed as actors. Our mother's life was told as a precursor to our own (a story of origins), our trajectory a continuation of hers. In a not always welcome sense, our achievements were built upon the pre-history of her life.

Our mother's stories

The 'umbrella narrative' over all our mother's stories was that of upward mobility – by dint of work and will-power she had bettered herself, escaping the poverty, misery and almost continuous pregnancy which had been her own mother's lot. Her childhood self is invariably described as snivelling and pathetic, a sickly, put-upon eldest girl with a 'mawky, shittin' look', kept off school to be 'Billy Muggins' until she could be found a job 'in service' at thirteen. The mother we knew was confident, stroppy, proud of her abilities as an organiser and impatient of the less assertive of her friends and relations. Her transformation was an achievement of which she was immensely proud, and one she assumed her daughters would build upon. In terms of confidence and 'character' we were to start out where she left off. Believing that Sue showed toddler tendencies to shyness (like her mother), nursery school and a full social diary were administered. Sara was diagnosed as cheerful and sociable from birth and therefore required no additional stimulation. What these stories tend to occlude is the contexts within which these character assessments were made and the salience of class to these. Just as Olive's account of pulling herself up by her own nurse's uniform is ignorant of the commonality of this particular route to social mobility for young working-class women in the 1930s, so her stories of our infant selves are unaware that views about what constituted the 'nature' of children, 'a good baby' or a 'good little girl' shifted between the 1950s and 1960s. The quiet, passive baby, who was the darling in large, impoverished families, lost status to the active and entertaining infant as family size continued to shrink and affluence to spread. Such public stories about ideal family life can be seen to interpenetrate the private praxis of our lives.

Escape

A good number of the stories we were told came from a series on the theme of 'escape'. Mother first discovered her desire to be more than a doormat in her first job in service as a daygirl – or maid-of-all-work. Her employer treated her 'like dirt', she made insulting and demeaning comments, called her 'girl' and expected a performance of deference which our mother was unwilling to provide. Called stupid and lazy, and unfairly accused of not doing a particular task properly, Olive threw a scrubbing brush at her employer and walked out. We must have each heard this story hundreds of times; it served a variety of purposes. It made us cheer for the worm that had turned, our mother as teenage rebel became the heroine of her own life, the maker of her own destiny, as we too wished to be. The story located us as inheritors of our mother's determination to prove she was 'no bugger's skivvy' (as if to further ensure against such an eventuality, she refused to teach us even rudimentary domestic skills and is consequently astonished that we are both competent cooks). As adults (and sociologists) we discovered that Olive had been part of a revolution in women's employment, one of thousands of refusnik girls of the early 1930s who fled from domestic service to the new employment opportunities of shops and offices – or in her case to the glamour of a job as a cashier at the newly opened Regal Cinema (see Beddoe 1989).

Some years later her further escape into nursing represented respectability and self-worth. She achieved this only as a result of having been in a fever hospital for two months, where she was 'taken up' by the staff, and after a long struggle to persuade her father to sign the necessary papers. This is certainly a story of an individual struggle against the odds, but again it was an increasingly common route 'out' of both family and class for many women of her generation (Garmarnikow 1978; Witz and Halford 1997). Olive's stories about this period of her life juxtapose gender rebellion and status conformity in complex ways. Many of the stories focus on the importance of her acceptance as a 'good' nurse, the first of her cohort to be made a staff nurse – she arrived back from 'off-duty' to find the new uniform laid out on her bed. She was fiercely defensive of the discipline of nursing as it used to be, the routines of patient care, the precision of bed-making (a sort of origami in starched sheets), the military-model hierarchy. These things were contrasted with the 'slovenly' housewifery practised by her own mother, the weekly dosing of the children with sulphur and treacle, and the somewhat arbitrary discipline of working-class family life. Her stories taught us

Figure 6   The family group

that 'knowing the rules' was crucial to class mobility, and 'doing things properly' most compatible with advancement.

In sharp contrast, in the stories which focused on gender she presented herself as positively stroppy, engaged in activities that ranged from bending the rules to outright rebellion. The 1920s and 1930s were crucial decades in the profession-alisation of nursing, and the virtue and respectability of young nurses was of considerable concern to their superiors, as it would continue to be into the 1970s. In our mother's accounts curfews, late-passes and rules concerning the wearing of hats and gloves were flouted as frequently as possible. A sympathetic gardener could be persuaded to leave a ladder against the hospital mortuary wall, on the other side of which waited a boyfriend on a motorcycle – late re-entry being effected by climbing the wall between the cemetery and the nurses' home. Discreet tucks raised the hemline of uniform dresses to show an extra inch of leg, and hair was curled around starched caps to the very limits of acceptability. Stronger stuff came in the form of stories about slapping the face of a senior registrar who 'took liberties', lying in wait for a 'peeping tom' (who turned out to be a young policeman), then breaking his arm with a heavy army issue torch, and 'curing' a priest who regularly visited Casualty complaining of an 'intimate irritation' with an application of Wintergreen ointment (a precursor of 'deep heat' creams such as Ralgex).

Such stories were among our mother's favourites – they portrayed her as a fighter passing on her gauntlet to daughters whose similarly sassy spirit was taken as given. (Indeed, Sue remembers returning from the cinema, aged thirteen, with a tale of jabbing her umbrella into the leg of a man who had fondled her friend's knee; a tale which was met with the delighted approval of her mother.) Escape from the impoverished working class and escape from an obedient femininity were both entwined and conflicting, requiring different strategies, which the stories communicated. Through the telling of these we were encouraged to be both 'dare devils' and 'goody two-shoes' – apparently contradictory selves which we both embody today.

Skills and knowledges

We have described above the importance of 'learning the rules' and respecting the overt order, systems and structures of the respectable classes, which Mam's stories conveyed. However, she also taught – from bitter experience – that such strategies were not enough. Until very recently, class mobility for women could only be properly secured through marriage and Mam had aimed to 'marry up'. She explained to us how she had fallen for the family she might marry into, their shop-owning respectability and their nice ways. In their son she was deceived, or chose to deceive herself, until she woke up to find herself entangled with a violent man who was entertained by her 'pretensions' and relished the prospect of 'putting her in her place'. This man, so different to the gentle man who is our father, ruptured the forward flow of Olive's 'progress'. It took her many years to recover from the trauma and 'shame' of this experience, during which time she was not fit enough for nursing or other war work and found herself again in domestic service, this time as a children's nanny.

The importance of detailed knowledge of other people and other classes, the skill of reading situations and behaviour so that sarcasm and superiority cannot be disguised behind studied politeness, was conveyed in the story of Mam's 'comeuppance'. As girls we squirmed over the account, feeling both outrage at her mistreatment and mortification at her 'delusions' and snobbery. We learned something about class and gender as autonomous but interacting systems of power a decade before we encountered 'capitalism' or 'patriarchy'.

Mother's stories concerning her return to 'service' centre on the importance of detailed observation, of finding a necessary role, and of staking a claim to some autonomy and status. Her 'capital' was her professional training, which gained her a position of 'nurse knows best' in relation to her employers as well as their children. Her general competence in response to wartime privations, and the gradual loss of other domestic help, ensured she was much relied upon and could come to occupy a status somewhere between employee and family member – a position which provided salve for her bruised ambitions.

Our favourite stories from this time are about 'passing' and the pitfalls that lie in wait for the unwary. We were taken to have already absorbed the knowledge she had gained from her near misses: not to straighten grapefruit knives, or cook beetroot with the mud still on (it makes the borscht gritty) or throw away food thinking it 'off' until sure it was not supposed to taste so. We were thereby positioned as superior 'knowers', already occupying a later chapter of the narrative and able to look back with amused compassion on this earlier 'self'.[2]

Discussion

The stories we were told were the same stories, repeated frequently over a twenty-year period. Mother's stories about her life were as much a part of our sense of where we had come from as the family stories about our own infancies. However, when we came to analyse what we had been told and what it meant we realised there had been a subtle shift of emphasis between the focus of 'the same' stories as they were told to each of us. Sue was primarily being taught the 'passing' skills for the middle-class Inverness society she was expected to grow up in; Sara was being encouraged to repeat her mother's fight and once again escape Middlesbrough and the working-class family context to which we had all returned.

Of course we had heard these stories in very different class contexts and it is impossible to completely unpick the telling from the reading, but we believe the versions were adapted to the different class contexts in order that they could best function to the same ends of securing our allegiances to the mobility project, and pass on the skills most relevant to achieving it.

It is interesting that in our mother's characterisations of our childhood selves Sue was timid and shy, Sara was robust and outgoing. Sue had to be 'sacrificed' to nursery school in order to encourage her to socialise, while Sara needed no such hardening practices, and might defer mixing with her Middlesbrough peers as long as possible. What this maps onto is the very different tasks which maximising our mobility potential presented in Inverness and Middlesbrough. Sue needed opportunities in the surrounding environment opening up; Sara needed them limiting! Even the ascription of character was appropriate to the different contexts of our childhoods – Sue needed to observe and pass, Sara would be better off fighting for her opportunities.

For Sue it seemed to be important that Mum's stories told her 'where she came from' in order that she could be recruited to the upward trajectory *and* appreciate the struggle which preceded her. For Sara they conveyed Mam's anxiety about slipping back, but also a sense of possibility. The stories Sue first associated with class when we began discussing this chapter were the cautionary tales, which might help her function as a class-mobile child entering middle-class homes. Whereas Sara immediately identified a sense of being recruited to stories of Mam battling to escape the confines of her class.

Unlike some of the more commonly discussed expressions of aspiration to social mobility, such as private education, piano and ballet lessons, stories cost nothing, and we have emphasised the importance we believe they had in linking our mother's aspirations for us and our subsequent class mobility. We recognise there were other strategies to the project: we were well groomed and good mannered, maternal labour maintained skin, hair, teeth and posture in forms that declared our current respectability and our future promise. However, even attempts to purchase the same 'cultural capital' for each of us had very different meanings and implications in Middlesbrough and Inverness. We were both sent to elocution lessons – Sue in order to gain an Invernesian accent (often claimed as 'the purest English') and fit better into the surrounding community, and Sara to lose an incipient Middlesbrough one, and thereby ensure her distance from family and peers.

Mum/Mam also embodied a parallel contrast between involvement with church, friends and neighbours in Scotland and relative isolation back in the northeast of England. There were a number of reasons for Mam keeping her distance from Middlesbrough in Sara's early childhood, but certainly one of them seems to have been her resolve to hold out a different class identity for her daughters than the one their (re)location supported. While Sue had been sent by taxi to the occasional party in a Scottish castle, Sara was always collected from friends' street and council houses by her dad. *He* might belong back in Middlesbrough, but *she* could not – at least not until our exit was secured. Once Sue had left home, and began to provide her little sister with access to the wide world of olives, avocados, tunes without words and plays without tunes, the job of ensuring Sara's class mobility fell to her. Mam settled back into the family and locality of her childhood, increasingly retiring from both motherhood and the mobility project as Sara's teens progressed.

Conclusion

Why does any of this matter? Why is it of sociological interest? We will highlight two main reasons. First, because it offers a way into understanding the detailed mechanisms – within the increased opportunities for social mobility afforded by modernity – which may render some more mobile than others. Sociological analysis of class mobility has been largely limited to examining external indicators and has rarely linked overall biography to work history or life-event history (see, for example, Sennett and Cobb 1977). Sociological theory tends to treat 'the family' as a unit in relation to class, and although this has been subject to a gendered critique, there is little on differences between siblings. By contrast, social mobility has tended to be studied as a trajectory of individuals (see Goldthorpe 1987; Gershuny 1983; Pahl 1984) and has failed to map changes across time within families. Consideration of family stories about class offers an opportunity to put experiential flesh on structural bones, and to examine the influence of desire and aspiration alongside the importance of cultural capital in (re)producing class distinctions. Such detailed analysis can also put flesh on the bones of more general lines of thought, such as that followed by Beck and Beck-Gernsheim, which locate children, in the context of modernity, as part of their parents' mobility project.

> With the future lying ahead the child confronts its parents with their own biographies and ambitions, disappointments and fears, including old dreams of being a huge success and making it to the top. Anyone suggesting that 'my child should have it better than I did' is not just thinking of the child, but mostly of him/herself.
>
> (Beck and Beck-Gernsheim 1995: 138)

Second, our considerations call for a better sociology of the intimate, one which explores the relationship between subjectivity, intersubjectivity and social networks, and, following from this, the relationship between such networks and the public sphere. We suggest that theoretical claims concerning the constitution of 'the self' in late modernity, and the relationship between public and private stories be subjected to more empirical examination. From our perspective Mum/Mam was involved in a set of reflexive practices in relation to our production as her daughters: the reflexive project of ourselves. We doubt that she was so very unusual, in which case the kinds of reflexive accounts produced within therapeutic encounters or displayed on Oprah Winfrey shows may be more continuous with previous constitutions of subjectivity than is often suggested.

There is a backlash against life-stories in the 1990s – there are too many, they all sound the same, the voices are too shrill, they cannot all be true. According to Elaine Showalter, we are currently subject to: 'Infectious epidemics of hysteria spread by stories circulated through self-help books, articles in newspapers, TV talk shows and series, films, the Internet, and even literary criticism' (Showalter 1997: 5). Feminists are at least partly responsible for encouraging the production of stories as revelation and confession: child abuse, anorexia, domestic violence. 'The silence' has been repeatedly broken and some complain the resulting cacophony is deafening. The educated cultural commentator can barely get a word in edgeways and some complain bitterly that this is so. The *privileged* position of the sociologist collecting such stories from the private realm and translating them for public – or at least academic – consumption has been usurped in multimediated social worlds. However, the task of analysing the part which different stories play in the development of identity, in the play of inter-subjectivity, and as vehicles for power, surveillance and resistance remains as interesting as ever.

We grew up with a story-teller for a mother, a teller of tales about her experiences of the gender and class transformations which have shaped the twentieth century. This may not be unusual in itself, but what is worthy of note is that the 'tellings' of these stories suggest a reflexive project of self with which Olive was consciously engaged.

We both 'tell' ourselves through stories as our mother did, and do so most particularly as part of a process of engagement and separation in relation to 'family', 'class' and 'gender'. We are the products of our mother's project, of her efforts to fit us for upward mobility and to be equal to men – efforts which have formed a major part of the wider project of late modernity. This may seem obvious, but not all women growing up in families like ours in the 1950s, 1960s and 1970s were so equipped; and if we are to explain the differences within broad patterns of social change it is to biography and its relationship with society we have to turn. The motivated aspect of 'family stories' and the ways in which they impact on class and gender identities may provide one of many productive answers to the question posed by Ken Plummer: 'what are the links between stories and the wider social world?'.

Notes

1 This distinction is captured by the fact that we call our mother by different names, to Sue she is 'Mum', to Sara 'Mam' – in conversation with each other we refer to her as 'Mother', a term we would never use to her face except in jest or mock exasperation. We have used all three terms in this text, as seemed appropriate to the 'voice' of the passage.

2 In literature this is a device exemplified in *David Copperfield* where the reader is recruited to the mature narrator's perspective on the young Davey:

> 'What is that upon your face?'
> 'Dirt,' I said.
> He knew it was the mark of tears as well as I. But if he had asked the question twenty times, each time with twenty blows, I believe my baby heart would have burst before I would have told him so.

(Dickens 1994: 49)

Bibliography

Beck, U. and Beck-Gernsheim, E. (1995) *The Normal Chaos of Love*, trans. M. Ritter and J. Weibel, Cambridge: Polity Press.

Beddoe, D. (1989) *Back to the Home and Duty, Women Between the Wars 1919–1939*, London: Pandora.

Bourdieu, P. (1977) *Distinction*, London: Routledge and Kegan Paul.

Burstein, J.H. (1996) *Writing Mothers, Writing Daughters*, Chicago: University of Illinois Press.

Chodorow, N. (1978) *The Reproduction of Mothering*, Berkeley: University of California Press.

Dickens, C. (1994 [1849]) *David Copperfield*, Harmondsworth: Penguin.

Garmarnikow, E. (1978) 'Sexual Division of Labour: The Case of Nursing', in A. Kuhn and A.M. Wolpe, *Feminism and Materialism*, London: Routledge and Kegan Paul.

Gershuny, J. (1983) *Social Innovation and the Division of Labour*, Oxford: Oxford University Press.

Giddens, A. (1991) *Modernity and Self Identity: Self and Society in the Late Modern Age*, Oxford: Polity.

—— (1992) *The Transformation of Intimacy: Sexuality, Love and Eroticism in Modern Societies*, Oxford: Polity.

Goldthorpe, J. (1987) *Social Mobility and Class Structure in Modern Britain*, Oxford: Clarendon Press.

Horney, K. (1967) *Feminine Psychology*, New York: W.W. Norton.

Jackson, B. (1968)*Working Class Community*, London: Routledge and Kegan Paul.

Jamieson, L. (1998) *Intimacy: Personal Relationships in Modern Societies*, Oxford: Polity.

Lasch, C. (1980) *The Culture of Narcissism: American Life in an Age of Diminishing Expectations*, London: Sphere.

Pahl, R.E. (1984) *Divisions of Labour*, Oxford: Blackwell.

Plummer, K. (1995) *Telling Sexual Stories: Power, Change and Social Worlds*, London: Routledge.

Sennett, R. and Cobb, J. (1977) *The Hidden Injuries of Class*, Cambridge: Cambridge University Press.

Showalter, E. (1997) *Hystories: Hysterical Epidemics and Modern Culture*, London: Picador.

Smith, D.E. (1983) '*The active text*', unpublished mimeograph, Ontario Institute for Studies in Education.

—— (1990) *Text, Facts, and Femininity: Exploring the Relations of Ruling*, London: Routledge.

Stanley, L. (1992) *The Auto/biographical I*, Manchester: Manchester University Press.

Suleiman, S. (1994) *Risking Who One Is: Encounters with Contemporary Art and Literature*, Cambridge, MA and London: Harvard University Press.

White, M. (1995) *Re-Authoring Lives: Interviews and Essays*, Adelaide: Dulwich Centre Publications.

Witz, A. and Halford, S. (1997) *Gender, Careers and Organisations: Current Developments in Banking and Nursing*, Basingstoke: Macmillan.

8   Matrilineal narratives revisited

Tess Cosslett

This chapter began in 1993, at a conference on Autobiography and Gender at Nijmegen. For that meeting, I wrote an open-ended, unfinished piece on 'matrilineal narratives' – attempts by some feminist autobiographers to 'reclaim' or 'recover' the mother's subjectivity by writing their mothers' stories, in conjunction with their own. In that paper, I noticed that these writers were often very ready to attribute thoughts and feelings to their mothers, to speak for them, but not for their daughters (where daughters did appear in the narrative). The daughter, I thought then, represented unknown potential, the unshaped future – it would be intrusive and limiting to try to write her thoughts, to inhabit her consciousness. This idea was partly confirmed at the conference, when Karen Klitgaard Povlsen (1993) performed an impressive Lacanian reading of the silencing of the daughter by the mother's narrative in the writing of Friederike Brun, a mother who insisted on narrating her daughter's life.

But couldn't the narration of mothers' stories be destructive too? The only reason it isn't, is that the mother has already lived, unhampered by daughterly fictions. A more sinister reason for the imbalance occurs to me now: the mother being dead, or so far estranged, or of a different culture, can't answer back. At the same time, the idea of the mother's unknowability has been impressed on me from different directions. At a seminar in the series that gave rise to this book, Griselda Pollock (1998) gave a video presentation centred around her inability to recover her dead mother, or to find any reconciling image for her own bereavement. I'd also been reading autobiographical MA essays, and had come across a disinclination to pry into or finalise mothers' lives in words: Maureen Fenton writes of her dead mother: 'our relationship is defined by my sense of her unknowability'; Serretta Bebb writes, 'Above all I find it hard to contain Mum within a fiction, to make a story stand in for who she is.' Her mother is still alive, and 'resisting the drive for endings and closure in her self narrative, my mother has remained open to new possibilities'. At the same time, I've been thinking about my own attempts to write about my dead mother – what stands out, is that they are about her irrecoverability. At the end of this chapter, I've appended a couple of poems that explore this. I'm also engaged in writing a semi-autobiographical novel in which I have no problem in satirising a figure based on my father (though I have no wish to enter into his consciousness), but my mother remains an absence, a black hole of longing. This unknowability of the maternal is over-determined: I could make use of a psychoanalytic differentiation between the semiotic and the symbolic; or a more historically based opposition of the private and the public; or poststructuralist theories about the unrepresentability of any 'reality' or 'self'; or the specificities of individual mothers.

The other impetus to this chapter has been Margaret Forster's book *Hidden Lives* (1996), which reconstructs the lives of her grandmother and her mother, from an autobiographical perspective. It is more of an interdisciplinary book than the matrilineal narratives I considered in the unpublished paper: *Hidden Lives*, as well as some degree of fictionalisation, also bases itself in oral history and social history, although it then obscures the route from data to story. In my reading of *Hidden Lives*, and the responses of my students to the text, I locate a sense of disquiet with the 'recovery' project, which reflects back on the earlier texts, though they all have ways of dealing with or pointing to similar problems. Here, first, is a version of my earlier paper.

There are three main points that delineate the focus of my argument in this paper. First, I'm interested in a feminist-inspired move by which contemporary women's autobiographies construct a matrilineage for their protagonists; the identity of the subject is assumed to be dependent on or in relation to the identities of her female ancestors. Second, because the matrilineage is often hidden, silenced or lost, it has to be reconstructed. Fictionality necessarily and overtly enters at this point, in this act of imaginative reconstruction (I say 'overtly', because all autobiography could be seen as necessarily fictional). In another way what's happening could be seen as *biography* – telling the story of another person's life. Third, there would be no need for these overt elements of fiction and biography if the autobiographer were merely presenting what she herself remembers about her female relatives, or what she's been told about them. She might limit herself to this if she were only interested in presenting the mother (and before her, the grandmother) as the grounds of her own being, the dispensable envelope of the *real* person, her, the autobiographical subject. But, in all the texts I'm interested in, there is instead a move to restore subjectivity to the mother, and other female relatives, as well as merely to show their influence on the protagonist. For various reasons (they are dead, illiterate, not writers) they can't tell their own stories – the autobiographer writes for or as them. Having set up this framework, I'm interested in exploring the narrative strategies used to execute this quite complex move – the telling of several interconnected life-stories at once, emphasising both the similarities and the differences, the interrelationship and the separateness, of their subjects.

I see these texts as a part of the feminist movement's recovery of the mother/daughter bond, after an earlier feminist phase of what Adrienne Rich calls 'matrophobia' – the fear of becoming like one's mother. The appearance of many texts, autobiographical and fictional, exploring and valuing the mother/daughter bond is not just coincidental with the rise of second-wave feminism. In 1976, Adrienne Rich, in *Of Woman Born*, pointed out that 'The cathexis between mother and daughter ... is the great unwritten story' (Rich 1976: 225). *The Woman Warrior*, also published in 1976, can be seen as an autobiographical exploration of this hitherto unwritten mother/daughter story. Since then, there have been many attempts, in theory, fiction and autobiography, to write that 'unwritten story' (Cosslett 1996; Chodorow 1978; Daly and Reddy 1991; Doane and Hodges 1992; Hansen 1997; Hirsch 1989; Steedman 1986; Walters 1992).

I want now to look at examples of this matrilineal move in three autobiographies: Maxine Hong Kingston's *The Woman Warrior* (1976), Audre Lorde's *Zami, A New Spelling of My Name* (1982) and Kim Chernin's *In My Mother's House* (1983). To call any of these three books 'autobiography' is to oversimplify. Maxine Hong Kingston's book recounts her own life-story in the interstices of stories about two of her aunts, her mother and a mythical Chinese warrior woman; throughout the book her mother's versions of these stories are mixed with Maxine's own retellings and reimaginings. Audre Lorde has called *Zami* a 'biomythography', and it mixes myth and poetry with autobiographical material. Kim Chernin's book is the story of her attempt to tell her mother's story, which also includes at points her mother's story about her own mother, and about Kim, her daughter, the writer of the text who is also within it. It could be described as her mother's biography, within an autobiographical frame, or her mother's autobiography, within a biographical frame.

All three books are explicitly concerned with matrilineage as a way of constructing the female subject: Hong Kingston writes of her aunt: 'Unless I see her life branching into mine, she gives me no ancestral help' (Kingston 1977: 10). Lorde gives us this reformulation of the Oedipal triangle:

> I have felt the age-old triangle of mother father and child, with the 'I' at its eternal core, elongate and flatten out into the elegantly strong triad of grandmother mother daughter, with the 'I' moving back and forth flowing in either or both directions as needed.
>
> (Lorde 1984: 7)

Chernin, like Lorde, sees the matrilineal story as having a different *shape* from the standard patriarchal stories:

> For here finally is the clear shape of the story my mother wants me to write down – this tale of four generations, immigrants who have come to take possession of a new world. It is a tale of transformation and development – the female reversal of that patriarchal story in which the power of the family's founder is lost and dissipated as the inheriting generations decline and fall to ruin. A story of power.
>
> (Chernin 1983: 16)

Chernin sees her role as torchbearer in this triumphant progress:

> I see generations of women bearing a flame. It is hidden, buried deep
> within, yet they are handing it down from one to another, burning. ... And
> now, in this very moment, my mother imparts the care of it to me. I must
> keep it alive, I must manage not to be consumed by it, I must hand it on
> when the time comes to my daughter.
>
> (Chernin 1983: 16)

The shape is both progressive and conservative of something valuable.

Another important similarity between the three texts is that all involve
American daughters with mothers from other cultures – China, the Caribbean, a
Jewish shtetl in Russia. I wonder if it's easier to see a matrilineage from another
culture (however patriarchal) as offering positive alternatives to the dominant
white, Western patriarchal culture, as well as or instead of reinforcing its values.
Matrilinealism offers a feminist way into the politics of cultural identity. An
important difference between the texts is Lorde's lesbianism: she presents her
matrilineal 'triad' as opening out at both ends into a community of women. She
does not pass on the matrilineal inheritance to a daughter as Chernin does, but
to her female lovers; and she mythologises a community of women friends and
lovers in the island where her mother was born. The other important emphasis
in feminist auto/biography, the rediscovery of the subject's network of female
friends (Stanley 1991), is here combined with the matrilineal project. Perhaps
this combination is based on a construction of lesbianism as a continuation of
love for the mother that was current at the time of writing (Rich 1980).

But now I want to suggest how these three autobiographies reconstruct both a
matrilineage and a maternal subjectivity. Hong Kingston's first chapter, 'No
Name Woman', famously reconstructs the story of her aunt (her father's sister in
this case), who has been erased from the family history because of her adultery.
Kingston both writes a biography for this lost aunt, and makes clear that she is
writing fiction by imagining the story in several different ways. At the same time,
as we've seen, she presents the aunt's story as directly relevant to her, as a
possible deviant woman in a patriarchal culture. Later, she similarly reconstructs
her mother's story and that of her other, maternal aunt. All offer possibilities for
what she could become, or should avoid: the first aunt commits suicide, the
second ends up in an asylum, but the mother, before coming to America, was a
strong, independent woman. Their stories are all told in close third-person
narration, their thoughts and feelings explored in the manner of a novelist.
While based on family stories, these versions go beyond what Kingston could
have known, into an imaginative sympathy and reconstruction of her female
relatives' subjectivities. It's interesting that in her final 'biographical' story, she
refers to her mother by her name, 'Brave Orchid', not as 'my mother'. Sidonie
Smith (1987) takes this to indicate a separation from the mother, a recognition of
her as a separate person with her own name and her own life. But it also indicates an *identification* with her as an equal, another woman like the narrator
herself.

This effect is also present in *Zami*: Lorde retells the story of her mother's arrival in America, referring to her as 'Linda'. The change from 'my mother' to 'Linda' occurs in the third paragraph of the first chapter: her mother goes to work as a scullery maid in a teashop – 'The owner told my mother that she ought to be glad to have the job, since ordinarily the establishment didn't hire "spanish" girls. Had the owner known Linda was Black, she would never have been hired at all' (Lorde 1984: 9). This develops on the third page into a novel-istic exploration of 'Linda's' feelings:

> Linda missed the bashing of the waves against the sea-wall at the foot of Noel's Hill, the humped and mysterious slope of Marquis Island rising up from the water a half-mile off-shore. She missed the swift-flying bananaquits and the trees and the rank smell of the tree-ferns lining the road downhill into Grenville Town. She missed the music that did not have to be listened to because it was always around. Most of all, she missed the Sunday-long boat trips that took her to Aunt Anni's in Carriacou.
>
> (Lorde 1984: 11)

The chapter alternates between referring to her as 'Linda', explaining her thoughts and feelings, and referring to her as 'my mother', who told Audre the stories on which these reconstructions must be based. The mother's stories include the grandmother and other female relatives. The naming of the mother as 'Linda' and the fictional exploration of her thoughts both credit her with her own subjectivity, emphasising her separateness, and, paradoxically, bring her nearer to the daughter who can sympathise and identify with the mother as a young woman, before she became a mother.

The willed, constructed nature of Lorde's recreation of her mother's subjec-tivity, and of her own matrilineage, becomes clear in a section of chapter 3, where, under the heading 'How I became a Poet', she writes:

> When the strongest words for what I have to offer come out of me sounding like words I remember from my mother's mouth, then I either have to reassess the meaning of everything I have to say now, or re-examine the worth of her old words.
>
> (Lorde 1984: 31)

The way her mother's relationship to her is represented in the rest of the book is as extremely harsh and repressive: Audre is a rebel against her mother's attitudes and leaves home early. Yet here Lorde stops and revalues her mother, and makes herself look back to her poetic debt to her mother's language, and to memories of physical closeness to her mother's body. In retrospect, the reader can now see the recreation of 'Linda's' story in chapter 1 as part of that process of recov-ering/making matrilineal connections, trying to explain/excuse her mother's behaviour by retrospectively imagining her point of view.

Kim Chernin's book incorporates the mother's story in a much larger way than either of the other two books. The story begins with Kim's mother, Rose, a communist activist, asking Kim, a poet, to write her, Rose's, story. Part of the aim of this is to recover the story of Rose's mother, Perle, and to pass the record on to Larissa, Kim's daughter. Rose, it is implied, is a brilliant oral storyteller, but needs the help of her writer daughter to record her life. Perle, too, it emerges, had a story-telling gift, which emerged in the letters (now lost) which she wrote. All the women are story-tellers, but Kim has the gift, and the sometimes painful responsibility, to write it all down. The book is constructed in alternating sections of interactions between Kim and her mother about the stories, setting the scenes in which they are told (these sections are told by Kim in the first person); and the stories themselves, told in the first person by her mother, Rose; later Kim's stories, in her first person, take over. The first-person sections told ostensibly 'by' her mother are in a different style from the other sections: her mother has an individualised 'voice', and the short sentences, simple vocabulary, and rhetorical questions reproduce the effect of oral story-telling. On the other hand, anyone who has ever recorded oral narratives can see that what's happening here is an extremely artful *representation* of oral story-telling: it gives the effect, but leaves out the repetitions, pauses and ungrammatical structure of speech. Once again, an element of daughterly fictionalising and reconstruction is added to the first-person testimony of the mother.

In the chapters that intervene between the 'stories' as such, the process of writing is foregrounded: in one scene, Kim is to read out the manuscript of her first story to a group of her closest friends. Her mother is also there, and prefaces the reading with an oral story of her own. At another, meta-fictional level, we have to remind ourselves that the whole scene, including her mother's story, has been written by Kim. As well as being about the process of writing the book, these between-chapters also show a gradual, sometimes painful coming together of mother and daughter, after some years of separation and antagonism, through the very process of telling and hearing the stories. They begin to see each other's points of view, to accept differences and to see similarities. Their fixed identities as 'politics' (the mother) and 'poetry' (the daughter) shift, change and merge.

I ended my paper in Nijmegen with a question about daughters: only Kim Chernin's book contains a representation of her daughter as well as her mother and grandmother. How do these dynamics work the other way round? Can mothers give their daughters a separate subjectivity? Larissa, the daughter in Chernin's book, is there, but peripheral: Kim's gaze is mostly back towards her ancestresses. Larissa appears as both wonderful and mysterious, full of an unknown potentiality. What I haven't been able to find yet is an example of an autobiographer exploring the subjectivity of her daughter. Could that be possible, or even desirable?

My reading of *Hidden Lives* has shown up some similarities to the earlier texts, but has also led me to question and develop my previous conclusions. *Hidden Lives* is as complexly intergeneric as the other books. It narrates the stories of Margaret Forster's grandmother, Margaret Ann, and then her mother, Lillian, both called by their first names. About half-way through, Margaret herself appears – but at first only referred to in the third person. Then, when she turns five, the narrative perspective changes, and Margaret becomes 'I', when 'my own real memory begins' (Forster 1996: 132). The narrator comments:

> So I can stop now, writing in the third person, stop retelling stories I was told about the years before I was born, about when I was under five, stop splicing oral history with local history, and start instead letting my own version of family lore come into play. I am there, at the centre. What a difference it makes, how dangerous it is.
>
> (Forster 1996: 133)

This suggests that what has been written before this is objective, is not 'my own' version. As I will explain later, I want to question this, and to suggest that it is the earlier absence of the 'I' that is most 'dangerous'.

As Forster says, up till this point she has been 'splicing' social history and oral history in a fairly neat and seamless manner. As both main protagonists are dead by the time she begins research for the book, the oral material must come from other family and friends, but its origins are not made clear, or marked off from the rest of the narration, which aspires to the lightly fictionalised status of good biography. So, in this account of her grandmother's funeral, there are a lot of details Forster can't have known about, perhaps elaborated from someone else's first-hand account:

> The same year, 1936, 22 July. A hot day, most unsuitable for a funeral. It seemed so inappropriate to be standing at a graveside when the sky was a holiday blue and the sun shone so festively. It would have felt better to the mourners if it had been raining ...
>
> (Forster 1996: 5)

But Forster puts a clear limit to fictionalising: one of the obsessions of the book is the story of her grandmother's secret illegitimate daughter, Alice, disowned by her mother, completely unknown to the family. Forster, as a good historian, pieces together hints and finally verifies Alice's existence from the records. But she cannot find out anything about the period of her grandmother's life from 1871 to 1893, up to the time of Alice's birth, and very little is to be discovered about Alice herself, who died in a mental hospital and whose records are inaccessible. Mysteries remain: Alice married and lived very near Margaret Ann, her mother, but was never acknowledged. Margaret Ann's husband was a witness at Alice's marriage. Unlike Maxine Hong Kingston, Margaret Forster does not fill this gap with her own fictions: she has in fact written a separate novel, *Shadow Baby* (1997), dealing with this material, clearly separating the fiction from the 'non-fictional' autobiography. In *Hidden Lives*, she tries out some theories which could explain the mysteries, but concludes: 'these theories, the romantic, the melodramatic, the sordid, all of them can be made to work but none of them can ever be proved. Round and round it goes, this circle of questions with no answers' (Forster 1996: 108). This is deeply frustrating for the reader, who has been following the story along like a detective mystery, waiting for the answers: but this frustration can be seen as salutary, reminding us just how inaccessible to even the most meticulous historical research the lives of 'ordinary women' can be.

As the title *Hidden Lives* suggests, Forster is, like the other autobiographers, trying to bring to light what would otherwise be lost. Apart from oral history and the official records, she also makes use of analogous stories from the time, as in the account of Margaret Ann's own birth as the illegitimate daughter of Annie Jordan:

> The same month Annie Jordan gave birth there was an inquest in Carlisle on the body of a baby found 'in the river Eden, among the branches between the bank of the river and some old weiring. A sod was laid upon it … a woman was seen near the place where the child was found, leaning against some railings, apparently in distress and crying.' The woman was arrested and when it was discovered she was the mother of the dead baby she was sent to prison for six months. Annie Jordan could so easily have been driven to that solution …
>
> (Forster 1996: 17)

As Forster comments, 'Pointless to hope to find out more about poor insignificant Annie, about what she looked like, what kind of a personality she had, but not pointless or hopeless trying to piece together the sort of life she led' (Forster 1996: 18). To this end, she reconstructs the social history of Carlisle, the setting for all of the stories. The lives narrated are partly determined by their social and historical circumstances – the coming of the railways, the building of working-class estates, the Education Acts. While this opens out the narrowly individual to the social, it also means the women are reduced to representatives, as Forster freely admits is her larger purpose: 'My grandmother's story seems to me *representative* in that kind of way …. her history was somehow essential to understanding not simply my own but that of a whole generation of working-class women' (Forster 1996: 13–14).

While the other autobiographers have problems (but also room for fantasy and mythology) because their mothers come from distant countries, the distance for Forster is one of class. Her education has effected a rise into the middle class for her, which has removed her from the domestic slavery of her working-class matrilineage: at the end of the book, she draws this ringing but blinkered conclusion:

> My personal curiosity may not have been satisfied but my larger curiosity, as to whether life had indeed improved for women like my immediate ancestors, is. And I am glad, glad not to have been born a working-class girl in 1809 or 1901. Everything, for a woman, is better now, even if it is still not as good as it could be. To forget or deny that is an insult to the women who have gone before, women like my grandmother and mother.
>
> (Forster 1996: 307)

The shape of Forster's story, like Kim Chernin's, is *progress*, but there is not a corresponding sense of preserving something valuable from the past. Instead, she wants to record these women's sufferings, their wasted lives. Unlike the other autobiographers, she does not look back and mythologise these women's stories in any positive way – though the concept of progress is of course itself a powerful myth. It is this myth that some working-class students in my seminars have found offensive. As they pointed out, life for the working-class women now living on the estates around Carlisle cannot be said to have 'improved' in this triumphalist way; it is just that Forster and her relatives have now left, freed by education and money. Besides the overt story of progress Forster tells, there is a more hidden story of the decline of the estate, from the shining 'garden city' image of the 1930s when her mother and father move in, to 'an estate getting rougher all the time for reasons no one understood', full of 'problem families' and domestic violence in the 1950s and 1960s (Forster 1996: 149). My students also objected to the 'representative' status of the women protagonists, the way in which they were allowed to think and say only the stereotypical. They felt the women were denied full subjectivity. There is a long and complicated issue here about the individual and the representative, and the limits of responsible fictionalisation. Maxine Hong Kingston has been attacked by Chinese-American critics for *mis*representing the community in her 'memoir', for creating characters who are not representative enough (Wong 1992). The 'representative' quality of Margaret Forster's characters is partly a consequence of so little being known about them, partly because she refuses to fictionalise as much as Hong Kingston, and partly in order for them to fit the narrative of progress she is constructing. This narrative itself is not just a convenient historical concept, but also part of the self-construction of Margaret Forster as autobiographer, at the pinnacle of the line of progress.

But *Hidden Lives*, despite appearances of caution and unwillingness to go beyond the historically verifiable, is more fictional than it looks. The smoothness of the fiction is undone in the second half, when the autobiographer as 'I' appears, in a relationship to a mother whose subjectivity is far more difficult and intractable than her biography has made out. The other autobiographers all foreground their difficult relationships with their mothers – the hatreds, the resentments – from the start, and then a retrospective forgiveness can grow that leads to biographical understanding. In *Hidden Lives* the order is reversed: all seems smooth and unquestionable till the second half. Paradoxically, it is the appearance of the 'I' that allows the mother as other, as different, to appear. Forster clearly wants her mother to fit into her narrative of progress: the 'biographical' section tells of her intelligence, her achievement at school, which goes no further than the higher grade school, since no-one suggested she should go to the high school, let alone university, as her daughter is later able to. What is focused on in her adult life is her delight in her job in the Public Health Department, how she loves the office, the money, the clothes she can buy. Again, this is cut short, as the marriage bar operates, and she is consigned to a husband who is her inferior in intellect, and to domestic slavery for her often ungrateful family. One of the book's strongest points for me is its recreation of the material details of domestic drudgery.

But in old age, recounted in the autobiographical second half of the book, the mother refuses to fit the story Forster is composing for her. To her daughter's exasperation, she has no interest in adult education; she is resentful and envious of her daughter, but, according to Forster, for all the wrong reasons:

> 'I wish I'd had your life.'
>   It was painful, somehow, hearing her say that. I didn't want her to want my life. I wanted her to have enjoyed her own. And what she was concentrating on, in her desire, were only the superficial things in my life. Given my income, my mother would have been a spender. .... She would have been a lady who lunched, at the Savoy Grill, at the Ritz. She didn't know anything about my real life, the part that *was* enviable, the hours spent writing and reading which put being a wife and mother into a different context. She was right, life *had* changed for women and I'd benefited from the changes, but the greatest change of all was not one she either saw or appreciated. I was having a career as well as everything else and that was what, if anything, she should have yearned for.
>
> (Forster 1996: 295)

'Should have' is revealing: the mother will not accept the story her daughter is trying to fit her into. After her mother's death, Forster begins research for the book – because 'I can't understand my own history unless I understand my grandmother's, my mother's and that of the women like them, the ordinary working-class women from whom I came' (Forster 1996: 304). On first reading, the biographies present themselves as objective, impersonal. But looking back from the end, Forster can be seen to be finding in her mother's life a reflection of herself, focused on education and career: this is what she can understand, sympathise with, write about. The shape of this life also fits into the myth of progress that not only justifies Forster's life, but explains and subsumes her mother's sense of resentment, envy and waste; and yet, the intractable mother insists on envying the wrong things. One of the interesting features of the autobiographical section of the book is that Forster's own story also doesn't quite fit her declared framework: at Oxford, it is not the educational opportunities that attract her – she is rather bored by the work. What is important and liberating is the access she and her friends now have to information about contraception and abortion. This links back to the grandmother's story of unwanted, illegitimate birth: again, a progress narrative. Is it that Forster is propelled to do what she does and value what she values because of the frustrations of her grandmother and mother, or does she now look back and focus on those because of her own preoccupations? We can't know – but the mother's recalcitrance suggests that the daughter is looking back to find what is *like her*, and is constructing the mother's story to fit this project.

Looking back now to my earlier texts, this could also be said of them. Audre Lorde reconstructs her mother as a link back to a mythical lesbian community, and a speaker of poetic language, like her daughter. Maxine Hong Kingston concentrates on her mother's ability to 'talk story', like her writer daughter, and the way they are both 'Women Warriors'. Kim Chernin finds in her mother and grandmother her own story-telling abilities. Of course, in all these books these accounts are problematised, by fictional frames, by opposing accounts of the difficulties and misunderstandings of mother/daughter relations. Chernin seems to me to have succeeded best in coming nearest to a *reciprocal* mother/daughter narration; and Kingston to an admission that the whole fabric is based on her own memories and fantasies.

I do not want to seem to be blaming these writers; what I am questioning is my first assumption that what is going on here is a recovery of the mother's subjectivity. Instead, we are being shown how the mother and the matrilineage function to give 'ancestral help', as Kingston says, to the daughter. Similarly, a mother may find support in her fantasies about her daughter and how she may be going to carry on the matrilineage, but it would be the grossest imposition to call these the daughter's story, or to limit her subjectivity to them. Mothers perhaps can't be harmed by our stories about them, but neither are they helped or empowered by them.

Looking back to my first prompts to maternal unknowability, there seem to be several different things going on. For Griselda Pollock and myself, the early death of the mother is a complicating factor that partly accounts for her irrecoverability. But thinking about my novel, constructed around the mother as absent centre, this is of course just as much my fictionalisation of my mother, to do with my needs, as Margaret Forster's detailed, first-name biography of hers. I was going to end with Maureen Fenton's and Serretta Bebb's refusals to confine their mothers to stories as 'the way forward', the most ethical and respectful attitude. This would imply a feminist progress narrative, from matrophobia, to speaking for the mother, to allowing her irreducible difference and mystery. But these respectful constructions too can be seen first of all as helpful and empowering for the *writers*, leaving them free of closure and undefined, with an 'unknowable' subjectivity as one of their own resources. To have an intersubjective bond with someone unknowable and full of new possibilities is an exciting idea.

Matrilineal

What shall I
Say about the
Complicated bond with
That dead woman
Who was so
Different from whom
I am now? – a
Scientist, atheist,
Believer in reason,
Not able to follow
The long English sentences
In *Middlemarch* –
She wouldn't understand

Poetry, and yet her
Words must be on
My tongue, and her
Body is my body's
Shape, and I
Sometimes see her
Face in my
Daughter's, who said
Yesterday, to her little
Friend, 'Leave me
Alone, I need some
Time on my own
Now': my words
She was parroting –
Which perhaps
I copied from
My mother: so
Why can't I
Leave her alone?

Looking for My Mother in Vienna

I thought I saw you in the Underground,
The woman opposite me with your face,
The face from those old sepia photographs:
Brown skin and browner coffee eyes.
But she was dressed too finely, holding a parcel
From some elegant shop: you hated shopping.
She got off at the Karlsplatz, carrying
Her box of riches.

The exhibition was on 'Red Vienna'
Before the war. I saw you in a picture,
Two women putting up a poster together:
'Frauentag, 1930' – you're the one
With bobbed hair, back to the camera,
Reaching high to pin the left-hand corner;
But you wouldn't turn around.

I knew I'd meet you in the Alpine garden,
Thinking of the mountains; but we wasted
Half-an-hour in the hot streets
Searching for the entrance; when we found it,
Hidden behind a yew-hedge, it was closed.

The marble hallway of the Physics Lab
Displayed a plaque, to tell us that the Nazis
Shot down your teachers on this very spot.
I got out quick, like you did.

Bibliography

Chernin, K. (1983) *In My Mother's House*, New Haven and New York: Ticknor and Fields.

Chodorow, N. (1978) *The Reproduction of Mothering: Psychoanalysis and the Sociology of Gender*, Berkeley: University of California Press.

Cosslett, T. (1996) 'Feminism, Matrilinealism, and the "House of Women" in Contemporary Women's Fiction', *Journal of Gender Studies* 5, 1: 7–17.

Daly, B. and Reddy, M. (eds) (1991) *Narrating Mothers: Theorizing Maternal Subjectivities*, Knoxville: University of Tennessee Press.

Doane, J. and Hodges, D. (1992) *From Klein to Kristeva: Psychoanalytic Feminism and the Search for the 'Good Enough' Mother*, Ann Arbor: University of Michigan Press.

Forster, M. (1996) *Hidden Lives, A Family Memoir*, Harmondsworth: Penguin.

—— (1997) *Shadow Baby*, Harmondsworth: Penguin.

Hansen, E.T. (1997) *Mother Without Child: Contemporary Fiction and the Crisis of Motherhood*, Berkeley, Los Angeles and London: University of California Press.

Hirsch, M. (1989) *The Mother/Daughter Plot: Narrative, Psychoanalysis, Feminism*, Bloomington: Indiana University Press.

Kingston, M.H. (1977 [1976]) *The Woman Warrior: Memoirs of a Girlhood Among Ghosts*, New York: Random House.

Lorde, A. (1984 [1982]) *Zami, A New Spelling of My Name*, London: Sheba.

Pollock, G. (1998) 'The Invention of Memory: Feminity and the Death Drive', presentation given at the 'Visual Selves: The Image and Autobiography' seminar, in the 'Autobiography and the Social Self' series, Institute of Women's Studies, Lancaster.

Povlsen, K.K. (1993) 'Women's Autobiography 1765–1830', paper given at the WINGS conference on Autobiography and Gender at Nijmegen Catholic University, The Netherlands.

Rich, A. (1976) *Of Woman Born: Motherhood as Experience and Institution*, New York: Norton.

—— (1980) 'Compulsory Heterosexuality and Lesbian Existence', *Signs* 5, 4: 631–60.

Smith, S. (1987) 'Maxine Hong Kingston's *Woman Warrior*: Filiality and Woman's Autobiographical Storytelling', in Smith, S., *A Poetics of Women's Autobiography: Marginality and the Fictions of Self-Representation*, Bloomington: Indiana University Press.

Stanley, L. (1991)'Feminist Auto/Biography and Feminist Epistemology', in Aaron, J. and Walby, S. (eds), *Out of the Margins*, London: Falmer Press: 204–19.

Steedman, C. (1986) *Landscape for a Good Woman*, London: Virago.

Walters, S.D. (1992) *Lives Together/Worlds Apart: Mothers and Daughters in Popular Culture*, Berkeley: University of California Press.

Wong, S.L.C. (1992) 'Autobiography as Guided Chinatown Tour? Maxine Hong Kingston's *The Woman Warrior* and the Chinese-American Autobiographical Controversy', in Payne, J.R. (ed.), *Multicultural Autobiography: American Lives*, Knoxville: University of Tennessee Press: 248–79.

9   The global self

Narratives of Caribbean migrant women

Mary Chamberlain

the faculty of imagination is the gift of interpolating into the infinitely small, of inventing, for every intensity, an extensiveness to contain its new, compressed fullness, in short, of receiving each image as if it were that of the folded fan, which only in spreading draws breath and flourishes, in its new expanse, the ... beloved features within it.

(Benjamin 1996)

The Caribbean is, perhaps, unique in the world for what Susan Craig-James (1992) terms its 'overlapping diasporas and intertwining roots'. Caribbean peoples have lived within and through a culture which historically as well as contemporaneously has gained its energy and creativity from the world (Braithwaite 1971; Mintz 1989; Harney 1996), from migrations to, within and from the region, a continuing tension between exile and return. Caribbean culture has absorbed its world influences and transfigured it into a new syncretic culture, as elements from Africa, Europe, Asia and the Caribbean became absorbed, worked and reworked into a new and distinctively 'Creole' culture, in which, as the anthropologist Sidney Mintz points out, 'origins matter less than the creative acts ... involve(d)' (1989: 326). It is a process which continues, within the Caribbean and beyond, in the metropolitan centres of London or New York, Toronto or Amsterdam. Caribbean people are no strangers to strangeness, nor indeed to being a stranger. It is not a dislocating or disabling condition but an opportunity for creativity, a continuing process of syncretism shaped by, and contributing to, the history of its diaspora.

The peculiar dynamics of Caribbean culture have inspired and shaped its literature and its philosophy. This side of the Atlantic, it has inspired many of the recent contemporary reflections on diaspora and cultural formations, one cultural and philosophical aspect of which was explored in Paul Gilroy's *The Black Atlantic* (1993). Part and parcel of this cultural enterprise has been a rethinking of the notion of identities, not as fixed entities or absolutes, enshrined in essentialist views of race or gender or class, what Foucault might describe as technologies or regimens of the self, but as a process of creativity, of self construction, of the production of self which, as Hall (1996) reminds us, is never centred, neither fixed nor closed. It reflects in symbolic language the material realities of 'migranthood' (Hall quoted in Jeater 1992: 115), of a journey, of double consciousness, of dispersal and fragmentation. Indeed, many of the issues raised by identity and the synthesis or harmony of the multiple 'voices' revisit at an individual and personal level the broader notion of cultural syncretism.

It is this issue of syncretism which I wish to raise here, by exploring some of the expressive representations of self in the life-story narratives of Caribbean women. A necessary part of this exploration, however, engages with other issues relating to the nature and value of the life-story narrative for the social historian and in particular with the question of 'realism'. My examples will draw primarily on recent work on West Indian families[1] and migration.[2]

Let me start with a story:

When I were at the age of twelve years old, my uncle ... said he want me to go to secondary school because the people in Panama who is educated get the best job. ... My grandmother had a brother who worked on the estate as the book-keeper. The white half could work there. ... So I was to go to Combermere. I had my money, my books, my khaki suit, everything ready. The money ... that my uncle send to pay for the school fees, it was eight dollars and eight cents. I will never forget this as long as I live ... I was home one evening ... and my grandmother sister came very dressed. Two sisters came, two aunts, and my grandmother get dress. I saw her boots, her umbrella, and they leave. I do not know where they were going. But the next thing I heard, my uncle that was the book-keeper ... they ship him to Canada. ... My grandmother took the money, with my two aunts, and ship my uncle to Canada.[3]

Charles began his interview (in Barbados) by stating that he only had one thing to tell, the story above. These were the opening words of his interview, and he began it with no prompting. What he later termed the 'robbery' of his education proved the driving force of what he subsequently told me of his life, dominating his life choices and those he made for his children. In that short story we understand what motivated this man; we can also understand many of the details of the social history of Barbados in the early decades of this century – the race, class and gender dynamics, the structure of the family and the impact of migration. By implication, we hear the legacy of slavery and the painful positioning of himself within the exclusionary structures of colonialism. We can perhaps leap ahead and argue that in this short passage we hear many of the rumblings of social discontent which finally erupted in the riots in Barbados, and elsewhere in the West Indies, in 1937. There is, perhaps, more history in that short anecdote than I could have elicited had I asked him, more formally, to contemplate and talk about race or class or colonialism, or any other of the categories which preoccupy social historians of colonial Barbados in the twentieth century.

But it is also a good story. It is aesthetically satisfying. It is complete. Charles's use of language, rhetoric and repetition provide it with a literary, almost musical, rhythm, while his sense of drama is heightened by his pauses and his diversionary detail: of his grandmother putting on her boots, picking up her umbrella; the mystery of why his aunts had arrived, or where they were going. It was a story which commanded, and anticipated, an audience. This was the story of his life by which he wished to be acknowledged. It was a well-rehearsed performance, both compelling and convincing; he chose the story and crafted its delivery. We could imagine the scene and fill in the details – perhaps it was a black umbrella, a white hat – and convert this into a realistic account.

Let me offer a different vignette, from another Barbadian, a woman, born in 1908. I asked her to tell me about her mother and she replied,

> My mother, my grandmother, we live together. My grandmother, when she took sick in 1921, hair, enough hair, pretty white hair like silk cotton and me and my sister would pick she hair and we did fair size children at the time, so my mother had the last baby she had born, and my grandmother took sick so. After she took sick, we had to go and pick pond grass and let me mother stay at her mother.[4]

In aesthetic terms, it lacks the narrative qualities of the first example. Indeed, it is not a story, but a fragment. For the historian, such an apparently jumbled and broken response may seem of little value. We have no idea of the size of the family, of class, of occupation, the usual suspects in the construction of social history. It tells us nothing about race or colonialism. There is nothing there which postdates slavery or prefigures social change. Even allowing for the 'interference' of transcription (including standard spelling) it is still possible to recognise that this speaker not only talks in a heavy Creole dialect, but – compared with the first story – this dialect appears to restrict expression. What, therefore, is its value as testimony?

Many of the early critics of oral history argued that oral testimony as historical evidence was unreliable because it was unrepresentative: the testimony of a handful of individual men or women was no more than that. It did not carry the scientific weight of what Lévi-Strauss (1963) called the 'anonymity of numbers'. Alternatively, it was argued that oral sources, far from being too individual, were, paradoxically, too social: individual memory was structured by the social environment and that if a memory could not be disentangled from the layering of, for example, contemporary or retrospective accounts, it was, as testimony, worthless.

There has now evolved a large literature around the social functions and nature of memory. The French sociologist, Maurice Halbwachs, for instance, in *The Collective Memory* (1980), argued that memory is never 'purely' singular or idiosyncratic. The memories of others, and about others – parents, grandparents and so forth – enter into our own memories; memories are both inherited and transmitted and as such form a central plank in the process of socialisation. What is prioritised or what is repressed relates at varying levels to the permissions or prohibitions of social, cultural and, indeed, as Alessandro Portelli (1990) points out, political values. Memory itself is part of a social dialectic as its emphases and resolutions shift with the vagaries of the life cycle, and that of others, responding to generational change and fashion, including representations of the past. As historians such as Raphael Samuel (1995) and others remind us, we are surrounded with reconstructions and re-memories of the past which are part of the rhetoric and metaphors and clichés of history, and shape both a public view of history and a private interpretation of one's position within it. The recollection of memory equally responds to the audience and its questions, whether the questioner is the historian, the ethnographer or the family. The interview itself is, therefore, essentially 'dialogic', mutually constructed by the interviewer and interviewee (see Bakhtin 1984). From fields other than history, anthropologists such as Elizabeth Tonkin (1992) and literary scholars such as Alessandro Portelli (1998) have argued that oral testimonies, like other narrative forms, are governed by genres which the scholar can identify and codify, and clue back into an understanding of historical reckoning and imagining. Far from memories being 'pure' and 'singular', it is precisely their impurities, their pluralities and their volatility which provide such valuable testimony for the historian.

Historians also choose a 'genre' of explication and presentation. This choice determines how a work is 'read', and the interpretation (and status) of testimony within it. But the choice of presentation privileges 'realism'. The codes historians choose to articulate their arguments, and the resources and sources they bring to back up those arguments, tend to favour the articulate account and exclude – and thereby silence – the 'surreal'. Elizabeth Tonkin (1990) wryly commented on how anthropologists assumed that the mode – or more correctly code – of 'realism' encountered in their fieldwork would often be taken as more reliable evidence of the past, as history, than retellings of the grand myths of origin or events which remained consigned to the interpretative arena of the fabulous or symbolic, even though there may be more 'truth' in myth, and much myth in apparently realistic accounts.

I want to focus, however, on the surreal, those testimonies which appear to lack more formal narrative structures. Much oral testimony accords with recognised conventions, linguistic and oral devices to which the listener is attuned, with which we are familiar and which are capable of replication. But if those devices or narratives are not available either to the informant or the researcher, can we recognise their value as testimony? In other words, despite the relative sophistication of the historian in 'reading' the sources, the use of new theoretical tools (which I am not so sure differ substantially from the old ones) and an awareness of the multi-authored voice of testimony, are there still absences, or silences, which we are not hearing, and which we are replicating?

Few social historians who utilise life-story narratives would now endorse Oscar Lewis's early (and perhaps naïve) enthusiasm for the tape recorder by which 'unskilled, uneducated and even illiterate persons can talk about themselves and relate their observations and experiences in an uninhibited, spontaneous, and natural manner' (Lewis 1964: xii). Nor, equally, would many historians exclude (for instance) gender. Our 'narratives' of history have moved with the times as they always do and gender (and other categories of analysis) have entered into the historian's theoretical lexicon. Nevertheless, in dealing with a foreign country, both literally and metaphorically, there are many of the pitfalls of the ethnographer or the dangers of what Gwendolyn Etter-Lewis (1996) describes as the 'one size fits all' approach to the practice of oral history, and the privileged position within both history and ethnography of the 'realistic' account both in testimony and historical representation. There remains, perhaps, a lingering sympathy with Lewis's early claims for a new 'social realism' for the historiographic record.

Life-story narratives – oral testimonies – necessarily extend beyond data of empirical interest to the core of memory, the imaginative structures which shape it and the language which articulates it. One of the legacies of Romanticism is to locate memory and imagination as unique to the individual. Indeed, what constitutes the 'individual' has been defined by the specific properties of memory. But this is an epistemological, and therefore a cultural, construct. Yet the preferred form for an interview is one-to-one, individual to individual, which prioritises a cultural practice that may be neither relevant nor appropriate in all interview situations. Yvette Kopijn (1998) points to this in her experience of interviewing elderly Javanese-Surinamese women, for whom story-telling is primarily a collective, communal event governed by particular norms and practices which influence the content and the context of communication. It is the antithesis of the one-to-one interview, for which that society had no cultural precedent. As a result, she had to abandon many of the conventions of the formal interview to accommodate these cultural practices, and the memories recounted only became meaningful when situated within these practices.

The forms in which we remember – the languages, the images, the sensations – are shared, and therefore social, and shape and structure internalisation, interpretation and articulation. They manifest a shared consciousness, akin to what Mikhail Bakhtin might describe as 'social dialect', part of social and cultural production, or perhaps to Bourdieu's notion of 'habitus'. And of course they shift over time. Memories in other words contain both tense and judgement, reflecting life experience and cultural practice as much as shaping it. Memories, too, have a history (Passerini 1996). Their production is not a fixed or essential process. 'Interiority' as Nikolas Rose suggests,

> is not that of a psychological system, but of a discontinuous surface, a kind of infolding of exteriority. ... [Folds] incorporate without totalizing, internalize without unifying, collect together discontinuously in the form of pleats, making surfaces, spaces, flows and relations.
>
> (Rose 1996: 142–3)

Memory has to be seen in its relation to the imagination and imaginative structures, as engaged in essentially a dialectical process of recall and recounting, where, depending on which way the folds swirl and flow, at any one point one detail or another is revealed or concealed, and where all experience and articulations contribute and continue to contribute to a constant revision of self and subjectivity – a process which is continuously engaging in creating anew from the retentions of the old.

Seen from this perspective, those illustrative anecdotes which appear to catch so much of the immediacy, power and authority of first-hand experience are perhaps aberrative of how we think of our lives. It is perhaps the surreal accounts which are the most socially 'realistic'. But the question becomes further complicated by the meanings implied by the forms of language itself. The use of metaphors, rhetoric and sayings (which so often punctuate conversational speech) all signify values and priorities, ways of looking at the world and interpreting it. They are often symbolic shorthand for a particular [cultural] worldview. People may speak in the same language but the symbolic structures may not be the same at all. Indeed, their use may be both inclusive and exclusive, endorsing shared assumptions and collective membership, while denying an outsider access to these communal values. Life-story testimonies can become an interpretative minefield.

Spiritual metaphors are a recurring theme in many West Indian narratives. Family members are often described in religious terms, mothers and grandmothers are 'saints', they are 'angels', they are 'blessed'. Such terms convey a meaning in European culture, a religious meaning that is partially shared in the context of the West Indies which is often enthusiastically Christian, and a secular meaning, the 'angel in the house', an ordering of gender roles, which is also part of a shared official heritage in the West Indies (although in practice less so). It would, however, be a mistake to assume that metaphors have a universal and literal translation, and to assume that terms such as 'angel' are *only* second-hand renditions of a colonisation of heart and mind, or simply expressions of endearment and character. Both old and young informants talk of themselves as 'spiritual' people. Saints and angels run in parallel with other metaphors, of duppies (ghosts) and the spirit of the dead, an interest in lineage, a reverence for the 'old ancestant', an abiding trust in kinship.

The response to the question 'Tell me about your mother' began 'My mother, my grandmother', myself. Time and again, in my West Indian narratives, I hear not the autonomy, but the collectivity, of the individual. 'When you are looking at me', a Jamaican woman born in 1935 remarked, 'you're looking at my mother. I am the image of my mother.' 'I was never lonely,' another informant remarked (about her migration to England), 'I carried my family within me.' 'I was a grandmother child', Beulah, a Barbadian woman born in 1950, told me, 'My great-grandmother was everything to me. I am a grandmother child. I can feel her presence even now.' Another (Jamaican) woman commented simply on her family, 'Is them me get me blessing from.'

The psychoanalytic literature suggests that identifications are part of the process of individualisation, a step prior to the separation by, and recognition of, the self as separate, autonomous. Yet in these interviews, the women knit into their narratives of self, powerful identifications with family, and in particular with mothers and grandmothers, suggesting that such identifications may be the end, rather than the beginning, of the process of individualisation. 'We were all full of my grandmother', the Trinidadian Dionne Brand wrote in her short story 'Photograph':

> she had left us full and empty of her. We dreamed in my grandmother, and we woke up in her, bleary-eyed and gesturing for her arm, her elbows, her smell. We jockeyed with each other, lied to each other, quarrelled with each other, and with her for the boon of lying close to her, sculpting ourselves around the roundness of her back. Braiding her hair and oiling her feet. ... She had left us empty and full of her.
>
> (Brand 1989: 180)

Images of mothers and grandmothers sometimes involved the elision of mothers and grandmothers – Anne-Marie was born in London in 1972 and referred to her grandmother as 'Mother' because 'everyone does. Her children do, her grandchildren do, her great-grandchildren do. Everyone does.'[5] The intimacy of their lives together – Mrs A, for instance, picking her grandmother's hair like silk cotton – recurs constantly in these narratives. Let me recap: when we look to narrations of the self, we need to think critically about the components which enter into that narrative, into the meanings of such components, to look at the various articulations of memory as providing a personal *and* a cultural authenticity. In other words we need to recognise the importance, among other things, of identifications and elisions – my mother, my grandmother, myself – to recognise their cultural specificity and to recognise also that narrations of the self may not necessarily be narrations of the individual.

These identifications represent lineage and tradition, explanation and validation, the roots of and the routes to identity: the 'grandmother child'; the lady in whom you see her mother; or the lady who never felt lonely because of the family within her. These were all migrant women who left behind, were absent from, their family and kin in the West Indies. This sense of the spirit of kin, and particularly ancestral kin, is a strong element in West Indian culture and acts as a powerful binding force and dynamic in families. Such metaphors both reveal a profound sense of self, of women, of the vitality of lineage, kinship and family in the construction of subjectivity, and offer us considerable insight into the values, forms and power relations of African-Caribbean families.

This could be important. There is no space here to review the vast historical and contemporary literature on the Caribbean family, nor is it relevant in this context. Permit me a crude sketch. Caribbean families have been frequently characterised in terms of absence: they lack structure, form and men, and consequently the ability to nurture, socialise or progress. As a result, Caribbean families have been categorised as matrifocal and with a high level of male marginalisation. In our research (Chamberlain and Goulbourne forthcoming) we have collected some very 'real' accounts of how Caribbean families operate in practice. But we also have surreal accounts, evocative ways of imagining the past, couched in symbolic, but ambiguous, language.

Let me now return to the second example with which I opened this discussion and present a different reading. What we have is a topic-associated response, or (perhaps more aptly) a single unitary vision, a graphic, textual and sensual description of her grandmother, her mother and herself within the totality of the relationship. There is no clear chronology, either of genealogy or of narrative. Neither is there a closure between the generations. Instead, we have an integrated sense of the context in which the woman's mother lived and the context in which, as children, they went out to work. It conveys the meaning of her mother's life, the relationship across the generations, the values and attitudes inherent within it, and the emotions generated by it. Phrases such as 'her pretty white hair' alert us to this, although it bubbles up as a stream of consciousness, rather than as a measured ingredient in her narrative. Her individuality and her memories were haunted and informed by the context of the family, and were inseparable from them. Indeed, the 'voice' is not just her voice, but the voices of her mother and grandmother. There is an ambiguity of tense, as the present and the past elide into the continuous. It has none of what Alessandro Portelli (1998) described as the 'ritual representation of historical experience', nor does it resemble what we recognise as 'realism'. It would be easy to turn a blind eye or a deaf ear – make absent – an example such as this.

But it is a valuable piece of testimony for the light it sheds on subjectivity within the Caribbean family, though its shape bears no resemblance to Charles's story. And the light it sheds may suggest, first, that Caribbean women may have a very different sense of self from that which Europeans, with their emphasis on individuality and autonomy, may understand. This may be termed a 'syncretic' self, which enfolds within it an acknowledgement of lineage, and their place within it. This place necessarily shifts along with their course in the life cycle. In this sense, it is as much to do with origins as continuity (Sutton 1997), an awareness of the roles women play in their own life cycle and that of their families – my mother, my grandmother, myself. Like the culture it represents, it says as much about origins as creativity. Women, in other words, may have a plural sense of self, fashioned by the roles they perform and their positioning as intermediaries in their lineage. Indeed, a sense of self emerges precisely out of the cooperation which is integrally involved (with younger and older family members) in the act of positioning. They may even invoke a variety of terms to talk about the self, as Gloria Wekker (1997) notes in relation to Afro-Surinamese women.

In this, women's roles as kin and mothers are shaped by a specific 'cosmology' which may place them at the centre of an exchange of lineage (Kerns 1997). As such, this may help reinterpret the much-vaunted 'matrifocality' of West Indian family life, and deflect attention away from what Constance Sutton describes as the 'power by default' thesis which centres women as powerful only because their men are absent through migration or poverty. It makes sense of, and gives cultural meaning to, a range of identifiable social characteristics such as the importance of consanguinal (as opposed to conjugal) links, of family reunions and rituals (notably funerals), of child fostering and so forth, all of which have been regarded in the literature as part of the default syndrome, which (analytically, at least) renders women's roles as secondary and derivative. In this reading, therefore, women are placed at centre stage, as the life bearers, the carriers of lineage and the ones primarily responsible for cultural and familial continuity. Mothers are angels and saints not (just) because they display abundant goodness or patience, but precisely because they represent a living link with the dead, and are the guardians of the future.

Our recent research (Chamberlain and Goulbourne forthcoming) on Caribbean families in Britain has indicated that as Caribbean families evolve into the second and third generations, many of the characteristics discernible in the Caribbean have become replicated here. Many of those characteristics – in particular the high incidence of single-parent mother-headed households (OPCS 1991), high rates of illegitimacy, and male marginalisation from both social mobility (Modood *et al.* 1997) and family life (Dench 1996) – have been taken as evidence of family disintegration and dysfunction. Yet our research reveals how close family ties are retained across the ocean (Goulbourne 1999), and across the generations, with little loss to family unity, and how many of the child-bearing and child-rearing practices continue to conform, in a modified or syncretic form, to patterns of family formation and life in the Caribbean. It is, as one young British-born informant suggested, 'as if we're carrying on a tradition that we're not even aware of'.[6]

The early studies of the West Indian community in Britain, following an avowedly assimilationist agenda, predicted that over time the emotional and material ties between West Indians in Britain and those 'back home' would be diminished rather than consolidated (see, for instance, Patterson 1964). At the same time, West Indians, unlike migrants from the Indian subcontinent, lacking distinctive cultural form (Banton 1967) could, over time, become 'like us', for 'they want to adopt British standards, to be accepted, to become inconspicuous' (Huxley 1964). Despite those early predictions, in the fifty years after the first West Indians arrived in Britain aboard SS Windrush, a distinctively Caribbean way of life has emerged. One of its most distinguishing (and distinguished) features has been the strength and vibrancy of its transnational connections, whether through the links of family and culture or art and ideas. New forms and old, new impulses and old, continue the processes of syncretisation whereby the cultural (and indeed the national) parameters of the Caribbean cease to be geographic but emotional and cosmic. The borders of the Caribbean remain conceptually open, and elastic, as indeed they must when every generation of Caribbeans has been touched by the processes of migration, of themselves or of someone close to them. Indeed, it is perhaps this ability to adapt and incorporate – to syncretise or indigenise – culture wherever the Caribbean hangs its hat which has been a central plank in the strategy for survival of the Caribbean and its peoples. Such a strategy engages with a notion of belonging not to, or as, a fixed position, but as being part of a moving continuum in which the family –

the 'transnational' family (Wiltshire-Brodber 1986) – simultaneously, and perhaps paradoxically, 'roots' its members. 'The family unit', as a British-born Caribbean described it, 'provides the solace and stability that is needed [in migration]'.[7]

This rooting – and readings of it – is however proscribed by both gender and scholarship. Elsewhere (Chamberlain 1997a, 1997b), I have explored the gender differences in the processes and accounts of migration, arguing that whereas men stressed autonomy and progress in their narratives of self, the women retold theirs through the cycle of the family. As a result, whereas the men presented their life accounts in the form of a linear chronology, in the women's accounts, detail, time and chronology were often conflated. For the historian, the chronology of their lives, and their specific migration stories, needed to be disentangled from the multiple voices which were constructing and shaping them. Of course a coherent thread could be pulled out, and a 'realistic' account, that was both readable and comprehensible could be presented, but to do so would have distorted the wider weave of their lives.

The identity of the protagonist is perhaps a more familiar problem for literary scholars than for historians. And for them, too, realism is one aesthetic convention among several from which a writer (or artist) can choose. The tools for the historian are more circumscribed (even when the subject under study is identity itself). Within Caribbean literature, however, – and particularly women's literature – the protagonists may often reflect (and reflect on) the multiplicity of voices which inform a single narrative. In her perceptive essay on Caribbean women writers, Denise de Caires Narain (1998) wrote of the Jamaican novelist Erna Brodber's protagonists that they,

> are so intimately and densely embedded in the contexts of their communities and the boundaries between the individual and community are so blurred that to use terms such as 'protagonist' or 'character' is, in some sense, misleading. … Narrative attention seldom settles for sustained periods on any one moment or subject position; instead, Brodber circles back and forth over the same terrain, so that meanings proliferate and any understanding of the text can only work cumulatively. These are difficult but truly polyphonic texts – *noisy texts*, as it were.
>
> (Narain 1998: 264, her emphasis)

It is perhaps no coincidence that Erna Brodber is also a sociologist – and oral historian. 'The voice', she writes of one of her characters, 'belongs to the family group dead and alive. We walk by their leave, for planted in the soil, we must walk over them to get where we are going' (Brodber, quoted in Narain 1998: 264). C.L.R. James, too, was struck by the poetry in the language of ordinary people (Harney 1996). In these 'noisy' narratives individuals spill into families – siblings, who often do not share paternity, nevertheless grow up together 'as part of the family … because that is the order of the day'[8]; 'in my mum's family, to be quite honest, I just lumped everybody together, if she's my auntie, she's my auntie'[9] – and families spill into the community.

> My mother was plump, gorgeous. She was everybody's mum … everyone would be crying out as they're passing 'Hallo grandmother' … or 'Hallo, mother' … she was a community person … and I was cherished … by my family, by the community … that I remember, the community love. People just love you … the community had a parenting responsibility.[10]

What seems to link the oral narratives and much of the fiction is the lack of boundaries – genealogical, political (see Basch *et al.* 1994) and cultural. The Martiniquian novelist Chamoiseau talks in his novel *Texaco* (1997) of the 'boundless' city. What links the experience of West Indians, of migration – of the migrant and those left behind – is this sense of boundlessness, of an ever-permeable membrane through which emotions, subjectivities, identities flow, so that the global identities fuse with the local, while the generations and the genders become repositioned, boundless, as grandmothers are reborn as mothers, mothers emerge as breadwinners, siblings are co-joined through their mother, and lineage, the 'old ancestant', unifies. My mother, my grandmother, myself.

There is perhaps no conclusion to this chapter, no closure. The narratives are full and empty of their mothers, grandmothers, their families and lineages, of the 'overlapping diasporas and intertwining roots' of the Caribbean. They were their global selves which created, from their roots in the black diaspora and their personal migratory routes, a new syncretic self, caught in, but enriched by, the dialectical process of memory. Their stories are in many ways distinctive to the Caribbean, personifying and transmitting the cultural practices which others theorise over. Their sense of self, as an historical self is revealed in transgenerational life-stories, in the importance of family, what Angelita Reyes (1996) termed the 'olden ways of kinship', in the construction of the historic self. Let me return, finally, to Benjamin and suggest that historians should perhaps, at least in reading and interpreting oral testimony, begin to interpolate into the infinitely small in order to see the new expanse. There is, perhaps, more than one way of imagining the past.

Acknowledgements

This chapter is based on research (with Harry Goulbourne) on 'Living Arrangements, Family Structure and Social Change of Caribbeans in Britain', funded by the ESRC Award No.: L315253009 to whom grateful acknowledgement is given.

Notes

1 (With Harry Goulbourne) 'Living Arrangements, Family Structure and Social Change of Caribbeans in Britain', funded by the ESRC and part of the ESRC Research Programme on Population and Household Change.

2 Mary Chamberlain, *Narratives of Exile and Return*, University of Warwick Caribbean Studies Series, London: Macmillan (1997)

3 B/3/1/A/3. Mary Chamberlain, 'Barbados Migration Project'. Tapes deposited with the National Life Story Collection of the National Sound Archive of the British Library. Quoted in Chamberlain (1997a: 58, 140).

4 B28, 'Barbados Migration Project'.

5 'Living Arrangements, Family Structure and Social Change of Caribbeans in Britain', tape no. TC 058/2/1/1/5.

6 'Living Arrangements, Family Structure and Social Change of Caribbeans in Britain', tape no. JF 022.

7 *Ibid.*

8 'Living Arrangements, Family Structure and Social Change of Caribbeans in Britain', tape no. JI 028

9 'Living Arrangements, Family Structure and Social Change of Caribbeans in Britain', tape no. JB 008

10 'Living Arrangements, Family Structure and Social Change of Caribbeans in Britain', tape no. JI 028

Bibliography

Bakhtin, M. (1984) *The Dialogic Imagination*, Austin: University of Texas Press.

Banton, M. (1967) *Race Relations*, London: Tavistock Publications.

Basch, L., Glick Schiller, N. and Szanton Blanc, C. (1994) *Nations Unbound. Transnational Projects, Postcolonial Predicaments and Deterritorialized Nation States*, Reading: Gordon and Breach.

Benjamin, W. (1996) *One Way Street*, London: Verso.

Braithwaite, E.K. (1971) *The Development of Creole Society in Jamaica*, Oxford: Clarendon Press.

Brand, D. (1989) 'Photograph', in *Her True-True Name: Anthology of Women's Writing from the Caribbean*, London: Heinemann.

Chamberlain, M. (1997a) *Narratives of Exile and Return*, Houndsmills: Macmillan.

—— (1997b), 'Gender and the Narratives of Migration' *History Workshop* 43.

Chamberlain, M. and Goulbourne, H. (forthcoming) *Caribbean Families in Trans-Atlantic Perspective*.

Chamoiseau, P. (1997) *Texaco*, New York: Pantheon Books.

Craig-James, S. (1992) 'Intertwining Roots', *The Journal of Caribbean History* 26: 2.

Dench, J. (1996) *The Place of Men in Changing Family Cultures*, London: Institute of Community Studies.

Etter-Lewis, G. and Foster, M. (eds) (1996) *Unrelated Kin. Race and Gender in Women's Personal Narratives*, London: Routledge.

Gilroy, P. (1993) *The Black Atlantic*, London: Verso.

Goulbourne, H. (1999) 'The Transnational Character of Caribbean Kinship' in McRae, S. (ed.) *Household and Population Change*, Oxford: Oxford University Press.

Halbwachs, M. (1980) *The Collective Memory*, New York: Harper and Row.

Hall, S. (1996) 'Who Needs Identity?', in Hall, S. and du Gay, P., *Questions of Cultural Identity*, London: Sage.

Harney, S. (1996) *Nationalism and Identity. Culture and the Imagination in a Caribbean Diaspora*, Kingston: University of the West Indies/London: Zed Books.

Huxley, E. (1964) *Back Streets, New Worlds*, London: Chatto and Windus.

Jeater, D. (1992) 'Roast Beef and Reggae Music. The Passing of Whiteness', *New Formations* 18.

Kerns, V. (1997 [1984]) *Women and the Ancestors*, Chicago: University of Illinois Press.

Kopijn, Y. (1998) 'The Oral History Interview in a Cross-cultural Setting', in Chamberlain, M. and Thompson, P. (eds), *Narrative and Genre*, London: Routledge Studies in Memory and Narrative.

Lévi-Strauss, C. (1964) *Structural Anthropology*, New York: Basic Books.

Lewis, O. (1964 [1961]), *The Children of Sanchez*, Harmondsworth: Penguin.

Mintz, S. (1989 [1974]) *Caribbean Transformations*, New York: Columbia University Press.

Modood, T., Berthoud, R., Lakey, J., Nazroo, J., Smith, P., Virdee, S. and Beishon, S. (1997) *Ethnic Minorities in Britain: Diversity and Disadvantage*, PSI Report 843, London: Policy Studies Institute.

Narain, D. de C. (1998) 'Body Talk: Writing and Speaking the Body in the Texts of Caribbean Women Writers', in Barrow, C. (ed.), *Caribbean Portraits. Essays on Gender Ideologies and Identities*, Kingston: Ian Randle Publishers/Centre for Gender and Development Studies, University of the West Indies.

OPCS (Office of Population Census and Surveys) (1991) *1991 Census. Ethnic Group and Country of Birth Great Britain*, 2 vols, London: HMSO.

Passerini, L. (1996) *Autobiography of a Generation: Italy 1968*, Hanover and London: Wesleyan University Press.

Patterson, S. (1964) *Dark Strangers. A Study of West Indians in London*, London: Penguin.

Portelli, A. (1990) 'Uchronic Dreams: Working Class Memory and Possible Worlds', in Samuel, R. and Thompson, P. (eds), *The Myths We Live By*, London: Routledge.

—— (1998) 'Oral History as Genre', in Chamberlain, M. and Thompson, P., *Narrative and Genre*, London: Routledge Studies in Memory and Narrative.

Reyes, A. (1996) 'From a Lineage of Southern Women', in Etter-Lewis, G. and Foster, M. (eds), *Unrelated Kin. Race and Gender in Women's Personal Narratives*, London: Routledge.

Rose, N. (1996) 'Identity, Genealogy, History', in Hall, S and Du Guy, P. (eds), *Questions of Cultural Identity*, London: Sage.

Samuel, R. (1995) *Theatres of Memory*, London: Verso.

Sutton, C. (1997) 'Foreword', in Kerns, V., *Women and the Ancestors*, Chicago: University of Illinois Press.

Tonkin, E. (1990) 'History and the Myth of Realism', in Samuel R. and Thompson P., *The Myths We Live By*, London: Routledge.

—— (1992) *Narrating Our Past*, Cambridge: Cambridge University Press.

Wekker, G. (1997) 'One Finger Does Not Drink Okra Soup: Afro-Surinamese Women and Critical Agency', in Alexander, M.J. and Mohanty, C.T. (eds), *Feminist Genealogies, Colonial Legacies, Democratic Futures*, London: Routledge.

Wiltshire-Brodber, R. (1986) 'The Caribbean Transnational Family', UNESCO/ISER Eastern Caribbean Sub-regional Seminar, Cave Hill.

Part III

Memory

10 Subjects-in-time
Slavery and African-American women's autobiographies

Alison Easton

I shall, of course, start autobiographically.

In 1981–2 I was on a teaching exchange at the University of Texas at Austin. After initial shocks of difference and some mutual amusement, my students apparently settled quite happily, and I felt confident with pupils so hungry for knowledge and willing to engage in a critical dialogue on the making of American culture. The course, though it predated the multicultural debates on the curriculum, at least employed perspectives of gender, race and class, and while there weren't many African-American students in a university which had desegregated only in the 1960s, there were five in my section of fifty students (the rest were white or Chicano). I had taught European-Americans before, but never black Americans, nor for that matter Latinos. So, as I launched into an analysis of poems from the Harlem Renaissance (the great cultural flowering of the early decades of the twentieth century), I faltered inwardly: I was no longer a white Scotswoman, I was simply white, and my carefully acquired knowledge was about to be tested. I asked the African-American students to read out the poems in the class: 'I don't sound very black,' one demurred – 'A lot blacker than me,' I responded, without admitting that I didn't quite know what she meant. I began exploring the images of an ancient tribal African world in the poems – a reconstituted identification for black Americans that had been politically necessary to legitimate a nascent black culture in twentieth-century racist society but that had inevitably an element of the imaginary. This is not to say that great African civilisations had not existed in the past, but rather that the radical discontinuities of black history in the Americas made direct transmission impossible. Aware that all this might sound like negative criticism, I was proceeding cautiously with my analysis when one of my black students broke in with, 'I know what you mean. It's taken years for me to accept that *slavery* is my past.'

She credited me with more understanding than I really had at that time, and for that reason her comment has stayed with me as one of those moments which both make one realise what one doesn't know, and point to where one might start the task of finding out. A few weeks later Maya Angelou spoke at the university, starting her presentation with the same 1920s poem with which I had begun my first class on African-American writing. 'You are disgracefully igno-rant,' she good-humouredly harangued her audience (she directed her remarks to her black audience – more African-Americans than I had ever seen in one place at UT, and outnumbering the rest of the audience). She urged them to read, to study their own literature and their history.

There had been another more immediate follow-up. After my second class on these literary texts, two of the black students came to my office hour apparently quite angry. Without preamble they asked how many Education students were in the section (that is, students undergoing teacher-training – there were about five): why then were they silent in class, did they not realise they would need to teach this material in schools? I noted the role they had implicitly given me. And it was true: my clever and engaged class, which was normally a mass of raised hands whenever I asked for comment, had gone awfully quiet. I told the two students what I thought I could see from my position in front of the class – the faces of students who knew they didn't know and were listening attentively. It's a silence I have subsequently encountered with my white British students, who eagerly discuss most black novels, but fall silent on first meeting texts on slavery. Lancaster, I tell them each year, was the fourth largest slave port in Britain for part of the eighteenth century; this is their and my history too.

'No it isn't easy to forget/What we refuse to remember' (Nichols 1983: 19)

This chapter explores some of the implications of being a subject-in-time: if history is constitutive of identity, then which past is to be acknowledged, what relationships might one have to this past and what forms might this take in writing? I want to focus this discussion through autobiographies by African-American women concluding with Maya Angelou, and I shall start by considering why US slavery has been such a problematic history to establish and own.

The reluctance evinced by that student in the early 1980s about a slavery past that had ended less than 120 years previously can be readily paralleled with other examples, the best known being Toni Morrison's fictional exploration of post-slavery memory, *Beloved* (1986). As Morrison has observed,

> I thought this has got to be the least read of all the books I'd written because it is about something the characters don't want to remember, I don't want to remember, black people don't want to remember, white people don't want to remember.

(cited in Matus 1998: 103)

As Morrison's narrator paradoxically insists at the end of the novel, 'it was not a story to pass on' (Morrison 1987: 275). The double meaning of 'pass on' (to die, or to transmit) captures crucial ambivalences. Similarly, interviewed in 1937 as part of a Federal Writers Project recording very elderly ex-slaves, one woman commented, 'it is best not to have such things in our memory', before going on, nonetheless, to describe that life (Jones 1995: 13).

Even those who seek to deny the importance of that past in their autobiography, must first destroy that narrative – for example Zora Neale Hurston's *Dust Tracks on a Road*, published in 1942. Hurston was raised in an independent black township in Florida. The vehemence of her direct attack (even in the version her editor toned down for publication) on the continuing relevance of the traditional slave story is testimony to the power of this story's presence:

> Therefore, I see nothing but futility in looking back over my shoulder in rebuke at the grave of some white man who has been dead too long to talk about. That is just what I would be doing in trying to fix the blame for the dark days of slavery and the Reconstruction. From what I can learn, it was sad. Certainly. But my ancestors who lived and died in it are dead. The white men who profited by their labor and lives are dead also. I have no personal memory of those times, and no responsibility for them. Neither has the grandson of the men who held my folks.
>
> (Hurston 1986: 282)[1]

As my Texas student had spotted, Africentricity, that is the recourse to discourses of Africa as the place of origin, identity and destiny, has been another way of erasing consciousness of slavery times, both in the early years of the twentieth century and during the heights of black nationalism in the 1960s. Paul Gilroy sees this recourse to Africa as mythic rather than historical, providing a shelter against racism, and states that in consequence, 'there is a danger that ... slavery becomes a cluster of negative associations that are best left behind' (Gilroy 1993a: 189). As bell hooks comments in conversation with Gilroy, 'We have very little work that tries to connect slavery to the periods that follow it. I would like there to be psycho-histories ...' (Gilroy 1993b: 215). Toni Morrison remarked on how slavery had not been strongly present in American literary writings (Gilroy 1993b: 179); it has been only with the acceptance of the full range of historical experience by post-nationalist black writers that there have been many novels about slavery in recent years (Byerman 1991; McDowell 1989).

Morrison ascribes some of this cultural amnesia to a more general lack of interest in the past that is an important element in the dominant ideology of the American nation:

> We live in a land where the past is always erased and America is the innocent future in which immigrants come and start over, where the slate is clean. The past is absent or it's romanticized. This culture doesn't encourage dwelling on, let alone coming to terms with, the truth about the past.
>
> (Gilroy 1993b: 179)

The cultural power of this notion can be gauged by the way it has flourished in spite of the fact that, unlike slaves from Africa, on entry to the USA European immigrants held onto a version of their ethnic cultures and identities over several generations. However, it is a convenient philosophy for those whose power or comfort is built on others' labour. Furthermore as Gilroy shows, the culture of modernity has omitted the history of slavery from its own narrative of the past, even though modern life began with chattel slavery (Gilroy 1993a): hooks concurs, 'the buried history that isn't about that vision of progress is never invoked' (Gilroy 1993b: 216).

But slavery was not simply forgotten: for the illiterate ex-slave with few if any possessions and whose people had no written history, all she or he had was memory (Gates 1986). Even when slaves had no connection with their father or had been irrevocably separated from mother, siblings or extended family, they were still surrounded by fellow survivors. Unlike the Holocaust, there were over four million survivors in 1865. There are records: not only the 115 personal narratives by former slaves published between 1760 and 1930, but notably the 2,000 oral testimonies gathered by the Federal Writers Project (also known as the WPA narratives), as well as other, often brief interview material. Although estimates as high as some 6,000 items of personal testimony have been contested, nonetheless a significant body of material exists, in spite of this being disproportionally small compared to the total slave population (Forster 1994: 21–2). Story-telling, too, went on, transmitting memories orally, although with the mass migration to northern cities and the dying out of the slave-born generation, this may have largely ceased as the twentieth century progressed.

Yet professional historians, setting out to reconstruct chattel slavery in detail (something which proved highly contested, given partial and ambiguous evidence), were wary at first of using such testimonies. Notoriously, Harriet Jacobs' *Incidents in the Life of a Slave Girl: Written by Herself* (1865) came to be considered a work of fiction until the 1980s (Jacobs 1987). Antebellum slave narratives made greater truth-claims than most other autobiographical forms, but there are several reasons why such autobiographical writings were sidelined historiographically. These accounts are hard to generalise from: 35 per cent of slave narratives were written by fugitives, yet only 5 per cent of the total slave population escaped successfully; slavery varied both by region (escaped slaves mainly came from the border states, the FWP narratives from further south) and by gender (because of family commitments far fewer women escaped to write their story). Moreover, published slave narratives were written for an entirely white audience and for distinct political purposes (abolition before the war, and then, post-Emancipation, negotiations about black Americans' new status). As for FWP interviewers, they were overwhelmingly white, some even related to former slaveholders, and the transcription of the conversations into written form was governed by guidelines heavily affected by white preconceptions about black speech (Yetman 1984; see also Parish 1989).

The horrific nature of that history is obviously another key factor both in the contested, incomplete nature of those memories and in the reluctance to embrace this past as constitutive of one's identity. The ex-slave Sethe's idea of 'rememory' in *Beloved* resembles less the common processes of memory than those of trauma, given the way she sees the past as intact and ever present. The effects were severe. As Nell Irvin Painter observes when she calls for a study of slavery's psychological costs, 'sexual abuse, emotional deprivation, and physical and mental torture can lead to soul murder'. Furthermore, the abusers wanted their victims to be silent (Painter 1995: 128; Fleischner 1996: 11–31).

Moreover, since trauma need not be caused only by a single unassimilated, overwhelming event, but may instead be the response to persisting conditions over a long period (Brown 1995), the conditions for trauma among slaves were widespread. This form of trauma, as Kai Erikson observes, has 'a social dimension': 'traumatic wounds inflicted in individuals can combine to create a mood, an ethos – a group culture, almost – that is different from (and more than) the sum of the private wounds that make it up' (Erikson 1995: 185). Characteristic also of trauma is the absence of the 'ordinary' world, and consequently the lack of immediate external witness (even though slave narratives, public debate and a civil war constituted generalised recognition). A more immediate problem is that the nineteenth- and early twentieth-century personal narratives that we might use to analyse psychological states of ex-slaves withhold so much: though stressing the centrality of these slavery writings for black readers, Morrison observes, 'they were silent about many things, and they "forgot" many other things. .... But most importantly – at least for me – there was no mention of their interior life' (Morrison 1987: 110).[2]

Some of this 'silence' must be ascribed to the writers' awareness of their first audiences. Autobiographies of ex-slaves typically veiled their experiences so that a sheltered, squeamish and sexually reticent white audience would read them. We can, however, ask whether the survivors of slavery were also literally silent, for example in the way survivors of the Holocaust have characteristically been for their children. Nadine Fresco in 'Remembering the Unknown' describes the experience of a number of French Jews born shortly after World War Two: 'Parents explained nothing, children asked nothing.' She notes that there were no mementoes, and where there was any speech at all about the past, the forbidden memory of death was concealed behind a 'screen of words ... always the same words' of a heavily selected narrative (Fresco 1984: 418, 419; see also Raczymow 1994).

I want to suggest that the children of those surviving slavery in the USA did not encounter silence in the same way. Consider, for example, the account that Ida Wells gives of her ex-slave parents. Wells, who led an important anti-lynching campaign in the 1890s, was born a slave in 1862. In the first chapter of her autobiography, *Crusade for Justice* (written 1928–31 and published posthumously), she describes both her mother who told her about her life in bondage, and her father who spoke of slavery just once and only in order to refuse to meet his ex-owner, who had asked to see his children. He remembered the beating that mistress had given his mother: 'I'll never forget how she had you stripped and whipped the day after the old man died' (Wells 1970: 10). The situation was made more complicated because the beaten woman, Wells's now free grand-mother, was caring for her former mistress. Wells comments:

> I was burning to ask what he [her father] meant, but children were seen and
> not heard in those days. They didn't dare break into old folks' conversation.
> But I have never forgotten those words. Since I have grown old enough to
> understand I cannot help but feel what an insight into slavery they give.
>
> (Wells 1970: 10)

This does not seem to be the same kind of silence as the one Fresco describes
above. Group trauma may not necessarily function in the same way as individual
trauma (even though, as Cathy Caruth notes, Freud's theorising implies that it
does, Caruth 1996: 136). In Wells's account we have a community, in this case an
extended family, working out how its memories will govern its present actions.
The child may ask very little, but knows at least something and can extrapolate
more. She is alert to the importance of her family past; the past is present. In the
case of slavery, nearly everyone in a community had shared and survived the
experience, even though they were permanently affected by it (many of the esti-
mated third of all slave families separated by auction never traced their lost
family members after the war). When Harriet Jacobs asks, 'O reader, can you
imagine my joy?', and continues, 'No, you cannot, unless you have been a slave
mother,' the point at issue is not simply that her white readers cannot grasp her
experience, but that her fellow slaves, though mostly unable to read her story,
certainly could understand (Jacobs 1987: 173).

Studies of how a community, for example Quiche Mayan women in 1978–85
Guatemala (Zur 1997) or Japanese Canadian Second World War internees
(McAllister 1999), may record their catastrophic experiences for a later generation may give us insights into the complex ways in which memories of US
slavery could have been transmitted. These include the 'remembering' of events
within one's own community which one did not directly experience. In the
context of a still hostile state or wider social indifference or amnesia such unoffi-
cial, secret memories are difficult to integrate. It may be dangerous even later to
recount them openly, yet they are nonetheless recounted to some extent. Given
generational change, migration and assimilation policies, collective memory is
not ready-made and transmitted whole within a community but is produced, as
Kirsten McAllister argues, with difficulty and dialogically between oral testimonies and later listeners (see also Kirmeyer 1996).

Marianne Hirsch's theory of postmemory addresses this question of how later
generations might relate to the traumatic experience of their forebears (though
Hirsch's analysis is primarily concerned with the second generation and the
Holocaust). Postmemory, as Hirsch conceives it, is a 'cultural act of identification
and affiliation' (Hirsch 1999: 7) whereby a strong connection is 'mediated not
through recollection but imaginative investment and creation' (Hirsch 1997: 22):

> it is a question of adopting the traumatic experiences – and thus also the
> memories – of others as one's own, or, more precisely, as experiences one
> might oneself have had, and of inscribing them into one's own life-story.
>
> (Hirsch 1999: 9)

Hirsch is describing a kind of memory that is cultural and communal (however individually inflected). Its constructed nature is clear: as Ernst van Alphen observes, '[m]emory is not something we have, but something we produce *as individuals sharing a culture*' (Van Alphen 1999: 37).

Postmemory is thus constitutive of individual experience and identity. For African-American autobiographers this particular act of identification is a way of making sense of their own lives. Furthermore, as it works communally, post-memory is one of the means by which 'counter memory', to use George Lipsitz's term, is formed:

> Counter-memory is a way of remembering and forgetting that starts with the local, the immediate, and the personal. ... Counter-memory looks to the past for the hidden histories excluded from the dominant narratives. But unlike myths that seek to detach events and actions from the fabric of any larger history, counter-memory forces the revision of existing histories by supplying new perspectives about the past.
>
> (Lipsitz 1990: 213)

Sites of memory

It is slave narratives that play the central role in the formation of African-American postmemory. The first major genre by black Americans and the earliest attempt to produce a historical record of slavery, these narratives had from the outset deliberately combined an individual life-story with a more gener-alised communal account of shared conditions and socially significant events. The aim was to expose the facts of slavery: first-person narration was chosen because it formed a personal testimony and because it proved the slave's full humanity. Although often edited and introduced by white abolitionists, these narratives were importantly an account by black voices. They testify to the communally experienced effects of 'persistent trauma', as well as demonstrating that combination of the personal with group experience characteristic of both postmemory and counter-memory.

Toni Morrison has testified to the importance of these narratives ('a very large part of my own literary heritage is the autobiography', Morrison 1987: 103). Morr-ison notes the absence even in the 1980s of national or state memorials to slavery:

> There is no place you or I can go, to think about or not think about, to summon the presences of, or recollect the absences of slaves; nothing that reminds us of the ones who made the journey and of those who did not make it. There is no suitable memorial or plaque or wreath or wall or park or skyscraper lobby. There's no 300-foot tower. There's no small bench by the road. There is not even a tree scored, an initial that I can visit, or you can visit in Charleston or Savannah or New York or Providence, or better still, on the banks of the Mississippi.
>
> (Matus 1998: 30)

The continuing importance of the slave narrative in the formation of African-American identities, however, was not always apparent to black Americans. After Emancipation slaves had expected to put slavery behind them. Before the war slave narratives had had a clear political purpose – abolition. Slave narratives continued to be written after abolition in order to show the courage, resourcefulness and moral stature of slaves and therefore their right to a place in mainstream society. In this context slavery was now seen as a school rather than a prison (Andrews 1989). Even then, slavery could be downplayed. Elizabeth Keckley's *Behind the Scenes: Or Thirty Years a Slave, and Four Years in the White House* (1868) devotes just three chapters to those thirty years (a sixth of the autobiography) and the rest to being dressmaker to President Lincoln's wife. Although Keckley begins with a highly conventionalised though greatly abbreviated repetition of the standard slavery topics (separation of parents, floggings, death, rape), she soon starts to revise her relationship with slavery, stressing that she bought her freedom, having refused to flee, and devoting a chapter to a loving reunion with her former owners. She ends the story of an uncle who killed himself to avoid punishment with the extraordinary statement, 'Slavery had its dark side as well as its bright side' (Keckley 1988: 30). The underlying Reconstruction political agenda of reconciliation with the South (a largely white and short-lived agenda) undermines the traditional narrative of liberation.

However, postbellum racism proved Keckley's aspirations to be local wish-fulfilment. By the end of the century most southern blacks were no better off than during slavery, and in the northern states African-Americans were almost universally regarded as inferior. Black Americans could not continue to write their lives in the classic way as a movement from bondage to freedom. As the turn of the century black leader W.E.B. du Bois realised, their lives had turned out to be a movement 'from a simple bondage to a more complex bondage' (Rampersad 1989: 118). As one commentator of the period remarked, they 'knew that what they got wasn't what they wanted, it wasn't freedom, really' (Jones 1995: 81). Arguably black women had long known this, since Emancipation had not dismantled patriarchal structures. The ways in which family life, paid work, the black community and relations with a violent, racist white community have been structured for African-Americans in the past century and a half since Emancipation can be directly traced to slavery, whether as continuities or choices made in reaction to previous conditions (see Jones 1995). Ida Wells's understanding of this informed both her 1890s campaign against lynching and her subsequent autobiography with its clear roots in the antebellum abolitionist narratives.

So slave narratives, oral and written, go on being the primary, possibly unavoidable shaping narrative for African-American experience, autobiography and fiction (see Stepto 1985; Gates 1986; Braxton 1989). They have become what Pierre Nora terms a *lieu de mémoire* (site of memory) (Nora 1989). Focusing on national memory (but clearly relevant to subsections of a nation), Nora argues that acts of memory proliferate round points where there is a sense of discontinuity with or loss of the past: 'the sense that memory has been torn – but torn in such a way as to pose the problem of the embodiment of memory in certain sites where a sense of historical continuity persists' (Nora 1989: 7). The intention to remember is central to such sites. These 'sites' may be written texts, public anniversary celebrations, buildings and other places, historical and imagined persons, artworks, political movements and other kinds of cultural object. Memory here is 'collective, plural, and yet individual' (Nora 1989: 9).[3]

These sites are subject to creative negotiation: as Nora noted, they have to be hybrid and permanently evolving or they lose their cultural function. Slave narratives and later African-American autobiographies constitute a dynamic, eclectic genre, capable of adaptation (Stepto 1985; Forster 1994). This process of adaptation and evolution started by taking discourses of the dominant white culture, in particular those of individualism and political independence, the picaresque, the spiritual autobiography and abolitionist fiction and polemic to make slave narratives, and continues in later African-American autobiography.

Black women are important adapters of the genre, negotiating creatively with a form written largely by men (only thirteen of the 115 personal narratives by former slaves published in the USA between 1760 and 1920 were by women). As Jean Fagin Yellin demonstrates in relation to Harriet Jacobs, instead of a story of the lone male achieving literacy, freedom and manhood, women's slave narratives are about sexual abuse, motherhood, the search for freedom for her children, and supportive family (especially female) networks (Jacobs 1987). Hardest of all to deal with was her sexual history, her history of a raced female body. Women had to negotiate their identity through highly inadequate discourses of conventional, white images of femininity; they eschew victimhood. Post-slavery black women's autobiographies have continued these complex negotiations in relation to lives that were different from black men's not only in the home and in the black community but crucially at work and in the white public space (see Jones 1995).

All autobiography is, of course, by its very nature an unfinished story, but slave narratives are particularly painful in their lack of conclusion. The legal freedom from chattel slavery that the narratives ultimately record is hollowed out by the endemic racism of the 'free' society the autobiographer has come to live within. Their journey continues. For Maya Angelou, born 1928, this becomes a literal travelling, criss-crossing the USA, touring in Europe and living in Africa, yet aware that a white psychiatrist could never understand that the American South, her childhood home, is a place that 'I left, yet would never, could never, leave' (Angelou 1977: 234). In her sequence of five autobiographical volumes, written between 1970 and 1986, Angelou continues, adapts and possibly alters the narrative begun by fugitive slaves, and with this changes both how the past is memorialised, and herself as a subject-in-time.

To see these changes we need all five volumes of her autobiography. The first volume, *I Know Why the Caged Bird Sings*, describing her childhood in Arkansas, seems to continue the female slave narrative, though crucially adapted. Although this volume makes little reference to slavery, for black Americans until the 1960s, the deeply segregated South terrifyingly embodied the past that they had hoped to leave behind, the effects of which persisted everywhere. This is a gendered account. Maya's sexual history (she is raped by her mother's black lover at the age of eight) is reminiscent of, yet also contrastive to the sexual violations endured by women slaves, and suggests the aftermath of slavery in damaged relations between black men and women. The adolescent Maya attempts some degree of autonomy, typical of that constructed in the male slave narrative, in seeking a white person's job, but she is constantly pulled from that trajectory by the demands of motherhood. Motherhood was the keynote of the female slave narrative: the slave mother fought to keep her children and often lost. Here Maya's mother has to send her children away to her mother. But Angelou herself becomes a mother (albeit by mistake at sixteen) and her fight to raise her father-less son is one of the key themes across all five volumes, as she seeks both to protect the fatherless child and encourage in him a masculinity that will neither oppress women, nor be destroyed by the white world.

While this work displays more candour than Jacobs's, Angelou still faces prob-lems: she is addressing a racially mixed audience, so her account of her rape attracted criticism from some black readers. Despite the appearance of openness her story has its silences; it is not safe to be too open. She quotes a black American saying, ' "If you ask a Negro where he's been, he'll tell you where he's going" ' (Angelou 1971: 164). It's an odd motto for an autobiographer, but in drawing attention to such a strategy she signals the existence of a black world that still cannot be shared.

Increasingly, however, Angelou does tell 'where she has been' in order to be able to see where she and her people are going. This is signalled early in the next volume, *Gather Together in My Name* (1975), when she revisits the South and refers to the lynching her brother had witnessed – she had told this obliquely in the previous volume, and this time we do glimpse the horror. Angelou is aware, and indeed in her first volume had demonstrated, how blacks had learnt when not to speak (she herself had refused to speak for a long time as a child). Angelou understands this self-silencing as having created a special subjectivity for women, who, in conditions of appalling brutality, had to find 'safety and sanctity' and self-forgiveness inside themselves because 'often their exterior actions were at odds with their interior beliefs': 'Lives lived in such cauldrons are either obliter-ated or forged into impenetrable alloys. Thus, early on, black women became realities only to themselves' (Angelou 1998: 42). As she comments later in her autobiography, 'Over centuries of oppression we had developed a doctrine of resistance which included false docility and sarcasm' (Angelou 1987: 158). She then immediately adds, 'We also had a most un-African trait: we were nearly always ready and willing to fight.' It is this fighting which comes to the fore in Angelou's life-story, told as it is in a series of outspoken encounters, confronta-tions, conversations – a life in dialogue with whites, with African-Americans, with Africans. This autobiography is not processed by white editors as the slave narratives and even Hurston's were.

Angelou did not originally set out to write her autobiography – 'I wasn't thinking so much about my own life or identity' (Tate 1985: 6). The four volumes dealing with her adult life, though preoccupied with her many achievements as dancer, singer, journalist and political activist, do not send out an individualistic message, since like the slave narratives before her, she is primarily concerned with the underlying commonalties in her experiences and the sense of a shared culture. The long string of anecdotes in these volumes are part of a larger narrative about 'slavery' of her people and freedom. Tensions between white and black are a constant given in her texts, and although, like the nineteenth-century narrative, her story represents a battle for freedom and justice, unlike that narrative it shows that, while battles can be won, the war against racism goes on and on. In consequence, these narratives cannot structure their material to a clear end as did the nineteenth-century autobiographies.

A sense of US history as a slaveholding history pervades the volumes as her means of understanding and responding to an always racialised present. There are scattered references to slavery in the third volume, *Singin' and Swingin' and Gettin' Merry Like Christmas*, and in the fourth volume, *The Heart of a Woman*, which deals with her Civil Rights campaign work, the slave past surfaces repeatedly and explicitly to connect with the present: ' "If you're black in this country, you're on a plantation" ' (Angelou 1986: 33).

A counter-memory is being formed for the reader. More than that, Angelou's experience of history finally changes. Whereas in the third volume she gains a renewed sense of a rich slave 'heritage' in singing spirituals (Angelou 1977: 170), it is her years in Africa, a world almost never present in slave narratives because lost to memory, that take her narrative to a new place in the final volume, *All God's Children Need Travelling Shoes*. Africa is not the imagined place of earlier African-American poetry, nor had Angelou consciously come to find her roots. She experienced herself as an American in Ghana. At one early point there she attempts with deliberate artifice to recreate in her imagination the slave-trade scene of capture, and fails. When she feels the past restored, it is not through the discourse of slave narratives. Indeed, she moves beyond the textuality of that memory to the body as history: 'descendants of a pillaged past saw their history in my face and heard their ancestors speak through my voice' (Angelou 1987: 207).[4]

Significantly placed as the culminating event of the five-volume autobiography is a visit Angelou makes to Keta, a town in northwest Ghana, most of whose population was once taken by traders, leaving only children to pass on the memory down the generations. After an experience of *déjà vu* on the road to the town, when Angelou feels dread in a place of long past disaster, she encounters in Keta market a woman who looks exactly like her grandmother and who misrecognises her for a Ghanaian acquaintance. When with difficulty the woman is persuaded that Angelou is American, she and then the other market people one by one in tears mourn their stolen ancestors with a particular gesture of grieving that Angelou recognises from her childhood in the American South (where its meaning has become simply bad luck).

The idea of postmemory seems useful here in looking at the power and meaning of this event for these African and American 'children' of slavery, alike in their displacement from a space of identity. Marianne Hirsch focuses on two possibilities within postmemory: a melancholic acting out, or alternatively a working through of these memories as a process of mourning (see Dominick LaCapra, cited by Hirsch 1999: 16). Keta's public mourning brings a 'curious joy' (Angelou 1987: 207): what is it about this space that makes such mourning possible?

Hirsch argues that the form postmemory takes is not that of testimony, but imaginative reconstruction; this facilitates mourning by restoring something of what was destroyed (Hirsch 1997: 247–50). In Keta the combined bodily presence of descendants of those taken in slavery and of those 'orphans' left behind obviate the need for *imaginative* reconstruction. This postmemorial act of grief finds a language of the body – Angelou's and the Africans' – with which to work through the shared trauma. Their survival on both sides of the Atlantic bears witness, each for the other, to continuities as well as losses. True, it leaves unresolved the issues of social justice that problematically haunt attempts at mourning by survivors of state persecution and mass slaughter (see Frazier 1999). Angelou will not remain in Africa. No longer exiled in spite of slavery ('for now I know my people had never completely left Africa', Angelou 1987: 208), she ends her autobiography at the point of return to the USA, where the fight against racism continues. As Cathy Caruth observes, at the heart of trauma lies not only the repetition of death but also that of survival (Angelou's key understanding at Keta), and with it the possibility of creative witness and a language of parting that moves the participant forwards into life (Caruth 1999).

Notes

1 See Lionnet (1993) and Raynaud (1992), for the complex underlying explanations of Hurston's position.
2 Historians of slavery have been reluctant to use psychoanalytic theories (see Fleischner 1996: 11–32), and there are problems of mapping theories of infantile sexual trauma onto such very different events and contexts.
3 See Fabre and O'Meally (1994), for an extended exploration of Nora's thesis in relation to black American cultural texts (including slave narratives: 263–4).
4 For the 'body as history', see Easton (1994). In my view, the Keta incident overrides the opposition created by Nora between such body-memories and other types of memory:

> [W]e should be aware of the difference between true memory, which has taken refuge in gestures and habits, in skills passed down by unspoken traditions, in the body's inherent self-knowledge, in unstudied reflexes and ingrained memories, and memory transformed by its passage through history, which is nearly the opposite: voluntary and deliberate, experienced as a duty, no longer spontaneous; psychological, individual, and subjective; but never social, collective, or all encompassing.
>
> (Nora 1989: 13)

Bibliography

Andrews, W.L. (ed.) (1988) *Six Women's Slave Narratives*, New York: Oxford University Press.

—— (1989) 'The Presentation of Slavery and the Rise of Afro-American Literary Realism, 1865–1930', in D.E. McDowell and A. Rampersad (eds), *Slavery and the Literary Imagination*, Baltimore: Johns Hopkins University Press.

Angelou, M. (1971) *I Know Why the Caged Bird Sings*, New York: Bantam.

—— (1975) *Gather Together in My Name*, New York: Bantam.

—— (1977) *Singin' and Swingin' and Gettin' Merry Like Christmas*, New York: Bantam.

—— (1986) *The Heart of a Woman*, London: Virago.

—— (1987) *All God's Children Need Travelling Shoes*, London: Virago.

—— (1998) *Even the Stars Look Lonesome*, London: Virago.

Braxton, J.M. (1989) *Black Women Writing Autobiography: A Tradition Within a Tradition*, Philadelphia: Temple University Press.

Brown, L. (1995) 'Not Outside the Range: One Feminist Perspective on Psychic Trauma', in C. Caruth (ed.), *Trauma: Explorations in Memory*, Baltimore: Johns Hopkins University Press.

Byerman, K. (1991) 'Remembering History in Contemporary Black Literature and Criticism', *American Literary History* 3, 4: 809–16.

Caruth, C. (1996) *Unclaimed Experience: Trauma, Narrative, and History*, Baltimore: Johns Hopkins University Press.

—— (1999) 'Parting Words: Trauma, Silence and Survival', paper given at 'Testimonial Culture and Feminist Agendas' conference, Lancaster University, May.

Easton, A. (1994) 'The Body as History and "Writing the Body": The Example of Grace Nichols', *Journal of Gender Studies* 3: 55–67.

Erikson, K. (1995) 'Notes on Trauma and Community', in C. Caruth (ed.), *Trauma: Explorations in Memory*, Baltimore: Johns Hopkins University Press.

Fabre, G. and O'Meally, G. (eds) (1994) *History and Memory in African-American Culture*, New York: Oxford University Press.

Fleischner, J. (1996) *Mastering Slavery: Memoir, Family, and Identity in Women's Slave Narratives*, New York: New York University Press.

Forster, F. (1994) *Witnessing Slavery: The Development of Ante-Bellum Slave Narratives*, 2nd edn, Madison: University of Wisconsin Press.

Frazier, L.J. (1999) '"Subverted Memories": Countermourning as Political Action in Chile', in M. Ball, J. Crewe and L. Spitzer (eds), *Acts of Memory: Cultural Recall in the Present*, Hanover: Dartmouth College.

Fresco, N. (1984) 'Remembering the Unknown', *International Review of Psychoanalysis* 11:417–27.

Gates, H.L., Jr (1986) *Figures in Black: Words, Signs, and the 'Racial' Self*, New York: Oxford University Press.

Gilroy, P. (1993a) *The Black Atlantic: Modernity and Double Consciousness*, London: Verso.

—— (1993b) *Small Acts*, London: Serpent's Tail.

Hirsch, M. (1997) *Family Frames: Photography, Narrative, and Postmemory*, Cambridge, MA: Harvard University Press.

—— (1999) 'Projected Memory: Holocaust Photographs in Personal and Public Fantasy', in M. Ball, J. Crewe and L. Spitzer (eds) *Acts of Memory: Cultural Recall in the Present*, Hanover: Dartmouth College.

Hurston, Z.N. (1986) *Dust Tracks on a Road: An Autobiography*, London: Virago.

Jacobs, H.A. (1987) *Incidents in the Life of a Slave Girl: Written by Herself*, ed. J.F. Yellin, Cambridge, MA: Harvard University Press.

Jones, J. (1995) *Labor of Love, Labor of Sorrow: Black Women, Work, and the Family from Slavery to the Present*, New York: Vintage.

Keckley, E. (1988) *Behind the Scenes: Or Thirty Years a Slave, and Four Years in the White House*, New York: Oxford University Press.

Kirmeyer, L.J. (1996) 'Landscapes of Memory: Trauma, Narrative, and Dissociation', in P. Antze and M. Lambek (eds), *Tense Past: Cultural Essays in Trauma and Memory*, New York: Routledge.

Lionnet, F. (1993) 'Autoethnography: The An-Archic Style of *Dust Tracks on a Road*', in Andrews, W.L. (ed.), *African American Autobiography: A Collection of Critical Essays*, Englewood Cliffs, NJ: Prentice Hall.

Lipsitz, G. (1990) *Time Passages: Collective Memory and American Popular Culture*, Minneapolis: University of Minnesota Press.

McAllister, K.E. (1999) 'Re-Building Historically Persecuted Communities: Re-Constituting Fixed Configurations of Community Life or Exploring Dialogic Possibilities', paper given at 'Testimonial Culture and Feminist Agendas' conference, Lancaster University, May.

McDowell, D.E. (1989) 'Negotiating Between Tenses: Witnessing Slavery After Freedom – *Dessa Rose*', in D.E. McDowell and A. Rampersad (eds), *Slavery and the Literary Imagination*, Baltimore: Johns Hopkins University Press.

Matus, J. (1998) *Toni Morrison*, Manchester: Manchester University Press.

Morrison, T. (1986) *Beloved*, London: Chatto and Windus.

—— (1987) 'The Site of Memory', in W. Zinsser (ed.), *Inventing the Truth: The Art and Craft of Memoir*, Boston: Houghton Mifflin.

Nichols, G. (1983) '*Taint*', *i is a long memoried woman*, London: Karnak House.

Nora, P. (1989) 'Between Memory and History: Les Lieux de Mémoire', *Representations* 26: 7–25.

Painter, N.I. (1995) 'Soul Murder and Slavery: Toward a Fully Loaded Cost Accounting', in L.K. Kerber, A. Kessler-Harris and K.K. Sklar (eds), *U.S. History as Women's History: New Feminist Essays*, Chapel Hill: University of North Carolina Press.

Parish, P.J. (1989) *Slavery: History and Historians*, New York: Harper and Row.

Raczymow, H. (1994) 'Memory Shot Through with Holes', *Yale French Studies* 85, 1: 98–105.

Rampersad, A. (1989) 'Slavery and the Literary Imagination: Du Bois's *The Souls of Black Folk*', in D.E. McDowell and A. Rampersad (eds), *Slavery and the Literary Imagination*, Baltimore: Johns Hopkins University Press.

Raynaud, C. (1992) '"Rubbing a Paragraph with a Soft Cloth"?: Muted Voices and Editorial Constraints in *Dust Tracks on a Road*', in S. Smith and J. Watson, (eds), *De/Colonizing the Subject: The Politics of Gender in Women's Autobiography*, Minneapolis: University of Minnesota Press.

Stepto, R.B. (1985) 'I Rose and Found My Voice: Narration, Authentication, and Authorial Control in Four Slave Narratives', in C.T. Davis and H.L. Gates Jr (eds), *The Slave's Narrative*, Oxford: Oxford University Press.

Tate, C. (ed.) (1985) *Black Women Writers at Work*, Harpenden: Oldcastle Books.

Van Alphen, E. (1999) 'Symptoms of Discursivity: Experience, Memory, and Trauma', in M. Bal, J. Crewe and L. Spitzer (eds), *Acts of Memory: Cultural Recall in the Present*, Hanover: Dartmouth College.

Wells, I.B. (1970) *Crusade for Justice: The Autobiography of Ida B. Wells*, ed. A.M. Duster, Chicago: University of Chicago Press.

Yetman, N.R. (1984) 'Ex-Slave Interviews and the Historiography of Slavery', *American Quarterly* 36: 165–210.

Zur, J. (1997) 'Reconstructing the Self through Memories of Violence among Mayan Indian War Widows', in R. Lentin (ed.), *Gender and Catastrophe*, London: Zed Books.

11 Memory frames

The role of concepts and cognition in telling life-stories

Magda Michielsens

This chapter is a reflection on the difficulties of remembering and narrating when the concepts that framed past experience have lost their meaning. Stories become difficult to tell when the frame of reference in which experiences were originally placed has evaporated. This is more than an emotional problem; it is a cognitive one. A paradigm shift makes this cognitive difficulty extreme. We are familiar with the examples of autobiographical stories of lives that have passed through wars and revolutions, but the same phenomenon arises in the case of less dramatic transitions too.

This is a particular case of a general problem in oral history research. The way that memory works, poses much greater difficulties than simply the process of forgetting. How is research on the reconstruction of life histories possible, given that remembering is inherently a selective process, guided by the life experiences of the subjects in the research? The combination of social reality, current ideology, personal capacity for remembering, language and cognitive mapping dictates the life-story. How is an academic use of life histories possible, given the relationship between memory, language and social reality?

My discussion of the cognitive difficulty of life-story telling has a specific focus on research which I did in the early nineties in Bulgaria. The main concern of this chapter is with the impact on memory and autobiographical practices of changes in the frame of reference. I shall approach the issue of memory-telling through the intersubjective dimensions of the research, that is those that relate to the interaction between researcher and respondent and their constructions of each other. Analysing the findings of this research was unexpectedly hard, not least because of the difficulties I had in understanding my experiences as a researcher while I was doing the fieldwork. The chapter itself is thus in part autobiographical. It is a narrative of the problems I had in trying to elicit memory stories from respondents who had rejected the concepts and cognitive frameworks of the past which I was asking them to recall. I will illustrate my points with fragments from the life histories of three women who took part in my research, and draw some conclusions concerning memory, concepts and cognition in research on the life histories of women.

The question

The methodological problem that has imposed itself on me each time I have done fieldwork for an oral history project, is the question of the (dis)continuity of the consciousness of the respondents. The problem is well known: as time goes by, the frame of reference, the vocabulary, the connotations of concepts and of value systems change. The content and structure of the cognitive maps that respondents use change so much that it becomes difficult to verbalise previous experiences so as to express what happened. The concepts that helped in modelling the experience lose their meaning. This is not primarily an individual process, as in the case of emotions and feelings that wither away. Rather, it is a social process in which, when the ideological context has changed, words lose their power to express earlier experiences. Without the contemporary concepts, stories become very difficult to tell.

These conceptual dynamics pose a methodological problem for all historians: how do you analyse an historical period using the theoretical framework of the moment of the research? The same problem appears in everyday life. It is a permanent challenge to create continuity in one's life, while social and cultural changes are happening all the time. Agnes Hankiss (1981, referred to by Daphne Patai 1991: 148) explains how, when speakers tell their life, they charge certain episodes with symbolic meaning. Telling the facts transforms them into myths. Hankiss argues that this process never ends. An adult always has to find new models and strategies to live. Telling the stories changes the memory of the stream of events.

Concepts are a necessary part of the strategy people use to create continuity in their life. In oral history we are confronted with the gap between the concepts of the present and the past, and with the strategies people use in their longing for continuity. As a researcher one meets, in the first place, the (implicit) view of the respondent about her position in the historical narrative: what does she think happened, what does she think the 'facts' were? Second, the story told will be highly dependent on the way the respondent creates (and has been creating) continuity in her life. This is the fundamental methodological problem of oral history. It is engaged in a struggle with 'framed experiences'. The double meaning of 'framed' is useful to elaborate this point: frames are the indispensable organisers of experience, but at the same time these frames inevitably transform and betray experience. From the start experiences and emotions are framed by cognitions, and to revitalise and recount memories (and tell them to researchers), cognitive frames must be mobilised and (re)constructed. The relationship between frame 1 and frame x depends on both the respondent's personality and the social, political and cultural circumstances.

In 1997 I edited a special issue of *The European Journal for Women's Studies* on 'Women, War and Conflict'. In the collected articles it was clear that for the authors (independent from each other) the question of the conceptual prerequisites of memory played a central role. War and conflict are events that in most cases imply a shift in discourse and ideology. Even the most motivated witnesses often don't have the words to tell how it all happened.

In the 'Women, War and Conflict' issue of the *EJWS* Halleh Ghorashi illustrates the impact of the conceptual frame upon the experiences of Iranian exiled women in the Netherlands. She reflects upon her own experience while doing the interviews.

> I discovered that I could travel back to the past because of the character of some of the interviews. I realised this in a rather strange way. During my fieldwork in the Netherlands I had nightmares on several occasions. I did not really ask myself why. I had in fact anticipated this, as I had expected some of the interviews to affect me deeply. However, I later realised that I did not have nightmares after all the interviews. I then became curious as to which of them had caused me to have the nightmares. I read the transcripts of the interviews again, and was amazed with the result. I noticed that some of the interviews created an atmosphere in which I travelled back in time. This was a result of the vocabulary which was used by the women. They were using the revolutionary words of the past, a vocabulary that for all of us belonged to the past. Using those old revolutionary terms took me – unconsciously – back to that past. But interestingly enough, even in those extreme cases in which I went back in time, the sentences were mostly shaped by the present. This was especially so in the cases in which the women had tried to analyse the past, but instead of relating the story as it had actually taken place, they had used the old revolutionary vocabulary to formulate the conclusions which they now held in regard to those past events. …
>
> For many weeks after conducting these interviews I felt completely exhausted, without at that time realising why.
>
> (Ghorashi 1997: 287)

Gorashi doesn't exaggerate. Recalling old cognitive maps is like shaking the roots of a person.[1] The stories come down like leaves from a tree. Not only do they represent 'the facts'; they also tell how a person has been working on the story of her life. Even in less traumatic interviews[2] I have been impressed, as a researcher, about what we inflict on 'our' respondents when we ask them to tell 'their' stories for 'our' research.

Women in Bulgaria: a research project

I experienced the methodological knot that I'm trying to explain here most dramatically in the research project about and with Bulgarian women which I undertook in the early 1990s. During 1992, 1993 and 1994 I visited Bulgaria repeatedly to research the experiences of women during and after the 'democratic' changes. I wanted to understand and describe their role in the changes, their experiences during the transition and their expectations for the future. For that purpose I interviewed about thirty women who were politically active. I focused on the main personalities in the political movement to overthrow the communist regime, and the women who took positions of political leadership after the overthrow of communism.

Some of the interviews were done during a period when I was a Women's Studies guest lecturer in Sofia. This situation gave me the opportunity to make many contacts with young Bulgarian women. The information I obtained by means of these teaching contacts was complementary to the material I collected by direct research interviews. With a professional crew from Belgian Television (BRT, the Flemish public broadcasting company) I was also involved in making a television documentary based on the insights gathered in my study. For the film we did additional interviews and some research of a more journalistic kind. The film was broadcast in February 1994, and presented at several festivals afterwards. Since then the situation in Bulgaria has changed, but the position of women during and shortly after the so-called democratic changes remains a historical issue. The lasting value of the research is to have recorded the history of women in this period and place. The research also generated considerable methodological problems focused on the cognitive difficulty of recalling and recounting past experiences.

The problem of clashing frames in life-story telling was enlarged by the (then recent) collapse of the communist regime.[3] The women involved in my research were living through a sharp shift of paradigm, in which every emotion and every thought seemed to lose the meaning it had had before. 'Les mots pour le dire'[4] were breaking down while we were speaking. I invited them to talk about the way they had experienced the transition from the communist regime to democracy, and how they had been actors in this process. This invitation evoked stories about a transition from a closed system to freedom, laden with old communist expressions and ideas. These stories were fraught with problems of the meaning of the transition, and specifically of the concepts in which it could be described. Thus 'freedom' meant to the respondents a transition from 'equality' to the right to be different. 'Equality' was associated with dictatorship and was contrasted with democracy, which itself evoked the move from a socialist welfare state to a wild capitalism. Thereafter there were growing contradictions between the expected valuation of the concepts used, and the lived experience of their meanings. Thus 'welfare' meant the transition from full employment to general redundancy, and 'efficiency' meant the displacement of hypocrisy by aggression. 'Comradeship' and 'power' had lost their meanings in the collapse of the regime and the succession of hope by despair. What could 'revival' mean, when the Mafia was taking over? What did 'restitution of property' mean, when machines were standing rusting on the huge farms?

The women were motivated to tell me their stories, but it was as if every word needed brackets. The nouns central to their recollections were painful to pronounce. The manifest ideological character of the communist regime made the methodological problems of remembering and reiterating all the more intense.

My research questions and the social position of my respondents meant that my undertaking shifted into a kind of 'advocacy oral history' (Gluck 1991: 205). I was speaking with the protagonists of a cause. They were working hard for the democratisation of Bulgaria and Eastern Europe. Even more, they were aiming to prevent a Balkan war while Yugoslavia was torn apart. Above all, the reason why the women were speaking to me was the fact that 'the West' had to know, and 'the West' had to help them. But 'the West' was never defined.

Because they were advocates of a cause they made me an advocate of the same cause. In general terms, I was prepared to be that advocate. I wouldn't have been doing the research if I hadn't been prepared to transmit their story. But as the project developed I realised that I could not accept the role of advocate for specific aspects of their case.

Intersubjective construction

Central to the production of memories in which I was engaged was the relationship between myself, the researcher, and the politically active Bulgarian women whom I was interviewing. In such an intersubjective relationship, mutual construction is inevitable. In my Bulgarian research these 'constructions' were made manifest, because of the combination of the high degree of personal familiarity and the total estrangement between researcher and respondent (between East and West). On the one hand, as women who were active in politics and/or social action, highly qualified, working at an academic level and occupying important positions, we thought we knew each other. On the other hand, women in the East and in the West were unable, at that moment of history, to even imagine the range of each other's positions.

The construction of others: me constructing them

In the course of making the documentary we inevitably engaged in the deliberate construction of the women protagonists of our film. As a social scientist involved in the filming process, I learned (better than in any scientific research seminar I ever followed or taught) how the researcher constructs the respondents, particularly in the process of editing the final reportage. Every cut in the film was based on the supposed representativity provided by the research or by the symbolic expressivity of the take. That is how the presentation of qualitative research works, and even in the best cases the protagonists become typecast. This is characteristic of qualitative research: whether filming or writing about research findings, it is part of the game; it is the case in Bulgaria, as it is everywhere else. The experience of being so constructed, however, was very hard to take, for women who were not accustomed to openness and to the heavy burden of expressing their meanings.

During the research I took a photograph of a girl of twenty-four, the first in her life: a special case of constructing the other. She spoke perfect English, with a posh accent; she worked in an American firm, where I could contact her by email; her university degree was of no use for her there, but she was earning some money. I took the picture with a feeling of being captured in an anachronism: how is it possible to have such an abundance of resources, without being accustomed to the social ritual of taking photographs?

I wanted to know, to understand, to deconstruct myths about so many things (socialism, socialist women, the revolution, poverty, the welfare state). My approach to them was strongly motivated by a desire to deconstruct (Western) opinions that I thought to be part of the Cold War. But eventually I had to conclude that my partners in the conversation wanted on the contrary to confirm the (Western) stereotypes.

I had problems in seeing the 'otherness' of the women I was working with. These women were seemingly so close to me: they were university trained, often fluent in English, well-informed on certain points, very self-conscious, leading the way, or frustrated after having undertaken brave and meaningful actions. But at the same time numerous cognitive automatisms, that go along with the feeling of closeness, did not function. Sometimes I had to mentally make myself feel the difference, to stop myself thinking that I understood because things were apparently similar, and to try to go beyond what I thought I understood. When I forced myself into the difference, I tried to imagine what it is not to have the Enlightenment in common when you are speaking about postmodernity.

I was, in my work, constructing (cooperating in the construction) of protagonists, even heroes, in the herstory of revolutionary changes. Here, everyone had many problems with 'the truth'. There was an edge of panic about some contradictory aspects of the history of the recent past, above all the possibility that it was not the effort of courageous people in the streets that had produced the collapse of the East European regimes in the late 1980s, but a cooperative action between the leaders of the West and the old élites, in an international scenario of power.

My task was to use the stories of the women to tell the relatively hidden history of the revolt and the changes. But there was a lot of confusion: the emotion, after three years, was still very fresh; most details of the transition were unknown; there was an atmosphere of distrust about the official version of its history; the women themselves were not sure what they wanted to tell – the history ('the facts') or their lives (their experience)? The answer was that they wanted to tell both, of course, and the 'why didn't we know?' question of every totalitarian regime was never far away. It was as if every individual testimony was that of a person knowing one piece of the general knowledge that had always been withheld from the public. And, constantly interacting with this complex production of memory, was the inevitable process of attributing value, the everlasting construction of 'the good one' and 'the bad one'. As an outsider I could only guess at who had 'god on their side'.

So I was struggling with the way I knew I was constructing my Bulgarian respondents. I also had to struggle with the way they were constructing me. It was a painful process, not only for them, but also for me. The intense feeling of discomfort which I experienced still hasn't disappeared completely. One lives for years with this kind of research, and I still have not come to terms with the (non-) dialogical character of my work.

The construction of the self: them constructing me

Feminist oral historians have frequently reported their concern to present them-selves to their respondents carefully. Accounts of their research speak of high aspirations for honesty and attention to a non-exploitative and reflexive method-ology and ethics, as well as of the surprised discovery that, over and over again, the respondent is not interested at all in these issues (see, for example, Sondra Hale on her work in Sudan, in Gluck and Patai 1991: 127). I knew this was the case, but nevertheless I found the gap between my preoccupations with feminist research and the responses I encountered disheartening. It was made all the worse by what both sides did share. This was an expectation that the interviewer would have what one might call a professional attitude, involving a certain self-effacement, and at least the appearance of an uncritical acceptance of the rights of the respondent. These consisted in the idea that respondents always have right on their side: they don't have to interact and engage in a respectful dialogue; they dictate the climate. This, combined with the ways in which the respondents constructed me, erased who I felt I really was, and made my experi-ences of interacting with them painful.

In their eyes I was a Western Feminist, thus I was by definition liberal. They could use what they thought to be the liberal discourse, and it went without saying that I would agree with their principles, and with the picture they constructed of me. The few exceptions, such as those discussed below, empha-sised the general response to me. Furthermore, to them I carried with me the smell of money. I was the precursor of 'money', and money was synonymous with emigration. I would have the knowledge to help them find an escape route. In fact I was an escape route. I was constructed as a person who was able to use the various influential channels of the West: universities, media, political parties. This was not completely untrue, but using these channels would have changed my academic intentions. Advocacy oral history was not my intention, neither was journalism or political action on my agenda. They couldn't be, because, as an outsider, the political aims and programmes of my respondents were not transparent to me.

The West as a symbol of what was 'good' and 'better' was difficult for me as a feminist to accept. Teaching feminist theories implies a critical analysis of Western thought and social organisation. As a result, the common ground for their feminism and mine was extremely difficult to find. It got lost somewhere on the road between Sofia and Plovdiv. As a Westerner, I simply could not have a problem, in their opinion. Because I couldn't have a problem, I couldn't have a story. Of course, I was not there to tell my story, so in a sense there was nothing wrong with that, but my idea of a dialogic interview technique faded away completely. What I thought I had in common with the women whose life histo-ries I studied was a knowledge of Marxist historical theory, a topology of social problems, a conceptual framework pointing to difference and equality, fairness, sharing and social security. But all this appeared to be taboo.

I found the way my respondents constructed me during the fieldwork nerve-wracking. If thinking about the strange phenomenon had not been so interesting, and if it hadn't been possible to work it through with one or two of the respondents and with my colleague, the director of the film, it would have been too much to bear.

The overall project was so difficult because of the mutual construction I have described. Not that the people as individuals were particularly 'difficult', but the historical and political load of the process was heavy. If I had been more congruent with their circumstances, there would have been less confrontation, but with my political, historical, feminist questions in mind, an open mind was not enough to understand what was going on in the women's lives. My questions confronted me (us) with the limits of an open dialogue.

Concepts

After completing the project and making the film, I was able gradually to reflect on what had happened, and on what I, as a left-wing feminist intellectual, had learnt about the present and future possibilities of dialogue between Eastern and Western Europeans. I found the work of Andrew Arato, a radical political scientist and long-term opponent of totalitarianism in Eastern Europe, helpful in formulating the ideas which I record below.

The changes in Eastern Europe have irrevocably and radically changed the world for all Europeans. Not wanting to know about them is no longer possible. Fundamental convictions about the balance of power, the armaments race and bickering amongst the major powers have been overturned. The opening up of Eastern Europe has made accessible to Western Europeans a materially under-developed world with a well-educated population. So there are enough interlocutors for those who really want to know, for those who want to understand what the problems have been and are likely to be in the future. There are enough people with whom to build relationships and understanding.

But it is certainly not easy. In the face of the desolation of life in Eastern Europe, left-wing intellectuals in both East and West find themselves with empty hands and, above all, with empty concepts. Open dialogue about the situation, which is new both in the East and in the West, is not an easy thing to achieve. In my research project, we constantly found how few concepts came to mind when trying to describe what had been overcome and what had been achieved: totalitarianism, dictatorship, revolution, democracy, freedom? It is difficult to define the framework clearly. Andrew Arato analysed in 1991 the way in which dialogue had by then become difficult between East European and West European intellectuals. Even those who previously made great efforts to meet each other, exchange ideas and formulate critical strategies, now had difficulty in understanding each other's point of view. Critical minds in the West had learnt a good deal in recent years from East European dissidents. Arato posed the question: 'Can social critics in the West learn something from the dramatic events in the East? Is there something that radical democrats in the East can learn from those in the West who in turn learnt something from them?' (Arato 1991: 24).

What Arato wanted to discuss were the same topics as before 1989, namely phenomena such as revolution, social justice, the market economy, civil society, the state and so on, both in the West and in the East. Thanks to the experiences and ideas of people from the East European states, new visions existed of, for example, revolution and basic democracy. He confirmed that after 1989 there was a rapid decline of interest in a critical examination of basic societal principles on the part of his East European colleagues. They were no longer interested in the critics of Western society, but preferred to learn from the protagonists of capitalist liberal democracy. If we still wish to work together, argued Arato, this presupposed that on the Western side:

> we fully understand the East European desire to choose second best, that being the existing model of society. It presupposes also that our friends in the East do not forget, or at least try to remember, that this second best in all its variations, is by definition a society which is the object of very fundamental criticism.

> (Arato 1991: 25)

Our research experiences in Bulgaria confirmed Arato's point. We met many people who said, often excusing themselves, that they did not want very much, not the very best, but just a normal life. They meant it in both the material and the ideological sense. For left-wing Western ears these quite understandable desires soon acquired a (cultured) right-wing tone. The kind of statements which were looked upon as progressive in Bulgaria in the 1990s were those which, in the West, one hears only in conservative circles, for example: 'People do not want to work'; 'those who do more should earn more'; 'by treating people as equals you stifle talent'; 'granting equal rights is unfair'; 'social services kill initiative'; 'you don't have to share with those who haven't earned it'.

Arato argued that we must make a serious attempt to understand such statements in their actual context. Westerners who are shocked by such assertions and refuse to listen to them deprive themselves of the chance to understand what communism meant in practice, a refusal which deprives East Europeans of feedback about what the welfare state, social security and democracy have meant and could mean, in principle and in practice. Taking these assertions out of context, as if the fall of communism demonstrates their validity, is grist to the mill of right-wing forces in the Western democracies. At the moment, East Europeans do not want to listen to Western criticism of liberal democracy, but that does not constitute a reason for stifling such criticism. Resistance to the decline in critical thinking, in both the East and the West, is one of the most important motives for listening very carefully to what people who are favourable to change in Eastern Europe are saying.

The absence of a common framework is a theoretical problem. It was illustrated with examples from everyday political practice in almost all the discussions held during the project. Words have an uncertain significance if their political context is ambiguous. Open dialogue between Bulgarians was something they had to rediscover in 1989. The vocabulary which formed the basis of left-wing thinking in the West had been tarnished by the communist experience in Eastern Europe. Even manifestly neutral sociological and political terms had to be used with caution. A few examples will demonstrate that this was more than a mere problem of language.

When she was vice-president of Bulgaria, Blaga Dimitrova could not and would not speak of a programme. She was allergic to the social technology which had been imposed in the name of programmes in the umpteenth five- or ten-year plan. But political activity becomes difficult if the word 'programme' may no longer be used and if the drafting of programmes is not considered to be a desirable or practical activity. The same applies to the stain on words such as equality and social justice. They no longer function as ideas which legitimise and mobilise plans for changing social organisation. Key concepts like these have been undermined by abuses perpetrated by the communists in the name of high ideals.

Compromise has also become a banished word. Meeting one's opponents half-way is a painful notion in a country which has just gained its freedom. The adherents of the Union of Democratic Forces (CDC) in Bulgaria soon became embroiled in internal quarrels. Every political compromise was labelled treachery so that strategic negotiations became totally impossible. Is democracy a question of give and take, or does it give one leave to refuse anything with which one does not agree?

Words such as 'natural' and 'normal' were given meanings in Eastern Europe which were hard for me to comprehend. It needs a certain worldview for a social phenomenon or evolution to be considered normal. In the Bulgarian context, it presupposed a vision of things which was no longer subscribed to by most theorists in the West. Forty-five years of communism deeply influenced the development of the country and the personality of the Bulgarian people. In criticising the regime, it was assumed that something like a natural development and a normal life that was antithetical to communism could exist. People in Eastern Europe did not seek a paradise on earth or the impossible; they just wanted to lead a normal life. That is perfectly natural, is it not? They did not have that normal life because of communism, which interfered with normal development. Objections that 'natural' and 'normal' do not exist and that a great deal of effort is required to pretend that liberal democracies are 'normal' and 'natural' did not help to further dialogue.

Freedom, the free market and the market economy are the best examples of concepts which lead to communication problems. These are words which have a meaning in Bulgaria which they do not have in the West. The uncontrolled freedom of the East European economy is unknown in the 'Free West'. The conclusion that such key concepts are not immediately useful in creating mutual understanding is not meant as a complaint. It is a useful eye-opener. If such concepts do not work, the interlocutors will be obliged to find out what is really the problem, in order to untangle the arguments and discuss experiences step by step. We have hardly started this process, either in the East or in the West.

As in every revolution there was a fascination in Bulgaria in 1989 with the idea of 'The Year Zero'. That this year seemed to have dawned for Eastern Europe was an attractive thought in both the East and the West. People felt that everything could begin again from scratch. Blaga Dimitrova, one-time vice-president, was preparing a new collection of poems on that theme. The title was 'And again. From the beginning'. But although radical things had taken place, the revival was in reality not starting again from zero. At the social and economic level, the former rulers were, in the mid-1990s, often taking new posts. At an individual level, it was clear to see how much everyone was affected by the revolution. 'At this moment too the way to change and democracy is by the personal road, by everyone's character. ... Now we are free we seem to be different and divided. It is as if freedom has divided us.' Blaga Dimitrova states that this is logical and normal, and goes hand in hand with a hazardous learning process. Daring to be different and defending difference is a new concept. The acceptance or assertion of difference has still not been attempted either individually or from the point of view of policy. Westerners are scarcely more experienced in this respect than the young democrats of Eastern Europe. The acceptance of the concept of differences between people in an honest and courageous manner, without short-changing the fundamental principle of equal rights is something which, to my mind, should receive top political and social priority. Speaking across the frontiers of the former Eastern Bloc countries means that people are obliged to discuss these questions without using the usual slogans, concepts and theories. Enthusiasm for such a dialogue did spring from the idea of 'The Year Zero'.

Both East and West are involved in the restoration of critical thinking, the winning back of theoretical insight and the building of a conceptual framework. Eastern Europeans are involved so that they may understand what they are doing and can determine where they want to make a connection. Western Europeans are involved because it is necessary to maintain and support the legitimacy of the criticism of liberal democracy.

Three women

Because I wanted to understand the role women had played in the transition to democracy, and how they were taking a lead in the social dynamics which followed the 'revolution', I interviewed many women who were known by name in Bulgarian public life. In reporting my research I had therefore to use the real names of public personalities. (One can hardly invent a surname for someone who clearly and bluntly was the vice-president.) For persons, however, whose name is not generally known in Bulgarian culture and history, I have used initials.[5] In what follows I shall concentrate on three of the women I interviewed, who illustrate that I am not inventing the problem and also that with some women a dialogue was possible.

B.D.

> What I find hard to forgive, is that the world is not what I thought it was.

B.D. (aged twenty-four at the time of the interviews) graduated from Sofia University. She was a fascinating mixture of modesty and self-confidence, erudition and ignorance, combining an amiable amour-propre with great readiness to be self-critical. She was warm, friendly, open and determined not to lose her way amidst all the upheavals going on around her. She studied philology and literature, but could not find a job in her field. She was critical about the so-called democratic revolution. The protests started while she was at the university. What she saw didn't inspire her confidence in the student leaders of the protest. To her, booze and egoism seemed to dominate over idealism. All these boys later studied or pursued a career abroad.

The memories she had of her school years were very precious: it was a period of hard work and serious study; she worked with other girls in a climate of discipline and orientation towards a studious future; they felt safe, motivated, and full of ambition; they responded to demands for high standards which they felt able to attain; and they received devoted support to gain what they were striving for. But in the end, it all turned out to be a pantomime. After 1989 everything had to be reconstructed, by her, without any support. Her mistake was not that she had been a little party-animal. Her mistake was that she had been so serious and so trustful.

> I do not feel bitter about the former regime. I see that others are bitter, but I can't bring myself to feel that way. I am just content that it is over and that it doesn't affect me any more. What I find hard to forgive, however, is that I had to go through the hard transitional period, that I have had to come to terms with my own personality, and that I have been forced to conclude that I am really alone now, and that it is no use expecting anyone else to help me. It needed time and a good deal of effort to rebuild my own consciousness, to learn to see that the world is full of all kinds of enriching things, and that ideology had distorted everything for us. I have to be honest and admit that when I was at school I thought only in terms of that ideology, for nobody ever taught me otherwise. Above all when I was in the upper classes … I learned a great deal and with pleasure, but I didn't know that something else existed outside, that the world could be different in any way. … I found it difficult to

understand that I had always thought within the boundaries of a single ideology and that the world is not like it seemed to be then.

Her efforts to construct continuity in her life were absorbing and authentic, and they were clearly driven by theoretical reflection. It was confusing for me, as a foreigner, that she, notwithstanding her critique of the fact that ideology had enveloped her completely, was equipped with all the necessary instruments for sharp self-analysis.

> I often think about the way I used to look at feelings and values, and how I look at them now. I am sure that there used to be a kind of hypocritical attitude towards the regime, and that everyone can recognise this hypocrisy in others. We were taught that we must be friendly, supportive, have faith in each other, and love one another. There was a continuous flood of hypocritical speeches, and these, as usual, were mere words. When they said that you had to be friendly with everyone, you could see that, on the contrary, there was a strict hierarchy, which effectively precluded friendship with everyone else. Everyone acted falsely towards everyone else, because Big Brother was watching. These were not the actual values anyway. Ideological thinking merely accepted that one just spoke about values; the communist ideology consisted of talking about values whilst actually doing something quite different. What we try to do now is to discover what lies behind words, what is their real meaning. Poverty is recognised as poverty now, and we can actually see it – social inequality stares you in the face, we see beggars in our streets and neglected children. Nobody takes care of these people, but at least nobody denies their existence.

Being enveloped by a dominant ideology is, indeed, a very absorbing process. What B.D. was telling us here gives a small elucidation of the process that most people in the post-revolutionary period were struggling with. Everyone had experienced a radical rupture in the way they were giving meaning to what happened in their lives.

Blaga Dimitrova

> That's why there are so many poets in this country.

The translated poetry of Blaga Dimitrova can be found in anthologies of the great Eastern European writers available in the West. In Bulgaria, her poetry belongs in every household and every heart. Since the 1980s more and more of her work has been translated. From 1990 until July 1993 she was vice-president of her newly democratic country. She was a member of the CDC, as was Zjelu Zjelev, the president (himself also a former dissident and intellectual). She resigned from office for exactly the same ethical and moral reasons that she had accepted it. In the interview she gave in our television documentary, from which

I quote at length below, she was open and reflective and recited several of her poems.

> When I was elected Vice-President they asked me why I became Vice-President. Now again they ask me why [I resigned]. I have to say that the answer is the same: because of moral reasons I accepted to carry the cross of being Vice-President of the Republic; because of the same reasons I resigned. This does not mean that I left politics. On the contrary, I made myself free to act in politics again, in a way that I want, to work for things I want.

Frost

> For us, there is only
> One possible escape
> From the white prison
> of winter
> to be our own freedom

Slowly I start thinking again about my books. I want to write a book, the dream of my life. A book about illusions. I went through a lot of illusions, my whole generation did. When I was young I was attracted to the communist ideas for a more perfect world.

Most

> I lived in the most golden of ages
> I lived in the fairest system
> Under the wisest doctrine
> with the highest morality
> amid the most eternal friendship
> in the happiest society
> towards the most wonderful future
> It's just that I don't know why
> my poems became so sad
> and sadder and sadder towards the end

Later we experienced the disappointments about these illusions. Now I, and everyone in my country, is again attracted to new illusions (maybe they are illusions) a new belief, about freedom and autonomy. But, as a philosopher said: ideals are like stars, we cannot reach them, but they are our guides. That is the kind of book I want to write: to show the windings of my time, of my generation, but at the same time a book of hope.

Face to Face

Who speaks the truth?
The words or the silence
The look or the voice.
The gesture or the hand
The pose or the spasm
The distance or the proximity.
We sit facing each other
With our backs to ourselves.
With hired faces,
A half-word from truth.
We get the meaning.

(1988)

That is the point of telling a life-story: to try to understand, above the windings of one's time, the meaning of what is happening. The advantage of oral history is that one does not need an exceptionally gifted person to apprehend the meaning.

R.V.

I'm a different person when I'm in the West.

R.V. (aged thirty-three) was full of enthusiasm for the economic aspects of the media world, in which she specialised and through which she wanted to build her personal link between East and West, between Bulgaria and England. She had both the theoretical background and the practical experience to be able to do so. At the time of the interviews she already had several research visits to the West to put on her curriculum vitae.

During the years of her academic education and in the period between her graduation and the democratic changes of 1989, she kept herself at a distance from the Communist Party. This, of course, marginalised her from intellectual and academic life in Sofia. This was the more explicit given the fact that her father was a prominent professor under the communist regime.

She explained that she suffered most from two things. First, there was the feeling that she and her husband were working so very hard (and had been working hard for a very long time) without much hope of seeing recognition or success. Second, she experienced a split consciousness between Western-style ambitions and her motivation to rebuild her own country. Doing one thing can make you forget another completely, because when doing it one feels like a different person. Only in Sofia did R.V. seem able to recall the experience of communism and the upheavals of the transition. The streets evoked the recollections. They carried the memory and dictated the feelings. When she was in London she lost that burden. There, she reacted differently, felt different and laughed a lot more often. Abroad she was more confident and even verbally she felt more powerful in English.

> I have definitely chosen the academic path now, although I am not yet sure where I am going to get the necessary money. I want to copmlete my doctorate thesis, and hope that it will be of some use to myself and a small section of the community. That is my long-term objective. I should like to study for my thesis in a foreign country and also defend it there. I should like to have a normal, objective professional experience and be able to judge my efforts by neutral and exacting criteria. I want to codify and make a generalisation of my own experience of the complicated East–West trade relations in the publicity field, from the point of view of the meeting between different cultures within the overall problem of the standardisation of advertising. That is my project for the next few years.
>
> Being able to work in another country for my doctorate is very important for me, not only in respect of my academic career but also for the human experience. It annoys me that in Bulgaria nobody seems to feel the need to comply with internationally recognised criteria. I feel trapped in the middle somehow: I have some knowledge of international criteria, but I am a product of Bulgaria. ... At this stage in my life I have to stop and think about things.

One of the things she wanted to work out was an assessment of her own potential, in an international context. Am I good? Do I say it to myself, because under the communist regime nobody was saying it to me? Are people saying it to me nowadays because at least I make things happen? Was I never good enough, and was there some validity in the criteria of the communist regime? Who am I? Maybe the West can tell me. ...

Her (meta-)questions were real. But they constantly ran into a loop within the life-story she told. It is like the feelings after a divorce: 'Has there ever been "love", did he/she ever respect "me"; did he/she – the way I constructed him/her in my mind and in my heart – even exist?; I have to involve myself in something completely different, to be sure that I can transcend the mediocrity of our troubled everyday life.'

> It is difficult to think about *equality* and *justice* in this country. Equality, for example, is a concept which has become debased in most people's minds by its links with communism. The concept of justice, which lies behind it, is important, and we are in danger of completely forgetting that fact. Perhaps it should be called something else; the equal right of choice, for example. In all the arguments about resolutions in the United Nations, it can be seen that equality is the most important question, a central concept in international attitudes towards justice. And that would be right too, if the tales told about equality were valid. There was no equality here under communism; there were just no options. The consequence of the lack of real equality,

which to me means equality of choice, was that many people simply did not make any choices. People just do not think about choices.

That is the point of a life history: taking the trouble to comprehend old choices, for yourself, and to make a fresh understanding for others, even if one has the feeling one never has made a real choice.

Memories of enlightenment

My research into the life-stories of Bulgarian women political activists left me with a set of disturbing questions: Will the future be silence, because they don't have the words to tell the past? Will the future be 'new speak', based on a *tabula rasa* vitalised with phrases from pop songs and wild capitalism? Will the future be forgetting and denial of the past?

Finally, the following two brief conclusions seem important to me. First, there are limits to the fragmentation a person can support. The women went through a dramatic period in their lives. It was not only that the difficult economic circumstances were hard. The cognitive chaos was almost a bigger problem. Fighting the confusion inside themselves was extremely difficult given the fact that the loss of singularity, coherence, vision and planning was what provoked the confusion. In this context the Western philosophical move to postmodernism is a dead end. You offer no philosophical support by explaining that dominant narratives have collapsed to people who are living through that collapse. A broadly accepted small 'big narrative' would be of more use, in order to prevent the barbarity and the madness.

Second, eliciting personal accounts of the recent changes in Eastern Europe is an extreme case of researching difficult memories, but it is not so different from any other case of investigating framed memory. The problems of memory and of finding the words to reconstruct the past are not typical only of the post-revolutionary experience. They are much more universal. They appear every time we ask people to recollect an important caesura in their lives. In many cases life-story research is about important ruptures. Most methodological attention is applied to the problem of the exactness of the recollection. Less attention is paid to the dynamics of the process of recollection itself. I have tried to make a start on exploring those dynamics here.

Notes

1 A possible interpretation of the psychoanalytic therapeutic technique is that the specific setting, and the associative talking cure, brings forward old cognitive frames, words, concepts, while the influence of the current cognitive map is reduced.

2 An example is a project involving about a hundred interviews with elderly Italian female immigrants in Belgium. In that research the women had gone through a culture shock many years earlier. Most of them, however, looked at their life as emigrées as a success story. But even without the drama of the moment equivalent to the case of Bulgaria, the interviews required a lot of the women.

3 In 1954 Todor Zjivkov came to power in Bulgaria. He remained the leader of
   Bulgaria in one capacity or another – party leader, president, prime minister – until
   10 November 1989. He was deposed under pressure from greatly increased popular
   opposition, which was at the same time a kind of palace revolution. Petur Mladenov,
   a new-style communist and former minister of foreign affairs under Zjivkov took over.
   The democratic elections held in June 1990 were won by the ex-communists. In
   August 1990 – under the socialist government – Zhelyu Zhelev (philosopher, former
   dissident) was elected president of Bulgaria by parliament. Two years later Zhelyu
   Zhelev and Blaga Dimitrova (poetess) were elected president and vice-president by
   popular vote. The elected parliament was a constituent assembly with a short-term
   working period. The Union of Democratic Forces (the former opposition to the
   communist regime) ruled the country for a short period after winning the October
   1991 elections. This government fell in November 1992. In February 1993 Berov
   came to power with a government composed of technocrats.
4 Marie Cardinal, *Les Mots pour le dire*, *The Words to Say It* (1983 [1975]), an autobiographical novelisation of Cardinal's psychoanalysis, in which finding 'the words to say
   it' constitutes the long process of healing the psychosomatic symptoms and the medi-
   calisation of the suffering of the protagonist.
5 All respondents agreed, of course, to the publication of their stories. In this chapter
   the names are hardly important.

Bibliography

Arato, A. (1991) 'Revolution, Civil Society and Democracy', *Praxis International* 10: 24–38.
Cardinal, M. (1983 [1975]) *The Words to Say It*, Cambridge, MA: Van Vactor and Good-
    heart (original: *Les Mots pour le dire*, Paris: Grasset & Fasquelle, 1975).
Ghorashi, H. (1997) 'Shifting and Conflicting Identities', *The European Journal of Women's
    Studies* 4, 3: 283–304.
Gluck, S. (1991) 'Advocacy Oral History: Palestinian Women in Resistance', in Gluck and
    Patai (eds), *Women's Words: The Feminist Practice of Oral History*, London: Routledge:
    205–19.
Gluck, S. and Patai, D. (eds) (1991) *Women's Words: The Feminist Practice of Oral History*,
    London: Routledge.
Hankiss, A. (1981) 'Ontologies of the Self: On the Mythological Rearranging of One's
    Life History', in D. Bertaux (ed.), *Biography and Society: the Life History Approach in the
    Social Sciences*, Beverley Hills, CA: Sage Publications: 203–9.
Patai, D. (1991) 'U.S. Academics and Third World Women: Is Ethical Research Possible?',
    in Gluck and Patai (eds), *Women's Words: The Feminist Practice of Oral History*, London:
    Routledge: 137–53.

12 Autobiographical times

Susannah Radstone

Is postmodernism a theory whose time has come for men but not for women?
(Nicholson 1990: 6)

A good feminist criticism, therefore, must first acknowledge that men's and women's writing in our culture will inevitably share some common ground.
(Kolodny 1976: 86)

Autobiography takes many forms. Though confessional autobiography continues to attract large numbers of readers and critics, this chapter will suggest that another form of autobiography – a form which I am calling 'remembrance' – has recently risen to prominence. This rise of literary autobiographical remembrance cannot be extricated, however, from a more general contemporary fascination with memory. Indeed, contemporary Western societies have recently been described as experiencing a memory 'boom of unprecedented proportions' (Huyssen 1995: 5) and of being 'obsessed by' (Hamilton 1994: 10) memory. This explosion of interest in memory (Radstone 2000: especially 1–12) has made itself felt not only in texts, but also in the academy and in popular practices (Samuel 1994) and has been associated by many with an epochal shift from modernity to the postmodern (see, for instance, Huyssen 1995). This association rests on an account of the divergent temporalities of modernity and postmodernity. While modernity is linked with a future-oriented temporality aligned with ideas of progress, postmodernity is connected, rather, with a temporality that folds the future back onto the past (*ibid.*). In this chapter, however, I suggest that contemporary autobiographies do not fit neatly into this account of epochal temporalities, since the latter takes no account of the temporalities of sexual difference. In offering a reading of contemporary autobiography, temporality and sexual difference, then, this chapter suggests that the very idea of an epochal shift rests on an unproblematised and reductive understanding of temporalities.

Autobiography and history

When women pick up their pens to write autobiographies, the shape their words take and the way their words are read form part of wider literary, cultural and social histories – histories of those who have written before; histories of those who have read before. Autobiography, one might say, has a history. But to suggest that autobiography has *a history* – a history that shapes individual autobiographies and that is shaped, in its turn, by the shape *taken by* autobiographies is already to take up a position *within* a particular way of thinking or theorising or making knowledge – a way of thinking informed by modern understandings of history and temporality. Thanks to the ever-expanding field of autobiographical studies it would now be possible, indeed, to write a history of historical studies of autobiography.[1] Unsurprisingly, such a history would, in its turn, reveal the influence upon autobiographical criticism of those literary theories which have, since the 1960s, unsettled the tenets of liberal humanist, reflectionist literary criticism. Few would nowadays agree with James Olney's view that autobiography reflects an *unchanging* human nature which desires to write about itself: 'there is no evolving autobiographical form to trace from the beginning through history to its present state because man has always cast his autobiography and has done it in that form to which his private spirit impelled him' (Olney 1972: 3). Today, few would accede, either, to Georges Gusdorf's suggestion that autobiography *reflects* a historically shifting rather than an essential and unchanging human nature (Gusdorf 1980: 28). For more recently, and under the impact of structuralism, poststructuralism and psychoanalysis, autobiographical criticism has shifted from an understanding of autobiography's history as a '*response* to changing ideas about the nature of the self, the way in which the self has been apprehended' (Spengemann 1980: 6–7) to an understanding of the part played by language, genre and discourse in the constitution of subjectivity. Under the impact, particularly, but not exclusively, of Lacanian psychoanalysis, autobiographical criticism took up the notion of the subject's *illusory* coherence, unity and autonomy. This idea of the subject's illusory coherence stems from the Lacanian understanding of infantile development as founded upon the misrecognition of the mirror-stage. According to Lacan, the mirror-phase, in which the infant perceives itself as an 'I' depends upon a splitting between the 'I' which perceives and the 'I' which is perceived. Entry into language arguably reinforces this first split, since it necessitates a second division between the 'I' which speaks and the 'I' which is spoken of (Benveniste 1971; Belsey 1980: 59).The impact of this body of theory upon the study of autobiography brought about a thoroughgoing reconceptualisation of the relation between the author – the writing 'I' – and the 'I' which is written about by that author. Once it had been posited that these two subject positions contradict, rather than mirror each other, it became impossible to argue that autobiography mirrored the experiences of its author: autobiography became, indeed a 'limit-case' for poststructuralist theory, which sought to overturn the powerful realist notion of autobiography as mirror of the author's soul by arguing that there is a contradiction between the self which appears in autobiography and 'the self which is only partly represented there, the self which speaks' (Belsey 1980: 64–5).

Much recent autobiographical criticism has concerned itself with autobiography's inherent contradictions – contradictions which led Louis Renza to conclude that autobiography constitutes a suicidal genre[2] since it 'presents the writer with an empty or discursive "self" – an "I" never his own because it makes present what remains past to him' (Renza 1977: 9). There are, however, at least two predominant positions within this overall critical concern with autobiography's contradictions – or even its impossibility. In the first position – a position exemplified by Renza – autobiography reveals an essential and apparently ahistorical truth concerning subjectivity: autobiography inevitably undoes itself, since its attempt to inscribe subjective coherence paradoxically reveals that coherence as illusory. More usually however, recent autobiographical criticism's perspective has been historical.[3] Earlier historical accounts of autobiography argued that the genre constituted a response to historically specific understandings of the self. Spengemann, for instance, argued that 'we need to understand the conditions that have led different autobiographers at different times to write about themselves in different ways' (Spengemann 1980: 6–7). Under the sway, however, of contemporary literary theory's stress upon the subject's constitution by and in language, historical criticism now asks, rather, not how a preconstituted self responds to historical understandings *of* the self, but how subjectivity is variously constituted *by* historically specific constructions *of* the subject. Unsurprisingly, there have been many and varied responses to this question. While for some, the historical 'development' of autobiography reveals the genre's increasing incapacity to sustain the (always) illusory coherence of the autobiographical 'I', others, such as, for example, Paul Jay, claim to be charting autobiography's history in relation to shifts in the ontology of the subject. Yet Jay's announcement that 'what I will be charting is the growing *recognition* of how complex and problematic is the transposition of the author into the autobiographical protagonist' (Jay 1984: 29, emphasis added) reveals, perhaps, some interweaving of the ahistorical deconstructionist emphasis upon the autobiographical 'I''s inevitable fictionality with a more historicised account of the ontology of the subject.

Recent histories of autobiography have moved from understanding autobiography as a reflection of historical shifts in the ontology of the subject to an emphasis upon the constitutive role of the autobiographical text in the production *of* subjectivity. The self is no longer understood, moreover, as constituted by a history which *then* shapes its autobiographical performance. Rather, it is autobiography itself which produces the subject: the subject, that is, is textually constituted and that textual constitution has a history. While histories of autobiography problematise earlier universalist, essentialist and reflectionist approaches to autobiography, these histories are themselves formed within a particular conceptualisation of history that informs their historical accounts of autobiography. Histories of autobiography locate individual autobiographies within historical epochs and their aesthetic, formal and thematic concerns – concerns which are inextricably tied to the historicisation of the ontology of the subject. These historicising moves make use of well-worn modes of historical and literary-historical periodisation: autobiographies are located in antiquity, modernity or late modernity and within literary-historical movements such as romanticism or modernism. And for all that the history of autobiography continues to be contested, the givenness of the terms of historical narrative remain unquestioned. Even when the problematisation of progressive and developmental models of history influence histories of autobiography (Marcus 1994: 154 and chap. 5 onwards) those 'counter-histories' remain tied to an understanding of historical *temporality*. This is perhaps especially or most obviously the case in treatments of marginal autobiographies – women's, working-class or ethnic autobiography, for instance. Thus Estelle Jelinek's feminist critique of autobiographical criticism argued that whereas the periods of greatest productivity in male autobiography have been aligned with important events in (American) history, women's autobiographies have not conformed to this history: historical turning-points, concluded Jelinek, are not necessarily the same for men and women (Jelinek 1980: 6). Similarly, Patricia Waugh's study of the relation between women's writing and literary modernism and postmodernism points to divergences as well as correspondences between the two fields (Waugh 1989: 6–7). Yet Waugh does conceptualise the fields of women's writing and literary modernism and postmodernism as occupying overlapping territories *within* 'history'. Likewise, although Jelinek concludes that the history of women's autobiography may be different to that of the male tradition, the divergent traditions that she posits appear to co-exist, for Jelinek, *within* history: history conceived of, in the words of Peter Osborne, as 'a homogeneous continuum of historical time' (Osborne 1995: 1). As Osborne points out, modernity 'can be used unproblematically to refer to some chronologically distinct span of historical time', while 'the question of the forms of time-consciousness produced within European societies during this period can be separated off from the question of periodization itself' (Osborne 1995: 1).

Modernity/postmodernity

Yet if autobiography has a history, or, as feminists, and others have insisted, histories, so too does this mode of historical theorisation and mapping. History's temporality – linear, progressive, 'a homogeneous continuum' – has been associated, indeed, with modernity. Historical temporality, that is, can be aligned with modernity's belief in progress as well as with modernity's colonialist and imperialist subsumption of all experience to its temporality. Recent writings on postmodernity, moreover, have debated whether postmodern temporality – variably characterised in relation to simultaneity, synchronicity or the folding of the present onto the past – represents merely the foregrounding of modernity's 'other' time/s or the emergence of the truly 'new' (Harvey 1989; Huyssen 1995; Osborne 1995). These insights concerning the history of 'history', or, better put, of historical temporality, might be taken up by autobiographical criticism.

Instead of an approach that maps autobiography onto its constructions of historical subjectivities, autobiographical criticism might, instead, attend to auto-biographical *temporalities*. Yet such an approach needs to avoid accepting unquestioningly what I'd want to call the dominant narrative concerning what, for want of a better term, I'll paradoxically call the 'history of temporality' – a dominant narrative that tends to set the linearity and progressivism of modern temporality against the simultaneity, or circularity or synchronicity, of post-modern temporality. In what follows, I want to offer one approach to the study of autobiographical temporality which attempts to avoid capitulating to this domi-nant narrative concerning modern and postmodern times.

The last half century has been dominated by two modes of autobiographical writing: confession and remembrance.[4] In the 1960s and 1970s confessional autobiography and first-person fiction enjoyed something of a heyday.[5] The 1960s saw a proliferation of sexual confessions from authors such as Philip Roth, J.D. Salinger, Kingsley Amis and Henry Miller. At the same time, confession too was shaping the feminist novel that 'changes lives' (Coward 1980), as novels such as Marilyn French's *The Women's Room* (1978), Verena Stefan's *Shedding* (1980) and Kate Millett's *Flying* (1975) rose to prominence. A little later, however, confes-sion's dominance began to be challenged by another mode of autobiographical and first-person writing that I'm calling ' remembrance'. Whereas, in confes-sional writing it is memory that arguably sutures over the break between the writing 'I' and the 'I' that is written about (Hodgkin 1999),[6] in remembrance, it is memory's relation to subjective coherence that comes under scrutiny. Instead of suturing the division between the writing 'I' and the 'I' that is written about, texts of remembrance tend rather to undermine the resilience of that suture, by emphasising memory's tenuous relation to the 'past'. Contemporary texts of remembrance to which I will later refer include Philip Roth's *Patrimony* (1991) and Eva Hoffman's *Lost In Translation* (1989).

A case might be made for aligning the ascendance of remembrance over confession with what many see as a shift from 'modernity' to 'postmodernity'. The confession's (often tortuous and torturous) quest for salvation as subjective truth depends upon a temporal distance – a sense of having moved on – between central protagonist and narrator. Furthermore, the confession's enactment of a purging of the past is in the service of 'becoming'. Since confession produces self-transformation, each act of confession alters the view of the central protago-nist offered to the reader by the confessing narrator. This process of continual self-transformation or 'becomingness' (Howarth 1974) arguably constitutes the defining feature of confession. The confession's quest for truth and its produc-tion of 'becomingness' align this autobiographical mode closely with definitions of modernity that emphasise an epochal concern with truth, linear progress and transformation (Berman 1989). In remembrance, the confession's quest for truth is superseded by an acknowledgement of memory's partiality, instability and impermanence. In place of the confession's 'becomingness', remembrance suggests, rather, that the subjective temporal horizon is constituted by memory's revision: whereas the confession's narration widens the gap between past and present, in remembrance, an acknowledgement of the narrator's *making* of memory weakens the boundaries between past and present. Remembrance's putting in question of memory's status as 'truth', together with its blurring of the boundaries between past and present align this autobiographical mode with definitions of postmodernity that emphasise an epochal fascination with memory (Radstone 2000), a loss of belief in the future and a blurring of boundaries between present and past.

Though an argument might be made, then, that aligns the emergence of remembrance and its arguable contemporary dominance over confession with an epochal shift from modernity to postmodernity, this mapping relies on a totalising and homogenising approach to contemporary temporalities, and risks reductive readings of the temporalities of contemporary texts. In what follows, my aim is to problematise this position by contrasting the temporalities of certain autobiographical texts of confession and remembrance. In place of the approach outlined above – an approach that pays no attention to the possible differences *between* confessions and *between* texts of remembrance – I want to introduce questions of sexual difference into discussions of 'the politics of time'. In so doing, I hope to show that the positing of an epochal shift from modernity to postmodernity rests on an unproblematised positing of history as a homogeneous temporal continuum – a view that is blind to the sexual politics of autobiographical time.

Temporality and sexual difference

Questions of temporality and sexual difference notwithstanding, there is certainly shared ground between autobiographical confessions and texts of remembrance that construct male and female narrating subjects. Both Marilyn French's *The Women's Room* and Philip Roth's *Portnoy's Complaint*, for instance, share the confession's recent obsession with sexuality and with suffering. Meanwhile Philip Roth's *Patrimony* and Eva Hoffman's *Lost In Translation* share the autobiographical remembrance's often self-reflexive yearning for a lost past and lost parental figures – a yearning that is represented by the faded family photographs that appear on both these texts' covers. But if there is shared ground between the confessions of French and of Roth or the remembrances of Roth and of Hoffman, an analysis of their temporalities reveals differences *between* confessions and *between* texts of remembrance – differences that might be explored, I want to suggest, in relation to what I'm calling the sexual politics of time. These differences cannot be explored, however, without first offering an account of temporality and sexual difference. In what follows, therefore, I propose to offer an account of the sexual politics of time that raises questions about what has, to my mind, been wrongly assumed to be 'shared ground'.

It seems indisputable to propose that an experience shared by all in early infancy is that of coming to an awareness of having a life – an experience which encompasses an acknowledgement of possibility and of limitations. Coming to life, that is, entails recognising the spatial and temporal bounds of that life.

Psychoanalysis suggests, moreover, that the beginnings of this awareness of temporal and spatial boundedness occur prior to the infant's awareness of sexual difference. A case might be made, then, that sexual difference has no bearing on subjectivity and time, since a dawning sense of separate, bounded being precedes the taking up of a sexually differentiated position. Yet though it can be argued that the infant's coming to time occurs in the early months of life, when the psyche has yet to undergo what Freudians term 'Oedipalisation', this view rests on an 'unpsychoanalytic' understanding of psychical temporality – an understanding of psychical temporality that aligns it with historical time's linearity and progressiveness, rather than with what Freud termed *Nachträglichkeit*.

Freud's concept of *Nachträglichkeit* has informed much later psychoanalytic thinking about temporality and the unconscious.[7] This concept refers to a process of deferred revision, where 'experiences, impressions and memory-traces may be revised at a later date to fit in with fresh experiences or with the attainment of a new stage of development' (Laplanche and Pontalis 1988: 111). Psychoanalysis deploys this concept to reveal that memories are not simply representations of past events. For psychoanalysis, memory's images are understood, rather, as complex representations. These representations do not reflect a remembered event. They are constituted instead by chains of associations made in the present – chains of association that produce the revisions otherwise known as memories. The argument that sexual difference is temporally undifferentiated, since coming to time occurs prior to sexual differentiation, takes no account of *Nachträglichkeit*. In place of such an argument, I want to suggest that the acquisition of sexual difference prompts a *revision* of 'coming to time'. But in place of an essentialist argument that links masculinity and femininity to different temporalities,[8] I want to suggest that the temporalities of sexual difference are always *themselves* open to revision – revisions that can be explored, *inter alia*, by autobiographical criticism. But before moving on to explore how contemporary autobiographical writing revises temporalities in the context of sexual difference, an account of the temporalities of sexual difference is required.

Both psychoanalysis and philosophy concur that it is the recognition of death – a recognition which comes from the other – which 'temporalizes time' (Osborne 1995: 80). Though there are varied understandings of the precise nature of this recognition (*ibid.*: chap. 3) and though it is sometimes argued that the death that is recognised as threatened, or represented, by the other is not a physical but a symbolic death, what seems clear is that at an early point in the child's development something is sensed in the other that represents 'death'. It is this recognition that instils in the small infant a sense of its own temporal finitude, and a sense too of time's passing. According to Peter Osborne's reading of Lacan, it is 'the otherness of the image of the child's body in the mirror phase ... which underlies the consciousness of death and hence of *time*' (Osborne 1995: 89).

Yet this account of the small infant's earliest recognition of death appears paradoxical, since what seems to be suggested here is that the small child recognises something in the other at a developmental stage that comes prior to its capacity to acknowledge the existence of others. What is this 'other' in which the child recognises 'death', then, given that this recognition is posited as occurring prior to object relations? Osborne's survey of philosophical and psychoanalytic attempts to answer this question dwells briefly on Julia Kristeva's suggested account of this process (Kristeva 1987). Kristeva's account revises Lacan's theory of the 'mirror-stage' in relation to the constitutive role of the mother's desire in the child's earliest stages of development. Kristeva rereads the Lacanian misrecognition of the 'mirror-stage' as the child's primary identification with the 'Imaginary father'. According to Kristeva, the small child attempts to compensate for the sense communicated to it by its mother that part of her desire lies elsewhere, by identifying with the object of the mother's desire, what Kristeva calls 'the Imaginary father'. Thus the child's earliest identification is with an image constructed to cover over or compensate for a felt loss of part of the mother. Whether the 'death' encountered here is understood as real physical death, or the sense of annihilation produced by non-recognition of the child by the mother, it is a 'death' threatened by the felt possibility of the complete loss of the mother's desire, a complete disregard or failure of recognition on the part of the mother. Yet at the same time, it is the child's identification with the 'Imaginary father' – representing a part of the mother's desire felt to be directed elsewhere – that implants in the child the beginnings of a sense of its *own* potential for independent existence. Thus does the awareness of death augur life.

Peter Osborne's study of time, death and recognition discards Kristeva's account of primary identification with the 'Imaginary father' on a number of grounds: he argues that this account fails to offer a clear enough explanation for why the 'Imaginary father' signifies death, and that it produces what he calls a 'paternal return' – that it constitutes a 'race back into the arms of the law' (Osborne 1995: 94). Yet in discarding Kristeva's account of primary identification with the 'Imaginary father', Osborne rejects too the potential this account offers for *linking* primary identification not only with 'coming to time' via a recognition of death, but also with a primary encounter with the Phallus, represented, in Kristeva's account, by that 'Imaginary father'. Though one might want to question the apparent immutability of the primacy accorded to the Phallus in Kristeva's post-Lacanian theory of *significance*, feminist work has taken up this theory, precisely because of the links it makes between phallocentricity, identification and language.

Osborne's quest for an adequate explanation of how the child's image of its body 'in the primitive imaginary …' is perceived as the 'image of death' (Osborne 1995: 90) leads him to reject Kristeva's account of early infancy's coming to time. Earlier, Osborne has pointed out that according to Lacan, the temporality acceded to at this point 'is an immanent temporality, an immanent mortality …'. Continuing, Osborne explains that, for Lacan, this temporality can only be *experienced* 'once the "register" of the symbolic *within* the imaginary comes into its own. This is a process which is associated by Lacan with the castration complex and the production of sexual difference' (Osborne 1995: 89). Given the explicitness with which a revised experience of temporality is here linked with the acquisition of sexual difference, it seems all the more surprising that Osborne's discussions of temporality avoid further mention of sexual difference. Yet Lacan's own account of the castration complex is *saturated* with temporality. Lacan's description of the Oedipus complex distinguishes between its production of masculine and feminine desire: 'in Lacan, the boy's castration complex joins desire to threat, whereas for the girl, desire is joined to nostalgia' (Radstone 1995a).[9] What emerges here, I want to suggest, is an account of castration and the Oedipus complex which reveals its *revision* of primary identification's imbrication with temporality and death along sexually differentiated lines. For the little boy, the Oedipal promise (having a woman *like* your mother) occupies the future. Meanwhile, though castration anxiety will arguably haunt this future, it was across the mother's body that castration was written – a body that, like Oedipal desire itself, can be located in the past. As Juliet Mitchell has argued, in a subjective sense, Oedipus inaugurates the past:

> The castration complex … introduces the command that the Oedipus complex be over and done with; if you accept it as past you will be able to have a new version (be a father in your turn with a woman of your own) in the future.
>
> (Mitchell 1986: 26)

Mitchell herself points to the phallocentrism of this account before concluding that: 'The castration complex, bearing the injunction of human history, inaugurates history within the individual' (*ibid.*). For the little girl, on the other hand, the worst (castration/death) seems already to have happened and her passage through the castration complex and Oedipus promises no future salvation. In place of the future promise inaugurated for the boy, the longings castration evokes in the girl are for the (fantasised) plenitude of the past. Once she has recognised, that is, that both she and her mother lack the Phallus, she seeks compensation not in the future, but by recourse to pre-Oedipal fantasies and myths of the Phallic mother.

Having established an account of how, under phallocentricity, Oedipus revises 'coming to time' along sexually differentiated lines, I now want to return to the subject of autobiographical writing. In what follows, my focus will be two-fold. I will be asking both whether these sexually differentiated temporalities appear to be shaping contemporary autobiographical confession and remembrance, and whether this account of the sexual politics of time might itself now be in need of revision.

Sexually differentiated temporality in confession and remembrance

The temporalities of narratives are complex. Questions of tense, of narrative point of view and of plot/story relations all demand careful and detailed analysis before anything can definitively be said concerning a text's temporality/ies.

Nevertheless I offer what follows, in the hope that what remains merely sketched here might be challenged, or even developed, by others, particularly in relation to the question of the temporalities of other differences.[10] I have already proposed both that the confessional outpourings of, say, Marilyn French and Philip Roth do share some common ground and that there are grounds for associating the contemporary confession with aspects of modernity. But as Rita Felski has argued, though feminism needs the category of modernism (Felski 1989), its aim should be to complicate that category. The same holds equally true of postmodernity and postmodernism.

One writer who has attempted to complicate, if not problematise the categories of modernity and postmodernity is Alice Jardine. Her book *Gynesis* (1985) asked whether or not American and French contemporary fiction written by men is participating in modernity (a term she uses to refer to what is more usually termed postmodernity). Jardine's understanding of modernity was influenced by continental literary theory, which, at the time of writing, was wedded to the promotion of 'feminine writing' – writing which was arguably displacing the masculine symbolic order by means of deploying formal strategies such as open-endedness, polysemy and the foregrounding of rhythm and texture over 'sense' and fixed meaning. For Jardine, the aim, then, of this 'continental' writing was the symbolic murder of the father: 'the task of modernity, as it has been programmed in France', she argued 'is to "kill the father" in all his disguises, whatever his function or form' (Jardine 1985: 229). Jardine's concluding comparison of male-authored French and American texts proposes that whereas in the French case, 'gynesis' and the 'killing of the father' are enacted through the disruption of language and narrative, producing 'feminine' texts, in American texts 'the first thing that strikes the imagination is that there would seem to be no father to kill … the father as figure, or as character, if you like, is already dead' (Jardine 1985: 230). Jardine later revises this position, arguing that in American fiction, the son punishes the mother for the father's death and that in American fiction gynesis operates not at the level of language and syntax, but at the level of *representation* (Jardine 1985: 236).

The turn from confession to remembrance *might* be read in relation to gynesis – in relation, that is, to 'killing the father' and the 'feminisation' of culture. For example, remembrance's substitution of revision for linear progress and its emphasis on the contingency and partiality of memory over the 'truth' and authenticity of confession appear in keeping with Jardine's account of gynesis. There are, however, reasons to be wary of too straightforward an assimilation of this shift with Jardine's account of literary (post)modernism and 'parricide'.

Jardine's comparison of American and French male-authored contemporary fiction produces a simultaneously complicated *and* universalising account of (post)modernity. *Gynesis*'s focus on the potential differences between male- and female-authored texts and between US and French male-authored texts raises crucial questions about (post)modernity and difference. Jardine seems to assume, nevertheless, that her findings do not necessitate a thoroughgoing complication of the epochal shifts that are her focus. Her thesis seems to assume that the differences she describes are differences occurring *within* the overarching category of (post)modernity. I want to offer two criticisms of this approach. First, my previous account of sexually differentiated temporalities problematises the assumption of changes occurring entirely *within* history's epochal categories. Second, Jardine proposes that 'killing the father', or reproaching the mother for her death, marks either the form of continental writing, or the themes, characterisations and plots of American writing – that these are indeed dominant tendencies across contemporary writing (and the universalising and homogenising nature of *this* assumption should not be overlooked). If, however, this analysis is accepted as a working hypothesis, then my questions become: first, how does this tendency *differentially* revise the sexually differentiated temporalities of the contemporary autobiographical 'I'? Second, what might this tell us about the relationship between the temporalities of the sexually differentiated subjects of contemporary autobiography and the historical mapping of epochal shifts that shapes so much literary criticism? Bearing these findings in mind, I want now to turn to a comparison of some contemporary autobiographical confessions and remembrances.

Confession, temporality and sexual difference

Like so many confessional novels of the 1960s and 1970s, Philip Roth's *Portnoy's Complaint* (1969) proceeds stream-of-consciousness fashion without chapter divisions. And like so many confessional novels of the period, its primary concerns are those of sexuality, suffering and parental relations. The first-person outpourings of the confessing narrator are directed towards an analyst-doctor whose analysing ear provides both the pretext for the narrative and a possible point of identification for the reader. As the paperback edition's backjacket suggests, Portnoy's confessional outpourings concern themselves largely with the narrator's mother and with the intolerably intense feelings that she evoked in the child and continues to evoke in the adult: 'Alexander Portnoy is a great comic character. He is going to be for many readers what his mother was for him "The Most Unforgettable Character I've Met".' In Portnoy's house, the narrator complains, things were not as they should have been 'if my father had only been my mother! And my mother my father! But what a mix-up of the sexes in our house!' (Roth 1995: 41). This narrator lays the blame for the sexual and relational problems that befall him as an adult at the feet of his overbearing and powerful mother, who, he feels, has usurped his father's rightful place and against whom he harbours murderous feelings. In Jardine's terms, the son reproaches the mother for weakening, if not quite killing, the father. Thematically speaking, then, Portnoy's 'complaint' is certainly directed towards the mother: it is she, the narrator implies, who has usurped the father's place. Yet though the novel's plot/story relations do depart from the strict linearity of modern progress, its typically confessional narrative confesses the past in order to redeem the future. This anguished story leaves the reader laughing and with the promise of future salvation: this boy might *yet* win the Oedipal promise and avoid its threat. For *Portnoy's Complaint* ends with an anguished scream followed by a punchline: 'So [said the doctor]. Now vee may perhaps to begin. Yes?' (Roth 1995: 274). In other words, though *Portnoy* concerns itself thematically with a father weakened by too powerful a mother, the text's circularity – its suggestion, at the book's end, that Portnoy is about to retell the future-oriented confession that has already formed *Portnoy's* narrative – offers the promise of a return to a linear, future-oriented temporality: the temporality of the father's Oedipal promise to his son. Though this ending suggests, not straightforward linearity, but layer upon layer of revision (the life-story we have read will now be revised, once more, in analysis), it also suggests that after that scream – which signifies, perhaps, the essence of subjective truth as constructed by confession, recovery and a way forward might have been found. The father's Oedipal promise and the future-oriented temporality of masculinity appear to be within reach.

What is the relationship between *Portnoy's* 'complaint', then, and its confessional, future-oriented 'return to the past'? What I am proposing here is that though *Portnoy's* themes, plot and characterisation appear in keeping with Jardine's findings, the text's temporality contradicts the idea that the father is weakened, if not dead. Portnoy's confessions return to the past in order to redeem the future and though the book's ending appears to fold the confession back upon itself, the analyst's promise of a beginning implies the future-orientation of post-Oedipal masculinity. It might be proposed that Roth's *Portnoy* constitutes simply an aberrant text that falls outside the field of gynesis's dominance. I want to suggest, rather, that Jardine's account of gynesis's 'killing of the father' *forgets* that the patriarchal father was always-already dead. According to *Totem and Taboo* (Freud 1913) it is precisely the son's murdering of the primal father which puts in place the patriarchal father of modernity. Having killed the father, remorse takes over, and the sons struggle to put in place a father who resembles the father they have killed. Freud's phylogenetic approach suggests, moreover, that infantile development constitutes a reprisal of this tribal history. Thus the Oedipal father, the father whose threat and promise are arguably constitutive of the temporality of masculine subjectivity is a father who has, if you like, 'risen again' from the son's parricidal impulses. Jardine likens the American 'sons' to Freud's fraternal clan, positing that this clan knows nothing of Oedipus. Jardine associates the American 'sons', that is, with the brothers, who, according to *Totem and Taboo*, killed their father to get access to 'his' women. While one might argue that the plotting brothers knew only of the archaic law of their father – a father who kept all the women for himself, Jardine's 'sons' blame the mother for the father's death. Jardine implies, therefore, that these 'sons' are post-parricidal, and free from the father's violent rule. But as Freud reminds us, murder prompted a remorse met with by the symbolic restoration of the father, in the form of the father of patriarchy and of Oedipus. On this Freudian account, killing the father *inaugurates*, rather than undoes, the Oedipal relations characteristic of patriarchy. Moreover, Freud's *Totem and Taboo* goes on to argue that in the totemic religions that were the forerunners to patriarchy, certain conditions demanded the re-enactment of the father's murder:

Thus it became a duty to repeat the crime of parricide again and again in the sacrifice of the totem animal, whenever, as a result of changing conditions of life, the cherished fruit of the crime – appropriation of the paternal attributes – threatened to disappear.

(Freud 1960: 145)

On this account, the 'father killing' associated by Jardine with feminisation and gynesis might be reread as a *revision* of the son's murder of the primal father aimed at restoring the son to a position modelled on his father's. Though the temporality of this second killing would appear to be backward-looking, its aim is future-oriented: to restore to the son that which the father once took as his own. Under threat, the reprisal of parricide offers the hope that men can once again become *more like* the powerful father.

Marilyn French's *The Women's Room* (1978) shares much with *Portnoy's Complaint*. Like *Portnoy*, *The Women's Room* places the reader in the position of knowing analyst while also soliciting identification with the text's central protagonist. Like *Portnoy*, *The Women's Room*'s stream-of-consciousness confessions concern themselves with sexuality and its apparently inevitable shackling with suffering, constructed here, as in *Portnoy*, as the core truth of the subject. Like *Portnoy*, *The Women's Room*'s narrator describes ambivalent relations with her mother, as well as with other maternal figures.[11] Like *Portnoy*, *The Women's Room* ends by doubling back upon itself as the narrator describes beginning writing the book that is now ending. But here the similarities end, for unlike *Portnoy*, this doubling back is accompanied by no promise of future salvation. The confessional impulse appears, rather, to have delivered this narrating confessant to the truth of her own ambiguous relation to time's future promise. Thus, although Roth's and French's confessions appear to share some ground, they construct markedly divergent temporalities. Here, we come face to face with questions concerning autobiographical history, temporality and sexual difference. Although *Portnoy*'s problematisation of the father's role arguably positions Roth's text at the boundary between Jardine's parricidal, (post)modern 'gynesis' and modernity, I am suggesting, nevertheless, that these two confessions arguably share ground – and arguably 'modern' ground at that. Yet the temporalities that emerge here are divergent. While the ultimately forward-facing, 'becoming' temporality of *Portnoy* remains in keeping with modernity's dominant temporality – the temporality of Oedipalised masculinity – this cannot be said of the bleak backwards look of *The Women's Room*, which bespeaks, rather, an acknowledgement of femininity's stranded position between a present that is always already suffused by loss/death and a revision of the past predicated upon the impossible fantasy of maternal plenitude.

Though the so-called 'crisis' of the postmodern may be challenging the 'social and familial' father's capacity even loosely to resemble the *primal* father, this challenge can be met with in a number of ways. In *Portnoy*, I have suggested, the son's endless complaints about the father's weakness constitute a revised 'killing' – a killing which aims to restore the son's capacity to *resemble* the powerful, primal father. For Portnoy, at least, furious melancholy represents nostalgia for a father who may still be redeemable for/as his own future. This ending's promise contrasts starkly with the 'futureless' future that opens up at the end of *The Women's Room*, which struggles, though ultimately comes adrift, I would argue in its attempt to redeem the future by confessing the past. For though the temporality of the confession directs its confessant towards the future, Mira, the central protagonist of *The Women's Room* remains haunted by the ghostly figure of her erstwhile friend Val, who represents, in displaced form, the impossible 'phallic mother' of feminine nostalgic desire: a fantasy figure who is condemned not to renewed life (like the murdered primal father resurrected by patriarchy), but to annihilation by the future. To speak simply of the (modern) ground shared by confessions is to miss this difference, a difference that problematises the very *idea* of that shared, homogeneous, continuum of time suggested by epochal divisions.

Remembrance, temporality and sexual difference

Eva Hoffman's *Lost In Translation* (1989) and Philip Roth's *Patrimony* (1991) remember, rather than confess, childhood. Both these texts are suffused with nostalgia, though while *Lost In Translation* is drawn back to and works through nostalgia for the past and for the motherland, revealing their past promise as 'myth', *Patrimony* remembers Roth's father in elegiac and appreciative terms, while seemingly demonstrating that this father falls short of the fantasised ideal of patriarchy. Yet, as *Patrimony*'s ending makes clear, this other father remains a powerful undercurrent. After his father's death, the narrator recounts a dream in which his father berates him for burying him incorrectly, before realising that:

> he had been alluding to this book. ... The dream was telling me that, if not in my books or in my life, at least in my dreams I would live perennially as his little son, with the conscience of a little son, just as he would remain alive there not only as my father, but as *the* father, sitting in judgement on what-ever I do.
>   You must not forget anything.
>
> (Roth 1992: 237–8)

Roth's *Patrimony* remembers the author/narrator's father, Herman, as he gradu-ally succumbs to a death brought on by the effects of a brain tumour. Interspersed with scenes which detail visits to specialists and Herman's deterio-rating condition, the author/narrator retells his father's life-story. *Patrimony*'s unflinching gaze dwells lovingly on a father decimated by the ravages of time, illness and decay. The narration describes the failing father's body in visceral detail: his loss of sight, his facial paralysis, his difficulty swallowing, his rectal fissures, his loss of bowel control. The narration of this deterioration, replete with descriptions of Herman weeping, or slumped, immobile, in a chair, are counterpointed, however, by memories of his stubborn determination, grit and guts, as well as examples of his present fortitude. In a phone conversation, the narrator, Phil, explains to his friend Joanna:

> He's been remarkable. I don't mean in some unusual way. I mean in his own mundane, bull-headed way. His strength amazes me. ... Anybody's helplessness is difficult ... but the helplessness of an old person who once had such vigor ...
>
> (Roth 1992: 123)

The qualification of 'remarkable' here – 'I don't mean in some unusual way' – exemplifies the narrator's continual and insistent differentiation between his father's *real* capacities and super-human or idealised qualities that his father lacks. In *Totem and Taboo*, Freud argued that though the brothers' parricidal remorse eventually produced patriarchal societies which sought to restore the father to his rightful place, a gap remained between the patriarchal father and the primal father – a gap that produced longing *for* that other father (Freud 1960: 149). Feminist-inspired cultural theory has argued that though Freud's account of the masculine Oedipal complex describes a passage from an identification with the 'other' father, the super-human primal father, to a recognition that neither the son *nor* the familial father can ever occupy that powerful position, this is a recognition defended against, rather than encouraged, by patriarchy (Radstone 1995b: 152). *Patrimony*'s descriptions of the dying father's frailty and of the younger father's 'mundane' strength remember the father in quintessentially 'earthly' terms – they seem, that is, to emphasise the gap between the real and the primal father. At the same time, *Patrimony*'s question becomes precisely that of the book's title: under these conditions, what is it that can be passed on from father to son? What is it that now constitutes 'patrimony'?

I have already suggested that the Oedipus complex's promise to the son – a wife like your mother; a life resembling mine – inaugurates, too, a future-oriented temporality. Clearing up after his father, the narrator responds to the book's question about *contemporary* patrimony thus: 'There was my patrimony: not the money, not the tefillin, not the shaving mug, but the shit' (Roth 1992: 176). In place, that is, of patrimonial inheritance's objects of economic, religious or familial symbolic exchange, *Patrimony* offers 'shit', which, in this context, signifies a reminder, to the son, of his father's and his own fallibility, mortality, earth-boundedness.

Portnoy's Complaint and *Patrimony* arguably return to the killing scene of *Totem and Taboo* with different emphases and with different results. *Portnoy* recollects the annihilatory and triumphant aspects of that scene. Its future-oriented confession of the past remembers and repeats parricide to secure a reappropriation of the primal father's attributes. *Patrimony* remembers, rather, the remorse inaugurated by that scene. Its literary act 'of memory, elegy and appreciation' (Roth 1992: backcover text) constitutes an act of totemic remorse. But in place of the totemic hope that remorse might undo murder and bring the primal father back to life, *Patrimony* consigns him to a mythical past. Though the narrator scans his memory for recollections of a more-than-mundane father, the strengths he does remember are always revised *as* 'mundane'. While it is the *myth* of the 'other' father which continues to drive this remembrance, the temporality of the narrative it produces seems inflected less by future-oriented promise than by the temporality of nature that returns life to dust, and that will bring the son to his father's fate.

Eva Hoffman's autobiographical work *Lost In Translation* (1989)[12] describes the narrator's experiences of childhood exiledom following her family's emigration from Poland to Canada. Like *Patrimony*, *Lost In Translation* is suffused with nostalgia, though in this instance that nostalgia focuses less on the father than on the lost motherland. The text is divided into three sections: part 1, 'Paradise'; part 2, 'Exile'; and part 3, 'The New World'. Like *Patrimony*, *Lost In Translation*'s nostalgic evocation of the past reveals the myths that constitute memory. Looking back to the years in Poland, the narrator comments: 'the wonder is what you can make a paradise out of' (Hoffman 1989: 5). Part 1 opens and closes with Ewa, the narrator, remembering standing on the deck of the *Batory*, about to sail off to Canada. Between the two rememberings of this moment, Part 1 describes a remembered Cracow childhood; Part 2 tells the story of Ewa's arrival in Canada, and her transformation into Eva, an immigrant struggling to learn 'life in a new language'; and in Part 3 Eva's narration is concerned with coming to terms with life in Canada, life in the 'new world', and the acknowledgement that 'No, there's no returning to the point of origin, no regaining of childhood unity.' The narration's ultimate acceptance of life in the new world is described in the following terms: 'The small space of the garden expands into the dimensions of peace. Time pulses through my blood like a river' (Hoffman 1989: 280). *Lost In Translation* dwells on loss. The loss that is dwelt on, the loss of home, of the place in which childhood was lived and the language that was first spoken, becomes, for Eva, 'the model of all loss'. But the losses nostalgically mourned in *Patrimony* and in *Lost In Translation* are, I want to insist, *different* losses productive of *different* temporalities. *Patrimony* nostalgically evokes a fallible and yet admirable father, a father who falls short of the 'primal' ideal. Its temporality is marked less by the future-oriented remembrance of the Oedipal promise than by a cyclical temporality that remembers the future as the past: the son will become the dying father. *Lost In Translation*'s nostalgia is self-reflexive and critical. Its aim is to work through the fantasies of plenitude that subtend a nostalgia prompted by the loss of the motherland. This nostalgia arguably revises, however, not 'all loss', but a specifically feminine loss: the little girl's Oedipal loss which, as I argued earlier, inaugurates not a temporality of future promise but one of nostalgic longing for a fantasised past. But just as *Patrimony*'s nostalgia undoes the fantasy of the primal father while acknowledging that his ghost still haunts, *Lost In Translation* insists that while the lure of nostalgia continues, the object of its desire is a myth. However, whereas *Patrimony* substitutes for *Portnoy*'s future-oriented confession a temporality that revises the future as the past, *Lost In Translation* delivers Eva not to the terrifying frozen time of *The Women's Room*, but to a new sense of life *in* time: having come to terms with the new world, Eva rejoices that 'time pulses through (her) blood like a river' (Hoffman 1989: 280). The last few pages of *Lost In Translation* consist of a meditation on the 'new' time inhabited, now by Eva. This time described, by the narrator, as 'middle time' is a time, she goes on to explain, which is 'neither too accelerated or too slowed down'; it is a time which offers a sense of the future 'to balance the earlier annunciation of loss' (*ibid.*). Yet 'middle time' fits neither into accounts of modernity's future-oriented progress nor into accounts of postmodernity's self-enclosed folding of the future back onto the past. In 'middle time' the future is no longer dreaded as terrifyingly unfamiliar – 'I lived with my teeth clenched against the next assault ...' (Hoffman 1989: 278) – but is anticipated, rather, in the shapes and forms of a recognisable world. This passage from the assault of the new to 'middle time' is not, in any simple way, the passage from modernity to postmodernity, for Eva's passage through exiledom is a passage shaped not simply by the repetition of primary loss, but by the revision of a sexually differentiated experience of loss – itself a revision – inscribed at a particular historical moment.

Neither *Patrimony*'s nor *Lost In Translation*'s narratives occupy, in any simple way, the temporality of 'history'. Yet neither do they occupy similar temporalities, for each narrative remembers its differentially temporalised past. Though it might seem that I have suggested that in *Lost In Translation* the female narrator appears to be born into modernity's historical time – a temporality in which the future beckons – while in *Patrimony* the future's promise seems harder to sustain, this would, I think, be too simple and reductive a conclusion.

While *Patrimony* remembers the masculine Oedipal promise, *Lost In Translation* remembers the temporality of an impossible nostalgia for a mythic past. Might there be a relation *between Patrimony*'s undoing of primal, phallic masculinity and *Lost In Translation*'s undoing of the myth of 'paradise' – the myth of the phallic mother? Such a hypothesis would need further substantiation. Suffice it to say, perhaps, that to think only in terms of modern and postmodern texts and times is to do the complexity of the sexual politics of time a great disservice.

Notes

1 One comprehensive study of autobiographical criticism (Marcus 1994) does already survey many histories of autobiography.

2 Though, in this chapter, I am describing autobiography as a genre, the question of whether or not autobiography can be said to constitute a genre has been much debated (see, for instance De Man 1979; Jay 1984: 15; Marcus 1994: 203; Radstone 1989: 23–4).

3 For a fuller account of the various tendencies within recent autobiographical criticism, see Laura Marcus's comprehensive study of the field (Marcus 1994, especially chaps 4 and 5).

4 It is now widely argued that it is not possible 'to arrive at any strict definition of autobiography, or clearly to mark it off from autobiographical fiction, or to make absolute distinctions between fiction and truth' (Wilson 1988: 23; see also Jay 1984: 15). In light of the immense difficulties presented by the task of distinguishing between the truly and the partly autobiographical, this chapter will use the term 'autobiographical' to

refer to a range of first-person confessions and texts of remembrance that have been read or that present themselves as autobiographical.

5 Confession's history is, of course, far longer than seems to be indicated here (Axthelm 1967; Radstone 1989).

6 I have to thank Kate Hodgkin for this understanding of the relation between confession, subjectivity and memory.

7 The work of Jean Laplanche, in particular, has been centrally concerned with the extension and development of Freud's insights concerning *Nachträglichkeit* (Fletcher and Stanton 1992).

8 Some feminist work has argued for an understanding of femininity's temporality that links it to, for instance, menstrual cycles, or the circularity of life and death, rather than to 'masculine' linearity. For an interesting selection of essays on feminism and temporality, see Forman and Sowton's *Taking Our Time* (Forman and Sowton 1989). Julia Kristeva's influential essay 'Women's Time' (Kristeva 1981) has shaped much thinking on this subject. Opinion has been split concerning the possibly essentialist analysis that it offers. My own thinking on questions of temporality and sexual difference has been shaped by an anti-essentialist reading of Kristeva's essay.

9 Here, I am glossing Jane Gallop's summarising of Lacan (Gallop 1985: 145–6).

10 Differences other than sexual difference might also be explored in relation to questions of temporality. How, for instance, does the recognition of ethnicity or colour *revise* the primary acknowledgement of temporal (and spatial) boundedness?

11 This analysis is a much-abbreviated extract from my PhD thesis (Radstone 1989), which offers a more detailed discussion of femininity's relation to confessional suffering and becomingness.

12 Elsewhere (Radstone 1995a) I have explored Hoffman's *Lost In Translation* in relation to questions of femininity, feminism and nostalgia.

Bibliography

Axthelm, P. (1967) *The Modern Confessional Novel*, New Haven: Yale University Press.

Belsey, C. (1980) *Critical Practice*, London: Methuen.

Benveniste, E. (1971) *Problems in General Linguistics*, Miami: University of Miami Press.

Berman, M. (1989) *All That Is Solid Melts Into Air*, London: Verso.

Coward, R. (1980) ' "This Novel Changes Lives": Are Womens' Novels Feminist Novels?', *Feminist Review*, 5.

De Man, P. (1979) 'Autobiography as De-facement', *Modern Language Notes*, 94, 5 (December).

Felski, R. (1989) *Beyond Feminist Aesthetics*, London: Hutchinson Radius.

Fletcher, J. and Stanton, M. (eds) (1992) *Jean Laplanche: Seduction, Translation, Drives*, London: Institute of Contemporary Arts.

Forman, F.J. with Sowton, C. (1989) *Taking Our Time: Feminist Perspectives on Temporality*, Oxford: Pergamon Press.

French, M. (1978) *The Women's Room*, London: Sphere.

Freud, S. (1960 [1913]) *Totem and Taboo*, London: Routledge.

Gallop, J. (1985) *Reading Lacan*, Ithaca: Cornell University Press.

Gusdorf, G. (1980) 'Conditions and Limits of Autobiography', in Olney, J. (ed), *Autobiography*, Princeton: Princeton University Press.

Hamilton, P. (1994) 'The Knife Edge: Debates about Memory and History', in Darian-Smith, K. and Hamilton, P., *Memory and History in Twentieth Century Australia*, Oxford: Oxford University Press.

Harvey, D. (1989) *The Condition of Postmodernity*, Oxford: Blackwell.

Hodgkin, K. (1999) 'Losing the Subject: Discontinuities of Self in Early Modern Writing', unpublished paper given at 'Frontiers of Memory' conference, Institute of Education, September.

Hoffman, E. (1989) *Lost In Translation: A Life In A New Language*, Harmondsworth: Penguin.

Howarth, W.L. (1974) 'Some Principles of Autobiography', *New Literary History*, 15 (Winter).

Huyssen, A. (1995) *Twilight Memories: Marking Time in a Culture of Amnesia*, London: Routledge.

Jardine, A. (1985) *Gynesis: Configurations of Woman and Modernity*, Ithaca and London: Cornell University Press.

Jay, P. (1984) *Being In The Text: Self-Representation from Wordsworth to Barthes*, Ithaca and London: Cornell University Press.

Jelinek, E. (ed.) (1980) *Women's Autobiography: Essays in Criticism*, Bloomington: Indiana University Press.

Kolodny, A. (1976) 'Some Notes on Defining a Feminist Literary Criticism', *Critical Inquiry*, 2 (Summer): 86.

Kristeva, J. (1981) 'Women's Time', *Signs*, 7, 1.

—— (1987) *Tales Of Love*, trans. Leon S. Roudiez, New York: Columbia University Press.

Laplanche, J. and Pontalis, J.-B. (1988) *The Language of Psychoanalysis*, London: Karnac Books.

Marcus, L. (1994) *Auto/biographical Discourses: Criticism, Theory, Practice*, Manchester and New York: Manchester University Press.

Mitchell, J. (1986) *The Selected Melanie Klein*, Penguin: Harmondsworth.

Modjeska, D. (1990) *Poppy*, Ringwood: McPhee Gribble.

Nicholson, L. (1990) *Feminism/Postmodernism*, New York and London: Routledge.

Olney, J. (1972) *Metaphors of Self*, Princeton: Princeton University Press.

Osborne, P. (1995) *The Politics of Time: Modernity and Avant-Garde*, London: Verso.

Radstone, S. (1989) 'The Women's Room: Women and the Confessional Mode', unpublished PhD thesis, Warwick University.

—— (1995a) 'Remembering Ourselves: Memory, Writing and the Female Self', in P. Florence and D. Reynolds (eds), *Feminist Subjects, Multi-Media: Cultural Methodologies*, Manchester: Manchester University Press.

—— (1995b) 'Too Sraight a Drive to the Tollbooth: Masculinity, Mortality and Al Pacino', in P. Kirkham and J. Thumim (eds), *Me Jane: Masculinity, Movies and Women*, London: Lawrence and Wishart.

—— (2000) 'Working with Memory: An Introduction', in *Memory and Methodology*, Oxford and New York: Berg.

Renza, L. (1977) 'The Veto of the Imagination: A Theory of Autobiography', *New Literary History*, 9, 1 (Autumn).

Roth, P. (1995 [1969]) *Portnoy's Complaint*, London: Vintage.

—— (1992) *Patrimony: A True Story*, London: Vintage.

Samuel, R. (1994) *Theatres of Memory*, London: Verso.

Spengemann, W.C. (1980) *The Forms of Autobiography*, New Haven: Yale University Press.

Waugh, P. (1989) *Feminine Fictions: Revisiting the Postmodern*, London: Routledge.

Wilson, E. (1988) 'Tell it Like it is: Women and Confessional Writing', in S. Radstone (ed.), *Sweet Dreams: Sexuality, Gender and Popular Fiction*, London: Lawrence and Wishart.

13 Circa 1959

Nancy K. Miller

I forced myself to keep my own figure fictitious; legendary. If I had said, Look here I am uneducated, because my brothers used up all the family funds which is the fact – Well they'd have said; she has an axe to grind; and no one would have taken me seriously.

(Virginia Woolf, letter to Ethel Smyth, 8 June 1933)

The con: a fable

I didn't go to Stratford-upon-Avon to study Shakespeare. That's not true either. I did want to study Shakespeare. I was an English major, after all. But mainly I wanted to get away from my parents and impress my boyfriend. David had given me a brown leather-bound diary with gilt-tipped pages for a going-away present. As soon as the boat pulled out of the harbour, I started recording my feelings and impressions. After some twenty pages of imitation travel writing, the diary abruptly stops with an arrow pointing towards Oxford. Not another line. And yet what happened at Oxford was the beginning of everything, which of course I couldn't possibly have known then. It was 1959 and I was eighteen – a literary girl in love with books (her boyfriend was an English major too).

The Shakespeare Institute offered a six-week summer course for foreign students. It took a while for me to understand that being an American in England was being a foreigner. I had begun reading Henry James and admired Isabel Archer. I knew this; I just hadn't made the connection. Famous Shakespeareans gave lectures at the Institute every morning. On performance nights, we would go to 'The Dirty Duck', the pub across the road from The Royal Shakespeare Theatre, and wait for the actors to turn up. Our teachers chatted with them about the performance, almost casually, over rounds of lager. We watched them out of the corner of our eyes. Was I impressed? I note my views in my diary, on 25 July 1959: 'Stratford: is a phony, artificial, contrived TOURIST TOWN. It is quaint but this really isn't enough.' Bored by school from the beginning, I wrote home daily aerograms complaining to my parents. Couldn't I please drop my classes and travel all summer?

'Dearest Doll', my father begins. Then comes a summary of paternal permissions and prohibitions:

1   The fees have been paid. Receipt is dated July 6.
2   You may rent a bike and ride it.
3   You may travel week-ends. Be discreet.
4   Tuition covers whole period. Don't judge course by partial early performance.
5   Passage back has been assured and extension of stay is out of question.

My father was one of the last patriarchs, and a lawyer to boot.

One weekend my parents, who were touring northern Europe, came to England and I took the train to meet them in London. There's a picture my father snapped on an excursion to Whitechapel we made together that weekend. I'm standing with my mother, wearing a navy blue print sleeveless dress that has a tight dropped waist with a matching bolero jacket. My frizzy hair (the bane of my existence) is pulled back tight in a bun and I'm wearing prescription sunglasses, light green lenses with pale, almost transparent pink harlequin frames that cast a v-like shadow on my cheeks. In the diary, I describe the unsmiling girl in the picture as she appeared a few weeks earlier that summer on the SS Rotterdam, where I documented my experiments in shipboard romance. 'Tonight I feel ugly. I've noticed this for some time. My figure looked quite good in the navy dress but there is something wrong with my face.' I seemed to be having a hard time having fun, even without the company of my parents.

One day toward the end of the summer course, Judy, another American girl in our group at Stratford, and I hitchhiked to Oxford.[1] The Bodleian and the Radcliffe Camera were high on the list that David had compiled for my instruction, though he had not yet crossed the ocean himself (not that we were competitive). A large part of my desire to visit Oxford was to report on what I had seen with as much architectural detail as I could muster. In the late afternoon, standing morosely under our umbrellas in the parking lot of one of the colleges, Judy and I were approached by a man in a long trenchcoat who asked if we needed help. A lecturer at King's College, just back from teaching in the States (Yale, no less) with an invitation to return, was how Peter Bradshaw presented himself. Americans had been very kind to him during his stay, he said, and he wanted to repay their generosity. Besides, he casually added on the way to the car, his family had their ancestral home, a castle, in Warwick, a town not far from Stratford. As we drove back in the rain, we made plans for the following week. Judy and I were to visit his chateau and meet his family. (Our children, I thought happily in the backseat, will have an English accent.) One night, after a week of meals and drinks, we all went back to one of the student's rooms to drink scotch, a newly acquired taste. Peter explained that he couldn't drive back to Warwick that night because his car was being repaired. I eagerly offered him my room, proposing to sleep with Judy and her roommate in theirs.

Flash forward. Reader, please remember this is the 1950s; we cut away from the bedroom to which I returned in stealth later that night. (It's also true that I can't see into that room anymore, beyond twin beds, a tall dresser, and a prolifer- ation of ruffles and antimacassars.) The next morning, unable to concentrate on the lecture, and fantasising about our romantic adventures to come – the castle, the moat – I reread the week's mail. My parents had finally sent me the money I'd been pleading for and I wanted to count it again. The envelope was empty. A small rush of panic made me sweaty. I turned to Judy: look in your wallet, I signalled wildly in pantomime. She gestured back that her money was gone too. Abandoning Coriolanus to his fate, we jumped up in tandem, hopped on our bikes, and raced back to our rooms at the Barwyn. No money anywhere. It wasn't quite 1 pm.

The afternoon dragged on. I felt sure my prince would return. So when the police arrived at tea time, called in by one of the other students who had disap- proved of Peter from the start, I refused to talk. (Once back in Stratford, Peter had shared meals with us, sometimes treating us to drinks, all the while politely cadging small sums of money from the students in our little group; quietly, one- by-one, each promising not to tell the others.) The officers were polite and kind – they were English, after all – but unbending. They threatened to tell our parents if we didn't cooperate. My parents will kill me, I thought, and in my case this was barely a figure of speech. I nodded when I had to admit in front of everyone that there were 'intimacies' between Peter and me, but I did not confess that he had proposed to me; the marriage proposal seemed the final humiliation rather than a mitigating excuse. We traipsed down to the police station at the edge of the village and grudgingly flipped through an album of mugshots, convinced

Figure 7   My father's snapshot

that this was a huge, not to say unjust, waste of our time, that Peter would reappear as promised – a gentleman's word.

We begged the policeman to phone him. But there was no Bradshaw teaching at King's College. Not only was the family not titled, its name didn't exist in Warwick. The worst was yet to come. I turned a page and my heart, as they say, stood still. Full face or in profile, I don't remember which, there was the face I had spent the night in bed with; but despite the evidence I still would not admit to myself that I had been caressed by a criminal. 'Peter' had recently been released from prison. I was a nice Jewish girl from New York who went to midnight concerts at Carnegie Hall and saw only foreign movies in black and white. How could I have daydreamed about life with a man who had spent most of his doing time for conning little old ladies?

Reader, did I really want to marry him? True, I wanted an adventure but then I couldn't manage to separate it from fairytale – lords, castles, being picked up out of your boring middle-class life and carried away to reign as the princess (eventually queen) you really were. The professor would have to stand in for the prince, the white car for the horse. I was still in the world of 1950s girls where whatever your ambition – to be smart, learn about Shakespeare, travel the world – that desire was usually harnessed to the marriage plot. I don't remember leaving Stratford but once I got to Paris, I closed the door on England and my stupid American girl secret, and changed my major to French. In the summer of 1959 I had already found my emotional style – a kind of desperate unknowing.

Black stockings

> Sexual intercourse began
> In nineteen sixty-three
> (Which was rather late for me) –
> Between the end of the *Chatterley* ban
> And the Beatles' first LP.
> (Philip Larkin, *Annus Mirabilis*)

At the beginning of the 1990s, I was invited to contribute to an anthology called *Changing Subjects: The Making of Feminist Literary Criticism*. The editors describe the book, as 'an effort of remembering and historicising, a collection of individual stories that, taken together, comprise a collective story – histories that make a history' (Greene and Kahn 1993: 1). These stories form an intellectual memoir emerging from a generation of American women with literary aspirations for whom the 1950s were 'the decade', the editors state in their introduction, 'that produced us and produced feminism' (2) – 'us', that is to say, academics, at various points on the graph of their middle age; most straight and white, and writing in the 1990s from tenured positions. My contribution to the volume was titled 'Decades', where the 1960s prelude to my 1970s coming-to-feminism story began, as it happened, in Paris. Ten years later I find myself writing what feels like the prequel to 'Decades'; but this time I return to the native grounds of my New York 1950s, to the years and yearnings that directly preceded the official narrative.

What is safe to tell? I'd like to sketch out the lines of a cultural narrative in which these histories and voices converge, a tapestry woven of academic feminist history and of private lives that took place in the American 1950s, of autobiographical silences and public statements. In the pages that follow I will be present as a participant/observer of a collective feminist past whose origins I locate in the late 1950s, and, as we've just seen, an autobiographical actor in my own drama of a highly regulated gender culture.

But which 1950s and whose? If there is a lazy consensus about how to date the moment at which the 1950s seemed over, it's of course in large part due to the magnitude of the presidential assassination in 1963. Less easy to pinpoint as traumatically is the beginning of its end. We could take the 1957 launching of Sputnik, or on the literary scene, the stunning success of Jack Kerouac's *On the Road*. For autobiographical reasons, as we've seen, I'm partial to 1959, when I first went to Europe and began, unbeknownst to me, of course, my feminist odyssey – fear of flying when we were still crossing the ocean by boat. The crossing changed my life. In 1959, the Barbie doll, weird harbinger of feminine futures and bodies, appeared on the scene. In 1959, Castro became Premier of Cuba. Such are the intimacies of the timeline.

Whatever shape you give to the arc of postwar culture, there's evidence in this period of transition pointing to a palpable if undefinable sense that in the realm of the social relations between men and women, but especially for American women, things were changing. *The Presidential Report on the Status of Women*, the result of the work of Kennedy's Commission on the Status of Women established in 1961, made front-page news in 1963; it addressed – with predictable ambiguity – questions about what were not then called gender roles and the social implications of women's work. And furtively but surely, ideas about what sex might mean for women were in the air. In 1960 the Pill was approved by the FDA. By 1963, 2.3 million American women were taking the Pill, and their numbers were rising.[2] The 'problem without a name' described by Betty Friedan became a popular national cry when it was diagnosed in *The Feminine Mystique*. She argues:

> Sex is the only frontier open to women who have always lived within the confines of the feminine mystique. In the past fifteen years, the sexual frontier has been forced to expand perhaps beyond the limits of possibility, to fill the time available, to fill the vacuum created by denial of larger goals and purposes for American women.

> (Friedan 1984: 261)

A radical social refiguration for girls took place in this window between Kerouac and Kennedy, Barbie and Betty, but what road could an adventurous girl follow? Sylvia Plath, an emblematic though not perhaps exemplary figure of the drama lived by ambitious girls of this era, left for England with Ted Hughes at the end of 1959 and killed herself in London in February 1963.

In the spring of 1959, I was a sophomore at Barnard College, the school for girls of Columbia University. In New York based literary culture, this was the year that Allen Ginsberg and his friends read their new poetry at Columbia University and got lots of attention. When she described the event in the *Partisan Review*, Diana Trilling looked down disdainfully from her perch as faculty wife with reserved seats at the girls who turned out for Ginsberg's performance – 'the always-new shock of so many young girls, so few of them pretty, and so many dreadful black stockings'. She did not think much of our male counterparts either – 'so many young men, so few of them – despite the many black beards – with any promise of masculinity' (Trilling 1964: 224).[3] And as though she was descending into the subway on a steamy summer afternoon, Mrs Trilling admitted that to her astonishment the audience of such poor specimens didn't smell bad!

This was one of two major national events related to the Columbia scene that year. The second had to do with the famous literary Van Doren family. Mark van Doren was retiring, but the possibility of continuity was present in the form of his son Charles, who was just finishing his PhD and had been newly promoted to the rank of Assistant Professor. Father and son had shared an office; now Charlie was to be on his own. But Charlie let the family down in a big way. He allowed himself to be seduced by a deal with NBC television to appear on the enormously popular quiz show *Twenty-One*. Van Doren's dazzling success as a contestant conferred instant national celebrity. But when his picture appeared on the cover of *Life* magazine in October 1959, it was not just because he was smart. *Twenty-One* had been rigged and Van Doren admitted his guilty role before a House Subcommittee in Washington.[4] Because it was about television – a young medium that inspired both fear and enchantment – and because Van Doren was a Van Doren, exposure was relentless. Charles Van Doren withdrew from Columbia and, for a long while, from the public eye. (This story was revived in the 1990s by the movie called *Quiz Show*.)

What does this American fable of lost innocence have to do with my own, you might be wondering? For one thing, Charlie's 'last and favorite' student (his words) was none other than David, my very own Renaissance man, whom we saw from afar in the Stratford episode, a senior at Columbia, forever ahead of me. That connection, I figure, makes it my story too. For now, let these few degrees of separation provide a metaphorical bridge to the snapshot of an era. In retrospect, it seems that what finally characterises those years for me is a sense of being *close* to what mattered, here by relation to a man, but somehow at an oblique angle to the real thing. David went to the poetry reading, he says; why didn't he take me? I always thought we went everywhere important together. Suddenly this event that I don't remember seems symptomatic. What else did I miss?

The *Life* magazine photospread on the Van Dorens shows a clan of WASP (*avant la lettre*) entitlement, where whatever else women may have accomplished –

and many of the Van Doren women were 'literary' too – they are of course called 'Mrs. Charles Van Doren' or, my favorite, 'Mrs. Spencer Klaw'. Babies are ubiquitous, even when the women have professional activities to their names. The men are the professors. In one photo, Charlie is sitting around a seminar table, index finger raised ominously, warning the class of all male students 'to expect a question on Milton in the M.A. exam'. In another, father and son bond in a book-lined office, talking of literature and baseball. Under the photo of Charlie's wife 'dandling' their baby daughter, the caption explains that he 'hired her as secretary to answer his *Twenty-One* fan mail and married her three months later'.

Life or *Life* magazine? If marrying literary royalty was not the destiny that the girls in their 'dreadful black stockings' had in mind, it's what framed their universe. Female ambition was rarely on display in its own form, or even visible to ourselves – not that we saw ourselves self-consciously as a group. On the contrary. This was the era of individual rebellions. The contingency that links the Van Doren scandal to the scene at the poetry reading makes another kind of sense when replaced in a retrospective narrative about a piece of Manhattan culture in the 1950s. But what *is* memory, if not a reconstruction? In her memoir about coming of age in this urban landscape, Hettie Jones recalls Trilling's 'Partisan' article with an amused edge: 'She didn't find us pretty, and hadn't liked our legs at all. "So many black stockings", she wrote with distaste.' But there's a nice twist to this recollection. A year later Hettie, who worked as a subscription manager at the magazine, encounters Mary McCarthy at a party. 'I like your stockings,' McCarthy says with a smile. Jones couldn't keep herself from telling the writer where she could buy them herself: 'on Fourteenth Street, at the Bargain Hosiery Center next to the Catholic Church' (Jones 1991: 129).

Did 'bad' sex produce 'good' feminism? or how did we get to the 1970s?

> So I began to think maybe it was true that when
> you were married and had children it was like being
> brainwashed, and afterward you went about numb
> as a slave in some private, totalitarian state.
> (Sylvia Plath, *The Bell Jar*)

What if you didn't want to marry the prince, or anyone else for that matter?

Looking at the 1960s as they modulate into the 1970s in a short history of literary criticism, Catharine Stimpson returns to the period in which Kate Millett's *Sexual Politics* came into existence, evoking that era, the mid-1960s when both Kates were teaching at Barnard, as a personal witness to it:

> Kate and I wanted to be accepted in the academy that we treasured, to have our degrees and lecterns. We also wanted to be different. Ambition, not the

desire to marry the boy next door, had taken Kate out of Saint Paul, Minnesota, and me out of Bellingham, Washington. Within a few weeks, we were sharing an office at Barnard. She looked more conservative than I, in her long skirts, pumps, and hair drawn back in, yes, a bun. I jumped around the corridors in miniskirts, tights, and unruly, unkeyed, naturally curly locks. The discrepancy between a woman's decorous appearance and flaring subjectivity – in a Jane Eyre, for example – was to become a theme for feminist criticism. I might have looked the more radical, but I was, intellectually, the more conservative, prudent, and buttoned-up.

(Stimpson 1992: 252)

Her account, Stimpson notes half-apologetically, while 'autobiographical', nonetheless 'reflects some of the cultural ferment in which *Sexual Politics* developed' (251). But for me, it's precisely the personal details of skirts, hair, shoes that make cultural history come alive: the inclusion of those daily issues of *style* that define a moment in a collective social pattern; pantyhose and tights have replaced the black stockings. I love having the hair and the skirts in my line of vision. (As I write this, 1970s fashions have returned – the ghosts of my emergent feminist days, bell bottoms, platform shoes, and little sweaters have appeared on the Barnard campus, I'm told. It's a form of haunting.)

Writing in the 1990s and providing the intellectual history of a young feminist from a post-1950s generation, Jane Gallop personalises the sexual in sexual politics. She describes the effect of reading *The Second Sex* in the early 1970s; she learned from Beauvoir's essay, she says, that women could masturbate. Then she went on to be fired up by her studies in college and graduate school; not surprisingly, she wrote her dissertation on Sade (Gallop 1997: 4). (Female perversions, we know, often begin in school.) What turned Beauvoir on? In the spring of 1997, the love letters Simone de Beauvoir wrote in English to Nelson Algren were published in France – translated into French by Sylvie le Bon de Beauvoir, Beauvoir's adopted daughter and literary executor. The letters, now available in the original English, begin in 1947 after Beauvoir's visit to America during the early stages of writing the essay that was to become *The Second Sex*.[5] In France the importance of the letters was discussed in a popular television programme ('Bouillon de Culture', 6 March 1997) devoted to contemporary writers – all men. A woman editor (and the only woman on the screen, including the host) from Gallimard, the publisher, who assured the viewers that men could be interested in this aspect of Beauvoir's life too, presented the letters. Philippe Sollers, the ubiquitous French man of letters, remarked with his usual authority that we would now be able to understand *The Second Sex* in a new way since we can see that it was thanks to her love for Algren that Beauvoir was empowered to write *The Second Sex* – thus proving that the book wasn't the 'catechism for feminists' it had been made out to be. In 1947 Beauvoir discovers America and orgasm, and writes a major book. 'We must put dates on things,' Sollers remarks, as though he had just discovered America himself.

Reviewers were especially enchanted by places in which Beauvoir showed she was 'just a woman' like all the rest of us, a hot heterosexual woman, not an amoral existentialist and lesbian:

> But for myself, I just know that I could not sleep with another man now until I meet you again. ... I'll be as faithful as a dutiful and conventional wife just because I could not help it – that is the way it is.
>
> (Beauvoir 1998: 69)

A few years later, the good wife model still prevails, despite the serious problems the two had already encountered in their transatlantic affair. Beauvoir writes in 1950:

> Oh Nelson! I'll be so nice and good, you'll see. I'll wash the floor, I'll cook the whole meals, I'll write your book as well as mine, I'll make love to you ten times at night and as much in the day, even if I feel a bit tired.
>
> (Beauvoir 1998: 324)

(We can note in passing the 1950s discourse of caring for one's man, along with the bolder but tranquil ambition of writing his book, while writing her own! An offer, sadly for Simone, he could refuse.)

Was Sollers right? It's true that Algren had encouraged Beauvoir to expand her 'essay on women' into a book. Deirdre Bair, Beauvoir's biographer, fleshes out the picture: Algren and Beauvoir 'had discussed the situation of women when they were in New York in May, sitting and smoking in the twin beds of their hotel room after they made love'. Bair writes, 'He had been fascinated to learn that French women had only just received the vote, and as his questions became more probing they had settled on the topic of "women's status throughout the world" as [her] possible theme' (Bair 1990: 353).[6] If Beauvoir discussed the project that became *The Second Sex* as pillow talk with Algren in New York, Sartre had played a catalytic (though perhaps not orgasmic) role earlier in the story by convincing Beauvoir to write about something he thought she knew about very well – 'the condition of women in its broadest terms' (in Bair 1990: 325).

The letters shed new light, too, on Beauvoir both as a literary critic and as a reader during the complicated climate of the postwar (she identified herself in public as politically feminist only in the early 1970s). Beauvoir writes to Algren about D.H. Lawrence in November 1948, reporting on her research:

> Among a lot of tedious or silly books I am reading about women, I read over Lawrence's novels. It is rather tedious: always the same sex-story, the woman brought to submission by a lover who looks like Lawrence himself, has to kill her own self so they can both be happy. Well, you didn't kill my self and we were pretty happy, were we not? Still, sometimes he speaks with real warmth about love life, of such things in love life nobody dares to speak about; it should be more simple, so it could be moving and good. The begin-

ning of *The Plumed Serpent* is a story of a bull fight in Mexico, but he doesn't feel it the way I did, nor the way you did neither. Tell me if you think anything about Lawrence?

(Beauvoir 1998: 236)

What's striking here is the explicitly autobiographical way in which Beauvoir describes her critical views on Lawrence. Unlike the forceful but abstract analysis of Lawrence's novels in *The Second Sex*, the letters to Algren reveal a Beauvoir present in the flesh as a physical and sexual being.[7] Beauvoir clearly separates her personal experience with Algren from the ideology that shapes Lawrence's apprehension of sexuality. In other words, she perceives, names and analyses in literature what Millett later, without, alas, acknowledging the insights of her precursor, would come to call 'sexual politics'.[8] But unlike Millett, Beauvoir also turned to women writers throughout *The Second Sex* as precious testimony to other views of the female condition.

The ten years that preceded the publication of *Sexual Politics* were, as we might expect from the decade of the 1960s, full of sex. But what kind? Or put another way, to what extent did 1970s feminism emerge from reading – or trying to read – literary texts that were banned or newly unbanned in the immediately preceding decades?[9] D.H. Lawrence's 1928 *Lady Chatterley's Lover* was first brought out legally and completely in the USA in 1959 (1960 in England); in 1959 Olympia Press published William Burroughs' *Naked Lunch* in Paris. Like Virginia Woolf, who refers in *A Room of One's Own* to the obscenity trial for Radclyffe Hall's *The Well of Loneliness*, and Sylvia Plath, who writes home to her mother in America about the trial for *Lady Chatterley's Lover* in England, the early feminist critics of sexual politics made literary theory from contemporary readings of male writers famous, not to say infamous, for their views on sex and women: Miller, Lawrence, Kerouac, Mailer, to name the usual suspects (the views were not identical but were not incompatible either).[10] Miller's *Tropic of Cancer* was published in the United States in 1961, *Capricorn* in 1962. Many 1950s girls had a hard time getting out from under, so to speak, these manuals of male pleasure and bonding, especially when the books came with an aura of rebellion and violation. What imaginative girl *wouldn't* want to know – or try on – what was in the books that were banned?

Banned books were indeed key to the zeitgeist and someone much less downtown and literary than Kate Millett would have dipped into an earlier edition of *Lady Chatterley's Lover*, even if she had already read it in an underground, pirated copy. In my senior year of high school, I note in my diary for 1957, 'I read Lady Chatterly's Lover [sic]. I sort of would like a lover. I don't know', I added nervously.

How do we live with the books that change our lives? Impossible to have come to intellectual consciousness between 1957 and 1967 without reading the Beats and hearing about the obscenity trials. And any girl's reading habits would include contradictions: bestsellers like Grace Metalious's *Peyton Place* or Herman Wouk's *Marjorie Morningstar*, along with the recondite poetry of T.S. Eliot and Wallace Stevens; the sexy novels of Kerouac, Lawrence and maybe even Mailer alongside *Seventeen* magazine and *True Confessions*, not to mention the romances of Taylor Caldwell. Plath, herself, was a studious reader of women's magazines and wanted to publish stories in their pages – the 'slicks' – for money. These perplexing reading experiences led some girls avid for transgression to try and make their lives resemble the books, or at least look for a different kind of life and world after reading them; for some that meant becoming many years later, though they surely didn't imagine it at the time, feminist critics.

I sometimes think we were the last generation to get the information we sought about sex from books, not from movies. What happened, for instance, when Millett met Miller on paper?

Sexual Politics opens (how could we forget?) with an excerpt from Henry Miller's novel *Sexus*, set in a bathroom, with the narrator in the bathtub.[11] Ida, the sex partner in question, enters the scene wearing a silk bathrobe and silk stockings. Millett then produces an *explication de texte*, focusing pedagogically on a crucial detail in the description of the woman as she brings the narrator towels. Here Millett makes an even bolder critical move than starting her book *in medium coitum* with a woman's pubic hair ('muff') viewed at eye level; she invokes the existence and reaction of a female reader:

> The female reader may realize that one rarely wears stockings without the assistance of other paraphernalia, girdle or garters, but classic masculine fantasy dictates that nudity's most appropriate exception is some gauzelike material, be it hosiery or underwear.
>
> (Millett 1970: 5)

Girdle or garters, ultimately the impact of the passage is not limited to the plausible or implausible detail of undergarments. It's the recognition of gendered reading, especially in the face of sexual representation:

> What the reader is vicariously experiencing at this juncture is a nearly supernatural sense of power – should the reader be a male. For the passage … is also a male assertion of dominance over a weak, compliant, and rather unintelligent female. It is a case of sexual politics at the fundamental level of copulation. Several satisfactions for the hero and reader alike undoubtedly accrue upon this triumph of the male ego …
>
> (1970: 6)

Millett stays focused on the masculine, what Gilbert and Gubar call the 'male male impersonation' of the 1960s and 1970s, 'men's uncertainty about their own potency' (1994: 321).

And should the reader be not only female but lesbian? In the essay I cited earlier, Stimpson rapidly alludes to Millett's autobiographical reticence in the book, commenting on the 'almost total erasure of lesbianism, especially ironic', she notes, 'since Millett's autobiographies were later to write the lesbian and women's sexual pleasure into contemporary literature' (Stimpson 1992: 265). In

Flying, Millett's first autobiography published in 1974 and republished in 1990, Millett herself revisits the writing contexts of *Sexual Politics*. In a brief introduction to the new edition, she describes *Sexual Politics* as a 'Ph.D. thesis composed in Mandarin mid-Atlantic to propitiate a committee of professors of English, a colonial situation' (Millett 1990: x). This echoes the language of 1974 where Millett returns in time to the Bowery, to the 'red table where I wrote a book, so long ago – writing for professors. Writing when I did not even want to be a writer, just burning with an idea that could make me do a book, call it a thesis, rip off a Ph.D.' (43). Looking back, after the fact of the book for professors, Millett revels in her well-earned autobiographical freedom. 'I'd never yet written', Millett admits in the introduction to *Flying*, 'in my own voice' (ix). *Flying* also represents what the so-called French feminists of this period liked to call 'coming to writing'.

The danger of expressing an individual autobiographical desire, even as late as 1970, here gets translated, I think, into the reinvention of the biographical, sexed and gendered reader. Like Woolf's fictionalised 'I' in *A Room of One's Own*, the author is present but at a literary distance. In the case of Woolf, Beauvoir and Millett, moreover, the biographical 'I' is also – in complex and singular ways – bisexual (at the time of publication, Millett was rather publicly married, kissing her husband for the cameras, etc.). Doubtless, the reception history of *Sexual Politics* (like Foucault's later *History of Sexuality*) would have been radically different had autobiographical material entered the author's arguments directly, regardless of the fact that those in the know, knew.[12] This is a variant of the fear Woolf expressed in the letter to Ethel Smyth that if she had identified herself autobiographically, her essay would not have been taken seriously, but dismissed as a family affair.

In 1970 *Sexual Politics* landed Kate Millett on the cover of *Time* magazine, as *Sexual Behavior in the Human Female* had done for Alfred Kinsey in 1953, because she too had hit an exposed nerve in the contemporary culture, a national culture obsessed with sex. This was a moment in American history when ideas about social change and new citizens were shot through with sexual fantasies, and in which, as Eve Sedgwick says about the century as a whole, 'the "sex appeal" of sexuality' dominated the imagination (Sedgwick 1992: 280). Critics have asked what would have happened if Millett had chosen other literary works through which to ground her claims for sexual politics.[13] Wouldn't she have had to write a different book? Maybe. But that's somewhat like saying that Henry Miller would have written the bathtub scene differently if pantyhose had been invented in the 1920s.

Did 'bad' sex lead to 'good' feminism? Yes and no. In a discussion published in the *Women's Studies Quarterly* at the beginning of the 1990s entitled '*Sexual Politics*: Twenty Years Later', Kate Millett, Alix Kates Shulman and Catharine Stimpson reflect on the anniversary of the book and celebrate the publication of a new edition.[14] Millett recalls the autobiographical context of the book's production:

> It happened because I got fired ... I'd been doing the reading for years; a whole summer for Lawrence. But what I mean is that this became the book it is, even that it became a book at all, taking off with that 'to hell with it' first chapter, rather than another Ph.D. thesis, because at the end of 1968 I was fired from ... a job I would have worked at gladly the rest of my life.
>
> (Millett *et al.* 1991: 37)

(Millett's participation in the Columbia strike eliminated that possibility – given Barnard's institutionally dependent relation on Columbia.) In the new introduction to the book, Millett emphasises the collective nature of the thinking that went into its making: 'I was', she writes, 'the scribe of many' (Millett *et al.* 1991: 39). Shulman wishes hopefully that the reissue of the book might 'provide a certain timely kick' (Millett *et al.* 1991: 36). Instead, the book is out of print again and Millett rather bitterly underemployed.

Bad sex, sex driven by male domination, as the phrase went, produced one strand of literary feminism, the one embodied first by Beauvoir then by Millett – the ideological critique of male-authored literature. There is, of course, another critically important current in the feminist tide, the question of women reading women's writing, that I will only mention here – emblematically.[15] By the time *The Bell Jar*, published under a pseudonym in England in January 1963, was republished eight years later in the USA, feminism was underway in the USA and England. In the month of April 1971 both *The Bell Jar* and Germaine Greer's *The Female Eunuch* were favourably reviewed in *The New York Times*. Seen through feminist eyes, the doomed girl of the 1950s suddenly made another kind of blinding sense both to reviewers and to readers. Not that the sex was so great, but at least Plath's heroine is, as we once said, the subject of desire. However.

A sentimental journey

At the end of 'Decades' I stop short when it comes to addressing the question of feminism in the 1990s, resisting the urge to predict how it might or should evolve. I had begun writing the essay in 1990, when I was looking hard at fifty, and thinking fearfully about ageing – my own and that of my cohort in feminism. I ended then on an anxious note about not wishing to *represent* feminism through my own involvement as a literary critic, turning instead to an autobiographical writing freed from what I took to be that burden, and leaving the future of redescribing feminism to new generations. I'm not now any more able to make amends, to say in retrospect what second- and third-wave feminism in the 1990s have been – beyond a vantage point from which a group of old girls get to review our salad days.

As I face down sixty, I'm irresistibly drawn back to the time of youth, here to the girl who got conned in 1959. When I examine the girl in my father's snapshot, I read the 1950s writ large, a decade in which stories like this happened – me thinking I was on the road when I was still waiting for the prince. I mean Grace Kelly married one, didn't she? A photograph in an October 1959 issue of

Life, the same number in which the fallen Van Doren prince appears on the cover, features Princess Grace of Monaco engaged in conversation with Charles de Gaulle, her smooth blond hair bound up in a splendid beehive. Conceivably the hairdo could be emulated even with dark hair, but the total picture was a girl's American dream come true.

So what finally is my relation to that girl who sees the world through harlequin glasses? The girl and I both belong to a genealogy that links in an uneasy chain, backwards and forwards, 1970s feminists to 1950s girls and 1990s matrons – ageing female citizens of our fin de siècle. I know by the documents that the girl is me, or at least that her pastness is *in* me (the dumbness and unknowing); and when I revisit that memory I wish equally to reclaim and disown her. Part of my autobiographical shame is remembering another episode from earlier that summer when I exchanged passionate kisses with a handsome stranger on the ferry from Calais to Dover – another Englishman. Sadly, he was met at the ferry by his beautiful, blond fiancée. 'Don't you ever learn?', my mother used to sigh with an edge of exasperation. I guess that's the thing about the girl – it took her so long to learn. As always, it's in the private stories behind the public statements, as much as in the collective pronouncements and manifestos, that the history of feminism continues to remain – however embarrassingly – alive. These autobiographical moments provide keys to the *emotional* logic at work in the culture that supplies the juice for any political movement. Stories like these have a special place in a collective feminist history, for they speak volumes about the brainless furtiveness of pre-feminist consciousness.

When I remind myself how thoroughly I was trained, I have more compassion for my younger self, and turn off the critical gaze. I manage to work up some sympathy for her, as I hope you will, if only as exhibit A of this archive. I like myself better as a generic American girl true to her time, than as 'myself'. Still, it's true that a founding irony runs through my writing whenever I encounter her face to face; I cringe – or at least wince – when I have to acknowledge our resemblance. But maybe it's time to give her a break. Maybe I can lure her into the more forgiving arms of academic memoir. (After all, I'm not her mother, am I?)

Could I have known that in 1959 Godard would make *Breathless*, a new-wave film that created a new role for an American girl, Jean Seberg, on her own in Paris with a real gangster and a sexuality of her own?

Almost forty years later, I decided to revisit the scene of the crime. I took the train from London and stopped at Oxford on my way to Stratford, looking for clues. I'm doing research, I would say when asked, on the 1950s. Victoria, my student, who was writing a dissertation on gender and architecture, studying floorplans and blueprints, accompanied me.[16] My memory work dragged her out of the library, but at least she got to see Stratford and Oxford, where she'd never been. I was spending a sabbatical year in Paris and she was in London on a grant; it was a piece of luck that we were able to make this journey into lost time together.

When we arrived at Stratford (we stopped at Oxford on the way back), we went directly to the police station. I wanted to see the record of my experience, maybe even the face of my con man again. The police were polite but discouraging, and permission to see the files, if files from 1959 there were, would have to be pursued by the mail. The visit to the Shakespeare Institute was equally fruitless. The records had been transferred to the University of Birmingham since that summer programme was now defunct; the secretaries at the Institute gave me a name and an address. The last stop was the theatre. We sat through a numbingly long modern-dress performance of *Macbeth* at the Royal Shakespeare Theatre in the company of solemn schoolchildren. Afterwards, the two of us braved the clouds of smoke at 'The Dirty Duck', and watched the actors come in, drink, unwind, flirt.

We stayed the night, still hoping for a piece of involuntary memory to bubble up from the dirty waters of the Avon. From Paris I had asked Victoria to try and book us a room at the Barwyn, the hotel our group of students had lived in during the summer of 1959. No one at the booking agency had heard of the Barwyn and the only room she could find was a wildly overpriced one at the Grovesnor House. When we checked out of the hotel, we inquired at the desk whether anyone knew what had happened to the Barwyn, only to learn that twenty years earlier, three hotels that had stood side by side – one of them the Barwyn – had been bought up and incorporated into a single entity. The Barwyn had vanished as a separate establishment but its previous existence was marked within Grovesnor House by a meeting room dubbed 'The Barwyn Room', a refashioned trace of its former self. Without knowing it, Victoria and I had spent the night with the ghosts of the Barwyn's old walls. Victoria took photographs of me standing in front of the hotel, pointing at the garden beds remembered from a slide my parents had taken that fateful summer. But what about the ghost of my former self?

In February 1997, I received two letters in response to my Stratford inquiries. The first from the Warwickshire Constabulary which reads in part:

> Unfortunately police records relating to that time and indeed up to more recent years, have all been destroyed as policy and procedure dictates. I can find no trace of X [I had given him the name Judy had recorded in her diary] and therefore must assume that the professional con man may also have used an alias. It is with regret that I am unable to assist you further with your memoirs however may I take this opportunity of wishing you well in your venture.

This letter is signed by a man appointed to the CRIME DESK, as he styled his function. The second arrived on my fifty-sixth birthday (a birthday I could hardly have fathomed then); it, too, closed the door on further evidential research.

Figure 8   The Barwyn then

Figure 9   The Barwyn now

Unfortunately because of storage space we do not keep records for so long: I have checked through the publicity leaflet for that year, but there is nothing there for the Stratford summer school. ... We are sorry that we are unable to be of any help, but wish you good luck with the memoir.

Both letters promptly answered my request for information; both correspondents courteously said that they found my project interesting. I still haven't written the memoir I had announced in my letter of inquiry, but somehow converting the con man fiasco into an artefact of 1950s culture has provided a small reward. If I started out too late to find the truth, at least I've recovered a piece of lost time. And for me, memory trumps history every time.

Did I ever learn? I'm not sure, but Reader, I didn't marry him – the con or the boyfriend. And yes, I've finally given up on the prince.

Notes

1 I am beyond measure grateful to Judith Fryer Davidov for generously sharing with me her memories of this episode – diaries and photographs – which in many cases were more detailed and useful than my own. I'm also grateful for her precious editorial comments.

2 In *The World Split Open: How the Modern Women's Movement Changed America* (2000), Ruth Rosen identifies 1963 as a 'banner year' for women's rights. In this illuminating account, Rosen cites the Equal Pay Act of 1963 and the Presidential Report as crucial markers of a 'growing sense of gender consciousness' in the USA (Rosen 2000: 71) – and as prelude to the 'turning point' legislation of Title VII, which was included in the Civil Rights Act of 1964 (72). For a brief history of the pill, see David Halberstam (1993: 605). The *New Yorker* article, 'The Annals of Sexology: Dr Yes', by James H. Jones about Alfred Kinsey, a key figure in any study of the 1950s (Jones 1997: 113) is useful here in mapping the turning points in sexual and gender history. Some examples: the 1957 Supreme Court Roth decision that:

> narrowed the legal definition of obscenity, expanding the umbrella of constitutional protection to cover a broader range of works portraying sex in art, literature and film. In 1961, Illinois became the first state to repeal its sodomy statutes. The next year the Supreme Court ruled that a magazine featuring photographs of male nudes was not obscene and therefore not subject to censorship.
>
> (Jones 1997: 113)

3 The tone of 'The Other Night at Columbia: A Report from the Academy' epitomises the sense of entitlement that characterised the New York intellectuals of this era.

4 In *No Respect: Intellectuals and Popular Culture*, Andrew Ross points to Van Doren's betrayal as a turning point in the history of television, and 'grist to the mill' for intellectuals concerned with the rise of 'mass culture' (Ross 1989: 104).

5 Simone de Beauvoir (1997, 1998). In the French version there is no way of gauging the correctness and charm of the letters.

6 Bair had relied heavily on the letters to Algren in the biography but they were not available to the general public.

7 In *Simone de Beauvoir: The Making of an Intellectual Woman* (1994), Moi underscores the 'startling originality of *The Second Sex*' (Moi 1994: 189) seen in its historical context:

'*The Second Sex* is nothing short of unique' (190). Moi too believes in the importance of the love affair with Algren, that Beauvoir was also 'more or less unwittingly – expressing many of the insights gained from her relationship with Nelson Algren. Moi writes:

> In so doing she infused her political discourse with personal concerns: while I would have preferred her to do so more openly, there is no doubt in my mind that the power of her sexual passion for Algren helped Beauvoir place sexuality firmly at the centre of her agenda. The result was a radical breakthrough in feminist analysis: Beauvoir is the first thinker in France explicitly to politicize sexuality.
>
> (Moi 1994: 190)

8 Stimpson mentions in a footnote that, in 'conversation Millett told me she now regrets not rereading Beauvoir more closely' (Stimpson 1992: 268).

9 James Joyce's *Ulysses* is the precursor of the banned history. On this and the history of obscenity trials, see Edward de Grazia's encyclopaedic *Girls Lean Back Everywhere: The Law of Obscenity and the Assault on Genius* (1992). Joyce was the writer to whom Hélène Cixous devoted her doctoral dissertation. The comparable figure for Julia Kristeva is Céline. In each case literary experiment is bound up with the masculine violation of bodily taboos.

10 November 6, 1960. Sylvia Plath, not yet a heroine for generations of feminists, from London writes home to her mother in Wellesley, Massachusetts that she was lucky enough to have been given a ticket

> for the last day of the Lady Chatterley trials at the Old Bailey – very exciting – especially with the surprising verdict of 'not guilty.' So *Penguin Books* can publish the unexpurgated edition – a heartwarming advance for D.H. Lawrence's writings!
>
> (Plath 1992: 399)

Like all politics, literary ones make for odd bedfellows. Lawrence also drew Beauvoir and Millett to his work, though in vastly different modes of appreciation. Sandra Gilbert, a passionate reader of Lawrence's poetry, shows the paradoxical connections between 'French feminism's' exaltation of *jouissance* and the cosmic orgasms assigned to Connie Chatterley in her introduction to a translation of Cixous and Clément's 1970s feminist *The Newly Born Woman* (Gilbert 1986). If both Lawrence and Miller have had their female fans, as critics and writers, Mailer seems to inspire mainly antipathy.

11 Several contributors to *Changing Subjects* name Millett's book as a turning point experience in their careers as feminists – myself included.

12 Millett describes her public outing at Columbia in *Flying* with Joycean echoes, 'Yes I said yes I am a Lesbian. It was the last strength I had' (Millett 1990: 15). On the effects of the *Time* cover, the creation of 'Kate Millett', and the public outing at Columbia, see Millett (1990: 14–15, 17–19, 76, 241).

13 In a fierce (Marxist) critique of *Sexual Politics*, Cora Kaplan suggests 'an alternative group composed, say, of James, Fitzgerald, Updike and Baldwin, novelists equally obsessed with the social and political implications of sexuality' (Kaplan 1991: 159). Despite her many caveats, she recognises the book's intervention: 'Once you have read Millett' she writes, 'an "innocent" enjoyment of the sexual in literature is almost sure to be lost. This breaking-up of an unthinking "broadminded", liberal consensus about sexual representation has been a major achievement' (158).

14 Millett *et al.* (1991: 3, 4). I'd like to thank Alix Kates Shulman for bringing this article to my attention.

15 Dubbed by Elaine Showalter in 'Feminist Criticism in the Wilderness' as the practice of 'gynocritics' (Showalter 1985).
16 Victoria Rosner's dissertation – 'Housing Modernism' – has since been completed and is now being revised for publication. I thank her for coming on this trip and reading this essay.

Bibliography

Bair, D. (1990) *Simone de Beauvoir: A Biography*, New York: Summit.

De Beauvoir, S. (1997) *Lettres à Nelson Algren. Un amour transatlantique. 1947–1964*, Paris: Gallimard.

—— (1998) *A Transatlantic Love Affair*, New York: The New Press.

De Grazia, E. (1992) *Girls Lean Back Everywhere: The Law of Obscenity and the Assault on Genius*, New York: Random House.

Friedan, B. (1984) *The Feminine Mystique*, repr., New York: Dell.

Gallop, J. (1997) *Feminist Accused of Sexual Harassment*, Durham: Duke University Press.

Gilbert, S. (1986) Introduction to Hélène Cixous, *The Newly Born Woman*, trans. Betsy Wing, Minneapolis: Minnesota University Press.

Gilbert, S. and Gubar, S. (1994) *No Man's Land: Letters from the Front*, New Haven: Yale University Press.

Greene, G. and Kahn, C. (eds) (1993) *Changing Subjects: The Making of Feminist Literary Criticism*, New York and London: Routledge.

Halberstam, D. (1993) *The Fifties*, New York: Villard.

Jones, H. (1991) *How I Became Hettie Jones*, New York: Penguin.

Jones, J.H. (1997) 'Annals of Sexology: Dr. Yes', *New Yorker*, 25 August and 1 September.

Kaplan, C. (1991) 'Radical Feminism and Literature: Rethinking Millett's *Sexual Politics*', in Mary Eagleton (ed.), *Feminist Literary Criticism*, London and New York: Longman.

Millett, K. (1970) *Sexual Politics*, New York: Doubleday.

—— (1990) *Flying*, repr., New York: Simon and Shuster.

Millett, K., Shulman, A.K. and Stimpson, C. (1991) '*Sexual Politics*: Twenty Years Later', *Women's Studies Quarterly*, 3 and 4.

Moi, T. (1994) *Simone de Beauvoir: The Making of an Intellectual Woman*, Oxford: Blackwell.

Plath, S. (1992) *Letters Home: Correspondence 1950–67*, (ed.) A. Plath, New York: Harper Perennial.

Rosen, R. (2000) *The World Split Open: How the Modern Women's Movement Changed America*, New York: Viking.

Rosner, V. (1999) 'Housing Modernism', dissertation, Columbia University, New York.

Ross, A. (1989) *No Respect: Intellectuals and Popular Culture*, New York and London: Routledge.

Sedgwick, E.K. (1992) 'Gender Criticism', in Stephen Greenblatt and Giles Gunn (eds), *The Transformation of English and American Literary Studies*, New York: MLA.

Showalter, E. (1985) 'Feminist Criticism in the Wilderness', in *The New Feminist Criticism: Essays on Women, Literature, Theory*, New York: Pantheon.

Stimpson, C.R. (1992) 'Feminist Criticism', in Stephen Greenblatt and Giles Gunn (eds), *The Transformation of English and American Literary Studies*, New York: MLA.

Trilling, D. (1964) 'The Other Night at Columbia: A Report from the Academy', repr., in *Claremont Essays*, New York: Harcourt Brace.

Part IV

Autobiography matters

14 Auto/biography and the actual course of things

Trev Broughton

In an early essay on 'Biography', the soon-to-be-renowned Victorian thinker Thomas Carlyle urged the readers of *Fraser's Magazine* to:

> Observe ... to what extent, in the actual course of things, this business of Biography is practised and relished. Define to thyself, judicious Reader, the real significance of these phenomena, named Gossip, Egoism, Personal Narrative (miraculous or not), Scandal, Raillery, Slander, and such-like; the sum-total of which (with some fractional additions of a better ingredient, generally too small to be noticeable) constitutes that other grand phenomenon still called 'Conversation.' Do they not mean wholly: Biography and Autobiography?
>
> (Carlyle 1972: 66)

The comment appears in an extended discussion of Boswell's *Life* of Johnson, which Carlyle reviewed in 1832. The publication of the essay coincided closely with that of Carlyle's *Sartor Resartus*, which has been seen as one of the inaugural moments of modern literary subjectivity, and hence of what the editors of this volume have called the autobiographical urge. Yet Carlyle's own project, in 'Biography' as, arguably, in *Sartor*, is anti-momentous. He takes it for granted that Life-writing is properly regarded as a practice or 'business' rather than simply or exclusively as literary text; that its role in everyday life – the 'actual course of things' – is what matters; and that how we consume, and how much we enjoy ('relish') it, are vital considerations. He goes further, insisting that personal narratives – even in the case of narratives of miracles – are of a piece with other more obviously fugitive, because apparently trivial forms of communication such as gossip and conversation. In other words, he is here unconcerned with purity of genre, preferring instead to situate biography among a heterogeneous assortment of 'kinds of things we say about ourselves' and 'kinds of things we say about other people'. And among the various kinds of things we expect from a written Life, good things, things involving a morally 'better ingredient', play, in practice, a very small part indeed. Finally, by bracketing autobiography and biography together, and linking both to a range of social practices, he implies that what is 'personal' about a life-narrative can be as private as reading and as public as scandal.

Carlyle's notorious racism makes him an unfashionable source of critique, but I offer this admittedly tendentious reading of his words because I find it disconcerting, not to say humbling, that it has taken auto/biographical studies so long to arrive at understandings and insights so commonsensical, so commonplace, that Carlyle could casually throw them down in passing. In fact, his comments could be said to encapsulate the agenda of much recent critical work in the field. Take, for example, Carlyle's point about the significance of Life-writing as a business and/or practice. For too long, the annexing of auto/biographical studies to literary criticism has had the effect of foreclosing the questions that could be asked of it. Until very recently, critics toiled relentlessly over narrow issues of genre (which autobiographies count as such and why), representativeness (which auto/biographers matter and why) or value (which Life-writers succeed or fail to represent their subjects according to one or other timeless standard of adequacy). It has taken a sustained onslaught from interdisciplinary scholarship, much of it feminist or feminist-inspired, to wrest Life-writing away from these wearying and largely unanswerable questions, or rather to prove that the questions are unanswerable in isolation either from each other or from larger issues of social movement and political process.

In Britain, Liz Stanley has led the way. She pioneered the use of the term 'auto/biography', now widely accepted, radically to contaminate the idea that a narrative produced by a self writing about itself, and one produced by a self writing about another being, were *formally* distinguishable from each other. As Stanley tersely puts it: 'This is not to deny that there are differences between different forms of life writing, but it is to argue that these differences are not *generic*' (Stanley 1992: 3). Her claim has been reinforced by Martin Danahay's study of the way in which autobiographical rhetoric actively elides the social implicatedness of individuals, thereby shoring up both the masculinist ideology of individualism and the notion of 'autobiography' itself (Danahay 1993: throughout). It is confirmed, too, by Regenia Gagnier's broad survey of a huge number of primarily 'first-person' British narratives, and by her observation that 'what is striking about the "mind" or personality is not its uniqueness or autonomy, but rather its profound dependence upon intersubjectively shared meanings and its profound vulnerability to the deprivations of the body' (Gagnier 1991: 58).

Such analyses form part of a belated but welcome *rapprochement* between the social sciences and the humanities. Liz Stanley, for instance, eschews a narrowly textual approach to Life-writing, characterising her own approach as 'cultural politics'. She stresses that her work 'provides a feminist discussion of the material production of biography and autobiography as ideological accounts of "lives" which in turn feed back into everyday understandings of how "common lives" and "extraordinary lives" can be recognised' (Stanley 1992: 3). Stanley's project throws the literary-critical agenda into disarray, by suggesting that the issue of *genre* needs to be historicised and refigured as a matter of representation, in particular as one of the ways in which *representativeness* and *value* are mutually constitutive.[1] Stanley's critique of existing work in the field has been compounded by Laura Marcus's study of nearly two hundred years of 'autobiographical criticism'. In this body of work, Marcus notes,

> Questions of the production and circulation of autobiographies are for the most part bracketed off, perhaps because the autobiography is perceived, like the life it narrates, to be 'unique' and singular. But the question of the perceived degrees of 'seriousness' of autobiographical texts is in fact not separate from perceptions of the literary market.
>
> (Marcus 1994: 4)

A different but often parallel tack is taken by Gagnier, who locates her survey of 'self-representation' in the field of cultural studies. Her aim is:

> To mark the conditions in which the texts were produced, whether as a relatively isolated event or part of a larger public event of representation, especially by seeing how conventional literary forms and figures are transformed by, or adapt to, concrete situations.
>
> (Gagnier 1991: 7)

As in Stanley's work, for Gagnier, 'the literary' figures as just one variable among many. Her emphasis is on processes and practices, and she attempts to take into account the material conditions of both production and consumption.

Gagnier's method, which she adapts from Critical Legal Studies, is to concentrate on what she calls the 'pragmatics' or rhetoric of texts: 'pragmatism seeks to locate the purpose an autobiographical statement serves in the life and circumstances of its author and readers' (Gagnier 1991: 4). This interest in the possible purposes of written Lives resurfaces in the titles of two recent volumes to have emerged from the UK and the USA respectively: *The Uses of Autobiography* (1995), edited by Julia Swindells, and *Getting a Life: Everyday Uses of Autobiography* (1996), edited by Sidonie Smith and Julia Watson. Julia Swindells was among the first literary historians in Britain to draw attention to the Life-writings of working women, and to point out their dialogical relationship to dominant narratives of class and gender. In *Victorian Writing and Working Women: the Other Side of Silence* (1985), she noted that the category of 'the literary', if it registered at all, was a problematic within, rather than a property of, most women's cultural repertoires. Hence *The Uses of Autobiography* moves beyond the aesthetic, and takes seriously the various educational and political uses to which Life-writing has and can be put. As her contributors demonstrate, written Lives have been used as elements of pedagogical strategy, as aspects of militancy, and as part of the currency of personal relations, to name just three possibilities. Evidently, this shift towards purpose opens up the field of autobiographical criticism to a range of 'non-literary' texts and approaches. Smith and Watson take this insight even further, showing the multiplicity of ways in which auto/biographies are deployed in daily life. For them the 'uses of autobiography' include getting a job, undergoing therapy, taking part in a talk-show, finding a partner via the 'personal ads', adopting a child and so on.

Equally, they include the various interpretive strategies adopted, and often imposed, by the other participants in each process: the appointments panel, the therapist, the audience, the media, the state.[2]

Clearly, the new focus on 'use' is not restricted to whether or not individual auto-biographers succeed in making sense of their own lives according to their own (or the critics') aesthetic criteria. Nor, on the whole, is it just about whether or not individual biographers assemble their findings according to some notional ideological template (such as liberalism, or femininity), and thus 'serve' or 'resist' the status quo. Rather, it takes into account how actual audiences respond, how audiences do or don't incorporate Life-writings into their daily lives, and crucially, how the producers and consumers of Lives relate to, and sometimes challenge, each other.

This move to think about the complex role auto/biographical texts play in 'the actual course of things' – in human lives and human institutions – seems to me the most promising recent development in auto/biographical criticism. However much work remains to be done if we are to catch up with Carlyle. For one thing, the question of enjoyment, of how we 'relish' Lives remains relatively unexplored. Carlyle's analogy with 'conversation' might provide one way forward. For me, it goes some way to explaining why the Life-writings enshrined by the literary historical canon – John Stuart Mill's *Autobiography*, for instance, or John Henry Newman's *Apologia Pro Vita Sua* – are not necessarily the ones I read, much less the ones I enjoy. The shame-less garrulousness of Boswell's *Johnson*, the wry confidentiality of Margaret Oliphant's *Autobiography*, even the soapy intimacies of Andrew Morton's *Diana*, compel me, where, if I'm honest, the worthy self-probings of a Mill or a Newman leave me cold. But even before we get to the dynamics of reader response, there are questions to be asked about what gets consumed and when. Without, it has to be said, offering up much hard evidence for the contention, commentators on autobi-ography and biography typically pay lip-service to the immense popularity of both genres. Indeed, such a claim is indispensable when one proposes a volume like the present one to publishers. If this is the case, why is Life-writing so seldom dealt with under the aegis of popular culture, as opposed to the literary, the historical or the anthropological? What does it mean to assert that Life-writing is popular? Or that it appeals to women? Do we mean it sells well? If so, to whom? Do we mean that it circulates widely, and if so how? Do we mean that it changes lives? Whose? How? Or do we simply mean that it is 'teachable' and hence widely taught? For all its popu-larity as a topic for essay collections and Women's Studies courses, the popularity of Life-writing with respect to non-academic readerships remains oddly unexamined.

While auto/biography has mattered, and continues to matter to me as a resource for feminist enquiry, as a tool for feminist pedagogy, and an engine of femi-nist change, I find myself increasingly interested in whether or not we can use Life-writings to develop new ways of thinking about how reading and writing communities evolve. Two lines of enquiry present themselves. The first is inspired by Gillian Fenwick's work on Leslie Stephen and the *Dictionary of National Biography*. Her patient work of ascription has uncovered a vast network of late-Victorian biog-raphers, all involved in a project of national self-commemoration. They were all, to some degree, participants in and producers of what I have called a 'culture of auto/biography': one in which reading and writing Lives, and imagining how one's own Life might be written or read, were day-to-day concerns (Broughton 1999: throughout). Yet how this auto/biographical culture worked (how it administered and regulated itself, how it figured in the business of securing a living and so on) and how it *felt* remains unclear. Other writing and reading communities – such as those engaged in proselytising, consciousness-raising or internetworking of various sorts, might also profitably be examined along these lines. *The New Dictionary of National Biography* is currently in the making: must we wait another century before this gigantic enterprise is examined for its role in the 'actual course of things'?

A second line of enquiry is suggested by current work on celebrity, controversy and scandal (Cohen 1993, Cohen 1996). Commentators on mass media and journalism have long recognised the complex reciprocal relationship between the workings of celebrity and the evolution of public opinion. Celia Lury, for instance, has argued that media representations of the ill-fated marriage of 'Charles and Di' took effect, not so much insofar as they could be proven to be true or false, but insofar as they were able to mobilise particular sections of the public as audience. Furthermore, not only was the 'public as audience' implicated in the narrative of the marriage (as harasser, as voyeur, as rival), but the narrative, and a certain 'mediatized reflexivity' it generated, created new ways in which 'the public' could take shape and agency in political debate (Lury 1995: 226–7). The story of the marriage, in other words, involved nothing less than a 'convergence between cultural and political representation' (225). As I have argued elsewhere (Broughton 1999), there seems to me to be every reason to extend this kind of analysis to encompass auto/biographical controversies. A case in point is the controversy surrounding John Bayley's account of his marriage to the novelist Iris Murdoch. *Iris: A Memoir* (1999), tells the poignant story of his wife's glittering career and gradual capitulation to Alzheimer's Disease. Widely and lavishly praised by reviewers, the book nevertheless generated questions about the ethics of auto/biography (who gets to speak for whom and why), and invoked and mobilised self-conscious readerships (the elderly, carers, sufferers from mental illness, the widowed, advocates of new ways of being married, husbands of successful wives) quite specific to here and now.

Attention is at last being paid not just to auto/biographical texts, but to auto/biographical practices. This involves interdisciplinary thinking, but also thinking about the role of auto/biography in the formation of disciplines (Amigoni 1993; Marcus 1994). My contention is that much work remains to be done. This work might involve investigating actual, rather than simply implied audiences. It might mean considering how auto/biographies work as material objects in the marketplace, how they function as part of wider cultural intertexts such as controversies, campaigns and curriculae, and how auto/biographical cultures are generated and sustained. The work already undertaken by Swindells, Stanley, Marcus, Gagnier and others encourages me, finally, to find ways of exploring the different and discontinuous ways in which Lives matter both to writers and to readerships.

Notes

1 The impact of interdisciplinarity, and the move away from a narrow focus on textuality, can now be felt even in volumes with a clear literary-critical orientation. Leigh Gilmore's *Autobiographics*, for instance, is less interested in *genre* than in the field of self-representation broadly construed: how and why individual autobiographers access, repudiate or challenge particular discourses of truth-telling and truth-withholding. These discourses range from religious confession to legal testimony and from political slogan to psychoanalysis.

2 See also Martin Danahay's observation that the individualist premises upon which literary autobiography, and indeed authorship itself, are based also informs a host of daily activities from signing a credit card slip, to filling out a census form (1993: 212–13).

Bibliography

Amigoni, D. (1993) *Victorian Biography: Intellectuals and the Ordering of Discourse*, New York: Harvester Wheatsheaf.

Bayley, J. (1999) *Iris: A Memoir*, London: Duckworth.

Broughton, T. (1999) *Men of Letters, Writing Lives: Literary Masculinity and Auto/Biography in the Late Victorian Period*, London: Routledge.

Carlyle, T. (1972) [1832] 'Biography', in Ian Campbell (ed.) *Selected Essays*, London: Dent: 65–79.

Cohen, E. (1993) *Talk on the Wilde Side: Toward a Genealogy of a Discourse on Male Sexualities*, London: Routledge.

Cohen, W. (1996) *Sex Scandal: The Private Parts of Victorian Fiction*, Durham and London: Duke U. P.

Danahay, M. (1993) *A Community of One: Masculine Autobiography and Autonomy in Nineteenth Century Britain*, Albany: Albany State University Press.

Fenwick, G. (1989) *The Contributors' Index to the 'Dictionary of National Biography 1885–1901'*, Winchester: St Paul's Bibliographies.

—— (1993) *Leslie Stephen's Life in Letters: A Bibliographical Study*, Aldershot: Scolar Press.

—— (1994) *Women and the Dictionary of National Biography: A Guide to DNB volumes 1885–1985 and Missing Persons*, Aldershot: Scolar Press.

Gagnier, R. (1991) *Subjectivities: A History of Self-Representation in Britain, 1832–1920*, New York and Oxford: Oxford University Press.

Gilmore, L. (1994) *Autobiographics: A Feminist Theory of Women's Self-Representation*, Ithaca and London: Cornell University Press.

Lury, C. (1995) 'A Public Romance: "The Charles and Di Story"', in Pearce, L. and Stacey, J. (eds), *Romance Revisited*, London: Lawrence and Wishart: 225–37.

Marcus, L. (1994) *Auto/Biographical Discourses: Theory, Criticism, Practice*, Manchester and New York: Manchester University Press.

Smith, S. and Watson, J. (eds) (1996) *Getting a Life: Everyday Uses of Autobiography*, Minneapolis and London: University of Minnesota Press.

Stanley, L. (1992) *The Auto/Biographical I: The Theory and Practice of Feminist Auto/Biography*, Manchester: Manchester University Press.

Swindells, J. (1985) *Victorian Writing and Working Women: The Other Side of Silence,*. Cambridge: Polity.

—— (ed.) (1995) *The Uses of Autobiography*, London: Taylor and Francis.

15 Doing Sym/Bio/Graphy with Yasna

Consuelo Rivera-Fuentes

This will be the synthesis of my life in which both the story of my family and my fantasies will be mixed. ... I will not be able to say that everything I write I lived, not even if I participated, as most of the situations will be the product of my fantasy combined with the facts ...(my translation from the Spanish).[1]

Dear Yasna, why did you begin by confessing to the fictionalisation of part of your life? Are you thus warning me not to believe everything I read? Or are you inviting me to share your fantasies? Are you telling me that in writing your life, it can become easily ripped apart, so by fictionalising it a bit, the pain of being torn will be less disturbing?

Whatever the answers, the 'truth' is that I like your openness and creativity and that I want to feel and construct meaning with you. I go on reading and unknitting the weaving of your life. You construct yourself by adopting different identities: Sometimes you are yourself, your own mother or your siblings. Very often, as you know, you adopt the role of the saviour of your parents' marriage and, at various points in the narration, you speak for both your parents and yourself, achieving thus a singularity and a plurality which allows both of us to cross the boundaries of a fixed, unchanging identity ...

Alex proudly showed me her breasts and I told her they were beautiful ... after the usual chat, we practised kissing as always, but then she made it last so long that I felt I was suffocating or drowning ... her tongue bothered me and I even felt some sort of disgust, but I did not want to disappoint her. ... Later, in a hurry, she asked me to kiss her breasts ... and the truth is that this seemed more interesting ... I mean, as a way to escape her exhausting mouth ... and I kissed them ... with a slower rhythm than the other kisses, while she arched her back to get deeper in my mouth, looking for my tongue ...

I feel wet, dripping ... I try to compose myself; to remind myself that I am reading this to make it public and that the confession of my body's reaction might not be as important to the academic environment this is going to be situated in as it feels to me. However, the electric wave that

*travels my whole body, from my temples down to my nipples and clitoris suffocates me, as well.
… This time it is me who doesn't want to disappoint you, Yasna, because I am evolving, with
you, in your re-memory, in my memory, in my present and in my past, in the love of a new lover,
in her tongue, in my tongue, in your tongue, embodying thus our alterities in the fleshy mountains
of our breasts, in the sucking waters of our desire …*

Sym/bio/graphy

I have, throughout my life, used silence in many different ways: to be in touch
with myself and my feelings; to push away pain; not to hurt those I love and very
often to resist authority. Academic knowledge can be full of deafening, authoritarian voices that I simply resist by going numb, stubbornly silent. This, of
course, presents a problem when trying to find a methodology with which to feel
comfortable. So the methodology I introduce in this paper explores my resistance to reading lesbian autobiographies in a detached, orthodox manner. I do
this by crossing the boundaries of interpretation of written texts in order to
experience not only the cognitive pleasure derived from solving a maze of
textual codes but also, and most importantly for me, in order to feel *with* the texts
and lives I am reading.[2] I started this chapter with a brief sample of the way in
which I interact with one of my Chilean lesbian friends who presented me with
the 'gift' of her written autobiography and asked me if my thesis would have *her*
in it as well.[3] This interaction takes the shape of a long letter addressed to Yasna,
my friend. Because we communicate mostly through snail mail, the letter format
seemed a good idea; one which would allow me to fulfil her desire, to feel *with*
her, as well as feel myself *in* her and her textual characters.

The combination of this reading process *with/in* the lesbian autobiographies[4]
I am interacting with and the physical sensations my body experiences whilst
doing this engaged reading led me to borrow the biological term *symbiosis* to be
able to go beyond interpretation. Biology is about *living* organisms who *feel* and,
most of the time, create positively.[5] Living organisms feel the cold and the heat,
most feel hunger and thirst, joy and pain; they experience dependency and/or
they co-evolve. Symbiosis, to put it simply, means the mutual dependence of two
or more organisms; and, as *The Oxford English Dictionary* explains, a living together
of, usually two plants or of an animal and a plant which contribute to each
other's support. I want to cross the boundaries of the traditional reading of autobiographies by calling my reading process *sym/bio/graphy*[6] because my friends,
their texts and I contribute to each other's support and search for identity in a
'living together', in a relating.[7]

Yet human relationships are full of disengagements, which explains why I
sometimes *disidentify* with my friends. When this happens, the only way I find to
remain loyal to my friends is through a meta-narrative within my
sym/bio/graphy in which I reflect on the various ways in which I enter texts but
also what happens on my arrival.[8] *Sym/bio/graphy* allows me to do this and transform knowledge into something more than the production of meaning. It allows

me to *feel* what I am doing, to think my *feelings*, *to feel* my thinking and to move beyond academic silences, especially when it comes to my lesbian identity.[9]

Having 'confessed' to this, and to the risk of falling into 'a complacent exhibitionism' as Elizabeth Fox-Genovese calls her dislike for this type of self-reflexive criticism and 'farce',[10] let me now go into yet another 'sin'.

The 'voyeur'

Dear Yasna, I am so sorry that I have to reduce and simplify your narration in order to share with the readers of this chapter the type of research I am doing at the moment. In another part of your narration you share with me your unspoken need for a woman's body. This time you reveal what happened on the last day of your stay in the south, when you slept with Paola, your best friend. Both you and I become voyeurs in this episode. But what is a voyeur?, *your voice in my head asks.*

There are many definitions, all of which carry some kind of ethical or moral judgement and I don't like being judged for something people do all the time (only that they don't admit to it!). Some people call it scopophilia, which 'refers to the pleasure derived from looking or gazing' says Ruth Waterhouse (1993: 119). You and I watch each other frequently in our interaction, we gaze into each other's desires and it feels fine, doesn't it? I prefer this to the Freudian interpretation of this act of human beings as objectification and control of other subjects. I am trying not to objectify you or Paola, rather I want to feel with you. So, we both watch Paola's rhythmical breathing as she sleeps, and I watch your gaze and wish to become air in order to enter Paola's dreams through her nose, so that our love, the listener of your fairytales, can take our essence in her lungs. My senses work in unison with yours, I can also see Paola in the darkness of that southern room, I can smell her fragrance, I can hear the sounds of her body ... and yours.

My breathing and the rest of my senses ached to manifest themselves and then I kissed her ... softly on her cheek, also her hands and her lips, right on the beauty spot she has in the middle of her lower lip; I touched her ... I tried to touch her completely ... gently, slowly and unafraid ... my senses were complete now and they enjoyed each other, one by one, joined like an orchestra in that wonderful symphony. ... I could taste the taste of her skin. ... Dawn came and I had to leave her ...

There is a lump in my throat which feels like sand, I do not cry with tears but with grains of sand which hurt my eyes, my throat and my chest. How did I get here? There I was happily being a voyeur, feeling excited at the prospect of some sexual fantasy or reality and suddenly the pain of leaving, of being separated because your parents took you away from Paola and academia takes me away from you. The whole of the Atacama desert, the driest one in the world, is in my throat now. Drained of tears, hot and confused I leave you and Paola for another day.

I leave them to reflect on what has happened to me while I was doing this implicated reading of Yasna as a child. I think that it is the way in which she constructs herself that is the source of my engagement with her text, not the people she makes up or remembers. Her fantasies are somehow similar to mine, only that she is more honest at times. I know now when a text becomes my own story and this is exciting. My excitement springs from the realisation that, unlike some other women, it is not a man who compels me to act and feel in close relation to Yasna and her first sexual experience. It is four women: Yasna, her cousin, my lover and myself. All of us making our sexuality and sexual desire a unique experience of interrelatedness in this *sym/bio/graphy* which occupies not only a textual/sexual space but also a time *warp*.

Dear Yasna, do you remember what I said about the voyeur in all of us human beings? Someone the other day asked me why I read and do research on autobiography and perhaps this is the answer. Reading about other lesbian lives is a form of voyeurism, but one that brings change to my life, one that is not sheer curiosity about other lesbians' ways of creating and understanding their self-construction of sexual identity. My voyeur wants not only to understand her own sexual-identity creation, but also to feel yours and others'; to hear the moans of our desires, to listen to the rustle and rattle of the leaves and seeds of our lives. That is why autobiography.

Notes

1 The different sets of type styles represent the three different voices present in this article.

2 In her book *Feminism and the Politics of Reading* (1997), Lynne Pearce comments on the fact that critical discourse treats reader and viewer *pleasure* as construed largely in relation to cognition, thus brushing aside feelings other than the pleasurable experience of interpreting a text. She mentions Roland Barthes' writings as an example of a case in which '*plaisir* or *jouissance* … is associated principally with the hermeneutics of reading' (Pearce 1997: 9) and not with the affective side of it.

3 Although I am only presenting this very brief example, sym/bio/graphy happens with all the autobiographies I am interacting with, as well as with two photo/bio/graphies I received when I asked my friends to narrate their lives for the purposes of my thesis.

4 My PhD research involves the reading of, and interacting with, five unpublished autobiographies written by British lesbians, plus two written by self-declared Chilean lesbians. Some of these autobiographies are narrated in prose, some are a mix of photographs and written text, some are a combination of prose and poetry. All of my lesbian friends involved in this research have given me an oral narration as well. Therefore, when I say 'the' lesbian autobiographies, I am only referring to these and not to some general concept around autobiographies written by lesbians.

5 The fact that I am borrowing a biological term does *not* imply that I believe in biological determinism. On the contrary, I strongly believe that biology is 'creative'. Moreover, there are no terms or concepts (that I know of) in other disciplines which can explain or cover what I am trying to do in my research. However, the biological concept of symbiosis to express similar methodologies in critical analysis has been used before. Linda Anderson, for example, in *Women and Autobiography in the Twentieth Century: Remembered Futures* (1997), when commenting on the model offered by Candace Lang (1982) as an alternative to the 'realist expressive' model of autobiography she is criticising, notices that this alternative is like a 'symbiotic merger between the autobiographer and the critic' (Anderson 1997: 2).

6 *Sym* (from the Greek) can mean 'with', 'together', 'similarly' or 'alike'. I do my reading 'with' my friends since they give me feedback and comments on this process, and I evolve 'together' with them as we interact. *Bio* (also from the Greek) can mean 'life' or 'way of living'. My friends' lives and my life are intertwined in the 'research' for my PhD. Our 'way of living' is a lesbian one. *Graphy*: 'some of the words with this ending denote processes or styles of writing, drawings or graphic representations', says the *The Oxford English Dictionary*. My friends' processes of writing or (photo)graphically representing their lives and/or ways of living are symbolised linguistically in symbiography and our cyclical interaction is represented by the slashes, hence sym/bio/graphy.

7 I am grateful to Lynne Pearce who, after reading a couple of draft chapters for my PhD thesis, advised me that I needed a new concept which could capture what I am doing in my research and suggested the term symbiography.

8 For a similar way of dealing with the problematic of 'loyalty' and 'identification', see Lynne Pearce's *Feminism and the Politics of Reading* (1997).

9 The concept of lesbian identity is, indeed, a very slippery one and, I believe, shaped by varying socio-historical contexts (cf. Markowe 1996). When I talk about *my* lesbian identity, I do it from a feminist perspective; one which challenges and resists definitions which seek to marginalise and silence my being and becoming in this world.

10 Cf. Elizabeth Fox-Genovese's article (1996: 68–75).

Bibliography

Anderson, L. (1997) *Women and Autobiography in the Twentieth Century: Remembered Futures*, London: Harvester Wheatsheaf.

Fox-Genovese, E. (1996) 'Confession versus Criticism, or What's the Critic Got to Do with It?', in Veeser, H.A. (ed.), *Confessions of the Critics*, London: Routledge.

Lang, C. (1982) 'Autobiography in the Aftermath of Romanticism', *Diacritics* 12 (Winter): 2–16.

Markowe, L.A. (1996) *Redefining the Self: Coming Out as Lesbian*, Cambridge: Polity Press.

Pearce, L. (1997) *Feminism and the Politics of Reading*, London: Arnold.

The Oxford English Dictionary (1978), vol. 10, Oxford: Clarendon Press.

Waterhouse, R. (1993) 'The Inverted Gaze', in Scott, Sue and Morgan, David (eds), *Body Matters: Essays on the Sociology of the Body*, London: The Falmer Press.

16 Bringing it home

Autobiography and contradiction

Ruth McElroy

[B]elonging expresses a desire for more than what is, a yearning to make skin stretch beyond individual needs and wants. ... While I am well aware that I walk a thin line that at any time may disappear into narcissism or endless auto-reflexivity, I maintain that the body that writes is integral to the type of figuring I wish to do. It is a body that is fully part of what it experiments with.

(Probyn 1996)

Nowadays, autobiographical criticism has come into general use. Granted, the autobiographical segment may occupy no more than forty seconds of a forty-minute talk. But the audience will ask questions only about the forty seconds. Autobiography triggers their startle reflex.

(Veeser 1996)

less said, more meant ...
... a coming home
to something brand new but always known.

(Lewis 1995)

Mindful of the criticism made by critics such as Nancy K. Miller that when we speak as feminists about autobiography we seem reluctant to do so autobiographically, I want to employ an explicitly personal, creative voice in this position piece. I approach autobiography positively as a process of contradiction rather than as a narrative of truth-telling, yet the experience of writing this piece entails a sense of loss. For all feminist literary criticism has celebrated gynocritical 'discoveries' of buried and silenced voices, what I feel most acutely now is the loss of my spoken voice in the act of writing. Why does this matter?

Autobiography's contradictions live on the tongue, find their ways into others' ears, inhabit and transmutate across the bodies of speakers and listeners. Autobiographical tellings – impelled, demanded and proffered – live through gestures, through tone, in the conjunctions and separations of the visceral, the intellectual, the spatial. The self moves physically in ways that are responsive both to its self and to the bodies of others, their words and claims. In talking autobiographically about the experience of being called (Probyn, 1996), what is most acutely lost here is the voice of that calling, not least when it is enunciated between Welsh women whose speech, both English and Welsh, is always already a response to a whole array of linguistic, and political callings. The autobio-graphical tongue in any bilingual context is unlikely to tell the kind of homogeneous and singular truth which critics of autobiography, quite contradic-torily, seem both to disdain and desire.

What follows is the result of attending a number of conferences in the latter stages of my doctoral years (1996–8) at Lancaster University, northwest England, which from my current position as a full-time, temporary lecturer in a Welsh college is a lifetime and a country ago. I myself cannot decide on the significance of my conference concerns. On the one hand, I am surprised at myself choosing to write about a series of events which are so public and academic. Given that my interest remains with the intersections of questions of gendered identity and constructions of home, both domestic and national, I am struck by my apparent refusal to set my writing self in the private domestic sphere. On the other hand, my working self is precisely subject to the academic narrative of the 1990s career structure which demands that, along with high productivity, I regularly place myself in a professional context that, for the most part, remains resolutely alien to me. Conferences seem to have become for me the most traumatic and enlightening catalysts for autobiographical turns as a way of thinking through my own locations and relationships to feminism, 'home' and Welsh women. For all they form a vital part of the academic apparatus, conferences and the stories we tell about them, as opposed to the papers which are published from them, remain something of a secret. So often relegated to weary talk on the journey home, the story of the conference is, nevertheless, the site where discourses of the professional self and the feminist subject meet and collide. As public, profes-sional arenas, conferences are marked by the constitutive imperative to perform a speaking voice. As chairs, speakers and delegates, we are promised transforma-tion and enlightenment only if we dialogue. As social locations, conferences are sites where professional story-telling occurs alongside the staging of a persona. The commodification of the speaking, sellable self, of one's voice through the *genre* of conference paper, is only the most obvious instance of this process. The very spatial organisation of conferences patently contributes to this theatre of the self. The bodies of speakers are set apart, isolated, made visible to a specu-lating audience. And haven't you noticed how bottles of water stand – the fragile limit between containment and embarrassment: God how you hope it isn't knocked over – and how often they go untouched – safe only when the perfor-mance is over. Cora Kaplan recently wryly suggested that if demonstrations were the dominant mode of feminist work in the 1970s, in the 1990s it is the series of conferences that now stand in their place (Kaplan 1997). I am not entirely sure I share Kaplan's pessimism but I do think that conferences are an interesting way of examining the intersecting narratives of the self as they are theorised, lived and performed by women who are differently positioned vis-à-vis the ethos of professionalism.

I am here trying to write about autobiography. I put the books down. Maybe the truth will out. A Welsh woman postgraduate at an English university, I find myself at my first academic conference in Wales – a border crossing which stands out from my own multitude. The shock of being here is physical. My palms are damp, my stomach is churning and my lips are dry. Entering another world, which is not home but is – the contradictions last. I am aware that there are some who regard any assertion of Welsh difference – including use of the Welsh language – as an elaborate fraud, designed to complicate simple matters and to wring subsidies from the English. Framed by this age-old charge of Welsh difference as fakery, my sense of national 'difference' in England had been lived as an unproductive battle between accusations of 'putting it on' and remaining unseen, silent, 'one of us' who is no different really because she doesn't stand out. Difference reduced to fakery vs authenticity and all trace of contradiction inexpressible; an impermissible complexity. And then I walk into another world. I am stunned by the simpler things: people talk to each other. I can understand what they say – I can read their signs, though coded. This is the first long conference I have come to alone and yet I am already socialising. I am speaking. This comes as a shock.

It is not idyllic of course – the contradictions remain. Two minutes into wine and I am surrounded by men. I am looking for a path to the women but the furniture is in the way. An argument erupts – literary prizes and judges, R.S. so familiar – an excuse to escape.[1] I am properly introduced by the only woman I know here. 'Mae Ruth yn siarad Cymraeg, wyddost ti.' That's it. A one line biography. Named. And I don't know what to say. I am trying to speak to two women in two languages – the contradictions remain.

Stepping into this world finally shows! 'You looked as though you were going to erupt in there!' My face lets me down again. I kept quiet, let it go. But if I can control my tongue, my eyes have a will of their own. How do I keep silent in this context? How do I deal with a lack of feminism? I feel again to be in two worlds – falling between.

At a conference on 'Passing' at the Centre for Women's Studies, Lancaster University, in 1996, delegates talked about the politics of passing and the gap. But it isn't a gap. This is a chasm – my stomach drops, I feel like I'm falling – I feel every fibre and muscle quake and contract. Another conference in an English university, the subject regionalism and marginality. Two Welsh women find each other. 'Where are you from?' The question is like a kick out of an aeroplane without a parachute. Like a dream sequence, no-one around us realises the horror of this act. I am about to be found out. Having been passing as an academic – performing my paper and seeming intelligent, the young feminist with the old Welsh men – I am found out. Exposed in public: the dream life erupts here again. I cannot sustain the role. Or rather, I don't know which role to play, which space to occupy. If it weren't you asking the question, I would be on solid ground – I would know how to respond: 'I'm from Lancaster, the Centre for Women's Studies.' But this woman is Welsh and so am I, so that must mean, 'Where are you from? Declare your location to me; let me place you in your region, your family, your school, which poets wrote of your valley.' But then she is an academic and I'm role playing one too. So maybe Lancaster is the answer. Falling between two worlds – a chasm, not a gap. If I answer wrongly, I'll be a fraud – I will not be who I am supposed to be. I will fail the code. And it will be awful to try and re-establish that ground. You will, I know, try helpfully to replace me on terra firma, but the replacement will be just that – standing in for someone else. A fraud again. So I am quaking and thinking and guessing. And, *clyw hyn*, all I can do, all my quivering arm can do is reach for a digestive! Stick something in my mouth and I don't have to talk. And as I do it, as my arm quivers there in the air across the table, you speak. You recognise the free fall and know that you are a part of it. The only recovery: recognition and declaration. 'Oh what a typically Welsh question, eh?' The chasm closes. 'Yes.' We laugh and just look at each other. 'Yes, from Llanrwst, a village nearby, Tal-y-Bont.' 'Oh right yes. I'm from …', 'Oh really well …'. I had lost my 'I', I really didn't know the subject, fragmentation was collapse. Only your eye, our meeting eyes brought me back.

So … if one of the things which autobiography can offer to do for us is to dramatise the misnamings, the collisions, the very performance of uttering a subject, how then to put into language this physical collapse, the bodily disintegration which it encompasses? And how to do this except to an addressee, a listener, who may not turn 'I' into a recognising 'eye'? As Nancy K. Miller (1991) points out in *Getting Personal*, the significance of autobiography is as much the putting into language – the sheer event of subjective speech – as the life history or situated position of which it seeks to speak. Seizing the language in which to say it is one of the founding dynamics and inherent conflicts of all autobiographical acts. This discursive, political dilemma is profoundly bound to the physical, if only because the experience of being speechless and of having too much to say is often imaged through our mouths and tongues. Finding the words to enunciate the self is a process of accommodation and conflict for the political and physical subject. Autobiography, when hailed as a response to the question 'Where are you from?', not only operates as a requirement to manage belonging, but it forcefully hinges the narrative of the self, the politics of identity and the contradictions of our relationships to our homes. 'Home' thus becomes a multi-dimensional place, a matrix of different national, political and professional homes which inhabit one another, even as the autobiographical subject never finds herself entirely at home in any single one of these.

The danger with autobiography is that its performative utterances are, of course, not definable, not contained. They are generically anarchic. One of my own greatest anxieties is when the act of autobiographising seems to transform into therapy. Teaching autobiography, and more particularly, attempting to read and mark students' autobiographies, is perhaps the most stressful readerly position I regularly occupy and it is one which inevitably sways on the cusp of the academic and the personal. Specifically, I find myself reading a sizeable minority of papers on traumatic accounts of abuse, disorders and anxiety-ridden sexualities. The 'I's I read know that it will be my eyes which read them, but do they know what kind of recognition they want? Having taught half a term's worth on the blurred boundaries of fact and fiction, how now to resist the need to discern truth from their often subtle fabulations? As a pedagogical strategy which Women's Studies tutors can adopt both to support women's voices and to cross boundaries, it is a profoundly risky one. The ethical urge to help sits very uneasily with the theorising of autobiography as fact and fiction.

So two texts emerge. The one, my official comments which the external examiner will see, the other a personal note in which I somersault around the question: offering phone numbers and simultaneously hoping not to be exposed as a fraudulent reader who has missed the point.

These two texts are a world apart and even in my teaching, the contradictions remain. That is perhaps what autobiography can offer us. It is less a net to support us – to give us confidence, to look down upon as a resource – but more a ropy bridge across a fearful and sometimes thrilling chasm, a chasm of legitimacy and discipline. Speaking the self is a risky business – especially when caged in confessional writing. But if the embarrassed self I now am in winter 2000 wishes that there had been 'less said' in this autobiographical piece – the cringes of an older self – I know that a good deal was and is meant by it. And I know too that its 'intimations of complexity' (Williams 1985: 18–31) have far more chance of being heard for having been authored on the English side of the border – a lasting contradiction which for many of us 'is brand new but always known'.

Notes

1 The Nobel shortlisted Welsh poet, R.S. Thomas, whose nationalist politics and fine English language poetry are always the subject of lively debate.

Bibliography

Kaplan, C. (1997) 'Feminism and Civic Society', paper delivered at the 'Identifying Feminism: Narrative Legacies' conference, University of Salford.
Lewis, G. (1995) *Parables and Faxes*, Newcastle-upon-Tyne: Bloodaxe.
Miller, N. (1991) *Getting Personal: Feminist Occasions and Other Autobiographical Acts*, London: Routledge.
Probyn, E. (1996) *Outside Belongings*, London: Routledge.
Veeser, H. Aram (1996) *Confessions of the Critics*, London: Routledge.
Williams, R. (1985) 'Wales and England', in Osmond, J. (ed.) *Wales: A Nation Again?*, Llandysul: Gomer.

Index